T0294820

The National Road and the Difficult Path to Sustainable National Investment

Also by Theodore Sky

To Provide for the General Welfare: A History of the Federal Spending Power
(Newark: University of Delaware Press, 2003)

The National Road and the Difficult Path to Sustainable National Investment

THEODORE SKY

UNIVERSITY OF DELAWARE PRESS
Newark

Published by University of Delaware Press
Co-published with The Rowman & Littlefield Publishing Group, Inc.
4501 Forbes Boulevard, Suite 200, Lanham, Maryland 20706
www.rlpgbooks.com

Estover Road, Plymouth PL6 7PY, United Kingdom

British Library Cataloguing in Publication Information Available

Library of Congress Cataloging-in-Publication Data

Sky, Theodore, 1933-
  The National Road and the difficult path to sustainable national investment / Theodore Sky.
     p. cm.
  Includes bibliographical references and index.
  ISBN 978-1-61149-020-6 (cloth : alk. paper) — ISBN 978-1-61149-021-3 (electronic)
  1. Cumberland Road. 2. National Highway System. 3. Transportation and state—United States—History. 4. Public investment—United States. I. Title.
  HE356.C8S49 2011
  388.1'220973—dc22   2011008715

∞™ The paper used in this publication meets the minimum requirements of American National Standard for Information Sciences—Permanence of Paper for Printed Library Materials, ANSI/NISO Z39.48-1992.

Printed in the United States of America

To Vera, Catherine, Victoria, Eric and Theo,
and to all their families
With love everlasting

Contents

Preface   ix

Acknowledgments   xi

PART I. THE GREAT DEBATES ABOUT
THE NATIONAL ROAD

1   Washington's Role   5
2   Jefferson, Gallatin, and the Legislation of 1806   15
3   Madison: Construction in the Shadow of War and the
    Bonus Bill Veto   29
4   Monroe's Compromise and the Tollgate Battle   39
5   John Quincy Adams and the High-Water Mark of the
    National Road as a National Road   49
6   Andrew Jackson and the Transfer of the National Road to
    the States   57
7   The National Road and the Law, Politics, and Policy of
    Internal Improvement   69

PART II. THE NATIONAL ROAD IN ITS PRIME

8   Laying Out and Building the National Road   85
9   Confronting Problems in Road Construction East of the Ohio in
     the Madison and Monroe Years: An Archival Account   101
10   The Culture of the National Road in Its Prime   117
11   The Road as a Microcosm of Early-Republic America   139

PART III. THE DECLINE AND REVIVAL OF THE ROAD, ITS ROLE AS A PRECURSOR OF THE INTERSTATE SYSTEM, AND ITS PLACE AS A NATIONAL SYMBOL

12   The Decline and Revival of the Road   151
13   The National Road, the Creation of the Dwight D. Eisenhower
     Interstate Highway System, and the Post-Interstate Period   167
14   The National Road as National Symbol   183

PART IV. TWENTY-FIRST-CENTURY LEGACY

15   The National Road and the Enduring Role of the Federal
     Spending Power   199
16   A National Road Perspective on America's Twenty-First-Century
     Infrastructure Challenges   211

Epilogue: The National Road, the American Recovery and
     Reinvestment Act, and Sustainable National Investment in the
     Twenty-First Century   219

Appendix: National Road Time Line   237

Notes   241

Bibliography   275

Index   285

About the Author   295

Preface

The Cumberland Road, also called the National Road, was the first federally assisted interstate highway built in the United States. When completed, it crossed six states: Maryland, Virginia, Pennsylvania, Ohio, Indiana, and Illinois. Federally appointed officers supervised the survey, laying out, and construction of the road under the direction of the president and laws passed by Congress.

Congress approved, and Thomas Jefferson signed, the first authorization for the road in 1806. Subsequent legislation to continue the road and provide funds for its construction was enacted during the administrations of James Madison, James Monroe, John Quincy Adams, Andrew Jackson, and Martin Van Buren. Frequent and sometimes acrimonious debates in Congress preceded these enactments. Members of Congress weighed constitutional, fiscal, sectional, and economic issues in the course of these debates. Political issues weighed heavily in these debates, and the future of internal improvements, the road among them, was an important, although not overriding, question in a number of presidential elections. Over a more than thirty-year period, the laws and presidential actions that affected the fate of the road established precedents for major court decisions in the twentieth century that influenced the direction of the United States.

After 1835, authority to administer the National Road was transferred in stages to the states through which it passed, and congressional appropriations ceased. Various states established tollgates to keep the road in repair and, where necessary, continue its construction. The era of the National Road as a direct responsibility of the federal government came to an end. As the railroads came to dominate surface transportation, the golden age of the road as an artery of interstate transportation travelers, emigrants, and haulers of freight also terminated.

Before that transpired, however, the road made a major contribution to the progress of the nation and became an indelible part of the American experience. It provided a viable means of transportation through the Allegheny Mountains to the heartland beyond. It facilitated a ceaseless flow of emigrants from East to West and hastened the settlement of the Midwest. It helped to unify the areas through which it ran by providing for easier transportation between them and accelerating the timely delivery of the mails. It became the avenue by which foreign travelers came to view and assess the state of the new nation. With the arrival of the automobile age that developed in connection with it, the National Road provided a foundation for a system of highways that ultimately evolved into the modern, federally assisted interstate highway system familiar to contemporary America. With that age came a "revival" of the National Road in the form of U.S. 40.

The year 2006 marked the two-hundredth anniversary of the first congressional enactment providing for the road. This book commemorates that event by taking stock of the National Road's history and its contribution to the growth and progress of the United States. A portion of this book focuses on the congressional debates about the road and the important constitutional precedents that were established with respect to its construction and maintenance. These precedents have had an important impact on both the well-being of the nation and its ability to provide for the general welfare of its citizens.

The story of the National Road, however, extends far beyond a discussion of constitutional considerations and congressional legislation. It embraces an account of its building, the unique culture that it represented, the movements and trends that transpired across its route, and the symbolic value that it held, and continues to hold, for the American people. These aspects are also reflected in this volume. It is hoped that a history of the road and its impact on the economy, politics, laws, and infrastructure of the United States, over two centuries, will serve to enhance the experience of traveling the National Road (in the form of U.S. 40), to preserve its heritage, and to assist schools, libraries, and museums dedicated to educating the present and future generations about that heritage.

Beyond its status as an American heritage symbol, the legacy of the National Road impacts the twenty-first century. It serves as a forceful reminder that the United States must continue to pursue the goal of sustainable national investment that began with the National Road and comparable projects during the early republic. This aspect of the National Road story is discussed in part IV and the epilogue.

Acknowledgments

I wish to express my deep appreciation for the contribution of the following individuals who, as students or former students at the Columbus School of Law, The Catholic University of America, have provided invaluable research, editing, and related services regarding this project: Ellen Berndtson, Barbara Burner, George Butler, Jennifer Crane, Kristin McGough and Maren Veatch. In all cases, these services were provided with skill, dedication, and commitment.

I also deeply appreciate all the efforts of Donna Holdorf, Executive Director of the National Road Heritage Corridor, Uniontown, Pennsylvania. Over the years, she has provided advice, encouragement, and support in the preparation of this book. Her efforts have contributed immeasurably to the completion of this project.

Dr. Donald C. Mell, chair of the editorial board of the University of Delaware Press, and Karen Druliner, have provided continuing and invaluable support, guidance and advice throughout the review and editorial process. The various readers for the University of Delaware Press have provided comprehensive, informed, and incisive advice regarding content and direction. For all assistance I am deeply grateful.

I am deeply grateful to my wife, Vera, and my daughters, Catherine and Victoria, for their support, advice, and insights on the text of the manuscript and on the illustrations, which has contributed greatly to the accessibility of this story of the National Road.

Particular appreciation is due to Ellen Berndtson, my student assistant during the spring 2011 semester. Her dedicated assistance in the final stages of the research for the book, in reviewing and editing the proofs, and in providing editorial and substantive comment was thorough, indispensable, and insightful. Nicole Picard, a former student at the Columbus School of Law, provided exceedingly helpful insights regarding issues pertaining to the concept of sustainable national investment. The staff of the Columbus School of Law, including the faculty support staff, the library staff, and the computer assistance staff, has been exceedingly helpful on the many occasions when requests for assistance were made by me or my student assistants during various stage of the work on this book.

I also wish to thank Johns Hopkins University Press for permission to quote material from *The National Road and the Guide to the National Road*, edited by Karl Raitz, published in 1996: pp. 104, 108–9, 112–13, 115–16, 124, 123–37, 139–43, 151–52, 155, 198, 203, 285, 289. I also thank the Overlook Press, New York City, New York, for permission to quote material from Merritt Ierley, *Traveling the National Road: Across the Centuries on America's First Highway*, as more fully set forth below in chapters 8, 9, and 10. The images in figures 1–5 are courtesy of the Museums of Oglebay Institute. I am grateful to Megan Clark, curator of the Museums, for her timely assistance in this regard.

I particularly thank my daughter, Victoria Sky, for taking the photograph of the author that appears on the back cover.

Christine Retz has devoted much time, thought, and effort to the preparation of an index for the work which greatly enhances its utility.

While I deeply appreciate all this assistance, I take full responsibility for all errors, omissions and lapses of judgment that may be reflected in this work. The views expressed in this work are my own and do not necessarily reflect the views of any institution or organization that I now serve or have served in the past.

The National Road
and the Difficult
Path to Sustainable
National Investment

Part I

THE GREAT DEBATES ABOUT THE NATIONAL ROAD

The Constitution of the United States

Article I.

Section 8.

The Congress shall have Power To lay and collect Taxes, Duties, Imposts and Excises, to pay the Debts and provide for the common Defence and general Welfare of the United States; but all Duties, Imposts and Excises shall be uniform throughout the United States;

To borrow Money on the credit of the United States;

To regulate Commerce with foreign Nations, and among the several States, and with the Indian Tribes;

To establish an uniform Rule of Naturalization, and uniform Laws on the subject of Bankruptcies throughout the United States;

To coin Money, regulate the Value thereof, and of foreign Coin, and fix the Standard of Weights and Measures;

To provide for the Punishment of counterfeiting the Securities and current Coin of the United States;

To establish Post Offices and post Roads;

To promote the Progress of Science and useful Arts, by securing for limited Times to Authors and Inventors the exclusive Right to their respective Writings and Discoveries;

To constitute Tribunals inferior to the supreme Court;

To define and punish Piracies and Felonies committed on the high Seas, and Offences against the Law of Nations;

To declare War, grant Letters of Marque and Reprisal, and make Rules concerning Captures on Land and Water;

To raise and support Armies, but no Appropriation of Money to that Use shall be for a longer Term than two Years;

To provide and maintain a Navy;

To make Rules for the Government and Regulation of the land and naval Forces;

To provide for calling forth the Militia to execute the Laws of the Union, suppress Insurrections and repel Invasions;

To provide for organizing, arming, and disciplining, the Militia, and for governing such Part of them as may be employed in the Service of the United States, reserving to the States respectively, the Appointment of the Officers, and the Authority of training the Militia according to the discipline prescribed by Congress;

To exercise exclusive Legislation in all Cases whatsoever, over such District (not exceeding ten Miles square) as may, by Cession of particular States, and the Acceptance of Congress, become the Seat of the Government of the United States, and to exercise like Authority over all Places purchased by the Consent of the Legislature of the State in which the Same shall be, for the Erection of Forts, Magazines, Arsenals, dock-Yards, and other needful Buildings;—And

To make all Laws which shall be necessary and proper for carrying into Execution the foregoing Powers, and all other Powers vested by this Constitution in the Government of the United States, or in any Department or Officer thereof.

CHAPTER 1

Washington's Role

Nemacolin and the Beginnings

In 1752, the Ohio Company of Virginia participated in a project to mark out a trail from Cumberland, Maryland, to Redstone on the Monongahela River (near present-day Brownsville, Pennsylvania). This was a portion of the route later envisaged in the 1806 act of Congress that established the framework for building the Cumberland Road, also called the National Road. Two colonial frontiersmen familiar with the region, Christopher Gist and Thomas Cresap, were engaged by the Ohio Company to join in the expedition. Nemacolin, a Delaware Indian chief, accompanied them. The party cut and marked a pack-horse trail from Cumberland to Redstone. It was known as Nemacolin's Trail.

Between 1753 and 1755, George Washington, then in his twenties, made at least three expeditions to western Pennsylvania that acquainted him thoroughly with the topography of the region as well as its economic potential. Road building was among the tasks that occupied him on at least two of those occasions.

In 1753, as an emissary of Governor Dinwiddie, colonial governor of Virginia, Washington was assigned to deliver a letter from the governor to the French commandant at Fort LeBoeuf (in northwestern Pennsylvania); the letter sternly warned France to abandon its plans to occupy British territory along the Ohio River. Major Washington, then twenty-one, accompanied by a small group of frontiersmen and Indians, traveled along a portion of the route that had been blazed by Nemacolin and his party—from Fort Cumberland in Maryland, across the Big Youghiogheny River to Chestnut Ridge (also known as Laurel Ridge) in Pennsylvania—before heading north to Fort LeBeouf in that colony. The return leg of the trip was, for Washington, "as fatiguing a Journey as it is possible to conceive."[1]

Fatiguing as it may have been, Washington's journey to northwestern Pennsylvania did not deter the French from pursuing their extensive ambitions regarding the Ohio Valley. In 1754, French forces occupied Fort Duquesne at the juncture of the Allegheny and Monongehela rivers (site of present-day Pittsburgh) and threatened the interests of Great Britain and its American colonies in the Ohio Valley. Further action was required. The young Washington was again called upon to play a role in protecting those interests. This time his efforts would include measures to improve the roads in the affected area.

Fort Necessity

In the spring of 1754, Washington set out for southwestern Pennsylvania, this time as commander of part of a regiment of Virginia soldiers assigned to drive the French out of their posts at Fort Duquesne. As part of their military duties, the expedition was to build a road to Red Stone Creek on the Monongahela near present-day Brownsville. This road would become a segment of the route from Cumberland to Wheeling later envisaged by the 1806 law that authorized the National Road. In May 1754, Washington and his regiment encamped at Great Meadows, another site along the future National Road. An encounter with a small group of French soldiers under the command of Joseph Coulon de Villiers, sieur de Jumonville, took place on May 28 at Chestnut Ridge, not far from Great Meadows. A number of the French soldiers, including young Jumonville, were killed. Anticipating a retaliatory attack from the French, Washington and his men returned to Great Meadows and fortified it with a circular stockade, which Washington called Fort Necessity. On July 3, 1754, a larger French force attacked Washington's troops at Fort Necessity. After a day's battle in which Washington sustained heavy losses, the French commander initiated a truce. Washington and his men were permitted to withdraw and return to Virginia with the honors of war.[2]

A more detailed account of the expedition suggests that military and road-building activities were intertwined. During the expedition but before the encounter at Fort Necessity, Washington and his force spent some time in road building in the same area that some fifty years later would became the site of the National Road in Pennsylvania. With directions from Governor Dinwiddie of Virginia to respond to French threats in the region of the Ohio River, Washington and his force left Alexandria on April 2. He made a report to Governor Dinwiddie from Wills Creek (Cumberland) on April 25, indicating that he was "destined to the Monongehela" with his detachment of 159 men. Part of his mission was evidently to widen Nemacolin's packhorse trail into a road that would be suitable for military vehicles. In a letter to Horatio Sharp, also written from Wills Creek on April 27, Washington communicated his intent to advance with his men and artillery "slowly across the mountains, *making the roads as we march*, fit for the carriage [of] the great guns. . . ." He expected to proceed as far as the mouth of Redstone Creek.[3]

On May 18, Washington wrote again to Governor Dinwiddie, this time from the Great Crossing of the Youghiogheny, reporting information he had obtained from the traders and the Indians. He had learned that it would be "almost impossible" to open a road "that a wagon can pass" from Great Crossing to Red Stone Creek (now from the Youghiogheny River to Brownsville). Apparently seeking a better alternative, Washington explored the Youghiogheny River for several days until May 23. By May 27, he was at Great Meadows where, on the same day, he wrote to Governor Dinwiddie that he had "prepar'd a charming field for an Encounter." Washington recorded in his journal the encounter with the French force under Jumonville, the death of Jumonville, and the capture of a number of the men under Jumonville's command. Washington justified the encounter in his letter to Dinwiddie, assuring the governor that Jumonville's group constituted a hostile force rather than a peace mission, as the French maintained.[4]

On June 3, Washington reported building a "small palisao'd Fort" to face the anticipated French attack in response to the Jumonville encounter. With Fort Necessity built, Washington was evidently prepared to return to road building. On June 21, he was "on the march to Red Stone." Six days later he recounted that he had detached several officers and sixty men to "complete building" the road as far as the mouth of that creek, on the Monongehela. Here, however, the journal entries on the expedition abruptly end. By July 3, 1754, Washington was, as mentioned, back at Fort Necessity (now with about four hundred men) to face the French and Indian force, which attacked his garrison there. After the battle, he was obliged to withdraw with his men and to return to Virginia. By August 11, he was back in Alexandria.[5]

Based on this account, the route that Washington traversed (and worked to improve) in 1754 from Cumberland to Great Meadows and then in the direction of Redstone Creek more or less followed the path said to be blazed by Nemacolin two years earlier during the expedition of the Ohio Company to the Monongahela. The surveyors who labored under the legislation signed by Thomas Jefferson some fifty-two years later generally selected the same route for the National Road.[6]

The Braddock Campaign

During the French and Indian War, the future route of the National Road again became the scene of a military campaign. This time, as an aide to British general

Edward Braddock, Washington accompanied a large contingent of British troops in an ill-fated effort to drive the French out of Fort Duquesne. Again, road building was a necessary aspect of the campaign. Braddock's engineers cut a wide road to facilitate the passage of cannon and wagons carrying military and other supplies to support the force and those who accompanied it. The road generally followed the route that Washington had taken in 1754 to the area of Fort Necessity, but then proceeded in a northwesterly direction toward Fort Duquesne. The delay involved in cutting the road prompted young Washington to complain that the British "were halting to Level every Mold Hill & to erect Bridges over every brook."[7]

Braddock's defeat and death, a result of the subsequent ambush by French and Indian forces (near the fort and north of the route of the future National Road), dealt a severe blow to the British and colonial forces. This initial setback, however, was ultimately reversed by a definitive British victory in the war, the French abandonment of Fort Duquesne and French withdrawal from North America.

Braddock's campaign represented the first major battle of the French and Indian War, a conflict that set the stage for the American Revolution. Despite reverses in the early stage of the war, Great Britain's victory in that conflict (and the conflict's European counterpart, known as the Seven Years' War) made it the dominant power in Europe. In winning, Britain paid a high price. Fiscally challenged, it began to impose taxes on its colonies in North America. That policy of taxation—without representation—eventually led to resentment, resistance, and a call for independence by the colonists. Washington, whose encounter with Jumonville in 1754 had helped to ignite the conflict, became commander of the American forces in the American Revolutionary War.[8]

A "Smooth Way" to the West

The experience of Fort Necessity and the Braddock expedition did not terminate George Washington's interest in a road leading to the west. Rather, it helped to convince Washington of the need for an adequate means of transportation across the Allegheny Mountains to the Ohio, both for economic and for military ends. Investment considerations were a factor as well. Washington owned large tracts of land in the region that demanded his attention.

In September and October 1784, Washington traveled to Virginia, Maryland, and western Pennsylvania in pursuit of his business interests, including the collection of rents and the inspection of his landholdings. In the course of his journey, he reflected deeply about the need for an adequate transportation route between the East and the West. Such a route would more closely bind western settlers to the new nation that had just emerged from the Revolutionary War. On October 4, at the completion of his journey, Washington committed these reflections to his diary. He was concerned that the western settlers might be drawn by trade considerations away from the new American Union and into the orbit of Great Britain or Spain, both of which held vast tracts in the North American continent. To prevent this, Washington was interested in finding a route that would connect his own state of Virginia with the West. He weighed the relative merits of various rivers in this context, including the Monongahela, the Youghiogheny, the Cheat, and the great Kanhawas.

In his diary, he observed:

> The Western Settlers—from my own observation—stand as it were on a pivet—the touch of a feather would almost incline them any way. . . . A combination of circumstances make the present conjecture more favorable than any other to fix the trade of the Western Country to our Markets. . . . The way to avoid [separation or war], happily for us, is easy, and dictated by our clearest interests. It is to open a wide door, and make a smooth way for the produce of that Country to pass to our Markets, before the trade may get into another channel. . . . So, if we [Virginians] are supine; and suffer without a struggle the Settlers of the Western Country to form commercial connections with the Spaniards, Britons, or with any of the States in the Union . . . we shall find it a difficult matter to dissolve them. . . .[9]

Interestingly, in this diary entry, Washington did not specifically address the possibility of a land route from Cumberland, Maryland, through Pennsylvania, joining the Potomac to the Monongehela and the Ohio, although he had traveled portions of that route during the military campaigns of 1754 and 1755 and, indeed, again visited Great Meadows and Uniontown during the 1784 journey. On the other hand, during the 1784 journey, Washington was carefully weighing various alternatives for such a route, apparently engaging on one occasion with a young surveyor, Albert Gallatin, with respect to the best alternative. It was Gallatin who was to play a major role in the establishment of a road that would serve Washington's objective. Judging from his diary, Washington's preference was for a route that would most meaningfully involve his own state of Virginia. Quite apart from the relative merits of individual routes, in 1784 Washington clearly recognized that, in order to serve vital economic, national security, and geopolitical interests, an investment in the making of a "smooth way" across the Allegheny Mountains that separated the East and the West was essential.[10]

Washington as Constitution Maker and President

Three years later Washington played a vital role in the establishment of the Constitution of the United States. He presided over the Constitutional Convention of 1787 and helped secure the ratification of that document in 1788. Within the framework of that charter, the "smooth way" contemplated by Washington was authorized by Congress in 1806 and subsequently built at federal expense. It joined the Potomac, the Monongehela, and the Ohio with a land route known as the National (or Cumberland) Road.

As the first president of the United States, Washington did not forget that adequate arteries of transportation were necessary for the well-being of the infant nation. In his first State of the Union address, he strongly recommended that Congress consider the need for "facilitating the intercourse between the distant parts of our country by a due attention to the post-office and post-roads." Washington's reference to post offices and post roads invoked a provision of the U.S. Constitution contained in Article I, section 8, of that document setting forth the powers of Congress. Clause 7 of that section confers on Congress power to "establish post offices and post roads." Washington did not specify whether he thought Congress should use this authority to conduct or assist in road building; he merely called the attention of the Congress to the constitutional provision in question. For a time in our history—namely, during the early twentieth century—the clause was cited as a constitutional basis, among others, for the federal investment in roads that essentially began with the construction of the National Road. However, James Madison, Washington's fellow Virginian and delegate to the Constitutional Convention, appeared to reject such a reading some twenty-eight years after Washington spoke of it in his message. In his Bonus Bill veto of 1817, discussed in chapter 3, Madison vetoed a bill that would have set aside federal funds for constructing roads and canals. Madison strongly denied that the Constitution afforded power to Congress to take such action. "[I]t does not appear that the power proposed to be exercised by the bill is among the enumerated powers," Madison said. He discussed the Commerce and General Welfare Clause in this context, but did not specifically discuss the Post Roads Clause. However, his blanket assertion appeared to cover that clause as well. In any event, in modern times the General Welfare Clause came to be recognized as the preferred or most frequently cited source of constitutional authority for federal aid to roads and canals, as well as other infrastructure needs.[11]

In addition to his observations regarding congressional attention to "post-roads," Washington included in his first annual message a strong plea for educational improvement through aid to "seminaries of learning" or the establishment of a "national university," thus linking the transportation and educational needs of the nation in his recommendation for objects of federal "investment." For Washington, adequate infrastructure for transportation and adequate institutions of higher education were both instruments of effective nation-binding. They were also instruments of the common good, and it was appropriate for the chief executive of the federal government to commend them to its legislative branch for enlightened consideration, even in an era when executive power was restrained.[12]

Equally compelling, a constitutional interpretation that would ultimately be important to federal participation in the building of roads and canals was proposed in Washington's first term. In 1791, Alexander Hamilton, Washington's brilliant and creative secretary of the treasury, conceived the constitutional theory under which federal financial assistance ultimately was applied to support the National Road (and other internal improvements) in the nineteenth century and to aid education on a broad scale in the twentieth. At the heart of Hamilton's thinking was a literal interpretation of the taxing and spending power found in Article I, section 8, clause 1, of the Constitution. This provision authorizes Congress to lay taxes to "provide for the common defense and general welfare of the United States." For Hamilton, the power of Congress to spend federal funds under this provision extended to "whatever concerns the general interests of learning, of agriculture, of manufactures and of commerce." Hamilton believed that it was constitutional for Congress to provide financial aid to any of these areas of endeavor, even if they were not specifically mentioned in the Constitution itself as areas to which the federal legislative power extended. Later, this theory was extended to justify federal support for internal improvement.[13]

Hamilton posed this interpretation in his *Report on Manufactures*, which he sent to Congress at its request. Hamilton urged that the United States take steps to strengthen its capacity to manufacture. For him a manufacturing base, as well as an agricultural one, was essential to the well-being of the new country. Among other things, that base would help the nation generate revenues that would enable it to pay the interest on the Revolutionary War debt. How would the United States encourage Americans to establish manufacturing enterprises that could compete with those in Europe that were long entrenched? Among other strategies, Hamilton proposed that Congress provide appropriate subsidies or bounties that would help the establishment of new or infant industries. However, in discussing the merits of these bounties and recommending them as fit subjects for legislation, Hamilton was obliged to address another question: what authority under the Constitution did Congress possess that would enable it to provide such financial assistance? None of the powers specifically assigned to Congress under Article I, section 8, of the Constitution gave it that power. In response, Hamilton pointed to the taxing power and the inherent related power to spend tax revenues for the "general welfare of the United States" contained in Article I, section 8, clause 1, of that document.[14]

Not all the officers in Washington's cabinet applauded this interpretation. On the contrary, Secretary of State Jefferson opposed it profoundly. Jefferson was devoted to the vision of an agrarian society in which yeoman farmers would preserve the values of the American Revolution. A strong central government was inconsistent with his vision. Moreover, he thought that vesting Congress with the enormous power that Hamilton was proposing (through the medium of the General Welfare Clause) was inconsistent with the Constitution and a danger to the preservation of liberty. Indeed, Hamilton's legal interpretation, together with his financial program, was regarded by Jefferson as a "subversion" of the Constitution.

Jefferson complained to Washington about the dangers that Hamilton's theories posed and pointed specifically to the interpretation of the spending power as the root of the problem. However, confronted with these accusations, Washington apparently remained silent. While he did not overtly embrace Hamilton's interpretation, he did not openly disavow it. Moreover, during his second term, although Hamilton had left the Treasury Department, Washington continued to look to him for advice and drafting assistance in making his recommendations to Congress, a number of which had a "public investment" thrust. None of this directly affected the National Road. The first legislation to deal seriously with new roads to the West was not adopted until 1802 after Washington's death. As mentioned, the first National Road authorization was not enacted until 1806. Although Congress never acted on Hamilton's bounty proposals, the battle over the issue during the Washington administration set the stage for a long struggle over the role of the federal government under the Constitution, a battle that would engulf the National Road. That battle also established a framework for the conflict of views between Hamilton's Federalist Party and Jefferson's Democratic-Republican Party, a conflict that was to characterize American politics during the early decades of the nineteenth century.[15]

Washington himself had no occasion to comment publicly on the constitutional issue, because no legislation emerged from the report in which Hamilton made his interpretation. It seems likely, however, that the president was satisfied with the flexibility the interpretation afforded the government; he was in favor of promoting national economic growth through the establishment of a viable transportation network. At the very least, Hamilton's constitutional observations appear to be consistent with Washington's own views in favor of federal public investment expressed in his State of the Union and other addresses.[16]

The Whiskey Rebellion of 1794 constitutes yet another event during the Washington administration that bears, in a sense, on the history of the National Road. In 1791, as part of Hamilton's program for funding the national debt,

Congress adopted an excise tax on domestic whiskey. The tax fell particularly hard on farmers and residents of western Pennsylvania who were "most economically dependent upon whiskey distillation." They resisted the tax forcibly. One of the leaders of the "rebellion" was William Bradford, a prominent lawyer and resident of Washington, Pennsylvania. When efforts to achieve compliance with the tax failed and some tax collectors were treated forcibly, President Washington, accompanied by Hamilton, led an army of some thirteen thousand troops into western Pennsylvania to quell the rebellion and ensure compliance with the law. Washington called this force the "army of the Constitution." He saw the expedition as a necessary effort to enforce the laws and ensure the flow of revenues required to meet the obligations of the infant government. The federal forces prevailed, and resistance to the tax subsided. While the administration's efforts had no direct bearing on the National Road, which was not legislatively authorized until more than a decade later, they did provide a foundation for the later efforts of the government to assist internal improvements with the proceeds of federal revenues.[17]

While the initiation of the National Road did not take place until the Jefferson administration, one action taken during Washington's tenure anticipated a federal role in the laying out and building of roads. In 1796 Colonel Ebenezer Zane, a veteran of the Revolutionary War, sought congressional authority to lay out a post road from the Ohio River to a town now known as Maysville in Kentucky. The purpose of the road was to help speed the delivery of mails and facilitate land travel. By the Act of May 17, 1796, in the last year of Washington's administration, Congress authorized the project and approved Zane's request for compensation. They permitted him to use his military land warrants to acquire land at three points in the Ohio territory where his road crossed important rivers. Zane's Trace, as it was called, amounted to little more than a packhorse-trail mail route. A portion of Zane's route, between Wheeling, Virginia (now West Virginia), and what is now Zanesville, Ohio, was later incorporated into the National Road. The role of the government in supporting the establishment of Zane's Trace is described as follows in a current article in the U.S. Department of Transportation's Highway History series: "Colonel Zane . . . appealed to Congress for permission to build a road and he received that permission in 1796 after he had already begun the project. Zane requested and received from the American government land grants where the Trace crossed the Muskingum, Hocking and Scioto Rivers to pay for his surveying costs. The government agreed to his request believing that a major road opened in 1797 would bring more settlers to Ohio and help increase trade." Presumably, the permission was sought because Ohio was then a territory of the United States subject to the authority vested in the federal government by Article IV, section 3, of the U.S. Constitution.[18]

In sum, as a young military officer, George Washington engaged in road-building activities along a part of the route that eventually became the National Road. As a leading figure in post–Revolutionary War America, he expressed a strong interest in a "smooth way" to the west that would bind the western settlers, facilitating their trade with the East and at the same time precluding any gravitation on their part toward Great Britain or Spain. As president he recognized the need for a federal role in establishing post roads. He also appointed a secretary of the treasury who conceived and articulated a plausible constitutional framework for federal assistance, both for the National Road and the multitude of infrastructure projects that followed it. Washington took a bold step to ensure the future enforcement of the federal revenue laws, those laws upon which federal assistance to the National Road and other internal improvements would come to depend. As indicated above, during Washington's administration, Zane's Trace, an early road project, was laid out, with government support, by Colonel Ebenezer Zane, to whom Congress had issued military warrants. The project anticipated that much more extensive investment commenced in 1806 by means of the federal legislation authorizing the initial steps leading to the construction of the National Road. In these respects Washington, or the administration over which he presided, played a critical role in the genesis of the National Road and set the stage for its initiation less then a decade after his leaving office.

Washington's contribution in this arena should be celebrated in another important respect that transcends but at the same time relates to the National Road. This is his contribution to the quest for sustainable national investment that runs through the course of American history. As military officer, military road builder, land investor, canal promoter, and advocate for a "smooth way" to the west, Washington encouraged and promoted what is called here "sustainable national investment," investment carried out by the federal government through funds appropriated by Congress under the spending power contained in the Constitution in order to serve the nation's economic goals in ways that could not be achieved without federal participation. President Washington recognized this aspect of the federal role throughout his administration. For example, in his annual messages he advocated or recommended, however discreetly, a federal role in education, the establishment of post roads, agricultural and commercial assistance, and other objectives of an investment nature. His tacit support for Hamilton's broad interpretation of the Constitution's General Welfare Clause (as expressed in the treasury secretary's *Report on Manufactures*) is an important part of Washington's implicit inclination in favor of the government's public investment role. That role was to become considerably more concrete and pronounced through the authorization and construction of the National Road as a federally funded project.[19]

CHAPTER 2

Jefferson, Gallatin, and the Legislation of 1806

The Act of March 29, 1806—Connecting Ohio

On March 29, 1806, President Thomas Jefferson signed into law legislation authorizing him to "make" a road from Cumberland, Maryland, to the state of Ohio. It also authorized him to appoint as commissioners three "discreet and disinterested citizens" to lay out the road according to its specified width (four rods). The law directed the commissioners to report to the president on any recommendations they had, as well as the probable expense of constructing the road. The president was free to accept or reject the report in whole or in part. If he accepted it, he was required to obtain the consent of the states through which the road would pass. This done, the act authorized the president to take prompt measures to cause the road (often called the Cumberland Road but referred to here as the "National Road") to be made.[1]

The Act of March 29, 1806 built upon an earlier law enacted in 1802 authorizing the establishment and admission of Ohio into the Union. That law provided that 5 percent of the proceeds of federal government land sales in Ohio could be set aside for laying out and making public roads leading from the navigable waters emptying into the Atlantic to the waters of the Ohio River, as well as roads within that state. Subsequent legislation appropriated 3 percent for roads within the state, thus leaving a balance of 2 percent of the proceeds for a contemplated portage road joining points of navigation on the Potomac and the Ohio River and establishing a route from the East to Ohio. Jefferson signed this law apparently without public comment.[2]

What steps led to the 1806 act's passage? In December 1805, during the first session of the Ninth Congress, Senator Uri Tracy of Connecticut, on behalf of the Senate committee to which the matter had been referred, submitted the committee's report to the Senate. The report discussed a variety of possible routes for the road in question. Roads from Philadelphia, Baltimore, Richmond, and Washington were considered, but the committee thought that federal funds for these roads might duplicate or complicate efforts of the states in question. What was most expedient was a route from Cumberland, Maryland, that crossed the Monongahela at Brownsville, Pennsylvania, and then reached the eastern bank of the Ohio in the vicinity of Wheeling. The committee estimated the distance at 156 miles. It also concluded that Maryland, Pennsylvania, and Virginia would be unlikely to build such a road from their own funds. Federal money was needed to stimulate the project.[3]

To carry out this ambitious plan, Senator Tracy reported a bill containing the provisions described above. The bill was dutifully read and ordered to a second reading. On Friday, December 27, 1805, the Senate passed it without debate and sent it to the House. "Duty," Senator Tracy urged, compelled this important step.[4]

The House waited until the spring of 1806 before taking up the measure. Representative Michael Leib of Pennsylvania moved to postpone the bill indefinitely, and several members spoke in favor of that motion, "fearing that the subject . . . would not be deliberately examined." Postponement may have been suggested as a means of delaying or defeating the legislation by those who favored a different route. Representative George Bedinger of Kentucky opposed postponement. He believed that the route prescribed in the bill would best serve the "general interests of the Union." Representative Jeremiah Morrow of Ohio also urged the House to reject postponement. The road, he said, would be "conducive to the interests of the Western people." The House must have been persuaded. On a roll call vote, Leib's motion to postpone lost, 51 yeas to 59 nays.[5]

On Monday, March 24, the measure was again taken up by the House. It passed, 66 yeas to 55 nays. In general, members of the House from the New England, Maryland, Kentucky, and Ohio delegations supported the measure, while Virginia and Pennsylvania members largely opposed it, apparently on the ground that the route did not cover major portions of their states. As Joseph Wood points out, "Jefferson and Democratic Republicans favored the bill. . . . The Federalists' successors, the Whigs, led by former Northwest Territory governor Arthur St. Clair, opposed, their concern being the West's too rapidly increasing importance with respect to the East's political power."[6]

Gallatin's Contribution

Jefferson's able and energetic secretary of the treasury, Albert Gallatin, played a major role in the enactment of this legislation. Joseph Wood ranks Gallatin high among those who contributed to the establishment of the road. "Of all the actors in the National Road drama," he observes, "Albert Gallatin may be the most important." Gallatin had been a staunch advocate of internal improvements since his days in the Pennsylvania legislature and his service, as a representative from western Pennsylvania, in the U.S. Congress. As treasury secretary, he had suggested inclusion of the provision for reservation of funds for road construction in the 1802 Ohio admission legislation.

Gallatin recommended to William B. Giles, chair of the congressional committee handling the legislation, that a bargain of benefit to the state and the nation be inserted into that legislation. On its part, the state would agree that the sale of federal land in the state would be exempt from state taxation for a period of ten years. In exchange the United States would agree that one of sixteen sections sold by the United States in a township would be reserved for education. It would also agree that one-tenth of the net proceeds of the lands sold by the United States would be applied to laying out roads first from the navigable waters emptying into the Atlantic to the waters of the Ohio and then through the state of Ohio. Clearly, schools and roads were both important priorities of the framer generation.

Gallatin advocated these specific provisions for several reasons. The school-based provision was originally in the Northwest Ordinance legislation and was desired by the inhabitants of the Ohio territory. "The roads," Gallatin said, "will be beneficial to the parts of the Atlantic States through which they are to pass" as well as to much of the Union and the Ohio territory. In sum, Gallatin thought the admission legislation would "contribute toward cementing the bonds of the Union between those parts of the United States, whose local interests have been considered as most dissimilar." During consideration of the 1806 act, Gallatin also worked tirelessly on behalf of the administration to ensure its passage. Again, Wood pays tribute to the treasury secretary: "[Gallatin's] National Road plan was part of a large scheme, not only for ensuring internal improvements but also for formulating a complete national plan."[7]

Gallatin's career included service in the Pennsylvania House of Representatives and Senate, the U.S. House of Representatives and U.S. Senate, the Jefferson and Madison administrations as secretary of the treasury, and the Madison administration as a principal negotiator of the Treaty of Ghent, which settled the War of 1812. He also served the Monroe administration as minister to France and the John Quincy Adams administration as minister to Great Britain. He has the distinction of being the longest serving secretary of the treasury in the nation's history. His contributions include, in addition to those related to the National Road, the financing of the Louisiana Purchase in 1803 and the Lewis and Clark Expedition of 1804 through 1806. He also conceptualized a major program of internal improvements during the Jefferson years, set forth in a landmark report to Congress.[8]

Jefferson's Quandary

Jefferson himself, while a proponent of limited government, proclaimed his enthusiasm for internal improvements in his 1805 second inaugural address. But Jefferson also had constitutional qualms about the authority of the federal government to make or fund such improvements. The Constitution contained no explicit provision authorizing a congressional role in "making internal improvements." Therefore, Jefferson thought, there was no constitutional authority to spend federal funds for such endeavors. Indeed, in his inaugural address, Jefferson advocated a constitutional amendment to provide the explicit authority he and his secretary of state, James Madison, thought necessary. Jefferson did not accept the interpretation of the Constitution that Alexander Hamilton had propounded in his *Report on Manufactures*, which justified, among other things, federal subsidies for manufacturing activities. On the contrary, as noted above, Jefferson had vigorously opposed that report's conclusions and protested its issuance.[9]

How then did Jefferson come to sign the Act of March 29, 1806? One may speculate that he believed it appropriate to commence planning the project (laying out the road) and assumed that an amendment would be proposed shortly thereafter by Congress and submitted to the states for ratification. Moreover, the use of the proceeds of land sales that Gallatin had advocated, together with the requirement in the 1806 law that the consent of the states must be obtained for the building of the road, may have convinced Jefferson that an argument for the constitutional validity of the project could be made even in the absence of an amendment. After all, under this "state compact" argument, Congress was merely carrying out the agreement with the state that had been written into the admission law with the consent of both parties. It was not using its appropriation power contrary to state wishes but rather to carry out the terms of a compact with the state in which the state had given up its right to tax the proceeds of land sales in the state. This "compact theory" at least for a time appears to have responded to Jefferson's concern regarding the lack of a specific enumerated power on which to base the federal aid legislation that he had signed.

Jeremiah Simeon Young, in his 1902 dissertation, "A Political and Constitutional Study of the Cumberland Road," commented upon this so-called compact theory as follows:

> The act of Congress in 1806 fixed only two points on the Cumberland Road—Cumberland on the Potomac and Wheeling on the Ohio. This immediately presented the question of the constitutional authority of the United States to lay out and construct a road through the territory of Maryland, Pennsylvania and Virginia. In other words,

had the United States the authority to exercise the right of eminent domain within the territory of a state? The treatment of eminent domain in connection with the early internal improvements is an interesting subject, as eminent domain is one of the great powers of sovereignty. The right of the United States to exercise this power was denied by the states as an infringement on their sovereignty; therefore, the practice in most cases was for the United States to exercise the right with the consent of the states, and by means of state methods and officers. . . . Since this was the prevailing view, the act of 1806 providing for the Cumberland Road empowered the President, after accepting the report of the commissioners on location, "to pursue such measures as he deems proper in *obtaining the consent of the states* through which the road may pass; and having obtained their consent, he is further authorized to take measures in having the road promptly made through the whole distance."[10]

This explanation is not satisfying insofar as it applied to the matter of appropriation of funds for the National Road project, as distinguished from the matter of eminent domain. The state compact argument apparently also assumed that a state could, by its consent, sanction the exercise of federal spending authority that the Constitution, according to Jefferson, did not expressly confer. However, it is doubtful that a state's consent would confer upon Congress the power to appropriate funds for a purpose for which appropriation was not authorized under the Constitution. Thus, the state consent argument masked what must have been a profound dilemma of politics, policy, and philosophy for Jefferson. On the one hand, as he had declared in his first inaugural address, he was dedicated to limited and frugal government. He believed that the state prerogatives should be preserved against federal encroachment. Like his friend and political partner, James Madison, he believed that the enumerated powers in the Congress must be faithfully observed. As we have seen, he had battled fiercely with Hamilton over that point in his days as secretary of state in the Washington administration. He had, as we have seen, denied that the spending power in Article I, section 8, clause 1, of the Constitution conferred power to appropriate for objects not contained within the enumerated powers in that section.[11]

However, Jefferson also wanted to promote western expansion and knew that internal improvements were essential to that cause. He wanted to see the West settled for economic and philosophical reasons. Filling up the land beyond the mountains would promote and protect the United States and give effect to the Louisiana Purchase that his administration had successfully negotiated. In his second administration, he had expressed, in a letter, the hope that "during peace we may chequer our whole country with roads, canals, etc." His secretary of the treasury was preparing a bold and ambitious report that amounted to a blueprint for nationwide internal improvement. He must have known that this would not be possible without federal assistance. How could he then reconcile these competing strands of his political philosophy and of the principles of his party?[12]

A call for a constitutional amendment to authorize Congress to assist such internal improvements might resolve the constitutional dilemma without the need for reliance on the state compact theory. In fact, Jefferson called for such an amendment in his second inaugural address and in his sixth annual message of December 1806.[13] Surely, he must have had the national road project in mind; he had signed that legislation in March, months before the delivery of the message. But when Congress did not propose such an amendment, how could Jefferson, nevertheless, continue the project? In doing so, he may have believed that he had performed his duty and stayed true to his political philosophy, while still moving the country forward, when he had clearly called for the amendment in formal state papers. After all, the Constitution placed the responsibility for initiating such an amendment on Congress, not the president, who had no formal role in the Article V amendment process. If Congress failed to heed his solemn counsel, it was not for him to deprive the nation of what was needed to open up the interior and stimulate commerce. Moreover, the compact theory discussed above could be seen as constituting a temporary expedient to address the period before a constitutional amendment could be secured as a result of Jefferson's advocacy in his second inaugural address and the subsequent annual message.[14]

Whatever may have been his motive or thinking, Jefferson's signature on the 1806 legislation set in motion a train of events that led first to the charting of a route for the Cumberland Road and thereafter to the commencement of road construction in 1811. It also set a key precedent for federal involvement in the financing and establishment of internal improvements during the years of the early republic and beyond.[15]

The Commissioners' First Report

Following the enactment of the Act of March 29, 1806, President Jefferson duly appointed three commissioners to lay out the road: Thomas Moore and Elie Williams of Maryland and Joseph Kerr of Ohio. Later that year they undertook their duties, conducting surveying activities with a company including "two surveyors, two chain carriers, a vane man, a packhorse man, and a horse." Elie Williams has left us with an account of the meeting of the commissioners in Cumberland, prior to the submission of their report to the president:

> From Fryday [sic] 28th November till Saturday the 6th December inclusive the Commsrs were engaged at Cumberland in comparing their several journals of their proceedings in exploring & examining the grounds from the commencement and in making a decision on the grand points to be located for the direction of the route and after mature deliberation determined that the route commence at a stone at the corner of lot no. 1 in Cumberland & near the confluence of Wills Creek & the North Branch of Potomac, to extend thro the street westwardly to cross the hill laying between Cumberland & Gwynns [Tavern] at the gap in said hill where Braddocks road passes. . . .
>
> Before the Commsrs came to this decision an unusual fall of snow at so early a period of the winter made it impossible for them to proceed in regulating & marking the route, they therefore concluded to relinquish further progress in the business till such a period in the Spring as the weather will permit them to resume and in the meantime to report to the President the progress made, and after instructing Mr. Thompson their Surveyor to prepare with all convenient dispatch a compleat & comprehensive map of all their work they left Cumberland under an engagement to meet at the City of Washington as soon as their journal & report could be made up to be presented with their plat to the President of the United States at the City of Washington.[16]

In December 1806 the commissioners submitted the report to President Jefferson. It described the steps they had taken to survey the terrain that a road from Cumberland might cross. It graphically portrayed the difficulties the commissioners faced in laying out a workable route from Cumberland to the West. The governing principle, the commissioners wrote, should be to achieve the "best mode of diffusing benefits with the least distance of road." With this in mind, they suggested a route from Cumberland, Maryland, across the "Big Youghiogheny" River, across Laurel Hill in Pennsylvania to Brownsville on the Monongahela (in that state) and from there to the east bank of the Ohio in the vicinity of Wheeling. While the route selected did not exactly duplicate Nemacolin's path in 1752 and Washington's military road of 1754, it generally ran parallel to them. Jefferson transmitted the report to Congress on January 31, 1807, informing that body that he had obtained the consent of Maryland and Virginia for the making of the road within their borders but had not yet received assent from Pennsylvania. He, therefore, deferred a decision on whether to accept the report until Pennsylvania consented.[17]

The Question of Uniontown

The route proposed by the commissioners in their first report failed to include two important communities in Pennsylvania: Uniontown and Washington, both county seats. In early 1807, that state's legislature responded to the invitation for its consent. It granted its consent subject to the qualification that the route must pass through those two communities. In a letter to Gallatin in April 1807, Jefferson noted this issue and expressed his willingness to accede to the deviation through Uniontown.[18]

Accordingly, in their second report the commissioners revised their proposed route to include Uniontown. With this revision, they had marked out the mountainous route from Cumberland to Brownsville. The commissioners included a table showing the various elevations along the way, with the summit of Negro Mountain in Maryland, at 2,328 feet, being the highest point and a point at Dunlop's Creek near the Monongahela being the lowest, at 119. Despite the difficulties of predicting such matters, the commissioners estimated that the construction of the road would cost the government approximately six thousand dollars per mile.[19]

In February 1808, Jefferson transmitted this second report to Congress, informing the legislature that he had now received the consent of all three affected states and had approved the proposed route as far as Brownsville, subject to a "single deviation" through Uniontown. Jefferson observed that the major purpose of the project was to join Washington, D.C., to St. Louis, an objective that would not be subverted by the proposed deviation. When complete, Jefferson told Congress, the road would "accomplish a continued and advantageous line of communication from the seat of Government to St. Louis, passing through some very interesting points of the Western Country." This comment in Jefferson's 1808 report to Congress seems to be the first official mention of the idea that the National Road was expected to terminate in St. Louis, although the concept of the road ultimately connecting the East with the Mississippi is hardly surprising and is consistent with Washington's general objectives as described in chapter 1. Jeremiah Simeon Young mentions the report in his study of the Cumberland Road but does not ascribe the St. Louis terminus idea to statesmen other than Jefferson.[20]

The Question of Washington, Pennsylvania: Politics, Economics, and Policy

Attention now turned to the remainder of the route—from Brownsville to the Ohio. In April 1808, Jefferson again wrote to Gallatin on the subject of the

Cumberland Road. The president reminded Gallatin that Pennsylvania was insisting that the road pass through the town of Washington in that state. This prospect perturbed Jefferson. "I know my determination was not to yield to the example of a State's prescribing the direction of the road," he told Gallatin. "I understood the law as leaving the route ultimately to me," he continued. "If I have misconstrued the law, I shall be sorry for the money spent on a misconstruction, but that loss will be a lesser evil to the United States than a single example of yielding to the State the direction of a road made at national expense for national purposes."[21]

Despite the emphasis that Jefferson had previously placed on state prerogatives and the limitations of federal authority, he was correctly anticipating the course of federal law on the subject. The law now clearly recognizes that, in granting federal funds, the government may insist upon conditions that are binding upon the recipient, whether a public or private agency. These conditions, however, must be reasonably related to the program in question and meet other requirements that the Supreme Court has set forth. This principle, however, was not so clear in 1806.[22]

The issue concerning the deviation to Washington did not generate an intractable barrier in connection with the charting of the Brownsville-to-Wheeling portion of the road. Gallatin sought to defuse the issue with some practical political advice not unlike that which occasionally figures in the resolution of such matters in our own day. The election of 1808 was looming. The embargo against commerce with Britain was generating great concern within the nation, and the anxiety was directed at the Jefferson administration. The loss of Pennsylvania in the coming election would be a blow. Gallatin took these factors into account in advising Jefferson to instruct the commissioners to survey a route that would pass through Washington, Pennsylvania. In a letter of July 27, 1808, to Jefferson, Gallatin wrote: "Permit me, however, to state that the county of Washington [Pennsylvania] with which I am well acquainted, having represented it six years in Congress, gives a uniform majority of about 2000 votes in our favor, and that if this be thrown, by reason of the road, in a wrong scale, we will infallibly lose the State of Pennsylvania at the next election. . . ." Gallatin considered the additional distance required to include Washington negligible. He also hastened to assure Jefferson of his view that the diversion would not to be contrary to the "public interest."[23]

Gallatin's Report on Internal Improvement and the Posture of the Jeffersonians

Gallatin may have also been moved by another consideration: with the backing of Jefferson, Gallatin, in his capacity as treasury secretary, had submitted to Congress, *at its request,* an ambitious and far-reaching report on a program of federally supported internal improvements for the entire nation. It proposed a breathtaking system of roads and canals, running north to south and east to west. This report was in keeping with both Jefferson's and Gallatin's belief in the importance of internal improvements as a means of unifying the country and stimulating its economic growth. But, in the absence of a constitutional amendment authorizing such a broad program of internal improvements, it was not consistent with the president's view of the limits of federal spending power. Accordingly, in his report, Gallatin had suggested such an amendment. Gallatin's effort has been called "a remarkably cohesive and forward looking document which, unfortunately, had little effect on U.S. transportation policy."

In his report, Gallatin stressed the economic value of a nationwide system of roads and canals. Gallatin was certain that only the general (federal) government could fund and execute such public works. The ambitious program of public works that Gallatin contemplated would cost the government $20 million at the rate of $2 million a year. To this end, he proposed a series of canals along the eastern seaboard, a highway from Maine to Georgia, a set of internal roads to Detroit, St. Louis, and New Orleans, and improved inland navigation between the Hudson and the Great Lakes, as well as other waterways. The National Road was also part of the system.[24]

Gallatin's report was entitled *The Report of the Secretary of the Treasury on Roads and Canals.* It was submitted to the Senate in the first session of the Tenth Congress in 1808. It was the most comprehensive executive-branch report on the transportation needs of the nation that had been submitted to that date. Together with Hamilton's *Report on Manufactures* in 1791, it remains a primary early-republic touchstone on the subject of national investment generally.[25]

In it Secretary Gallatin advocated a bold and ambitious plan of infrastructure development and improvement designed to demonstrate the economic, military, and political advantages of a comprehensive program of national investment in roads and canals substantially financed by the fledgling federal government. Gallatin's plan included a proposal to connect Washington, D.C., with the West—among other ways, through the launching of the already authorized Cumberland Road that would connect the Potomac with the Monongehela and, later, the Ohio.[26]

In advocating his plan, Gallatin first proposed a formula for determining the advantages of infrastructure investment. He related that investment to its impact in increasing national wealth. He wrote: "It is sufficiently evident that, whenever the annual expense of transportation on a certain route in its natural state, exceeds the interest on the capital employed in improving the communication, and the annual expense of transportation (exclusively of the tolls) by the improved route; the difference is an annual additional income to the nation." The community as a whole would be the beneficiary.[27]

Gallatin also discussed the circumstances that he believed warranted *federal* financial assistance to support such investments. "There are . . . some circumstances, which, whilst they render the facility of communications throughout the United States an object of primary importance, naturally check the application of private capital and enterprise, to improvements on a large scale." Among these were the great demand for capital in the United States, the extent of its territory, and the objects for which it was required. The difficulty of obtaining sufficient capital to complete a large project within a reasonable time was also a challenge. Under these circumstances, Gallatin concluded, "[t]he general government can *alone* remove these obstacles." Thus, Gallatin identified an essential role for public infrastructure investment by the federal government, within the broader framework of Jefferson's preference for a frugal and limited federal enterprise.[28]

Gallatin did not doubt the capacity of the general government to address this challenge. "With resources amply sufficient for the completion of every practicable improvement, it will always supply the capital wanted for any work which it may undertake. . . ." Moreover, other considerations justified its participation. "Good roads and canals," he wrote, "will shorten distances, facilitate commercial and personal intercourse, and unite by a still more intimate community of interests the most remote quarters of the United States." Nor did he fail to invoke the national defense implications of such investment. He proclaimed that "it would tend to strengthen and perpetuate that union, which secures external independence, domestic peace, and internal liberty."[29]

These points made, Gallatin proposed and discussed in detail four categories of internal improvements: (1) great canals, from north to south, along the Atlantic seacoast; (2) communications between the Atlantic and the West; (3) communications between the Atlantic and St. Lawrence; and (4) interior canals. The National Road fell into the second category.[30]

Gallatin did not spare his readers (mainly members of the U.S. Congress) an account of the anticipated cost of the project. He was certain that federal resources were available to pay for such a project. From Gallatin's perspective, his plan set forth a program of sustainable national investment in the area of transportation infrastructure. To this end, he first recapitulated the cost of the project, concluding that it amounted to $20 million. He then proposed that an annual appropriation of $2 million would accomplish the objective in a period of ten years. Gallatin explained why he believed that these resources were available. The national debt was in the course of being expeditiously discharged. The annual revenues of the nation were sufficient to meet its operating expenses and still leave room for the investment program that the secretary was proposing, at least in time of peace. Gallatin took pains to note, in this connection, that the "facility of communications" was itself a national defense consideration. He also pointed to the possibility that sales of public land would provide a ready resource for the necessary appropriations.[31]

Gallatin personally believed that Congress possessed authority to make such investments under the federal spending power. However, he couched his report in such a way as to make it consistent with Jefferson's deeply held constitutional views (as discussed above in this chapter). Gallatin noted that the constitutional amendment that the president had proposed had not yet been secured; pending the adoption of such an amendment, Gallatin argued that the consent of the states for the projects in question must be secured and that this consent would suffice in lieu of an amendment. Only in the case of the National Road (from Cumberland to Brownsville) had such consent been secured.[32]

In sum, Gallatin balanced the need for his ambitious infrastructure agenda, the alternative priorities that challenged the nation at the time (defense and national investment), the aggregate costs of the program, and the available resources to produce an overall blueprint that Congress and its constituents could consider. It was a matter that ultimately the people would have to resolve.

Although Gallatin outlined the purpose, the costs, the available resources, and the authority for his comprehensive infrastructure investment plan, his report was never fully implemented. However, the National Road component was executed, and that road was completed, in one fashion or another, largely through federal appropriations. Gallatin's report represents an early large-scale governmental blueprint for a bold, essential national investment in the nation's infrastructure in the form of roads and canals, the principal investment objective of that day. Despite the concession to Jefferson on the constitutional question, the report was in danger of being sidetracked by the conflict with Great Britain. In December 1807, faced with continuing harassment from Great Britain, such as the forced induction of Americans into the British navy, Jefferson recommended that Congress adopt a trade embargo of indefinite length with Britain, as a means of persuading Britain to cease its hostile actions. The administration of the embargo and the efforts to respond to its critics absorbed Jefferson for the final full year of his administration and distracted him from devoting his full energies to the issues of public investment reflected in the National Road.[33]

In light of this background, it may be that Gallatin at least wished the Cumberland Road project to proceed (as one of the elements of his grand plan). This consideration as well as the political ones that he mentioned may have moved him to recommended that Jefferson satisfy Pennsylvania's request to include "little" Washington on the road from Cumberland to the West. With Gallatin's counsel digested, on August 6, 1808, Jefferson duly advised the commissioners that the route through Washington, Pennsylvania, to Wheeling would be "advantageous." He told them: "The principal object of this road [was] communication directly westwardly." However, he observed that if "inconsiderable deflections' would "benefit particular places," they could take these considerations into account. Pragmatism had prevailed once more, but in a way that would serve the infrastructure interests of the nation and its people.[34]

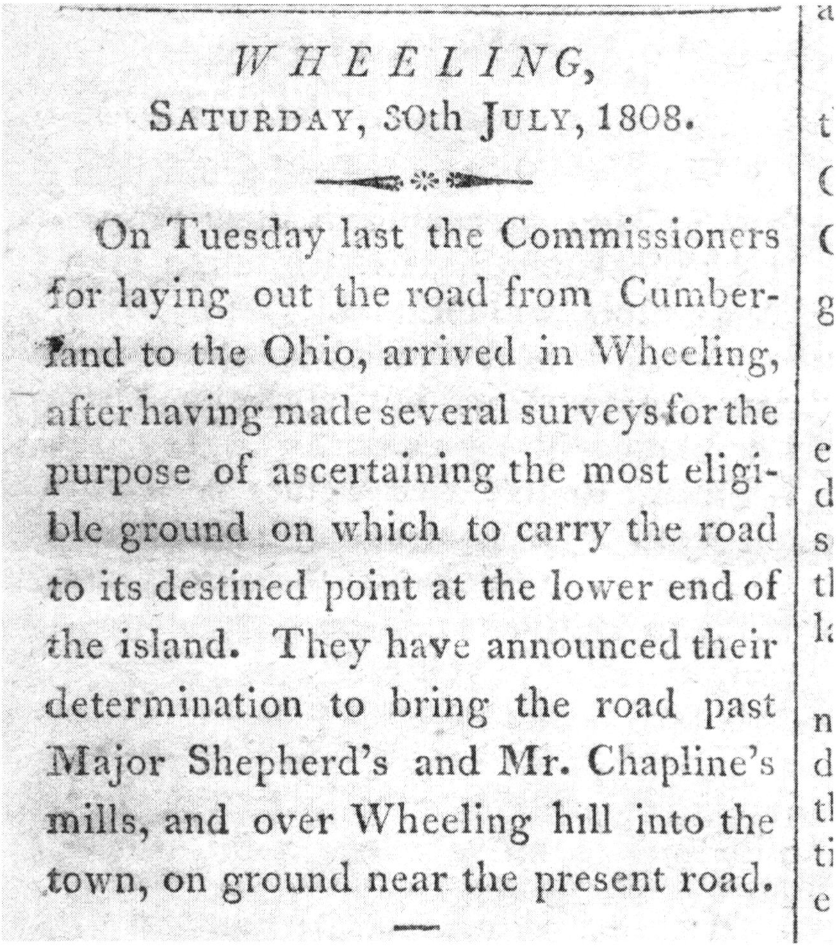

WHEELING,

SATURDAY, 30th JULY, 1808.

On Tuesday last the Commissioners for laying out the road from Cumberland to the Ohio, arrived in Wheeling, after having made several surveys for the purpose of ascertaining the most eligible ground on which to carry the road to its destined point at the lower end of the island. They have announced their determination to bring the road past Major Shepherd's and Mr. Chapline's mills, and over Wheeling hill into the town, on ground near the present road.

Figure 1.   Announcement of the National Road that appeared in the July 30, 1808, issue of the Wheeling *Repository* (courtesy of the Museums of Oglebay Institute).

In their final report to Jefferson on August 30, 1808, the commissioners responded to the instructions in the August 6 letter. They noted their conversations with officials of Washington, Pennsylvania, but observed that the route through that town was still three miles longer, a factor that militated "against" the Washington route. As to the overall construction strategy, the commissioners carefully counseled against an effort to construct a new road the "whole way." Instead, they recommended "the improvement of a few difficult places," a step that would make the road more passable. Jefferson conveyed this report to Congress in December 1808, after the election of that year had made James Madison his successor. Jefferson offered no further counsel to the legislators, evidently having taken the position that he would leave such matters to Madison.[35]

In February 1809, a bill was committed to the whole House that would have appropriated federal funds for the road between Cumberland and Brownsville. The bill contained a limitation that no part of the appropriation be expended for those parts of the road located within the limits of Uniontown and Brownsville. The Cumberland Road would lead travelers west, but it would not finance the cost of local streets along the way. The matter of Washington was to be definitively resolved in its favor by legislation in 1811. On March 4, 1809, responsibility for the road as a whole fell to Madison.[36]

After his second term had ended, in a letter of October 1809, Thomas Jefferson paid tribute to the man who had served him so well as secretary of the treasury and who had played so key a role in Jefferson's internal improvement program, particularly that aspect of it which concerned the National Road. In his letter to Gallatin, Jefferson took due note of their "joint exertions to promote the common good. . . ." The former president continued: "I feel particularly for myself the consideration of gratitude which I personally owe you for your valuable aid during administration of public affairs, a just sense of the large portion of the public approbation which was earned by your labors and belongs to you."[37]

Joseph Wood summarizes the role of the National Road in the Jeffersonian vision as follows: "In the context . . . of Jeffersonian republicanism and the economic and political tensions of the Jeffersonian era, the National Road must be viewed as a device for Western development—potentially a generator of profits as well as a tool for managing and defending territory beyond the Appalachians. A road would enable land sales and settlements and it would enable troops to move west to quell any uprising that might occur there."[38]

The National Road also constituted a species of essential national investment comparable to the other forms of such investment that Jefferson urged Congress to consider in his sixth annual message and in other public documents. In that message, despite his devotion to limited and frugal government as expressed in his first inaugural address, Jefferson clearly saw the uses and benefits of national public investment. He did so as well in his administration's adherence to the Louisiana Purchase, his active support for the Lewis and Clark Expedition, his recommendations regarding infrastructure enhancement (checker the country with roads and canals), his pursuit of educational improvements, and his approval of the legislation to initiate the National Road project. That he had constitutional reservations about these initiatives he candidly conceded both in public and in private, but he did not let these reservations preclude his support for the approval of the Louisiana Purchase or of the implementation of the National Road legislation. Jefferson was at heart a pro-investment president.

CHAPTER 3

Madison

CONSTRUCTION IN THE SHADOW
OF WAR AND THE BONUS BILL VETO

Construction Begins

Despite the threat of war and the initiation of hostilities with Great Britain in the War of 1812, a significant number of appropriations for the construction of the National Road were made during the Madison administration. These appropriations called for funds to construct the road from Cumberland to Brownsville. The funds appropriated would be repaid from the proceeds of the sales of land in Ohio, as called for in the 1802 legislation described above. In this way, at least $180,000 was appropriated through four separate acts in the eight years of the Madison administration.[1]

A wide array of potential obstacles confronted supporters of the road in their efforts to steer individual appropriations through a sometimes dubious and sometimes hostile Congress. Should priority be given to domestic internal improvements in a time of war? Should a highway that served one geographic area of the county be given the benefit of federal funds when other areas were bereft of such assistance? Would sufficient funds be available to complete the road as it was contemplated in 1806? Should a new, good road be built, or should the limited funds be spent merely to improve the existing road? The battle over these and other issues was resumed each year as annual appropriations were considered. Progress was measured as funds were made available for each ten-mile span and the superintendent of the road reported the completion of construction on that span. Each bridge became a focal point of controversy. Moreover, as the Madison administration proceeded, there seemed to be little likelihood of smooth sailing for these appropriations as the project wended its way from the Potomac to the Ohio.

29

In June 1809, a short debate in the House provided a preview of the political and fiscal issues that would frame congressional consideration of the future of the National Road for the ensuing decades. The House was pondering a bill from the Senate that would have funded the beginning of road construction. For this purpose, the bill called for an appropriation of $60,000. Rep. John G. Jackson of Virginia proposed an amendment that would have authorized the president to apply these funds to the "improvement" of the existing road without contemplating a "turnpike." A debate ensued. Congressmen in favor of Jackson's amendment argued that sufficient funds to make a "turnpike" road would never be available. Such a road would cost from $6,000 to $10,000 per mile. Thus, the $60,000 appropriation would at best cover no more than ten miles of turnpike. Instead, the existing road should be improved.

Opponents of the amendment responded that the law "pledged" them to a turnpike road. The amendment would be tantamount to repealing a "solemn law." Congressmen were legally bound to make a road that would be passable in winter as well as summer. The $60,000 would complete a new road across the mountains west of Cumberland. The Committee of the Whole rejected Jackson's amendment. The short debate captured the dilemma facing Congress, apart from the ever-lurking constitutional issues: to minimize the National Road project by merely "improving" the existing road or to move forward in full vigor with a modern road. The legislation that emerged early in the Madison administration, the acts of February 1810 and March 3, 1811, evidently followed the latter course. (At the same time, it does not appear that Congress, in considering either of those options, contemplated a turnpike or toll road. Nor did the original act of March 29, 1806, authorize the laying out of a turnpike or toll road.)[2]

Piecemeal Progress in the Debates and on the Ground

With these funds in hand, the Madison administration began to award contracts. In January 1812, Secretary Gallatin reported to President Madison on the progress. Four contracts had been let for the first ten miles of the road. With these funds spent, money would still be available for an additional seven miles. David Shriver, Gallatin reported, was urging that an additional eleven miles be funded. Shriver was a Maryland native, a businessman, and an engineer who had been appointed to superintend the survey and construction of the National Road. His reports provided a framework within which Congress could view current progress and determine next steps to take on the project.[3] This addition of the eleven miles would, Superintendent Shriver advised, permit the new road to join the Braddock

Road, the old road traversed by Washington in his trips west, and thus make the project useful in the event no further appropriations were made.

The following April, the House committee of Rep. Jeremiah Morrow of Ohio, to which the Gallatin report had been referred, provided its thinking in a report of its own.[4] The committee informed the House that, despite the needs of the war, an appropriation of $30,000 was justifiable to complete the road to Tomlinson's tavern in Grantsville, Maryland, which would connect it with the Braddock Road. Morrow's report took note of the national security needs that faced the country and denied funding for a bridge over the Youghiogheny, although the main appropriation won support. This presumably paved the way for the Act of May 6, 1812, which appropriated the needed funds. Thus, despite the war, which was declared in June 1812, Congress remained dedicated to the National Road as a new state-of-the-art highway.[5]

In December 1812 Shriver again reported to Gallatin, informing him that, with a few minor exceptions, the contracts for the first ten miles had been completed. The road was in use. Shriver also reported that progress was being made on construction of an additional ten miles covered by the second set of contracts. The next ten miles, he urged, should be contracted for in the spring of 1813. Madison transmitted the report to Congress without comment.[6] In December 1813, with Gallatin now at the peace conference in Ghent, Belgium, Shriver informed the acting treasury secretary that the first ten miles had been completed and that the second letting would be completed in the summer. On the third letting, involving an additional eighteen miles, little progress had been made. That still left a further twenty-one miles to Uniontown. For it $160,000 would be needed from Congress.[7]

In light of this report, transmitted to Congress by Madison, in January 1814 Senator Samuel Smith of Maryland delivered to the Senate a committee report reviewing the amounts that had been appropriated. Smith estimated the amounts necessary to move the project beyond the Big Youghiogheny to the foot of Laurel Hill and finally to Uniontown. The committee thought the funds requested were adequate to the object and recommended an appropriation to join the new road to the existing road and to construct a bridge over the Big Youghiogheny.[8]

Shriver's year-end report of 1814 reviewed the ensuing progress on the second letting and construction under the third letting, which was taking place in some sections but not others. The cost was running about seventy-five hundred dollars per mile, an increase over the estimate due to the rugged terrain over the mountains.[9] (Chapter 9 contains a detailed explanation of the challenges faced by the road superintendents and the contractors during the construction of the eastern portion of the road from 1811 to 1818.) In January 1815, Senator Smith's committee responded to this information in its own report to the Senate. The committee recommended funding for an additional ten miles beyond the Big Youghiogheny, the seven miles to the western foot of Laurel Hill, and that last three miles to Uniontown. These reports led to the Act of February 14, 1815. It provided an additional $100,000 for construction of portion of the road between Cumberland and Brownsville, the sum again to be defrayed from the sale of lands in Ohio.[10]

Madison's Seventh Annual Message: Optimism in the Aftermath of War

In December of that same year, Madison delivered an optimistic State of the Union address. It extolled the virtue of federal assistance for internal improvements but softly reminded Congress of the need for a constitutional amendment to resolve the underlying issues to which such legislation might give rise. By February 12, 1817, with only a few weeks remaining in Madison's second term, more than half of the 133 miles of the National Road between Cumberland and Wheeling had been completed or was under contract.[11]

The War of 1812 formally came to an end in 1815 with the signing of the Treaty of Ghent, although the battle of New Orleans was fought some months after that event. The war may have delayed but it did not ultimately deter Congress from continuing to pass legislation funding the Cumberland Road project and President Madison from continuing to sign such legislation, despite the fiscal issues and sectional concerns that had figured in the debate. Inexorably, the nation had felt compelled to overcome obstacles to the funding and building of a national road across the mountains. It had done so on a ten-mile segment-by-segment basis, always under the threat of termination of funding. In so doing, the nation had come down on the side of continued public investment. It was seemingly driven by the mystique of the West beyond the mountains and the knowledge that a continent lay open for domestication. With the war at end, the nation's efforts could be focused on that goal, as Madison's seventh State of the Union Message clearly proclaimed.

Jefferson had counseled that Congress should "chequer the country with roads and canals" in a time of peace. In Madison's administration, the process of supporting internal improvement had even progressed, at least as far as the National Road was concerned, in a time of war. Did this pertain to other internal improvements? Did it reflect a conclusion that "good roads" had a military as well as a domestic application? Madison's message discussed the defense as well as the domestic needs of the nation and the role of good roads in responding to those needs. He said: "Among the means of advancing the public interest the occasion is a proper one for recalling the attention of Congress to the great importance of establishing throughout our country the roads and canals *which can best be executed under the national authority.* No objects within the circle of political economy so richly repay the expense bestowed upon them; there are none the utility of which is more universally ascertained and acknowledged; none that do more honor to the governments whose wise and enlarged patriotism duly appreciates them."[12]

Despite the positive and progressive tone of Madison's plea for internal improvement, the constitutional issue related to such improvement was about to ignite a breach between Congress and the White House as Madison's second term came to an end. Whether it was because of the need for progress on the National Road or because the administration had been preoccupied by the press of the international crises that it faced, Madison had not emphasized the imperative of the constitutional amendment that previously he had intimated was a necessary precondition to continued progress on the issue of internal improvements. Events, however, were to provide an occasion for him to reinforce that point before he left office.

The National Road and the Bonus Bill Veto

In March 1817, President Madison was spending the last days of his administration in the White House. He and his wife, Dolly, were preparing for retirement on his beloved estate, Montpelier, in Orange, Virginia. The arrival of another bill regarding internal improvements intruded on Madison's plans to return south. The Fourteenth Congress had sent to his desk a measure that would provide for a broad program of internal improvements not unlike that proposed by Albert Gallatin in 1808 but never fully acted upon. The funds would come from a bonus or dividend generated by the Second National Bank of the United States. The bill was thus referred to as the Bonus Bill. Its champion in Congress was Rep. John C. Calhoun, an energetic and eloquent young Jeffersonian Democrat from western South Carolina who spoke strongly in favor of the legislation. Rep. Henry Clay of Kentucky also expressed the hope that Congress would "[lay] the foundations of this great work" of internal improvement. If enacted, the bill would have provided over $500,000 per year from the proceeds of the Bank "dividend" for appropriation by Congress for internal improvement. It presumably would have provided, from this amount, funds for the repair of the National Road as well as other improvements. Madison had watched the progress of this measure warily, as he wrote in a letter to Jefferson. Madison described the bill to Jefferson as one "of a very extraordinary character." He emphasized to Jefferson that the "object" of the bill was "to compass by law only an authority over roads and Canals." In other words, in addressing the bill, Congress had apparently not heeded Madison's advice, provided however delicately in the seventh annual message, that any legislation regarding roads, however welcome to the president, be accompanied by a related constitutional amendment.[13]

In one sense, a bill providing for road repair must have seemed a positive idea to the fourth president. In 1815, in his seventh State of the Union message, Madison had extolled the advantages of internal improvements as a unifying force and sought to make a case for applying federal funds to help make them.[14] Nevertheless, when the Bonus Bill arrived on his desk, Madison vetoed it. In a brief message, the president explained his views. He did not veto the bill because he opposed federal money for roads in general or for the National Road in particular. Indeed, he repeated his policy support for this type of spending. However, he found no constitutional basis for it. He did not believe that the Commerce Clause authorized the measure; it was focused on the *regulation* of interstate and foreign commerce, not their promotion. The most likely source of support, he acknowledged, would be the General Welfare Clause because it authorized Congress to lay imposts and taxes to provide for the common defense and general welfare of the United States. However, Madison found no comfort in this language. He firmly believed that clause to be no more than a reference to the other powers of Congress contained in Article I, section 8, of the Constitution, not an independent grant of authority. That section contained no language authorizing Congress to deal with roads or transportation.[15] Therefore, a constitutional amendment was needed to authorize the legislation in question. Madison urged that Congress propose such an amendment.

Madison did not explain in his veto message how he had justified signing the previous appropriation bills for the construction of the National Road described above. Perhaps it was because the Bonus Bill called for a general, nationwide system of internal improvements, while the National Road legislation provided funds for only one project, one begun during the administration of Madison's friend and predecessor, Thomas Jefferson, and continued in his own administration through successive but limited appropriations. Perhaps he had considered those bills as different from the one he vetoed because they derived from the original National Road legislation in 1802 involving the Territory of Ohio or because the appropriations were to be "repaid" from the proceeds of land sales in Ohio under a "compact" with the state. As mentioned, the bill in question made funds available from a different source, a "bonus" declared by the Bank of the United States. The National Road and the program contemplated in the Bonus Bill both provided for funding for internal improvement drawn from federal appropriations, but Madison did not address that point in his veto message.

Clearly, Madison felt compelled to deliver a pointed reminder as to his constitutional concerns as he left office, leaving a legacy for his successor. He evidently believed that his dramatic veto action would stimulate Congress to start the constitutional amendment process that Madison favored by sending a proposed amendment to the states for ratification. As it happened, Madison's veto came as a surprise to those members of Congress who supported the bill, Clay and Calhoun among them. They had urged him to leave the matter to his successor. He declined to do so, desiring, as historians have described it, to leave a last testament as to his views on government and its limitations.[16]

To fully understand Madison's perspective and his predicament, one must return to the Constitutional Convention of 1787. There Madison had defended the need for a strong central government that would be vested with a power to tax and thus pay the debts incurred during the Revolutionary War. He had strongly advocated the need to abandon the weak Articles of Confederation, pointing to state resistance to requisitions from the central government for funds to meet its financial obligations. After the convention, in the *Federalist Papers*, he had argued that the people should fear anarchy far more than they should fear the strength of the newly proposed federal government, and he had pointed to the weakness of the ancient Greek confederations as an example of this danger.[17]

At the same time Madison had tempered his support for a strong federal authority with an insistence that the legislative authority of the federal government be limited and circumscribed. The instrument of that limitation would be the enumerated powers. The power of Congress to legislate would be spelled out in detail in Article I, section 8, of the Constitution, which specifically defined those areas on which Congress might legislate, such as national defense and interstate and foreign commerce. Madison felt strongly that the enumeration should be observed and not expanded through "ductile" interpretation. For this reason, he had opposed Hamilton's broad interpretation of the General Welfare Clause in the *Report on Manufactures*, in much the same vein as Jefferson's complaints about that interpretation. For the same reason, he declared in the Bonus Bill veto that the General Welfare Clause and its taxing-spending power could not support the Bonus Bill. In his veto message he explained that the Bonus Bill could not be saved on the theory that spending legislation was different from legislation adopted under other legislative power granted to Congress in the Constitution under Article I. "A restriction of the power 'to provide for the common defense and general welfare' to cases which are to be provided for by expenditures of money would still leave within the legislative power of Congress all the great and most important measures of Government, money being the ordinary and necessary means of carrying them into execution."[18]

Furthermore, in his veto message, Madison seemingly rejected, as constitutionally improvident, at least one theory upon which the constitutionality of internal improvement legislation had been posited. This was the consent or compact theory reflected in the 1806 legislation that had initiated the National Road project. As to this proposition, Madison said, in the veto message: "If a general power to construct roads and canals, and to improve the navigation of water courses, with the train of powers incident thereto, be not possessed by Congress, the assent of the States in the mode provided by the bill can not confer that power. The only cases in which the consent and cession of particular States can extend the power of Congress are those specified and provided for in the Constitution."[19]

Furthermore, Madison rejected by implication one possible interpretation that was to be considered in the twentieth century—namely, reliance on the Post-Roads Clause in Article I, section 8, clause 7. He said: "The legislative powers vested in Congress are specified and enumerated in the eighth section of the first Article of the Constitution, and it does not appear that the power proposed to be exercised by the bill is among the enumerated powers. . . ." While not specifically discussing Clause 7, this broad statement would appear to embrace it.[20]

In sum, as Jeremiah Simeon Young puts it: "[Madison] denied the power of the United States to appropriate money for or to construct such improvements; nor could either of these be done even with the consent of the states."[21]

This, however, left Madison with same dilemma that confronted Jefferson when he signed the initial National Road legislation in 1806. Madison recognized that internal improvements were necessary. His veto of the Bonus Bill should not be interpreted as a statement on his part that Congress, as a matter of policy, should decline to provide financial support for a system of internal improvements, as Albert Gallatin had proposed in the Jefferson administration. On the contrary, in 1815 Madison had carefully explained why federal participation in internal improvements was necessary and desirable.[22]

The dilemma could be resolved only through a constitutional amendment, which, as mentioned, Madison recommended in the Bonus Bill veto and as he had, however obliquely, recommended in the seventh State of the Union message. With such an amendment adopted, there would be clear constitutional authority for appropriations for internal improvements, including the National Road. As Jeremiah Young summarizes it in his 1902 dissertation, "[Madison] strongly urged such an amendment, as he was favorable to a national system of internal improvements."[23]

Moreover, such an amendment would have other advantages. It would signify that other forms of federal aid (for example, to aid schools or manufacturing establishments) must be preceded by a constitutional amendment. It would, by implication, convey a message that Madison's and Jefferson's interpretation of the Constitution was correct; otherwise no amendment would have been needed. It would both provide for internal improvements and provide a precedent for adherence to the four corners of the enumerated powers, thus achieving the Democratic-Republican constitutional vision and simultaneously advancing the cause of internal improvement so necessary to westward progress and expansion.[24]

Ralph Ketcham, in his comprehensive biography of Madison, explains the action in the following way: "Though to Clay and others Madison's last-minute scrupulousness was painful and unnecessary, the retiring President considered it an important 'last testament' in favor of exactly the form of limited republican government he had just praised in his annual message as responsible for the free, prosperous state of the nation. . . . Madison meant to make clear that truly republican, truly federal government had to remain in vital ways 'defined and limited.'"[25]

These objectives were indeed worthy and were no doubt heartfelt. However, there was virtually no specific legislative history of the General Welfare Clause upon which to base a conclusion as to where that clause fit into the goal of a "defined and limited" federal government. The language was initially offered by Roger Sherman of Connecticut. He proposed that the taxing power (in what is now Article I) be modified by the language "to pay the debts and provide for the common defense and general welfare" as a means of defining the purposes for which tax revenues might be used by Congress. His proposal was initially defeated, without debate, on the floor of the convention. Subsequently, a committee, in which Sherman among others participated, reported out the language now found in the Constitution ("to pay the debts and provide for the common defense and general welfare of the United States"). Again, there was no debate. In *Federalist No. 41*, Madison interpreted this language as a mere cross-reference to the enumerated powers, denying to Congress any general authority to legislate for the general welfare. However, there was no specific colloquy on the floor to support his view. Madison later explained that it must have been the intent of the delegates, given their aversion to a broad grant of federal power. The literal language supported Hamilton's broader interpretation in the *Report on Manufactures*.[26]

Under Article I, section 7, of the Constitution a bill may become law over the president's veto if, after considering the president's objections, two-thirds of both houses of Congress agree to pass the bill. Clay and others mounted an attempt to muster the necessary two-thirds vote of both houses of congress to override the Bonus Bill veto. The needs of the Cumberland or National Road were no doubt on their minds. In the House of Representatives, Clay took the dramatic step of leaving the Speaker's chair to vote in favor of an override, but to no avail. The vote in the House to override was 60 to 56, a majority but not enough to produce the required two-thirds. The effort to override Madison's veto had failed. At the same time, it seemed clear from the vote that there was

not the two-thirds majority required to send to the states for ratification a constitutional amendment on the subject, as Madison had recommended.[27]

Congress and the president were thus at an impasse at least with respect to
legislation to provide for repair of the National Road. If presidents continued
to veto road legislation and Congress continued to decline to propose a constitutional amendment, the National Road would sink into disrepair, whatever its
merits. The road was thus at the center of a major political stalemate involving
grave questions of national authority and constitutional interpretation as they
related to internal improvements. Madison's veto message did not explain how
such an impasse should be resolved. How, if no constitutional amendment was
adopted, could one still maintain a federal enterprise that was "defined and limited"? The answer to that question would be left to his successor.[28]

The battle over the Bonus Bill and its constitutional dimensions may serve
to obscure that part of Madison's thinking related to national investment. In his
seventh annual message Madison had expressed his strong support for national
investment while perhaps soft-pedaling his views on the constitutional limitations on the authority of Congress. In that message, Madison had explained that
infrastructure investment by the federal government was at times essential and
that some of it could not be expected to be undertaken by the states or by private
entities ("roads and canals that can best be executed under the national authority"). But in his Bonus Bill veto Madison was unable to craft the two strands
of his preferences—for federal investment and for a limited General Welfare
Clause—into a sustainable framework that would support such investment. The
"solution" was an appropriate constitutional amendment, but Congress did not
provide it. Alternative strategies to promote that investment had to be found.

CHAPTER 4

Monroe's Compromise and the Tollgate Battle

The President and His Predecessor Share Views on the Scope of the Spending Power under the Constitution

James Monroe inherited the impasse posed by Madison's Bonus Bill veto when he took the oath of office on March 4, 1817. Monroe was of the same party and generally of the same political persuasion as that of his Virginia predecessors. Although he favored federal assistance for internal improvements as a matter of policy, he held doubts, similar to those of Jefferson and Madison, as to the constitutionality of such measures. In his inaugural address and in his first State of the Union message, Monroe recommended a constitutional amendment to solve the problem. Madison, writing from Montpelier, encouraged him in this course, which would pave the way for both internal improvements and seminaries of learning. At the same time, Monroe wanted to clarify the significance of the laws relating to the National Road that had been enacted prior to his entering office. He wrote to Madison questioning him about the basis for the string of laws to provide for the National Road that had been enacted during both Jefferson's and Madison's terms of office. Monroe was curious as to whether the legislation concerning the Cumberland Road might serve as a precedent for further legislation of this type without a constitutional amendment.[1]

In response, Madison sought gamely to justify the National Road bills with his own position on the Constitution. He noted that he had not been directly involved in the events leading to the 1806 legislation and speculated that Congress had given little thought to the subject. Because the road was "a measure of singular utility," he related, continuing appropriations had been made in both

Jefferson's and his administrations "with less of a critical investigation . . . than was due the case." Nevertheless, Madison tried to distinguish the National Road legislation from that before the Congress in Monroe's time on the grounds that the former legislation was undertaken for the "accommodation" of the Northwest Territory. Congress had a more general rule-making power for that portion of the country. Madison, in his response to Monroe, did not try directly to justify his own approval of the earlier National Road bills on the ground that Congress had passed them on the basis of the state compact theory invoked under the Ohio admission legislation of 1802. One may speculate that, among other things, his reluctance on that score grew out of a concern that reliance on this theory would have perpetuated federal spending for internal improvements without the constitutional amendment that Madison perceived as necessary.[2]

Monroe was not wholly convinced by these explanations. Henry Clay of and other pro-improvement legislators had criticized Monroe's constitutional views on the road. To respond, in 1819 Monroe began to prepare a long memorandum explaining his legal position. Dissuaded by members of his cabinet from sharing the memorandum in his first term, he put it aside. However, in 1822, when Congress passed a bill for the preservation and repair of the National (Cumberland) Road, the issue rose again. The bill, sometimes referred to as the Gates Bill, called for the establishment by the federal government of turnpikes and tollgates to enforce the collection of tolls to provide proceeds for the road. Monroe saw this legislation as providing for federal control over the road, a power he thought lacking. He vetoed the bill.[3]

In the course of his communications with Madison during 1817 over the scope of the spending power, Monroe also queried the former president regarding his views as to the status of education as a fit subject for federal assistance, whether through a constitutional amendment or otherwise. Indeed, Monroe's first annual message contained a recommendation for a constitutional amendment embracing not only roads and canals but also "seminaries of learning," for whose benefit President Washington had recommended some forms of federal assistance. In response to Monroe's questions, Madison had written: "The expediency of vesting in Congress a power as to roads and canals I have never doubted, and there has never been a moment when such a proposition to the States was so likely to be approved. A general power to establish seminaries being less obvious, and affecting more the equilibrium of influence between the National and State governments, is more a critical experiment." Thus, in the context of their discussion regarding efforts to resolve doubts regarding the constitutionality of federal assistance, Madison and Monroe considered both infrastructure and education as potentially fit subjects for congressional interest. As it turned out, no constitutional amendment on either infrastructure or education emerged from Congress for ratification by the states. It seemed clear that Congress was not going to provide a constitutional amendment through the Article V process. Thus, the question of state ratification, about which Madison speculated in his letter, would never arise. Monroe thus felt obliged to share with Congress his thoughts on alternative means to resolve the impasse over constitutional authority and thus permit the National Road to be repaired.[4]

Monroe's Memorandum

Accordingly, Monroe accompanied his veto message regarding the 1822 Gates Bill with a copy of the memorandum that he had previously filed in his desk. In the memorandum, Monroe reiterated his position that Congress lacked authority under the Constitution to take jurisdiction over a road within a state and charge tolls for travel on it. However, in a long analysis, he concluded that Congress did have power merely to *appropriate* federal funds for internal improvements. These funds could be used for building or repairing roads but not in a way that gave Congress the power to collect tolls.

Monroe's interpretation of the federal spending power in the Constitution in his 1822 memorandum represented an important departure from the thinking of his predecessors in the White House, Jefferson and Madison. It also represented an important change of heart in Monroe's own views on the matter. This he frankly conceded in the memorandum. In short, it meant that Congress could provide financial assistance to internal improvements, like the National Road, as long as Congress did not at the same time assume "jurisdiction" over the internal improvement by, for example, setting up federal tollgates. Where did Monroe find this authority? He found it in the General Welfare Clause of the Constitution, which reads: "Congress shall have power to lay and collect taxes . . . to pay the debts and provide for the common defense and general welfare of the United States."[5]

This was the same language that Madison, in his Bonus Bill veto, had concluded did not provide such authority. On what basis did Monroe reach this conclusion in his memorandum? First, he pointed out that the language of the provision literally supported his interpretation. There was no specific limitation in the phrase "to provide for the . . . general welfare of the United States." If the Constitution's writers had meant to confine it to the enumerated powers, Monroe urged, they could easily have said so. Furthermore, Monroe pointed to the long list of appropriations for the National Road (which both Jefferson and Madison had signed) as providing precedent for his position.[6]

Monroe stated his conclusion as follows: "My idea is that Congress have an unlimited power to raise money, and that in its appropriation they have a discretionary power restricted only by the duty to appropriate to the purposes of common defense and of general, not local, national, not State, benefit." This formulation was sufficiently broad to cover appropriations for the National Road as well as other nationally oriented internal improvements.[7]

In reaching his conclusion regarding the scope of the General Welfare Clause and its availability to support congressional appropriations for roads and other internal improvements, Monroe, like Madison before him, took pains to reject the applicability of other provisions in Article I, section 8, of the Constitution that from time to time have been put forward as possible sources of that authority. These include the Post-Roads Clause in section 8(7) and the Commerce Clause in section 8(3) of Article I of the Constitution. Respecting the Post-Roads Clause, Monroe took several pages to explain his difficulties. The core of his analysis is contained in the following paragraph:

> If we were to ask any number of our most enlightened citizens . . . what was the import of the word "establish" [in the Post-Roads Clause] and the extent of the grant which it controls, we do not think there would be any difference of opinion among them. We are satisfied that all of them would answer that a power was thereby given to Congress to fix on the towns, court-houses, and other places throughout our Union at which there should be post-offices, the routes by which the mails should be carried from one post-office to another, so as to diffuse intelligence as extensively and to make the institution as useful as possible. . . . The idea of a right to lay off the roads of the United States on a general scale of improvement, to take the soil from the proprietor by force, to establish turnpikes and tolls, and to punish offenders . . . would never occur to any such person.

Moreover, Monroe argued that the terms of the clause had appeared in the Articles of Confederation and had been understood to convey the power as he described it. With respect to the Commerce Clause, Monroe invoked the same argument that Madison had used in his Bonus Bill veto: the clause involved a power to regulate interstate and foreign commerce, not a power to appropriate funds in a way related to that commerce. In sum, having fixed upon the spending power as a broad multipurpose source of authority to provide federal "investment" dollars, Monroe, like Madison, evidently felt no need to try to construct an alternative source of authority.[8]

Henry Ammon, a Monroe biographer, has called the memorandum an "ungracious work on an ungrateful subject" but conceded that it did establish "clear guidelines" for internal improvement measures. It also provided a basis for Monroe to approve legislative measures that he considered necessary for the growth of the country, even in the absence of a constitutional amendment that he, Jefferson, and Madison had all earlier recommended.[9]

How did Monroe's compromise memorandum accord with Madison's core argument that the federal government should be "defined" and "limited"? Monroe had insisted that his reading permitted only the appropriation of funds to assist an internal improvement. It did not authorize the federal government to take control of the improvement in a way that ousted state authority—for example, by charging tolls and enforcing their collection.[10]

Monroe's compromise had important ramifications for the cause of internal improvements, and for other causes. His view recognized that Congress could spend on any matter that it considered to fall within the phrase "the general welfare of the United States," even if the matter was not specified in the enumerated powers of the Constitution as a matter regarding which Congress could legislate directly. More than one hundred years after Monroe wrote his memorandum, the Supreme Court in effect adopted his position in *United States v. Butler* (1936) regarding agricultural subsidies. The Court in that case relied upon Alexander Hamilton, who, as secretary of the treasury under Washington, had taken a similar position. The Court also relied upon Joseph Story, a Supreme Court Justice and revered law professor who, in a set of law commentaries first published in 1833, had supported both Hamilton's and Monroe's interpretations. Monroe offered a pragmatic approach to both a political and a legal problem; Story furnished a comprehensive legal analysis that in many respects tracked that of Monroe. Both Monroe and Story emphasized the literal language of the Constitution that was in question. The *Butler* case also recognized Monroe's contribution to the debate, favorably citing his 1822 memorandum on the National Road appropriation bill.[11]

However, for purposes of the National Road, Monroe's memorandum, taken with his 1822 veto action, made an important distinction. Joseph Wood puts it as follows: "Toll collection implied to Monroe a power of sovereignty that was not granted to the federal government by the Constitution and could not be unilaterally conveyed to any state without a constitutional amendment. It was one thing, in other words, to make appropriations for public improvements, and another to assume jurisdiction where improvements were made." This distinction was to assume greater importance as the debate over the National Road proceeded.[12]

The Congressional Debates on the Gates Bill and Congress's Effort to Override Monroe's Veto of It

In 1818, the National Road reached Wheeling. (For a fuller account of the administrative decisions surrounding the building of the road from Cumberland,

Maryland, to Wheeling, Virginia, between 1811 and 1818, see chapter 9; for an account of the problems relating to the building of the road and traveling upon it west of Wheeling, see chapter 8 and chapter 10.) In 1820 appropriations were made to extend it from Wheeling west into the state of Ohio. Why did Congress pass the Gates Bill in April 1822? Did Congress attempt to override Monroe's veto and with what result? Was the road ever repaired? To answer these questions we must look to the records of the congressional debates on the bill and the text of Monroe's significant 1822 memorandum.

In early 1822, supporters of the National Road in Congress began to push for legislation to repair it in the states through which it ran east of the Ohio River: Maryland, Pennsylvania, and Virginia. They also sought a mechanism that would give Congress a reliable source of revenue that could be dedicated to this purpose. At the time, customs duties and excise taxes were major sources of revenue, but they were required to meet all the needs of the government. Drawing upon them to maintain the National Road would compete with demands from other projects with equal claim to recognition. It would always be problematic. A better method would involve the collection of tolls from those who traveled the National Road, whether by wagon, stage, or other conveyance.

Was the federal government, which had financed the road, authorized to set the tolls, establish tollgates or tollhouses, and enforce the tolls through prosecutions of violators, or were the states through which the road passed solely authorized to do this? Supporters of the road took the former position. If the federal government was empowered to finance the building of the road, they argued, it was also empowered to collect tolls to keep it in repair. Others saw this kind of action as federal usurpation of state jurisdiction over state property.

In January 1822, Rep. Andrew Stewart of Pennsylvania, a champion of the road, reported to Congress on the state of its "dilapidation." In April, the House took up the Senate bill providing for the collection of tolls under federal authority. A solid majority in the House favored the bill and beat back all amendments. The bill provided that the United States, under the direction of the president, could erect tollgates and collect tolls. The final vote on the bill in the House was 87 to 68. The House bill was sent to the Senate for concurrence.[13]

On May 3, 1822, the Senate considered the House bill. The short conversation that ensued between Senator James Barbour of Virginia and Senator Rufus King of New York reveals some of the crosscurrents at play. Senator Barbour reminded the Senate that he had earlier sponsored a constitutional amendment to provide specific constitutional authority for internal improvement legislation. The amendment had failed to get the necessary two-thirds vote in the Senate. It had failed, Senator Barbour recalled, because some senators saw no need for the amendment; they believed that the Constitution already conferred on Congress the authority to provide funds for roads and canals. Other members had voted against the amendment because they did not wish to give that explicit authority to Congress.

Senator Barbour saw the Gates Bill as a chance to solve the problem by providing for tolls that would generate specific and dedicated revenue to pay for the repairs, rather than making repairs dependent on federal appropriations. This, he reasoned, would avoid the constitutional problems that had been raised by Madison and Monroe about federal appropriations.

Senator King shared another perspective. He declared that he had always believed that Congress had the authority to appropriate for roads and canals and that the consent of the states was not necessary. This contrasted with the 1806 National Road authorization legislation, which called for the president to obtain the consent of the states through which the road would pass when he accepted a report of the road commissioners regarding the route of the road. (See chapter 2 above.) King was apparently looking to the Gates Bill not as a means of avoiding constitutional controversy but as a source of revenue to relieve the pressure on federal appropriations as a fiscal matter. King spoke on the subject with a certain degree of expertise. Earlier in life, he had been a delegate from Massachusetts at the Constitutional Convention of 1787 and had participated frequently in its debates. He had served in the U.S. Senate in 1789, and in 1813 he was elected again, as a member of the Federalist Party, serving until March 3, 1825. King, it appears, was expressing a view flatly contrary to that of Madison in the Bonus Bill veto: Congress had authority to appropriate for and/or construct internal improvements and did not need the consent of the states to activate this authority. Following the exchange between Senator Barbour and Senator King, the Gates Bill finally passed the Senate by a vote of 29 to 7.[14]

When the final bill was sent to President Monroe, as we have seen, he vetoed it.

The president's short veto message focused on the provisions of the bill regarding the establishment of tollgates and the collection of tolls under federal authority. President Monroe said, "A power to establish turnpikes, with gates and tolls, and to enforce the collection of tolls by penalties, implies a power to adopt and execute a complete system of internal improvement." He regarded it as involving "a complete right of jurisdiction and sovereignty" unlike the power vested in Congress "to make appropriations, under which power, with the consent of the States through which the road passed, the work was originally commenced." Monroe could not find the power respecting tolls in the Constitution. He subsequently sent to Congress the longer memorandum described above, stating his views on the authority of Congress to appropriate.[15]

While his memorandum did not alter his conclusion regarding the tollgate provisions, it did make clear that, in Monroe's view, Congress was empowered to appropriate funds for the building and repair of the road as long as it did not take jurisdiction or perform acts that amounted to the assumption of sovereignty. In so doing, he established a framework that guided national transportation policy over the course of the nation's history. In 1976, the U.S. Department of Transportation, in its history of America's highways during the period from 1776 through 1976, observed: "President Monroe's position has continued to be the Federal position on highway matters to the present day." Monroe's legal thinking also paved the way for federal appropriations to provide financial assistance in a host of areas other than transportation, including such areas as education, agriculture, commerce, the arts, social welfare, social insurance to cover retirement and disability needs, and health care.[16]

That degree of flexibility, however, did not help the proponents of the Gates Bill. For them, the question was whether they had enough votes in the House to make up the two-thirds vote necessary to override the president's veto. On May 6, they tried and failed. The vote to pass the measure over the president's veto was 68 yeas to 72 nays, clearly not enough to override the veto.[17]

Congress and the President Come Together on a Legislative Solution

This failure led to further proceedings on the question of how to repair the road. The president's message had foreclosed the use of tollgates and toll collections for this purpose, though it had left open the possibility of appropriations. If "mere" federal appropriations unaccompanied by efforts to assert sovereignty were constitutional in the president's view, was Congress prepared to furnish these funds through an appropriation? This issue became the business of early 1823. In January of that year, the Senate considered a new bill providing for the repair of the National Road from Cumberland to the Ohio River. This bill was unencumbered by the provisions for federal toll collection that had characterized the 1822 Gates Bill. The Senate debate was framed by a conversation between Senator John Taylor of Virginia (known as John Taylor of Caroline), who opposed the bill on constitutional and policy grounds, and Senator Isham Talbot of Kentucky, who supported it fully. Senator Talbot's responses relied upon precedent and the Interstate Commerce Clause as the source of constitutional authority. The bill passed by a large margin (26 to 9) and was sent to the House, which approved it as well.[18]

With his comprehensive legal memorandum delivered and his constitutional compromise fully described, President Monroe now felt comfortable signing the repair legislation. Though he had continued to plead for a broad constitutional amendment giving Congress power to create a national system of roads and canals, Congress was unmoved. However, in December 1822, Monroe conceded in his sixth annual message that Congress had the power to appropriate to keep the National Road in repair, even if no specific constitutional amendment had been adopted on the subject. "Surely," he said, "if [Congress] had the right to appropriate money to make the road they have a right to appropriate to preserve the road from ruin." He was obviously relying on his own memorandum of 1822 for authority.[19]

The Act of February 28, 1823, that Monroe signed to carry out this policy appropriated $25,000 from the Treasury Department for the purpose of repairing and improving the road from Cumberland to Wheeling. The funds were not appropriated to the states. Rather they were to be used under the "direction" of the president, who was again directed to appoint, with the advice of the Senate, a superintendent of the road to contract for and supervise the repair and improvement. The act did not specify that the funds in question must be repaid from the proceeds of Ohio land sales.[20]

In light of this legislation, it appears that Monroe, on the basis of the long legal memorandum that he had provided to Congress, felt justified in signing legislation appropriating federal funds for the purpose of repairing the Cumberland Road. A clear precedent had thus been set for the appropriation of federal funds for purposes not strictly specified in the enumerated powers in Article I, section 8, of the Constitution. In the course of providing for the repair of the National Road, a significant obstacle had been overcome to the use of such funds for broad, "general welfare" purposes. In March 1825, on his last day in office, Monroe also signed legislation that appropriated an additional $150,000 to extend the National Road from Wheeling to Zanesville, Ohio. The new addition would extend the road beyond the Ohio River into the Midwest, just as Jefferson had contemplated.[21]

Jeremiah Simeon Young summarizes as follows the situation as it stood at the end of Monroe's two terms: "During the two administrations of Monroe a great constitutional battle had been waged. Using the doctrine of implied powers, Congress asserted its authority (1) to enter upon an extensive system of internal improvements; (2) to exercise jurisdiction over the Cumberland Road. Monroe's policy, as outlined in his veto message of May 4, 1822, denied both propositions. He suggested (1) an amendment to the Constitution which should grant power over internal-improvements; (2) the appropriation by Congress for internal-improvements of a national character under authority of the 'general welfare' clause of the Constitution."[22]

Through his memorandum and the legislation he signed, Monroe established a major precedent for broad use of the General Welfare Clause in the Constitution to justify federal financial assistance in a wide variety of areas. In this same way, the National Road and its need for extension and repair provided the occasion for the establishment of a precedent that has played such an important role in the history of the country.[23]

These momentous events did not go unnoticed along the National Road. William Blane, an Englishman traveling the road from Cumberland to Wheeling in October 1822, alluded to them in an account of the road's conditions:

> The road became worse and worse all the way from Brownsville to Wheeling. The truth is, that as travelers coming from the Atlantic cities, with the intention of descending the Ohio and going into the Western States, prefer this road to the one which leads from Philadelphia to Pittsburgh, and which was made by the State of Pennsylvania. The traffic of the Pennsylvania "turnpike" is very much diminished; and therefore all the people of that State, as well as of many of the other States, who do not derive any immediate benefit from it, are opposed to any grants being made by Congress for keeping it [the National Road] in order. Thus, for the want of a few thousand dollars expended annually, this great national undertaking was allowed to go very much out of repair. It would indeed in a year or two have become entirely impassable if, as I was informed on my return from the West, the advocates for internal improvements had not made a great effort, and obtained a grant of 25,000 dollars. This however is by no means enough for repairing the road at present, whereas a few years ago the same sum would have been more than sufficient.[24]

Under the reasoning Monroe had put forward in his 1822 veto, Congress lacked power to collect tolls on the road. Congress still had to depend upon general revenues for repair and maintenance of the road. The difficulties of such a course came more fully to light in the succeeding administrations: the single term of John Quincy Adams and the two terms of Andrew Jackson.[25]

At the same time Monroe had been able to take the two strands of Madison's policy (pro-public investment but limited authority under the Constitution) and bind them together in a coherent strategy for national investment that provided forward momentum for the National Road project west of the Ohio River. Monroe had shared the vision of his predecessors in support of national investment by seeking a constitutional means for keeping the National Road in repair. In the absence of the constitutional amendment that both he and Madison had sought, Monroe proposed a compromise constitutional theory that would sustain a federal role in funding the road at least for a time: Congress could appropriate funds for its construction but it could not assume jurisdiction over the road. On this basis, the road became a sustainable national investment for the better part of the next two decades and until it reached central Illinois. However, in the long run, it would become unsustainable for a combination of constitutional and fiscal reasons.

CHAPTER 5

John Quincy Adams and the High-Water Mark of the National Road as a National Road

J. Q. Adams, the Era of Internal Improvement, and the National Road

For John Quincy Adams the National Road was a lifetime concern. As a senator during the Jefferson administration, Adams supported legislation to fund the road. During his presidency, he signed legislation to extend the National Road in Ohio. As the only president to serve in the House of Representatives after leaving the White House, he participated in the congressional debates on the future of the road.

However, Adams's role in this history goes even further. During his troubled one term, Adams was a strong supporter of federal investment in internal improvements. He praised Monroe's efforts to support the National Road and other internal improvement projects and sought to extend them. His administration was to be a shining "era of internal improvement." He enthusiastically sought federal funds for roads, canals, and educational institutions. He did not see the need for a constitutional amendment to justify this program. Adams's efforts were often stymied by opposition in Congress, largely by supporters of Andrew Jackson and their allies. Despite these setbacks, Adams's vision of the federal government helping to improve the "condition" of the American people contributed to establishing meaningful precedents for the future.[1]

Adams won office in the presidential election of 1824, although Jackson had a higher popular vote. None of the candidates had a majority of the Electoral College vote. The election was thrown into the House of Representatives. The support of Henry Clay helped Adams to gain the votes of a bare majority of the state delegations. In his inaugural address and in his ambitious first State of the Union message in 1825, Adams sought to make a case for federal aid for internal improvements.

He recognized the constitutional dispute but thought that it could be resolved by compromise. Unlike his predecessors, he openly encouraged Congress to send him internal-improvement legislation unaccompanied by a constitutional amendment. "Liberty is power," he told Congress; through its exercise, Congress could "improve the condition of the governed." This could be partially accomplished by a bold program of internal improvements promoted by the White House and sanctioned by the Constitution.[2]

When one of his allies in Congress, Rep. John Bailey of Massachusetts, proposed to support a constitutional amendment to specifically authorize this legislative program, President Adams told him privately that such an amendment was not necessary and was indeed "dangerous." On a previous occasion, before his election, Adams had made known his view that a constitutional amendment to authorize Congress to spend money for internal improvements was superfluous. On that occasion, he said to Senator James Barbour, later to be a member of his cabinet: "Since the Act of Congress establishing the Cumberland Road, there had been no constitutional question worth disputing about involved in the discussion."[3]

Adams also gave support to the building of the Chesapeake and Ohio Canal, which complemented the National Road by providing a means of water transportation from Washington, D.C., to Cumberland, Maryland. In 1828, the last full year of his presidency, he proudly presided over the inception of work on the canal. In that same year, Adams signed legislation further appropriating funds for the extension of the National Road to Zanesville, Ohio. After his presidency, Adams praised James Monroe in an emotional eulogy for the constitutional compromise that he had crafted in his 1822 memorandum. It was the compromise that enabled Monroe to sign the 1823 legislation providing for repair of the National Road and the survey legislation that followed. In this respect, Adams again used the road and its funding legislation as a strong precedent to support his own policies in favor of a broad program of internal improvements that would provide for the growth of the nation and jobs for its people.[4]

Adams signed into law a number of road improvement projects, including several important measures to extend the National Road, but his grand design for a federally sponsored, federally administered system of roads and canals was never fulfilled. Toward the end of his life, Adams thought that the "great effort" of his administration—"to mature into a permanent and regular system the application of all the superfluous revenue of the Union to internal improvement which would have afforded high wages and constant employment to hundreds of thousands of laborers"—had failed. Time has, however, vindicated him. The nation has effectively pursued just that course in many walks of American life. In this respect, Adams was one hundred years ahead of his time.[5]

This foresight may have been recognized in 1837 when Adams, eight years beyond his White House tenure, visited Uniontown on a trip back from Cincinnati, Ohio. Adams was traveling back to Washington on the National Road. Dr. Hugh Campbell of Uniontown was appointed by the community to deliver the address of welcome to Adams upon his arrival in the town and thanked the aging former president for his continuing support for that road as well as other improvements. As Thomas Searight describes it, after paying homage to the former president's accomplishments, Dr. Campbell observed: "'We stand here, sir, upon the Cumberland Road, which has to some extent broken down the great wall of the Appalachian mountains which served to form so natural a barrier between what might have been two great rival nations. This road constitutes, we trust, an indissoluble chain of Union, connecting forever as one, the East and the West.'" Dr. Campbell attributed this achievement to the American System, the program of the Whig Party to support, through federal financial support, the establishment of internal improvements in the United States, a cause that, as Dr. Campbell noted, had "always received the support" of Adams. Surprisingly, Adams's generally copious and informative diary provides no mention of the occasion.[6]

National Road Debates in Congress during the Adams Presidency

James Monroe's resolution of the constitutional quandary respecting the National Road and the entry into the White House of John Quincy Adams, a president friendly to internal improvements, might have been expected to disarm congressional opponents of ample appropriations for the road. But it did not. During the course of the Adams administration, Congress did approve a number of bills appropriating funds for the continuation of the road first to Zanesville, Ohio, and then beyond it to Indiana and Illinois; it also provided funds for its repair. However, acrimonious debates accompanied the passage of each of these bills in both the House and the Senate. Each proposed appropriation for the road entailed a massive struggle. Supporters of the road complained that they were forced to "beg" for funds for every inch of the road despite the solemn undertaking of the Congress to fund it. Opponents of the road complained of the incessant appropriations that were draining the federal treasury for the benefit of one project and one portion of the country.

It was an old story played out in the national legislature of the early republic. Who should pay for a project that seemed to benefit one area of the nation but which arguably was of benefit to the nation as a whole? How should proposals to advance the "common good" be adequately funded? Sometimes the opposition took the form of direct assaults on the constitutionality of the measure in question. At other times, the high costs and the lack of funds to defray them were the source of the complaints. Objections concerned both bills to continue the road and those aiming to repair it.

Defenders of the road (of which there were many) countered that the constitutional problem had been solved, because appropriations were based on a compact between the states and the federal government at the time of admission of Ohio, Indiana, and Illinois. Moreover, the deal was a good one for the federal government. After all, had not the states, as part of the bargain, given up the right to tax federal land within their borders? Moreover, had they not pledged a percentage of the proceeds of land sales within their borders for both within-state and out-of-state portions of the National Road?

Even as the constitutionality of direct appropriations came to be accepted, particularly in light of the Monroe Memorandum, conflict arose over the right to impose tolls to keep the road in repair. Some legislators favored tolls to defray the repair cost out of the pocketbooks of those who traveled the road rather than all federal taxpayers. Opponents argued that the federal government lacked authority under the Constitution to charge tolls.

Representative James Buchanan of Pennsylvania, for example, in a lengthy speech on the subject, pointed to Monroe's Memorandum on the matter. Buchanan conceded that Congress had the power merely to appropriate for the road. However, Buchanan argued, it would be a usurpation of state authority for the federal government to charge tolls on a road over which the state had jurisdiction. Buchanan therefore urged Congress to cede authority over the road to the states, which could then legitimately erect tollgates and charge tolls. Proponents of the road regarded this as a fatal step likely to put an end to the road and the progress it represented.[7]

Without a legitimate means to raise funds from the users of the road, its proponents recognized that, despite their pleas, congressional financial support for the project would eventually dry up. The survival of the road thus depended on the willingness of a president to sign both appropriation legislation and an authorization for federal toll collection. Proponents of the road presumably had such a president in John Quincy Adams. After all, Adams had pressed for a program of internal improvements without the need for a constitutional amendment. He had also taken a dim view of the limitations on the exercise of federal power in the Monroe Memorandum. With the election of Andrew Jackson in November 1828, it was not clear what the future held for the funding of the old pike.

The National Road was the subject of a number of debates during the Adams administration, pitting friends of the road against opponents of the road from other sections of the nation, particularly the South. In March 1826, for example, such a debate took place in the Senate regarding a bill to provide $110,000 for the continuation of the road. A motion by Senator Thomas W. Cobb of Georgia to strike the appropriation as too costly brought to the floor Senator James Noble of Indiana. Noble defended the appropriation on the ground that Congress had the right to make roads in the territories and that the federal government had solemnly undertaken to build the National Road under the compact between Ohio, Indiana, and Illinois at the time of the admission of those states.

This initial debate stimulated a long and opaque conversation between Senator John Randolph of Virginia and William Henry Harrison, who had been elected to the Senate from Ohio in 1825. An archdefender of states' rights since the days of Thomas Jefferson, in a long and rambling discourse Senator Randolph argued that the National Road was a bad bargain in which southern states were surrendering their rights. Senator Harrison recognized that some members of the Senate believed that Congress could not appropriate for internal improvements. He argued, however, that the bill involved no more than a loan (secured by funds from land sales) for an important public purpose. The road was of great benefit to the United States because it strengthened the bond among them by facilitating travel between the states, uniting families, and encouraging emigration from east to west.

After the debate, the motion to strike the appropriation for the road was defeated and the bill was passed. The law in question was the Act of March 3, 1826, which made, among other things, appropriations for the continuation of the Cumberland Road. In 1827 Congress provided an additional $30,000 for repairing the road from Cumberland to Wheeling. In 1828, Congress provided an additional $175,000 for the completion of the road to Zanesville, Ohio.[8]

The 1828 legislation was preceded by an acrimonious debate in which senators mainly from South strongly opposed further appropriations for the road, while senators from the road states staunchly defended it. On January 23, 1828, Senator William Smith of South Carolina crossed verbal swords with Senators Hendricks and Noble from Indiana. Said Senator Smith: "[L]et every state make its own roads; and, if they reap advantages let it be from their own industry and perseverance." Senator Noble declared heatedly in response: "[B]y a compact with the Western States, Congress is bound to do this work. The Government cannot avoid it; its pledge has been given, and it must be done." If the Constitution was the problem, Noble argued, the provisions of the Constitution in Article IV that permit Congress to set rules for the admission of new states were the solution. Noble charged that opponents of the road were preventing progress: "Do all you can," he thundered to Smith, "the Western world has got the start of you, and will defy illiberality to overtake it or stop its progress." At the end of that speech, a vote was taken in the Senate. The bill to fund the road passed, 25–18, those from the western states generally voting in the affirmative and many from the South voting in the negative.[9]

The Tollgate Proposal Again

An advocate of internal improvements, John Quincy Adams readily signed all these bills. However, these bills left unanswered this central question: even if one conceded the authority of Congress to finance initial building of the road west of the Ohio River, once revenues on the sale of state land were depleted, on what reliable source of revenue could the continued repair of the road depend?

The key legislative debate on this issue came to a head in late 1828 and the early months of 1829, when both the Adams administration and the second session of the Twentieth Congress were in their final days. The Adams presidency would end on March 3, 1829. Before Adams left office, an appropriation bill had to get to his desk to ensure funds to repair the rapidly deteriorating road and to ensure its continued construction in Ohio, Indiana, and Illinois. Some acceptable means of charging tolls was essential to the future of the enterprise. A bill authorizing the federal government to establish tollgates and charge tolls for travelers on the road had passed both houses of Congress in 1822, only to be subsequently vetoed by President Monroe.[10]

While it took a broader view of the appropriating power than Madison's, the Monroe compromise left no room to finance the road through the use of tolls. Once more, in late 1828, strong advocates of the road as a national project tried to mount support for legislation that would authorize federal tollgates. On January 19, 1829, the House went into Committee of the Whole to debate Rep. Charles Fenton Mercer's bill, which would preserve the road and included the tollgate provisions. (Formerly a Federalist, Mercer had been elected to the Nineteenth Congress and the Twentieth Congress from Virginia as an Adams Republican.) Before the committee was Congressman James Buchanan's amendment proposing to strike out the tollgate provisions. At this stage Buchanan delivered a long speech explaining his position. He did not oppose an appropriation for repairs, but he did oppose the tollgate provisions largely for the reasons that President Monroe had stated seven years earlier. In the meantime, on January 20, 1829, the Senate approved a bill for the extension of the road westward from Zanesville to St. Louis. The bill was ordered engrossed for a third reading.[11] (Bills when near completion are normally engrossed—that is, put into final form— and then read for a third time in order to achieve final passage.)

On February 18, the House took up the Mercer proposal again. The question involved Representative Buchanan's amendment proposing that the road be ceded to Maryland, Pennsylvania, and Virginia on the condition that they establish tollgates. When it was rejected, Buchanan proposed another amendment authorizing the president to enter into arrangements with the states for the erection of tollgates. After some debate in opposition, it was withdrawn. Another motion was made to strike the toll gate provision in its entirety. The motion was defeated 107 to 87. On a roll call vote to engross the bill and read it for the third time, the bill passed—105 to 91. A bill containing the federal tollgate provision thus again went to the Senate.[12]

On March 2, the Senate again took up the repair bill, called up by Senator William Hendricks of Indiana. Hendricks was a constant supporter of the road—an unsurprising fact, as it was designed to join his state with Ohio and Illinois. Hendricks entered the Senate in 1825 and was to serve during the duration of both the Adams and Jackson administrations. On March 2, he was expecting to see a new tollgate bill pass the Senate. To his surprise, Senator Thomas Benton of Missouri offered an amendment that would preserve the appropriation, strike the federal tollgate language, and then transfer the road to the states. The motion to strike the tollgate language was passed. The motion to adopt the proposal to transfer the road to the states lost. The bill was thus passed in the form of a mere appropriation for repair. The Senate had ducked the issue of real long-term financing, presumably on the ground that the authority of the federal government to charge tolls was too questionable or too controversial.[13]

The House of Representatives now faced a dilemma. Should it insist upon its tollgate language? If it did, some supporters of the road thought, an appropriation might be lost for the year. Representative Andrew Stewart of Pennsylvania took a pragmatic view of the matter. To save the road from "total destruction," he urged the House to line up with the Senate on the issue. Some members opposed the appropriation without provision for gates and tolls. Representative Buchanan again proposed his amendment to vest the president with authority to negotiate arrangements with the states for gates and the collection of tolls. It met defeat. In the end the House blinked, declining to disagree with the Senate amendments. The two houses came into agreement. A bill could be sent to the president. It would not contain the federal tollgate provision.[14]

John Quincy Adams had joined the two strands that potentially made for sustainable national investment in the case of the National Road: strong support for the road as a policy matter and a constitutional reading that did not require a constitutional amendment to support a broad federal role. But Adams was unable to bring Congress along with him to the end of making the road fiscally sustainable by providing for a federal system to collect the tolls that would reduce the need for direct federal appropriations.

CHAPTER 6

Andrew Jackson and the Transfer of the National Road to the States

Jackson's Perspective on the National Road and Appropriations for It: The Maysville Road Veto

Unlike John Quincy Adams, whom he defeated soundly in the presidential election of 1828, Andrew Jackson was not a proponent of a broad, expansive *system* of federally funded internal-improvement projects. On the contrary, he undertook to draw back from the internal-improvement policies of Adams and to limit what he regarded as profligate spending on roads and canals. Throughout his administration Jackson urged fiscal restraint, the primacy of state authority, and limitations on internal-improvement projects, even if constitutionally authorized.[1]

As to the constitutional issue that had confronted proponents of the Cumberland Road and occasionally suspended its progress, Jackson's most significant action was to veto a bill to assist the Maysville Road in Kentucky by government subscription to shares of stock in the company established under state law to build the road. Significantly, in the accompanying veto message in 1830, Jackson maintained that Congress did not lack authority to assist *all* road projects. He believed that those projects that were "national" rather than "local" in scope qualified for financial assistance from the federal treasury, if Congress so determined. Jackson, however, found the Maysville project fell into the local category rather than the national one. That road, Jackson noted ominously, began and ended in Kentucky and, for the seventh president, was clearly *local* in scope.[2]

For authority to fund truly "national" roads with federal appropriations, Jackson looked to the multiple precedents established during the administrations of his predecessors—Jefferson, Madison, and Monroe. Among these precedents, the laws related to the National Road were paramount. Perhaps, Jackson reflected, it was unfortunate that the nation had by practice abandoned the "strict" construction of the spending power promoted by Madison and Jefferson before 1800. Nevertheless, the precedents that reflected a "more enlarged construction" of that authority had a force of their own. The people had spoken definitively on the matter.[3] Jackson explained: "[T]he public good and the nature of our political institutions require that individual differences should yield to a well-settled acquiescence of the people and the confederated authorities in particular constructions of the Constitution on doubtful points. Not to concede this much to the spirit of our institutions would impair their stability and defeat the objects of the Constitution itself."[4]

The position that he took in this 1830 veto message neatly enabled Jackson to veto road legislation that he disliked and sign road legislation that he favored. As Joseph Wood points out, "Jackson was not personally hostile to internal improvements." On the same day that he vetoed the Maysville project, Jackson signed appropriations for two other projects, one being a bill to extend the National Road to Indiana and Illinois. During his eight years in office, Jackson signed a number of bills concerning the National Road. All told, he outspent all his predecessors combined. In the aggregate Jackson's internal-improvement spending doubled that of his predecessor and much maligned antagonist, J. Q. Adams. Nevertheless, Jackson's Maysville Road veto did establish, to use Wood's words, that, "even to those who held a national view, it was unconstitutional for the federal government to support internal improvements that were of local importance."[5]

What is Jackson's legacy regarding the National Road? It is to confirm that, as a legal matter, the National Road was an appropriate *national* project for application of the federal spending power, for it is presumably on that power that Jackson relied in signing the internal-improvement measures that he did approve. However reluctantly, he concluded that successive enactments for the National Road had, in the aggregate, forged a solid precedent for the exercise of the authority.

As a result, despite his antipathy to what he regarded as "loose" construction and his opposition to uncontrolled spending, Jackson was confirming what John Quincy Adams had proclaimed: there was a legitimate public investment role for Congress to play under appropriate circumstances. The National Road represented an example of such an investment. At the same time, Jackson saw a role for the states in this process as well. At one point he favored (but later disavowed) a proposal to send revenue back to the states for their use in infrastructure projects. In general, he looked for a broader state role in the administration of federal funds.[6]

With respect to the National Road itself, Jackson commenced the step-by-step transfer of the artery to the states through which it passed. This policy was reflected in a congressional resolution of July 3, 1832, agreeing to state collection of tolls on the road in order to derive revenue for keeping it in repair. In 1831, Pennsylvania enacted legislation to provide for this takeover and to appoint commissioners to supervise the road. Maryland and Virginia also passed comparable legislation.[7]

Jackson's contact with the National Road was not merely legislative or administrative. He traveled the road on his way between Washington and his home at the Hermitage near Nashville. Searight gives an account of Jackson's preference for Hart's Tavern in Uniontown. There he stopped on occasion during his trips between his home and Washington, despite the identity of the tavern as a Whig establishment. Politics, it appears, did not preclude Jackson from exercising his preference for hostelries along the National Road.[8]

The Debates in Congress during the Jackson Administration: Moving to State Takeover

With the failure of the Twentieth Congress in 1829 to pass a Cumberland Road repair bill that would have sanctioned the building of tollhouses and the collection of tolls on the road under federal authority, the opportunity to provide a ready source of revenue through a federal user tax was lost. During Andrew Jackson's two terms, debates on the road often involved discussion of such a step, but appropriate legislation was never passed by both the House and the Senate. Moreover, it is unlikely that Jackson would have signed it; he took a more narrow view of the constitutional options regarding the collection of tolls than members of Congress who had voted for the legislation in 1822 and in 1829. Jackson's views were close to Monroe's on the issue. As he warned after his veto of the Maysville Road veto, Jackson would sign bills that appropriated funds for national projects but not bills that vested jurisdiction in the federal government. This left Congress with two choices from 1829 through 1835: (1), continue to appropriate funds from the federal treasury to repair the road without the help of federal tolls; or (2), turn jurisdiction over to the states to care for and maintain the road through the toll revenues that they could themselves collect.[9]

While the second option might have seemed desirable, many opposed it. A number of congressmen believed that the federal government had the responsibility for a national project of this sort, especially one that generated economic growth. They also saw the federal government as a more responsible steward of the road than individual states with their more limited interest. This was the position taken by Senator Henry Clay in the important debate of 1835. The Senate, albeit reluctantly, adopted the second solution in that year. It approved legislation that would turn the road over to the jurisdiction of the states and abandoned the annual debate to secure federal appropriations from an increasingly reluctant Congress. The final debate thus pitted against one another distinguished senators and representatives, future presidents, aspirants for the presidency, and even one former president. In addition to Buchanan and Clay, John Quincy Adams, James Knox Polk, and Daniel Webster participated in the debate.[10]

From 1829 to 1835, at least three major debates took place, leading ultimately to the transfer of the road. They illustrate the tensions that Congress confronted in its debates about the National Road. It may be useful to convey their substance in order to provide a better grasp of what was involved. On March 2, 1831, legislation was enacted that provided for the continuation of the road in Ohio, Indiana, and Illinois, west of Zanesville. A small amount was also appropriated for repair in Ohio. However, the issue of providing federal funds for repairing the entire length of the road, including the portion that ran from Cumberland to Wheeling, remained unresolved. Moreover, the direction of federal legislation regarding the road was driven by legislative action taken by the states. In 1831 and 1832, the state legislatures of Ohio, Pennsylvania, Maryland, and Virginia agreed to accept and maintain their portions of the National Road by charging tolls, provided that the road was first put into suitable repair.[11]

The May 3, 1832, Debate in the House: Repairing the Road for Transfer to the States

On May 3, 1832, Rep. Thomas M. McKennan of Pennsylvania, another devoted friend of the National Road, proposed on the floor of the House an appropriation of $329,000 for completing repairs on the road, the erection of tollhouses and the transfer of the road to the states through which it passed. McKennan represented Washington County, Pennsylvania, in the House. He was a native of Delaware; moved to Washington, Pennsylvania; attended Washington College (now Washington and Jefferson College); and was elected to Congress in 1830 and served there from 1831 to 1839, his terms spanning much of the Jackson administration. In the 1833 debate, he spoke eloquently of the progress that had been generated by the road, which by that time extended from Cumberland to Zanesville. The road passed through "one continued village." The traveler could hear "the din of life and business." Mail could move from Baltimore to Wheeling in sixty-eight hours rather than eight or more days. The constitutional question had been "settled," McKennan proclaimed, by the repeated appropriations for the road. As authority, he cited Jackson's own Maysville Road veto message.[12]

However, appropriations for the repair of the road had been difficult to obtain and were often so delayed that they were of little use. The solution lay in the acts of Maryland and Pennsylvania (noted above), which would provide for state tollgates, state collection of tolls, and state takeover. Tollgates had been erected in Ohio in 1831 with the consent of the federal government; more were needed in the part of the road from Cumberland to the Ohio River. They were designed to provide a dedicated source of state revenue, in light of the considerations reflected in the Monroe Memorandum, short of outright ceding of control to the states. McKennan pressed for an appropriation that would put the road in good repair prior to its transfer without delay.[13]

Rep. Thomas H. Crawford of Pennsylvania agreed with the principle established in the Act of March 2, 1831, providing the assent of the United States to an Ohio law providing for the establishment of tollhouses and the charging of tolls in the Ohio portion of the road. However, alluding to the many appropriations for repairs during the period from 1823 through 1831, he regarded the $329,000 appropriation before the House as "extravagant." He cited a number of reports that sustained the view that a lesser sum would suffice.[14]

Andrew Stewart of Pennsylvania represented Fayette County, through which the road passed. He was a dedicated and consistent supporter of the road and a frequent advocate for its preservation and extension. On this occasion, he spoke to the issue warmly and countered that Crawford's suggestion regarding a smaller appropriation would ensure the destruction of the road. Stewart was a native of Pennsylvania, born in 1791 near Uniontown. There he taught school, studied law, and was admitted to the county bar in 1815. He became district attorney but resigned his seat to enter the House in 1820, where he served until 1829, when the John Quincy Adams administration came to an end. He was reelected to Congress as a candidate of the Anti-Masonic Party and served from 1831 to 1835. Subsequently, he was elected as a Whig to the Twenty-eighth Congress; he then served from 1843 to 1849. His membership in Congress spanned the major debates over the National Road, and he was a constant and vigorous advocate for its continuation and repair. But for a procedural complication, he might have been nominated as the Whig vice-presidential candidate in 1848; and he, rather than Millard Fillmore, would have succeeded Zachary Taylor and served as the thirteenth president of the United States.

In the 1832 debate on the future of the National Road, Stewart professed that it would be utter folly to spend money on the continuation of the road through Ohio, Indiana, and Illinois if the road were not kept in repair from Cumberland to Wheeling. Instead, the three eastern states should be put on an equal footing with Ohio: appropriations for repair that would enable the states to take responsibility for the road should be provided by Congress. The road was in poor condition, and the full amount in the measure proposed by Representative McKennan was necessary. Because federal appropriations were too precarious and the establishment of federal tollgates had been rejected, the only viable option was the one adopted for Ohio: state tollgates and state takeover after adequate provision for repair. The McKennan amendment was eventually defeated, but it did serve to sharpen the issues.[15]

In 1833, the Senate adopted a measure that sought to define the western terminus of the road. In February of that year, a bill to continue the road from Vandalia, Illinois, to Jefferson City, Missouri, was considered and passed, 18 to 16. Senators Thomas Benton of Missouri, George Dallas of Pennsylvania, Thomas Ewing of Ohio, William Hendricks of Indiana, and Daniel Webster of Massachusetts were among the backers of this measure. Despite this support, enacted legislation never emerged from Congress. The western terminus would remain Vandalia, Illinois. What did pass on March 3, 1833, was a more general appropriation bill that included funds to continue the road in Ohio, Indiana, and Illinois and to repair it in Ohio and Virginia. The road would end in the prairies of Illinois. The question of repairs for the portion of the road from Cumberland to Wheeling remained in limbo.[16]

The 1834 Debate: Nickels and Dimes

In March 1834, the Senate took up an appropriation bill to continue the road in Ohio, Indiana, and Illinois. Senator Thomas Ewing of Ohio spoke in favor of an amendment to repair the road east of Wheeling. In order to give the road up to the states, it first had to be repaired. An appropriation had been made for the purpose, Ewing explained, but this was insufficient. The sum of $650,000 was now being requested for the purpose, in order to facilitate the complete transfer of the road to the states. Senator Hendricks of Indiana reviewed the situation to the same effect, noting that constitutional problems prevented the establishment of tollgates by the federal government. Because the states could build them, state takeover was necessary. Senator Ewing urged the adoption of the amendment and assured the Senate that the states would assume responsibility only if the road was put into "perfect" repair.[17]

The debate resumed on April 1, 1834, with Senator John M. Clayton of Delaware speaking in opposition to the bill. Clayton had been elected to the Senate in 1829 as an anti-Jacksonian and served there until 1836. Later, he would become secretary of state in the cabinet of President Zachary Taylor. Clayton had been a staunch friend of the system of internal improvements and had voted for the road. In the 1834 debate, he declared his strong "[disapproval] of throwing the road into the hands of the States." He was concerned that they might charge what they wished at the tollhouses. "Congress would have no power to control them." In the same vein he would oppose putting the Delaware breakwater, if completed, into the hands of the states. The bill amounted to taxing the states for the full amount of the repairs. Though the bill failed to pass at that stage, 20 to 22, on May 9, 1834, it was taken up again. The new version provided for transfer of the road after the appropriated sums were expended, and the United States would not be subjected to further expense. In this form the bill passed, 21 to 13, with Benton, Ewing, Frelinghuysen, Hendricks, Southard, and Webster all voting in favor.[18]

The matter then came to the House, which engaged in a lengthy debate focusing on proposed legislation that would appropriate $650,000 to repair the road east of the Ohio. Maryland, Pennsylvania, and Virginia had already passed state legislation assuming responsibility for the road and providing for state toll-gates. The state law provided that these things would happen, however, only if the road were first put in good repair. The purpose of the bill before the House, therefore, was to furnish an adequate appropriation for repair in order to satisfy this condition.[19]

Rep. James Knox Polk of Tennessee, later to be elevated to the presidency in the election of 1844, moved to reduce the amount in question to $300,000. He believed $650,000 was extravagant; the work could be done for less, he thought, and available resources in the federal treasury would not support the appropriation of such a sum. Representative Stewart opposed Polk's amendment as an inadequate response to the problem. Other speakers alluded to the massive expenditures previously made on the road, the burden it placed on the taxpayers, and the concern that the states would not be bound to take over the road or keep it in repair.[20]

At one point, Rep. John Quincy Adams of Massachusetts objected that it was improper for the legislation to suggest that the United States would "carry into effect" the state laws, as that was not the role of Congress. Other speakers from the South objected that the legislation could not "cede" the road to the states, since it did not belong to the federal government in the first place. Ultimately, Representative Stewart suggested, the argument was between those who supported the American System (Henry Clay's vision of high protective tariffs, the proceeds of which could be used for internal improvements) and those, such as the Jacksonians, who opposed it. Indeed, the federal treasury shortfall that left an insufficient amount for internal improvement could be blamed on the lowering of the tariff and a consequential drop in revenues. The road, Stewart declared, had opened the West and, as a result, long since paid for itself by re-ducing the cost of transporting goods from east to west and vice versa.[21]

Ultimately, the House acceded to Polk's amendment as a means of getting some appropriation out and continuing the momentum of the movement to state takeover. The resulting Act of June 24, 1834, appropriated $300,000 for the "entire completion" of the repair of the Cumberland Road east of the Ohio River. This was done, the act recited, in order to "carry into effect" the laws of Pennsylvania, Maryland, and Virginia, where the repairs would be made. Once the repairs were made, the states would take responsibility for the road. A significant step had been made in that direction. Would it be enough?[22]

The 1835 Debate: The Transfer Effected

In February 1835, the Senate considered a bill to extend the National Road in Ohio, Indiana, and Illinois and to make repairs over the entire road. The proposed appropriation was $346,000. John Quincy Adams had been right when he predicted that the 1834 appropriation for that purpose would be insufficient. Senator Hendricks put the matter squarely: the additional sum was needed to bring the funds available for repair up to the $650,000 level approved by the Senate in 1834 and thus induce the concerned states to make good on their promise to take over the road.[23]

Senator Buchanan, as he had in past debates, recapitulated. He reiterated his long-held view that the federal government had constitutional authority to provide funds for the building of the road but lacked constitutional authority to build tollgates on the road, administer toll collections, and effect enforcement of the toll requirements. Such actions, he argued, would amount to a "perfect consolidation" of federal and state authority, a concept that he profoundly opposed. Canons of federalism thus lay at the heart of the matter. Buchanan would vote for the appropriation as a means of turning the road over to the states and once and for all preventing a "federal" tollgate approach to its funding. He assured the Senate that once the appropriation was made available and the repair completed, Pennsylvania would carry out its part of the bargain.[24]

Senator William C. Preston of South Carolina objected to the cost of the bargain. Senator Ewing of Ohio disagreed. The road, Ewing said, had its origins in the Ohio admission legislation of 1802 in which 2 percent of the proceeds of land sales in Ohio were set aside for roads leading to Ohio, with the added provision that Ohio would not tax U.S. lands for a period of years. By failing to keep the road in repair, the United States would break its promise implicit in this bargain. The states in question were now prepared to take the road and to build tollgates. They should receive it in "perfect" repair. Ohio was now charging tolls on the road and had refrained from charging excessive tolls. Mr. Preston was not persuaded and moved to strike out the key sections of the bill.[25]

To this, the venerable senator Daniel Webster of Massachusetts rose in response. He maintained that the road was fundamentally a "national" project.

Perhaps it had cost more than necessary, but it had been of great benefit. The object of the road, to open access to new states, was a *national* rather than a state undertaking. Though it had been "a most extraordinarily expensive undertaking," Webster confessed that he saw "no better mode of legislation for the Congress to adopt than to follow up the course indicated in the bill of last year": to transfer the road to the states. He argued that it was "prudent and proper" that the federal government be charged with the "duty of preserving the road," but he understood that the states in question were prepared to spend the proceeds of the tolls on the maintenance of the road. It was time to "get rid of the road" by putting it into a condition that would render it acceptable to the states.[26]

Senator Henry Clay of Kentucky then rose to join the battle. He was of a different persuasion, but he would vote for the bill as the only viable option. The project was a national one. While the federal government was no longer obligated to repair the road, because the fund derived from the Ohio land sales was depleted, he believed it was in the interest of the federal government to do so. Clay disputed the position of Senator Buchanan with respect to the lack of authority enabling the federal government to build tollhouses and collect tolls. Clay believed the federal government possessed such authority. "[I]f the power to make a road were conceded, it followed, as a legitimate consequence from that power, that the general Government had a right to preserve it." And, if the right to preserve the road was recognized, "there was no mode of preservation more fitting and suitable than that which resulted from a moderate toll for keeping up the road, and thus continuing it for all time to come."[27]

Clay observed that the national objective represented by the road was of benefit to all, but that it now was to be confided to states having no special stake in its preservation. He saw this principle as "fundamentally wrong." Nevertheless, he would vote for the appropriation in question, compelled to do so by force of circumstances over which he had no control—namely, the unwillingness of Congress to continue funding in the absence of a reliable source of revenues derived from users of the road. The only mode of preserving the road was "by a reluctant acquiescence" in a "course of policy" from which "there lay no appeal."[28]

So the matter rested. Senator Preston's motion to strike the operative provisions of the bill failed, 32 to 14, with Senators Benton, Buchanan, Clay, Hendricks, and Webster, among others, voting against it. The bill itself then passed.[29]

What Andrew Jackson signed as a result of this key debate was the Act of March 3, 1835, providing for the continuation of the road in Ohio, Indiana and Illinois. It also provided $346,000 for repair of the road east of the Ohio. Under section 3 of the Act, before funds could be spent for repair of the road, the road had to be surrendered to the states through which it passed. If states wanted the repairs to be made, they must accept the road and the responsibilities that went with it. The act thus began the final process of road transfer to the states east of the Ohio.[30]

The Final Appropriations and Transfers

The following year, in 1836, Congress again appropriated funds for the continuation of the road in Ohio, Indiana, and Illinois. A final proviso in the act required that the moneys expended for construction in Ohio and Indiana be used in completing "the greatest possible continuous portion" of the road in those states, to the end that the finished parts of the road could be "transferred" to those states. There remained one final step to complete the process. The Act of May 25, 1838 provided funds to continue the road in Ohio, Indiana, and Illinois so as to pave the way for final state take over in those states. By that time Andrew Jackson had left the White House and been succeeded by Martin Van Buren. The 1838 legislation involved the last major federal appropriation for the road; with its enactment, by Searight's account, $6.8 million had been appropriated for the road by Congress since the 1806 act. Further efforts to gain federal financial support for the road west of the Ohio were unsuccessful. By the Act of August 11, 1848, the road in Indiana was formally transferred to that state, and, by the Act of May 9, 1856, the rest of the road was transferred to Illinois. By the time of the Civil War, the transfer of the National Road to the states through which it passed was complete. It had ceased to be a sustainable national investment.[31]

Craig Colton summarizes the impact of these legislative actions on the National Road and on the status of internal improvement in the pre–Civil War United States as follows:

> As work on new Road sections progressed in the western states, repairs commenced in the East. The Road also passed from federal to state control. Maryland's governor insisted that federal repairs include a complete road-way resurfacing in his state. The Army engineers inspected the route and found that it needed extensive repairs and recommended a macadamized surface. They oversaw the laying of a thirty-five foot wide macadamized surface between Cumberland and Wheeling by 1837. Upon completion of these and other improvements, the federal government turned the Road over to Maryland and Pennsylvania. The transfer enabled Congress to avoid a prickly constitutional issue while providing a means for the states to collect revenue for ongoing maintenance. Maryland took possession of its segment of the Road in 1835 and set up two tollbooths thereafter. Pennsylvania followed suit and gathered significant revenues

from the toll system over the next few decades. . . . By midcentury, both Ohio and Indiana had taken over their road segments, but they opted to lease the road to private toll companies. What had begun as an integrated federal project now passed back into state hands, with greater authority held at the county level or by private leasers. Therefore, by the mid-1830s, the National Road had lost its continental complexion and tended to serve local traffic, particularly west of the Ohio River.[32]

CHAPTER 7

The National Road and the Law, Politics, and Policy of Internal Improvement

The National Road and Internal Improvement Politics

In a sense each of the participants in the key 1835 debate was engaged in a familiar political duel that went well beyond the particular issues of continuing or repairing the National Road. James Buchanan, the Jacksonian Democrat who later became the last Democratic president before the Civil War, maintained his party's position on federal spending. Merely providing federal funds for road building was constitutional as long as it did not compromise state sovereignty or evolve into a "national system" of internal improvements. Henry Clay, leader of the Whig Party and its unsuccessful presidential candidate against Andrew Jackson in 1832, was the arch-advocate of the American System of high tariffs and generous federal funding for internal improvements. James Knox Polk, soon to be the eleventh president of the United States, was an ardent foe of the American System and what he regarded as profligate expenditures for such improvements, against which he would rail in his farewell message as president. Daniel Webster, the Whig Party's oratorical giant and strong supporter of its positions on internal improvements, saw the road as a national responsibility but saw as well that transfer to the states was the only path to its salvation.[1]

The compromise reflected in the 1835 legislation (and the succeeding laws of 1836, 1837, and 1838) provided appropriations to fully repair the road and then transfer it to the states. It brought all these statesmen together because they saw it as the only viable option for the immediate problem that the National Road posed. Without the authority in the federal government to set up tollhouses and charge tolls, there could be no dedicated source of revenue to keep it in repair. Only the states could establish such tollhouses; the road, once repaired, must be transferred to them. If this inevitably meant a loss of federal participation, so be it. It was presumed that, after the events of 1829, Congress would never authorize federal tolls and, even if it did, it was unlikely that Andrew Jackson, steeped in states' rights and a supporter of the limitations in the Monroe memorandum of 1822, would ever approve a bill providing for such authorization.[2]

However, the compromise left unanswered many questions. If the road was transferred, why should Congress provide continuing appropriations for the road? The states could charge tolls, but would they be obligated to keep the road in repair? Even if the federal government wished to support the road, what would be the source of a dedicated fund of federal revenues that could be made available for the purpose? On what basis could the federal government contribute such funds to all the states in a fair manner? Would tolls be sufficient to maintain the road even if the states in good faith tried to keep it in repair? The compromise would serve to "get rid" of the road, as far as Congress was concerned. It would not, however, solve the problem of achieving adequate infrastructure for the nation that would promise economic growth. That would be left for future generations. Nevertheless, the road had eliminated one barrier. The experience with it had established a precedent, accepted even by stalwart conservative Democrats like Buchanan: Congress could, under Article I, section 8, clause 1, of the Constitution (the General Welfare Clause) appropriate funds for building the road, even though road building was not specified in the enumerated powers of the Congress. That proposition would be of enormous significance to the economic and social progress of the nation.[3]

What was needed, in addition to Monroe's useful interpretation, was a framework for a viable and effective state-federal partnership in which that interpretation could play a role. The 1835 legislation did not provide the basis for such a partnership. It merely dropped the road in the laps of the affected states without providing for a continuing federal financial and leadership role in the framework of state administration of the road. In the wake of all the wrangling of 1835, such a framework was established, but decades would pass before that happened.

Early-Republic Political Parties and the Internal-Improvement Puzzle

A brief summary of the history described above may help to clarify how the debates about the National Road from 1806 to 1836 fit into and reflected the broader picture of internal improvement politics and policy in the era of the early republic. The Federalist Party that evolved during the Washington administration had envisaged a significant role for the federal government in the economy. Its leader, Alexander Hamilton, had supported federal bounties to encourage manufactures. He had also recognized it as desirable that the government should assist in the development of so-called internal improvements such as roads and canals. Thomas Jefferson came to the White House in March 1801, as a result of the election of 1800, vowing to preside over a more limited and fiscally frugal government in which both taxation and expenditure would be substantially constrained. This was the substance of his first inaugural address and State of the Union message. However, as his administration progressed, the tone changed. In 1803, his administration negotiated the Louisiana Purchase, which doubled the size of the country, and it was a step in which the president took great pride. It was clear that a way to the west must be opened if only to seize upon the great opportunity that this acquisition afforded.[4]

Jefferson's second inaugural address, while sounding themes of the first, called for federal participation in a network of roads and canals and support of other internal improvements. The theme was repeated in the sixth annual message of December 1806, as well as in the 1806 act authorizing the Cumberland Road, as discussed above in chapter 2. The theme of internal improvement was also reflected in the report submitted by Albert Gallatin, calling for an ambitious program of national investment in transportation infrastructure. During his eight years in office, James Madison also championed the benefits of internal improvements in various annual messages, including the seventh, delivered after the cessation of hostilities in the War of 1812. Both Jefferson and Madison were reflecting the desire of the people for better roads. They tried valiantly to harmonize that goal with their perceptions of the limited role of the federal government and the U.S. Congress under the Constitution.[5]

In sum, as Joseph Wood concludes, "Jeffersonianism reflected an attempt to cling to traditional agrarian notions without disregarding imperatives of modern commercial society. Such republicanism, premised on free exchange and complementary interest, was meant to manage national territory and foster economic development for all while minimizing sectional rivalries. Mutually beneficial trade would produce a durable bond of union, encouraging Easterners to anticipate prosperous returns from new western markets and western farmers to cultivate strong ties to the East." Such was the vision that guided the first steps to establish the road. However, as Wood points out, "[t]he [National Road] was only a small portion of the geographical vision for the nation."[6]

The fifth president, James Monroe, saw the need for internal improvements and spent considerable energy in crafting a constitutional compromise that would enable him to sign appropriate legislation. This he did in the form of the National Road repair bill of 1823 and the survey legislation of 1825. His successor, John Quincy Adams, praised Monroe's efforts on behalf of internal improvements and vowed to continue and extend them under what Adams called the "era of internal improvement" that he hoped would characterize his administration. Thus, he readily signed legislation providing for a breakwater in the Delaware, harbor improvements, and road and canal legislation, including legislation authorizing the construction of the Chesapeake and Ohio Canal. He signed a number of bills calling for road extension, among them extensions of the National Road in Ohio. While Adams did not have an opportunity to fully implement his legislative vision, his administration was not bereft of any milestones. He was the first president to openly support infrastructure investment without preconditions, such as a constitutional amendment or a ban on federal toll collections.[7]

Perhaps by way of contrast, Andrew Jackson stressed fiscal constraint, state prerogatives and the need to avoid profligate public-work spending. Nevertheless, he found it expedient to sign into law some projects that he regarded as "national projects," while vetoing those he regarded as "local" projects (for example, the Maysville Road project).

These presidential-level efforts were reflected in party politics. Hamilton's Federalist Party supported internal improvements in Congress. As we have seen in the context of the National Road, legislators like Rufus King of New York were supporters of internal improvements and a broad reading of the Constitution in the debates on the National Road. Henry Clay of Kentucky was another strong proponent of internal improvements and of a political philosophy known as the American System, which embraced high protective tariffs and the use of the money derived from them for internal improvement. Clay became a leader of the Whig Party, which evolved from the Federalist Party to challenge the Jackson forces in the elections of 1832 and 1836, in both of which Clay ran for president and lost. Jackson Democrats opposed the American System and, while supporting some internal improvement legislation, made the limitation of internal improvement a party standard. Thus, changes in political philosophy in the White House were reflected, among other things, in the stance that the occupant of the White House took toward internal improvements generally and the National Road in particular.[8]

The Whigs and Internal Improvements: One Newspaper's Perspective

A survey of the National Road–related articles in the *Springfield (OH) Republic* provides the reader with a window on these internal improvement politics and their effects on one Midwestern community leading up to the 1840 election in the last years of Van Buren's tenure in the White House. Little Van, as he was called, followed Andrew Jackson to the White House in the election of 1836 with Jackson's strong support. During the years covered by those articles, construction of the National Road was continuing toward the Ohio-Indiana line, and residents of Springfield were strongly interested in the progress of the road. Thus, one article, of October 4, 1839, pointed to the importance of the National Road in serving western interests and deplored its retardation due to lack of appropriations in the administration of President Van Buren. Another article indirectly chided the administration by noting that, on the question of engrossing (finalizing) an appropriation bill for the road, eighteen "administration" senators voted against the bill, while only four Whigs did so.

Yet another article accused Martin Van Buren of never casting a "a single vote" in favor of the National Road. On April 3, 1840, the *Springfield Republic* reported another failure of appropriations for the National Road and reported as well a speech of Henry Clay defending his vote against the appropriation on the ground that it should be deferred until the Harrison administration took office in March 1841, as well as on the ground that such appropriations were bankrupting the federal treasury. The *Springfield Republic* blamed the failure of the appropriation on the Van Buren administration, which had not requested the appropriation and, at the same time, criticized Whigs for failing to vote for the appropriation on spurious fiscal grounds. In a similar piece, the paper accused Van Buren of never supporting a road appropriation and documented the accusation with excerpts from the record. Sectional favoritism lay at the heart of the problem, the paper suggested. The people of western Ohio had "nothing to hope" from this "New York President." The solution was to put a "Western man in a place where he can look after Western interests."[9]

The paper continued to press for a Whig president and a Whig Congress as the only means of securing support for the road. This in effect happened with the election of William Henry Harrison as president in 1840, an election in which Harrison's support for the road played a role. Harrison ran on a Whig platform that, in the tradition of Henry Clay, strongly supported internal improvements. He defeated Van Buren roundly, gaining 234 electoral votes to Van Buren's 60. However, Harrison never had an opportunity to influence policy on internal improvement or any other issue. He contracted pneumonia at his inaugural ceremony where he spoke for over an hour in cold weather. Within a month, the first Whig president was dead. John Tyler, a Democrat from Virginia who had been elected as vice president in the election of 1840, became president. Again road appropriations languished. In a November 28, 1841, column, a now frustrated *Springfield Republic* asked whether the people should abandon the effort to complete the road. To do so would be a breach of faith, the article opined. The paper doubted the success of an appropriation but urged that western representatives should continue fighting for the appropriation. New representatives would be elected from the West as a result of the new census. Opponents of the American System would be defeated. The question should be kept before the Congress so that a subsequent Congress "possessed of a larger degree of Westernism" would "do justice to the great West." Thus, the issue of the National Road, as the *Republic* saw it, was dependent on the election of a Whig president, Whig legislatures, and the bolstering of the legislative clout of the West. The settlers streaming across the road to the heartland would settle the matter.[10]

However, these aspirations were not destined to be fulfilled. In 1844, the Democrat James Knox Polk won the White House. He expanded the size of the nation through the annexation of Texas and the Mexican War, but strongly opposed the American System touted by the Whigs, along with its pro-internal-improvement planks. In the election of 1848, Zachary Taylor, the Whig candidate, ran against the Democrat Lewis Cass; Taylor again cited internal-improvement considerations as an important factor. Taylor was elected but died after one year in office and was succeeded by his Whig vice president, Millard Fillmore of New York, who supported internal improvement legislation where he could, but had a limited impact in his three years of service; he was not renominated. Succeeding Democratic presidents Franklin Pierce and James Buchanan were strongly opposed to expansive internal-improvement legislation and to the role of the federal government in funding education and welfarelike measures.[11]

The inability of the Whig party to wield national power during the period of the National Road's prime influenced the history of that important artery. The Whig presidents won the presidency only after the decision of Congress to transfer the National Road to the states and after the last federal appropriation for the road. Moreover, their tenures were so brief as not to provide sufficient momentum to affect the course of the National Road or other internal improvements. The inability of Henry Clay to gain the White House, despite three attempts, also represented a lost opportunity for a more profound national role in internal improvement. Nevertheless, during its time upon the national stage, the Whig Party provided a philosophical home for many of those members of Congress who took up the cause of the National Road and internal improvements generally, including such proponents of the road as Andrew Stewart, T. M. McKinnon, Jonathan Knight of Pennsylvania, and J. M. Clayton of Delaware. One may speculate that the Whig Party's affinity for the National Road in particular and internal improvements in general, through its championing of the American System, naturally drew to that party those legislators whose political fortunes were aligned with the success and advancement of the National Road.[12]

Lincoln as a Proponent of Internal Improvement

Having spent his early political life as a Whig before becoming the leader of the Republican Party, Abraham Lincoln came to implement the Whig philosophy on internal improvement during his transcendent tenure in the White House. By that time the railroad rather than the turnpike had become the transportation mode of choice, and Lincoln's contribution, in the form of advocacy for such improvements as the transcontinental railroad, reflected that reality.

The late Paul Simon, who served Illinois with distinction from 1985 to 1997 in the U.S. Senate, explored Abraham Lincoln's Vandalia and Springfield periods in the state legislature in a book entitled *Lincoln's Preparation for Greatness: The Illinois Legislative Years.* Simon's study illustrates the degree to which those early years Lincoln spent in the Illinois House were dominated by issues pertaining to internal improvements. Indeed, it appears that Lincoln got his start in politics through the issue of internal improvements.[13]

Lincoln was first elected to the Illinois House from Sangamon County in 1834. During his first term in that body, Simon recounts, Lincoln favored state support for internal improvements as well as legislation to authorize the spending of state funds for railroad projects. Lincoln was also a strong proponent of federal financial assistance for roads and other internal improvements. In the Illinois legislature, he voted for a resolution requesting the federal government to make a land grant to the state of 500,000 acres. The proceeds of the land sales from the grant would be used for internal improvements.[14]

Reelected in 1836, Lincoln served a second term in the Illinois House in Vandalia and was again a proponent of internal improvements. This was not surprising, as there was a fair degree of public pressure for such improvements within the state as a means of getting products to market. As described by Senator Simon, the result was the state's Internal Improvements Act. Lincoln voted for the measure and voted to override the governor's veto of it. The same session of the legislature voted to move the capital to Springfield, a move that Lincoln supported. Despite a growing financial crisis that affected the state as a result of the enactment of the internal improvements legislation, as Simon describes it, Lincoln "firmly stood on the side of internal improvements."[15]

Some years later, when elected to the U.S. House of Representatives as a Whig in 1846, Lincoln continued to express his support for internal-improvement measures. In a significant speech, delivered on the floor of the House on June 20, 1848, he challenged President Polk's veto of an internal-improvement measure. Polk's veto message had cited both constitutional and policy objections. Lincoln defended the measure both on constitutional and policy grounds. With respect to the constitutional issue, Lincoln surveyed the legal precedents as described by Chancellor Kent, including the views of former presidents Jefferson, Madison, Monroe, and J. Q. Adams. Lincoln concluded: "This constitutional question will probably never be better settled than it is, until it shall pass under judicial consideration, but I do think no man, who is clear on the question of expediency, needs feel his conscience much pricked upon this." In sum, in his House speech, Lincoln supported the view that federal aid to internal improvements was constitutional but recognized the need for judicial clarification; as to expediency, he supported aid for internal improvements, as he had in the Illinois House.[16]

Lincoln's interest in this issue ultimately gave way to his participation in the larger debate over the extension of slavery and the preservation of the Union, an issue that convulsed the nation and brought Lincoln to national prominence in the famous Lincoln-Douglas debates of 1858. Lincoln's participation in those debates helped to catapult him into the White House following the election of 1860 and leadership of the nation during the Civil War. Despite that war, during his presidency Lincoln gave strong support to federal aid for railroads and canals. After that conflict had been resolved and the Union was preserved in the framework of a "new birth of freedom," it became inevitable that the issue of internal improvement would again confront its lawmakers. By that time, the National Road had long since ceased to exist as a federally funded turnpike, but the issues that it had raised in the great debates in Congress during the early republic remained relevant. Among those issues was that of constitutional authority for internal improvement projects financed by federal appropriations.[17]

In his first annual message of December 1861, for example, President Lincoln recommended congressional support for the construction of a railroad connecting east Tennessee, western North Carolina, and Kentucky with other "faithful parts of the Union." Lincoln saw the project not only as a useful in the war effort but also as a "valuable permanent improvement." Similarly, in his second annual message, President Lincoln expressed strong support for federal assistance in the building of the transcontinental railroad and the Illinois and Muskegon Canal. Lincoln connected these internal improvements with the battle that he was waging to preserve the Union. He saw them as contributing to "one national family," not two. "Steam, telegraphs, and intelligence have brought these to an advantageous combination for one united people."[18]

Thus, Lincoln, like Monroe, J. Q. Adams, and Joseph Story, aligned himself with those who believed that the Constitution enabled Congress to appropriate for the general welfare of the United States in a way that would advance national objectives and promote unity. Jefferson and Madison did not agree with them regarding the legal analysis of the Constitution, preferring a constitutional amendment route as a means of achieving these policy goals with which they were in accord.

Internal Improvements and the Constitution: The Prominence of the Spending Power and the Possible Place of the Commerce Clause; *Wilson v. Shaw*

That constitutional politics was part of this mix during the early republic seems clear from the discussion of the debates on the National Road. Indeed, the National Road played a major role in helping to frame that constitutional debate. When Jefferson and Madison failed to induce Congress to propose a constitutional amendment to support internal-improvement legislation, Monroe felt obliged to craft a compromise interpretation in order to keep the road in repair. In effect, the political need to maintain the road trumped a preference for the strict reading of the Constitution maintained by the three Virginia presidents who followed Washington: Jefferson, Madison, and Monroe. That compromise established a constitutional precedent for John Quincy Adams's staunchly pro-internal-improvement program, as well as a basis for Jackson to sign the internal-improvement legislation that he favored while maintaining a conservative stance on the internal-improvement issue generally. Lincoln strongly supported that compromise (or its result). His speech on internal improvements before the U.S. House of Representatives in 1848, referenced above, so indicates.[19]

As the technological scene shifted with the advent of the railroad and the decline of the road in the late 1850s and the 1860s, the focus of internal-improvement legislation shifted as well. Lincoln's successors continued to support federal legislation to assist the building of a transcontinental railroad with land grants and other forms of assistance. The constitutional objection seemed to wane as the nineteenth century marched on. The compromise worked out for the National Road appears to have paved the way for the railroad to the extent that constitutional concerns represented a barrier to the extension of that mode of transportation. By the time the advent of the automobile ushered in the revival of the need for roads in the early twentieth century, it seems to have been conceded that Congress had power to aid state road-building activities under the Highway Acts of 1916 and 1921 (discussed below) before the Supreme Court definitively addressed the issue of federal spending in a comprehensive way. Indeed, during the nineteenth century, as the history of the National Road indicates, the constitutional issues relating to the federal financing or making of internal improvements were largely the subject of congressional debates and presidential papers rather than of Supreme Court decisions.[20]

This changed in the twentieth century. The constitutional battle over the scope of the spending power was fought in the Supreme Court in 1936 not in the context of an internal improvement (such as a canal, road, or railroad project) for which federal assistance was sought but in the context of New Deal legislation providing subsidies for farmers who agreed, in exchange for the subsidies, to curtail agricultural production. While striking down the program in question, the decision in *United States v. Butler* broadly upheld the power of Congress to legislate under the Spending Clause (or General Welfare Clause) for purposes that were not confined to the four corners of the list of enumerated powers granted Congress under Article I, section 8, clause 1, of the Constitution. Congress could use its spending power to provide federal aid in areas of national (not local) interest that fell within the ambit of the "general welfare of the United States." Significantly, the *Butler* decision on that score rested in part on the conclusions that James Monroe had reached in his presidential memorandum of 1822 regarding appropriations for the repair of the National Road. The same taxing and spending power that figured in the *Butler* case was suggested to those in Franklin Roosevelt's administration who were planning the Social Security program as an adequate basis for such a program. The legislation that they proposed became the foundation for the Social Security Act of 1935. In the 1937 case *Helvering v. Davis*, the Supreme Court upheld the authority of Congress to enact Title II of that act, affording Social Security retirement benefits to all Americans. The program now accounts for a substantial portion of each year's annual federal budget. The constitutional basis for the Court's decision, as announced in the majority opinion by Justice Cardozo, was the taxing and spending power found in the General Welfare Clause of the Constitution.[21]

The focus here on the spending power in the context of the National Road seems warranted by the view of Monroe and others who concluded that it was the soundest constitutional basis for the road's construction; it seems warranted as well by modern decisions of the Court that rely on that power for contemporary legislation providing federal highway aid. However, before it decided the *Butler* and *Helvering* cases in the New Deal era, the Supreme Court also opined in the 1907 case of *Wilson v. Shaw*, 204 U.S. 24, that Congress had the authority to construct interstate roads or highways under another constitutional provision. Citing the precedent of the National Road, among others, the Court concluded that the Interstate Commerce Clause provided the necessary authority for this construction. In that opinion, the Court did not deal with the view of Madison or Monroe that the Commerce Clause did not afford such authority and did not mention the Spending Clause (Article I, section 8, clause 1) in its decision.

In view of its reliance on the National Road precedent, it seems appropriate to quote Justice Brewer's opinion on the subject in *Wilson v. Shaw*:

> The power to construct, or to authorize individuals or corporations
> to construct, national highways and bridges from State to State, is

essential to the complete control and regulation of interstate commerce. Without authority in Congress to establish and maintain
such highways and bridges, it would be without authority to regulate
one of the most important adjuncts of commerce. This power in
former times was exerted to a very limited extent, the Cumberland
or National Road being the most notable instance. Its exertion was
but little called for, as commerce was then conducted by water, and
many of our statesmen entertained doubts as to the existence of the
power to establish ways of communication by land. But since, in
consequence of the expansion of the country, the multiplication of
its products, and the invention of railroads and locomotion by steam,
land transportation has so vastly increased, a sounder consideration
of the subject has prevailed and led to the conclusion that Congress
has plenary power over the whole subject.[22]

While historically interesting, particularly in light of the heated contest over the
constitutionality of the Cumberland Road during the congressional debates on
that artery, the *Wilson v. Shaw* precedent has had relatively limited applicability,
as Congress has played its major role in fostering interstate highways through the
spending, rather than the interstate commerce, power. Through major federal-
aid programs, such as the Federal Aid Highway Act of 1956, it has provided
massive federal aid to states which have then constructed the highways, while
abiding by the aid conditions. *Wilson v. Shaw* seems to have been relegated to
a historical footnote in the story of the constitutional debate regarding internal
improvement. Moreover, Justice Brewer's opinion never adequately confronted
the objection raised by Madison and Monroe that the Interstate Commerce
Clause was not available for such improvements as the National Road because it
was a regulatory rather than an investment power. Furthermore, the case dealt
with a taxpayer suit challenging the expenditure of federal funds to pay for
property to be used for construction of the Panama Canal. Nevertheless, *Wilson
v. Shaw* does present the possibility of an alternative constitutional theory to
support direct federal construction of a road should the occasion arise—namely,
that state participation under a federal aid program is not available for maintenance of an interstate or primary highway that is deemed essential to facilitate
interstate commerce and the federal government finds it necessary to assume
direct responsibility for the repair of the highway.[73]

Turning again to the nexus between the Spending clause and internal improvement, one must fast-forward more than fifty years after *Helvering v. Davis*, the case sustaining the Social Security program under that power. In 1987,
the Supreme Court finally came to formally extend the reasoning of the New
Deal–era spending-power decisions to uphold conditions imposed under the
interstate highway program pursuant to the Federal Aid Highway Act of 1956,

as amended. The case *South Dakota v. Dole* concerned a requirement in the federal road legislation requiring South Dakota to maintain a minimum drinking age of twenty-one. Chief Justice Rehnquist, writing for the majority, said of the fundamental authority for the program: "The breadth of [the spending power] was made clear in *United States v. Butler* [citations omitted], where the Court, resolving a long standing debate over the scope of the Spending Clause, determined that 'the power of Congress to authorize the expenditure of public moneys for public purposes is not limited by the direct grants of legislative power found in the Constitution.' Thus, objectives not thought to be within Article I's 'enumerated legislative fields' [citations omitted] may nevertheless be attained through the use of the spending power and the conditional grant of federal funds."[24]

It should be emphasized that in this case, the Supreme Court relied upon the Spending Clause, not the Interstate Commerce Clause, to uphold the authority of Congress to provide *financial aid* to the states for the construction of the massive interstate highway system. It is appropriate to recall that it is upon the basis of that clause that James Monroe justified his signature on the 1823 legislation providing federal funds for the repair of the Cumberland Road. At this same time, it is of historical interest that the post-Civil War Court found authority in the Interstate Commerce Clause for the United States to engage in direct construction of an interstate road, a function that it had carried out in the case of the National Road, suggesting that both sources of authority are relevant to the subject. The spending power under Article I, section 8, clause 1, of the Constitution is available for federal assistance to the states; the Interstate Commerce Clause under Article I, section 8, clause 3, is available for direct construction. What is left open is whether the Court would have, as Henry Clay argued in 1835, sustained the imposition of a federally set and federally administered user toll. After all, if the federal government could have constructed a road, as *Wilson v. Shaw* decided, it presumably could have also charged a toll to help repair it.[25]

Be that as it may, in 1987, two hundred years after the framing of the Constitution, the Supreme Court came formally to extend the Spending Clause in Article I, section 8, of the Constitution to uphold congressional action in connection with a program of federal assistance to aid in the building and maintenance of a system of interstate highways. It did so largely on the same line of reasoning that Monroe had applied in his long memorandum of 1822 explaining his veto of a National Road repair bill. In this context, it should thus be remembered that the underlying precedents for the Court's most definitive constitutional decision respecting interstate highway legislation had been made in the context of much early congressional legislation respecting the National Road.[26]

Internal Improvement as an Enduring National Interest

The National Road's significance in the broader realm of the history of internal improvement in the United States is, therefore, not confined to the resolution of constitutional issues or federalism or states' rights issues. It was about the needs and uses of infrastructure as a national concern and as a distinct national interest. The experience of the National Road in the first half of the nineteenth century taught the nation a number of lessons about adequate infrastructure. First, it taught that an adequate system of surface transportation was essential to national survival and economic and social growth. Second, it taught that federal assistance is necessary for the construction of such a system. Even in 1806 it was recognized that the states (or private enterprise) could not alone defray the expense of building such a system. Federal assistance was needed—at least for some key arteries.

Finally, the National Road experience taught that it is not enough for Congress to simply aid the construction of roads and other internal improvements. Congress must also establish a reliable mechanism to ensure that once roads are built with federal assistance adequate means are found to keep them in repair. In the case of the National Road, the solution was to return the road to the states, which then had authority to charge tolls in order to maintain the roads. Whatever the merits of that solution in 1835, it was clearly not sufficient for the twentieth century. The broader message of the National Road experience, with respect to internal improvement, putting aside the constitutional and federalism debates, is that American growth and prosperity depend upon the establishment of a reliable framework for both building and maintaining an adequate system of surface transportation to be financed on a fiscally sound, pay-as-you-go basis. The experience of the United States in the twentieth century in seeking to establish such a system, on the basis of the foundation laid by the National Road experiment, is discussed in chapters 12 and 13. The challenges faced by the nation in maintaining and extending that system on a viable and sustainable basis in the twenty-first century are discussed in part 4. It should be remembered that this saga began not in modern times, but before the founding of the nation with Washington's crossings and with the events that unfolded in the course of the planning and construction of the National Road. In addressing today's challenges, the issues at hand should be considered in that context.[27]

Part II

THE NATIONAL ROAD
IN ITS PRIME

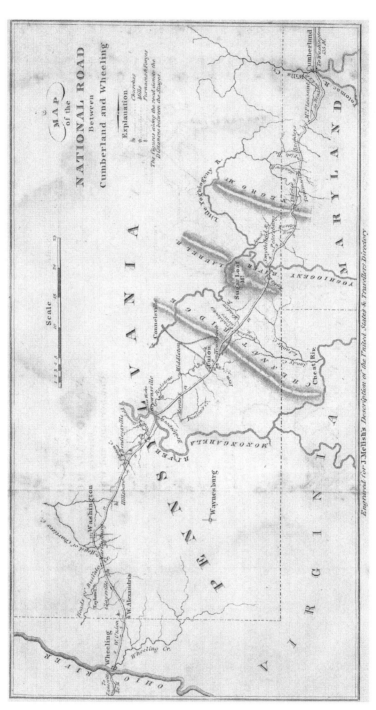

Figure 2. 1822 Map of the National Road from Cumberland to Wheeling (courtesy of the Museums of Oglebay Institute).

CHAPTER 8

Laying Out and Building the National Road

The story of the National Road is more than an account of the political debates in Congress over the routing and funding of the road. It is as well a story of the construction of the road and its culture during the period of its prime in early-republic America. That story also embraces the role of the National Road as a microcosm of that America and the social and political crosscurrents and movements that characterized it. To these matters we now turn. We start with the routing, laying out, and construction of the road.

The Routing of the National Road

The routing of the National Road involved decisions at the highest levels of the national councils in Washington. Those decisions reflected the geographic, fiscal, engineering, economic, and political issues that typically affect great public works. The considerations that influenced Thomas Jefferson in agreeing to approve the communities of Uniontown and Washington in Pennsylvania as points that the road would traverse were not unlike those that affect the placement of public works in our day.

The Eastern Portion

In charting the portion of the road east of the Ohio River, Jefferson's commissioners had selected what they regarded as the most direct route: from Cumberland, Maryland, to Wheeling, West Virginia (then Virginia). As built, and as displayed in an 1822 map of the road between Cumberland and Wheeling (see figure 2), the National Road began in Cumberland (135 miles by road from the capital at Washington, D.C., as specified in the 1822 map) and then proceeded in Maryland to Mount Pleasant (present Frostburg), crossed the Little Youghiogheny River (now the Casselman), passed Tomlinson's (present Grantsville), crossed the formidable Negro Mountain, and then entered Pennsylvania just east of Petersburg (now Addison). It then crossed the Youghiogheny (Great Crossings) at Smythfield (later Somerfield and now underwater by virtue of dam construction in the area), proceeded past the remains of Fort Necessity and Braddock's grave in what is now Farmington, climbed over the daunting Chestnut Ridge and Laurel Mountain, not far from where Washington had encountered Jumonville in 1754, and descended the very steep and winding grade into Union (now Uniontown).

The road then proceeded in a northwesterly direction to Brownsville on the Monongehela. Once across that river, the traveler would continue through Hillsboro to Little Washington and Claysville and exit Pennsylvania at West Alexandria (now West Alexander). The road then proceeded through the panhandle of Virginia to Wheeling, where it stopped at the east bank of the Ohio. The route covered approximately 32 miles in Maryland, 90 miles in Pennsylvania, and 11 miles in Virginia, for a total of 133 miles.

Construction of the eastern portion of the road began in Cumberland in 1811, reached Wheeling in 1818, and was complete by 1821. At this stage, the National Road provided a valuable land route from the eastern-flowing Potomac in Cumberland to the western-flowing Ohio at Wheeling. From there the road was designed to head due west through the states of Ohio, Indiana, and Illinois, thus providing a reliable and more expeditious land route to the West, opening it to commerce, travel, and settlement that would not have otherwise been possible.[1]

The Western Portion

Construction on the portion west of the Ohio started in 1825, after the enactment by Congress of legislation providing appropriations for westward charting and construction in the wake of James Monroe's message and memorandum of 1822 proposing the constitutional "compromise" that enabled him to sign that legislation with a certain degree of serenity. The road was completed to Zanesville by 1830.[2] Columbus had replaced Zanesville as the capital of Ohio, and the road reached that city by 1833, passing in front of the state capitol building. West of Columbus, the road reached Springfield, Ohio, and the Indiana line by the early 1840s. In Indiana construction began in 1824 from Indianapolis, simultaneously proceeding in both easterly and westerly directions. The road was largely completed in that state by 1838, linking Richmond, Greenville, Indianapolis, and Terre Haute, as well as many small pike towns in between. In Illinois, the road was laid out to Vandalia, then the state capital.

The National Road was expected to link the three Midwestern state capitals in Ohio, Indiana, and Illinois—Columbus, Indianapolis, and Vandalia, respectively—giving effect to the intent of the 1802 legislation providing for the admission of Ohio and the comparable bills for Indiana and Illinois. Abraham Lincoln and his colleagues in the Illinois statehouse in Vandalia complicated this picture. In 1837, despite extensive exertions on the part of Vandalia, the state legislature directed that the state capital of Illinois be moved to the more centrally located Springfield. Lincoln, then a member of that body, played a key roll in this action. The "old pike," as built, thus united the Midwest with the East, the Atlantic coast with central Illinois, close to, if not exactly the same as, the prescription of Thomas Jefferson when he signed the 1806 original authorizing act.[3]

The Never-Built Portion

The road was originally intended to proceed on to St. Louis, but agreement could not be reached on funding. Therefore, the federally financed part of the road ended in Vandalia. At one point, Congress considered extending the road beyond St. Louis to a fourth state capital, Jefferson City, Missouri. This prospect moved John Quincy Adams to rapture. He proclaimed in his diary: "This Cumberland Road from Vandalia in the State of Illinois, to the Mississippi, and from the Mississippi to the city of Jefferson in the state of Missouri—how it sounds! What a demonstration of the gigantic growth of the country, in population and in power, is contained in those few words." However appealing it may have seemed to the aging advocate of internal improvement, his fellow members of Congress never authorized the step. Evidently, building the National Road—the first federally funded interstate—to Vandalia was itself a "gigantic" enough task.[4]

Why was the National Road not extended to St. Louis, as Thomas Jefferson had contemplated in his 1808 report to Congress? The answer to that question illustrates some of the problems that confronted proponents of the road during the period of its routing and its construction, particularly in the three states west of the Ohio River. In sum, a combination of legislative and sectional challenges forced the federal government to terminate the road at Vandalia, Illinois, instead of extending it to Jefferson City, Missouri, as had been contemplated at one point during the period 1834 to 1844. The direction of the road in Illinois was substantially influenced by two pieces of federal legislation: the Act of May 15, 1820, and the Act of March 3, 1825. Both of these acts were adopted during the administration of James Monroe, an administration, as we have seen, that had a major impact on the construction of the National Road. The first act directed that the road should traverse Ohio, Indiana, and Illinois, running from the city of Wheeling to the Mississippi at some point between the mouth of the Illinois River and the city of St. Louis. The Act of March 3, 1825, called for the road to join the three state capitals of Ohio, Indiana, and Illinois.[5]

In Ohio, the route was drawn so as to join the capital, Columbus, with the town of Springfield and then to proceed to the Indiana state line at the town of Richmond, Indiana. Thus, Dayton and Eaton, Ohio, were bypassed, a result that offended backers of those two communities. Supporters of Dayton made economic and political arguments in order to obtain a rerouting, but to no avail. President Jackson supported the original route, and the House declined to change it.[6]

In 1825, the law provided that the road would extend to Jefferson City, Missouri, but without setting forth the exact route by which the road would arrive there. Two possibilities were considered in 1834. One involved routing the road through Vandalia and then to St. Louis. A second would have had the road cross the Mississippi at Alton, Illinois. The controversy simmered for the next ten years without resolution. In 1844, the appropriate Senate committee finally opted in favor of the Alton option, but Congress never passed legislation. By that time, the responsibility for administration was in the process of being transferred to the states, and Congress had ceased to have a strong voice in the matter. Given the impasse, the road was simply left to terminate in Vandalia.[7]

Jeremiah Simeon Young, in his study of the Cumberland Road, describes the impasse in the following passage: "A struggle which lasted for eighteen years was waged between Missouri and Illinois over the point at which the Cumberland Road should cross the Mississippi; Missouri stood for the St. Louis crossing; Illinois for the Alton." Young then proceeds to describe the various memorials and countermemorials from the legislatures of Illinois and Missouri regarding the controversy and the arguments made in Congress by the representatives of these states in defense of their respective positions. The last exchange took place in 1847 but led to no resolution. As Young observes, "The question was never decided by Congress, and the road was not located west of Vandalia, Ill."[8]

Even if the road never penetrated Missouri, it had a profound impact. In effect, at the time of its completion and the gradual takeover by the states in the mid-1830s, if one took into account the privately built roads (not part of the National Road) linking Baltimore and Washington with Cumberland, the National Road provided a viable means of transportation between the commercial East and the capital in Washington and the heartland in central Illinois. It facilitated water transportation between the East and the Mississippi by enabling stagecoaches and wagons to move people and goods to Wheeling, where they could proceed down the Ohio by steamer to Cincinnati, St. Louis, or other river ports, or in the opposite direction. It embraced six states. As laid out and built, it was both national and interstate. However, by piercing the difficult Allegheny Mountains through Maryland and Pennsylvania, the most feasible route, as it was thought, the road was also a "northern" artery. Most of its length was to be found in the four northern states of Pennsylvania, Ohio, Indiana, and Illinois. This regional characteristic, as we have seen, complicated its reception during the decades of debates. That same characteristic also made it largely a "free" state road.[9]

Billy Joe Peyton summarizes the overall impact of the first federally funded interstate: "No other transportation corridor has played a larger role in this nation's history than our first interstate highway—known alternately as the Cumberland Road, National Road, Uncle Sam's Road, Great Western Road, or simply the Road."[10]

Superintendents and Surveyors

The laying out and construction of the National Road was under the general supervision of a set of commissioners and a superintendent. Elie Williams and his fellow commissioners (Joseph Kerr and Thomas Moore) were appointed by President Jefferson to propose an initial route pursuant to the first authorizing statute in 1806. They conducted their surveys and made their periodic reports to Jefferson, contributing substantially to the laying out of the portion of the National Road between Cumberland and Wheeling. In his essay on the building of the road, Billy Joe Peyton pays tribute to the work of these first surveyors: "In the final analysis, [the team of surveyors] and the other expedition members whose identity will never be known should be remembered for their collective contribution to this country's history and development."[11]

DAVID SHRIVER

The first road superintendent, as previously mentioned, was David Shriver, a native of Maryland who was a businessman and an engineer. Shriver was first appointed during the administration of Thomas Jefferson. He was responsible for the series of reports to Albert Gallatin during the Jefferson and Madison administrations that essentially guided and nurtured the construction of the Cumberland-to-Wheeling portion of the road. Peyton observes: "Shriver is an unheralded figure who is scarcely mentioned in Thomas Searight's or Archer Hulbert's classic works on the subject, but deserves to be recognized for his dedication to the job. Indeed, Shriver merits a rightful place in the annals of the National Road, alongside such well known names as Henry Clay and Albert Gallatin, men who are generally given the credit for getting the Road built."[12]

Peyton candidly describes the duties of the superintendent and the challenges that that officer faced: "The superintendent's duties included letting contracts, supervising construction and insuring contractual obligations were successfully carried out. His job was not without travails, however. Keeping [contractors] supplied with proper tools and materials presented a constant problem, as did the quest to find competent labor. Moreover, the superintendent stood by as workers grumbled about their pay, spring freshets made rivers of creeks and swept away survey markers, and contractors swore their work was too difficult to complete."[13]

JONATHAN KNIGHT

The actual fieldwork in mapping or charting the path of the road was carried out by surveyors who might also be commissioners. One such individual was Jonathan Knight. Knight's career exemplifies the role of many able Americans of the early-republic era who lived on or near the National Road and contributed directly to its progress along a number of its major segments. It also illustrates how an individual's contribution, in the capacity of a surveyor, to the progress of the road might lead to success in business, local politics, or the Washington scene.

As a child, Knight was brought by his parents to southwestern Pennsylvania. He lived in Washington County in that commonwealth, attended common schools there, and supplemented his education by teaching himself mathematics and surveying. Knight served variously as a teacher, a surveyor, a civil engineer, and a county commissioner in his home county. He assisted in the preliminary surveys of the Chesapeake and Ohio Canal. He also carried out surveying duties on the portion of the National Road between Cumberland and Wheeling. In the 1820s, Knight was named a commissioner of the National Road, in which capacity he surveyed, or supervised the survey, of its route in Ohio and Indiana. In recognition of his service, the town of Knightstown in Indiana was named in his honor.[14]

Knight's contribution to the road led to service in the Pennsylvania legislature, which in turn led to work for the Baltimore and Ohio Railroad as its chief engineer. In 1855, Knight was elected to the Thirty-fourth Congress and served from that year until 1857. Not surprisingly, Knight adhered to the Whig Party, the party of Henry Clay, which favored internal improvements to be financed, at least in part, with federal funds derived from high tariffs.[15]

Presidential appointments of individuals to these important road positions required the kind of consultations between the White House and Congress that characterize political appointments in general. Members of Congress wanted input into the selection of officeholders who would survey the route of the National Road in or near their communities. For example, in March 1825, on the eve of his inauguration as president of the United States, John Quincy Adams received from Jonathan Jennings, a member of the House of Representatives, a communication, dated March 3, 1825, noting that a commissioner was required to be appointed to "survey and locate a road from Zanesville in Ohio through Indiana and Illinois to the Seat of Government in Missouri." The letter politely but pointedly observed: "We [desire] that you will not act on this subject until we shall have the honor of seeing you in reference to it."[16]

The National Road Bureaucracy

The construction of the road and its supervision generated the establishment of a small bureaucracy generally under the supervision of the area superintendent. In the early years of construction in the eastern portion, from 1811 to 1821, the Army Corps of Engineers did not play a major role. However, with the enactment in 1824 of the survey legislation, signed by President Monroe near the end of his administration, that agency was given a greater role. In the later years of road construction, the Army Corps of Engineers became responsible for construction, particularly in the three western states. Members of the corps held high-level positions in the road's administrative structure and necessarily became involved in the daily administrative tasks of reviewing or receiving vouchers and making payments. For their services, the officials involved in the supervision or construction of the road were paid by the responsible officer of the superintendent of the Cumberland Road. For example, on August 31, 1838, Otho Gapen, superintendent of grade in the middle division of the Cumberland Road in Indiana, signed a voucher indicating that he had received in Terre Haute, Indiana, on August 31, 1838, from Captain C. A. Ogden of the Corps of Engineers, superintendent of the Cumberland Road in Indiana and Illinois, the sum of $77.50 for services rendered from August 1 through August 31, 1838. The rate of pay for Mr. Gapen was $2.50 per day.[17]

Long after the road had been transferred to the states, positions in supervising its construction or upkeep were still vigorously pursued. For example, in 1862, citizens of Somerset County in Pennsylvania submitted to then governor Curtin of Pennsylvania a petition supporting the appointment of Jonas Augustine, Esq., as superintendent of the road in that county and Fayette County.

Because the road ran through Somerset County the petitioners urged that the appointment should be made of one of its residents.[18]

Of Building Methods, Contracts, Contractors

Two building methods dominated road construction in the early nineteenth century. The Tresaguet method (named after a French engineer, Pierre Tresaguet) involved "a bottom layer of stone seven inches thick laid on end and hammered in place." On top of this was a "layer of hammered-in smaller stones." The surface "consisted of small hard stones" and "had a central crest with each side sloping down to the edge." The other system, developed by the English engineer Thomas Telford, involved a "level subsurface" with smaller stones "added on top to a depth of seven inches in the center sloping to three inches on the sides." The portion of the National Road between Cumberland and Wheeling was constructed in accordance with a "regional variation" of the Tresaguet method.[19]

Where did the famous McAdam method fit into the construction of the Cumberland Road? Billy Joe Peyton provides an answer: "A commonly held myth about the National Road is that it originally had a macadamized surface. This is not the case . . . McAdam's principles had not yet spread to North America by 1821, the date of the Road's completion to Wheeling." Peyton takes care to add that the road "did eventually get a macadam surface, but not until the government funded repairs in the 1820s and '30s."[20]

What was the essence of McAdam's method and how did it differ from Tresaguet's and Telford's? Again, Peyton supplies an answer: "First, he advocated a flat foundation, which contrasted with Tresaguet's crowned surface. Because he did not have rigid rules for construction, the number of necessary layers varied by road. An imperviousness to water was paramount, inasmuch as moisture destroyed a road's weight-carrying capability if allowed to penetrate to the natural soil beneath the road."[21]

Peyton supplies further details about McAdam's method: "McAdam enforced the use of a two-inch ring for sizing stones that he claimed should not exceed six ounces in weight. . . . He did not roll his roads, but preferred applying stones in thin layers and allowing traffic to compact each successive application. He also sought to keep the road as level as possible to avoid sharp ascents and descents detrimental to proper drainage."[22]

In 1811, in his capacity as secretary of the treasury, Albert Gallatin initiated the award of a number of federal government contracts for the building of the first stages of the Cumberland Road in the state of Maryland. The contract awarded to a Mr. McKinley provides us with a sense of the specifications for the building of the road and the type of materials used in its construction. The contractor was required to clear trees to a width of sixty-six feet. The bed of the road was to be leveled for a width of thirty feet. Then the contractor was required to cover the road, twenty feet in width, with crushed stone. The contract called for the stone to rise to a level of eighteen inches in the middle, diminishing to twelve inches on the sides.[23]

The contractor was also obliged to assure that the upper six inches of stone (on the twenty-foot portion) was broken so as to fit within a ring three inches in diameter. The remaining stone was to fit within a ring seven inches in diameter. The contractor also undertook to enforce the use of the rings, although the practice was later abandoned during the course of road construction.[24]

The Gallatin-initiated contract called for a completion date. In the case of McKinley's contract, let in May of 1811, that day was August 1, 1812. If the contract terms were not met, provision was made for contract termination. Peyton describes other aspects of the contracting process: "Prospective contractors submitted bids for work as advertised in the local papers and on posters displayed in public places. They included samples of materials they planned to use (e.g., stone and mortar) and stated the total price of their work in their bid. Specifications were to be adhered to and all work completed by the date specified in the contract."[25]

The government used local newspapers to keep prospective contractors apprised of opportunities to bid on potential contracts to work on the road. The federal government or the state, depending upon which level of government was responsible for building the road at the time, would announce these opportunities in such advertisements. For example, the *Springfield Republic* printed an announcement by James Patterson, resident engineer, dated May 28, 1841, calling for sealed proposals for furnishing limestone or gravel for repair of different sections of the road to be received at various houses designated in the advertisement. Specifications described the degree to which the stone or gravel must be broken and provided information as to its quality and the details regarding pricing and delivery. Bidders were required to supply letters of recommendation.[26]

Problems complicated the administration and execution of these contracts during the laying and construction of the National Road, and differing perspectives made matters more difficult. As Peyton recounts: "Construction did not always proceed smoothly. . . . Once awarded a job, contractors had their own way of carrying out a contract, which sometimes led to quarrels with surveyors over angles and grades. Most contractors were builders, not engineers, who cared little for the consequences of a one- or two-degree difference in a grade to a horse pulling a heavy load over the mountains."[27]

At times, the help of high-level state or federal officials was required by contractors in order to pursue their claims for payment or other matters related to the construction of the road. For example, in 1844, one contractor wrote to Gov. Joseph A. Wright of Indiana profusely thanking him for assistance (in the form of papers and information) in helping to present his claim against the "general government" for "work done on the Cumberland Road."[28]

The road's construction from Cumberland to Wheeling cost the government approximately $13,000 per mile, more than twice the commissioners' original estimate of $6,000. This has been attributed to extravagant and "too-liberal" contracts. On the other hand, for the western portion of the road, the cost was much less, roughly $3,000 per mile, perhaps reflecting the flatter terrain.[29]

The Builders

Contracts and contractors, surveyors, superintendents, and commissioners were all necessary elements in the construction of the National Road. They were, however, not the only ones. Tradesmen and other workers were the true builders. Many were Irish and Welsh immigrants who left a life of poverty and unemployment in their own countries and emigrated to the New World to find work on the National Road. They were among the "hundreds of thousands of laborers" who, John Quincy Adams observed (in his diary), would be "afforded high wages and constant employment" by the "permanent and regular system" of internal improvement that he so eloquently advocated. However, his program would be largely discarded in the administrations that followed his own.[30]

Adlard Welby, an English tourist traveling west through western Pennsylvania to Wheeling in 1819 in a Dearborn Wagon, leaves us with a vivid description of these brave and resilient early builders: "Almost all the labourers employed here upon the roads are either Irish or English, and it is not certain that these republicans have not a secret pride in beholding the natives of the old world toiling for their benefit; however, the earnings of the men are I believe sufficient to render them in time independent, and I must say they look in general well fed, well clothed and comfortable."[31]

Welby describes the type of work in which these workers were engaged: "We passed one party employed in ploughing down part of the uneven road with a strong machine drawn by eight oxen, while two others drew a large wooden scoop to shovel up and lead away the ploughed up soil; it appeared to save much labour."

He also recorded his own interaction with them:

> The Irish here have not lost in our esteem; two or three times we have been beholden to individuals of that nation for good-natured little services: one of them lately aided me successfully to get along part of the new road where we had met with some opposition; another actually accompanied us about nine miles on a like occasion, not with a view

to remuneration, for I could not persuade him to take any thing for his services but some refreshment at the tavern. I heartily return them the good wishes they so frequently expressed as we passed them. One of the above men had acquired some property; he told me that seven years ago he bought land at six dollars per acre, and that he had just sold a part of it at fifty, and some even so high as seventy dollars per acre. The proximity of the new road had increased thus the value of his land.[32]

It was generally understood that these laborers would work hard for relatively modest wages. This was confirmed in a letter of May 1818 that Ebenezer Fitch wrote to his family from Washington, Pennsylvania, regarding the challenges faced by a road contractor. Fitch was evidently working on the building of the National Road bridges in that area, as the project moved closer to Wheeling. Apparently urged to send money home, Fitch was concerned about when he could draw money for the work. "Our Contract is moving quite well," he wrote, "and I hope we shall be able soon to draw money." Urged to return home when his work was completed, Fitch wrote: "I have not much to do after a short time except to dig the foundation for one bridge, which will be very wet, and bad." He continued: "We can get Irish Men to dig it cheaper than others."[33]

How well did the builders perform? Uria Brown, traveling the road from Cumberland to Brownsville, at a time shortly after it had opened (and before it was completed to Wheeling) provides a heartfelt picture of its state, its promise as seen in June 1816, and the quality of its workmanship, as he perceived it. Brown gives us first a sense of his itinerary in Maryland and the first miles of the Pennsylvania portion:

> 22nd of the Month & 7th of the Week [June 22]. This morning set out from Cumberland and road 5 Miles up the Potomac & on the Cumberland Turnpike road to Carters at the foot of the Aleghany Mountain fed & refreshed—$0.37 ½[.] Several little farms appears this far on the Potomac & amongst the Hills: thence 16 miles on this Great Western Turnpike road on the Allegheny mountain to Tomlinson's fed & dined—$0.68 ¾ thence 13 Miles to the Widow Janas and fed—$0.12 ½[.] this is near Somerset County in State of Pennsylvania, thence in Somerset County 6 Miles to Phillip Smith's Sine of General Jackson [tavern] & Lodged.[34]

Then, Brown furnishes his assessment of the quality of workmanship and its significance—in glowing terms:

> This great Turnpike road is far superior to any of the Turnpike roads in Baltimore County for Masterly Workmanship, the Bridges & Culverts actually do Credit to the Executors of the same, the [Casselman

River] Bridge over the Little Crossings of the Little Youghegany River is positively a Superb Bridge; The goodness[s] of God must have been in Congress unknownst to them; when the[y] fell about to & Erected a Lane [*sic*] for the making of this great Turnpike road which is the Salvation of those Mountains or Western Countrys & more benefit to the human family than Congress have any knowledge or any other Tribunal on the face of the Earth.[35]

In particular, Brown, like others after him, appreciated the straight lines with which the road had been constructed and the freedom from tolls that it represented.

I have seen no place on the Aleghany Mountain where they have Carried this road through but that has been done with as little Difficulty as making the Turn-pike Road up Joneses Falls, & one place in particular on this Mountain the road is carried on a Direct straight line for 3 Miles & I believe more & many other places from ½ a Mile to 1 & 2 Miles in a Strait line; this Great Western or Cumberland Turn Pike Road is free from Toll, it is not only good & handsome but is Ellegant & is & will be of more benefit than the Idea of man can possible have any knowledge of.[36]

Thomas Hulme, an English reformer and sharp critic of English society who emigrated to the United States and traveled extensively in its western states in 1818 and 1819, described the road as it had recently been built in Wheeling in terms similar to those of Brown. He provided a journal in which he recorded, among other things, his observations of his travels through the western country of the United States. His journal contained an account of his visit on July 28, 1819, in the company of a Quaker resident of Wheeling, to see the "new national road" near that city. On the occasion, Hulme wrote: "[The national road] is covered with a very thick layer of nicely broken stones, or stone rather, laid on with great exactness both as to depth and width, and then rolled down with an iron roller, which reduces all to one solid mass."[37]

Hulme, perhaps influenced by his revulsion for things English and his high regard for American society, expressed his unreserved enthusiasm for this construction. "This is a road made for ever," he wrote, "not like the flint roads in England, rough, nor soft or dirty, like the gravel roads but smooth and hard." He continued: "When a road *is* made in America, it is *well* made." As the National Road had reached Wheeling in 1818, Hulme was in a good position to assess its state at that stage.[38]

Farmers, along with the laborers described above, contributed to the laying out, construction, and maintenance of the road. Typically farmers received no compensation for the taking of the land and frequently donated the land that ran through their farms; at the same time, they hoped to prosper by opening businesses, hotels, or restaurants beside it. Roadside farmers provided food for the workers and rented out their own labor for 62½ cents per day, higher than the going rate. English and Irish laborers were typically paid $6 per month for such tasks as breaking limestone.[39]

Of Bridges

Uria Brown's enthusiastic comment on the quality of the Casselman River (Little Crossings) Bridge helps to underscore the significance of bridge construction in the laying out and building of the National Road. Indeed, the early progress of the road can be measured in the construction of its bridges.

During the Madison administration, David Shriver's reports to Secretary of the Treasury Albert Gallatin emphasized the particular challenges represented by the bridge-building agenda for the National Road in terms of both cost and technical difficulty. His report of 1813, for example, described efforts to contract for the construction of a bridge on the Little Youghiogheny River. It is still in excellent condition, having benefited from a restoration. Shriver contracted for the building of the original bridge in 1813, and it was built evidently between that year and 1816, when Uria Brown crossed it. It was an impressive arched structure built of sandstone that spanned the Casselman just east of Grantsville, Maryland. General Braddock and his army had been forced to ford the river in the 1755 campaign—hence the name Washington's Little Crossing. At the time of its construction, the bridge was the nation's longest arched bridge.[40]

Uria Brown also responded positively to the National Road bridge over the Big Youghiogheny in Pennsylvania at the point of Washington's Great Crossing of 1754 and 1755. Brown wrote; "[A]t this intended Town [Smythfield] they have commenced the erection of the Bridge over this River, no doubt but from the specimen of the work already on the road, but this Bridge will be a superb & Magnificent Building. . . ." The structure was a triple-span arched masonry bridge, built between 1815 and 1817, that carried road traffic over the broad river, from which it headed up the road to the site of Fort Necessity toward Uniontown.[41]

In Brownsville, the Dunlop Creek Bridge, built in 1849 by the Corps of Army Engineers, became an important landmark because it represented the first metal bridge in the United States. For years travelers over the road to Brownsville were obliged to ferry across the Monongahela. Once across the Mon and past Washington, Pennsylvania, travelers would encounter a handsome stone S-Bridge just outside Claysville, Pennsylvania. A frequently visited landmark on the road, the S-Bridge, as described by Peyton, "is so named for its curved approaches that meet the arch at opposite angles resembling the tails of the letter S and thus allow the stream to be crossed with a straight arch, an easy alternative to the more technologically complicated skewed arch."[42]

After Claysville and West Alexandria, National Road travelers would soon find themselves crossing several bridges in Elm Grove, Virginia, and then reach Wheeling, on the east bank of the Ohio River. There those heading west by land transportation were obliged to board the Zane Ferry for transportation across the river into Ohio, sometimes having to wait until the winter ice had cleared.

In 1849, the crossing was made easier with the construction of the Wheeling Suspension Bridge to Wheeling Island in the middle of the river and then to its west bank. The bridge was designed by Charles Ellet, a distinguished American engineer who had studied in Europe and become a champion of the wire suspension bridge. It was built by the Wheeling and Belmont Bridge Company. At the time of its construction, the Wheeling Bridge was the world's longest clear-span bridge. Its dedication in 1849 was a major event in the history of Wheeling.[43]

In the 1850s the Wheeling Suspension Bridge brought the National Road into potential conflict with another provision of Article I, section 8, of the Constitution—the Interstate Commerce Clause. Interests in Pittsburgh brought suit, charging that the bridge was an obstruction of interstate commerce because certain steamboats were unable to pass beneath it due to the height of their smokestacks. The court issued an injunction. At the behest of supporters of the bridge, Congress entered the picture and passed legislation that in effect legalized the bridge under the Commerce Clause and made it a post road. The plaintiffs in the litigation sought to overturn the legislation on the ground that it invaded the powers of the judiciary contrary to the principle of separation of powers in Article III of the Constitution, but the Supreme Court sustained the law, reasoning that the court's early injunction was subject to later legislative action by Congress reversing the court determination that the bridge constituted an obstruction of commerce. The precedent so established figured in a 1990s suit in which Justice Sandra Day O'Connor issued an opinion for the Court sustaining a congressional enactment known as the Prison Litigation Reform Act and rejecting arguments that it constituted an invasion of the prerogative of the courts under Article III. Thus, the Wheeling Suspension Bridge, joining the eastern and western portions of the National Road, gave rise to engineering, transportation, and legal precedents of the pre–Civil War era.[44]

Once on the road in eastern Ohio, travelers would encounter a number of S-bridges. One of these was an S-Bridge just west of New Concord, known as the Fox Creek S-Bridge. It crossed the creek at a point where the National Road intersected Zane's Trace. Some of these were covered bridges, a restored example of which may be found just outside Greenup, Illinois. With the exception of the Great Crossings Bridge, all of these structures, some rebuilt or refurbished, are

Figure 3. 1851 Engraving Showing the Wheeling Suspension Bridge drawn by K. Lankwity (courtesy of the Museums of Oglebay Institute).

still to be seen and enjoyed on today's National Road and are available for crossing, at least by foot. The Great Crossing Bridge lies submerged, the victim of the damming of the Youghiogheny River that created the lake of the same name, several miles beyond Petersburg (now Addison), Pennsylvania. Taken individually or collectively, these surviving bridges of the old National Road represent an abiding link with the past.[45]

Ultimately, the National Road was built from Cumberland to Vandalia. The nation's legislators were willing, sometimes grudgingly, to lay the foundation. The problem, as previously discussed, was how to maintain the artery once it was constructed. Unable to satisfactorily solve that problem, Congress was forced to transfer the road to the states, particularly following the inability of Congress to enact legislation providing for federal toll collection. A viable means of financing repair and maintenance became an essential need. Despite the efforts of commissioners, superintendents, contractors, and builders, the road as a federal enterprise came to an end approximately thirty years after it had begun. However, before that end came, in that thirty-year period of laying out and construction, the builders constructed an artery that carried thousands of travelers to the heartland—some to stay, some to visit, some to go further west. These travelers enhanced populations of the states through which the road passed and contributed to the national growth of which John Quincy Adams proudly took note.

CHAPTER 9

Confronting Problems in Road Construction East of the Ohio in the Madison and Monroe Years

AN ARCHIVAL ACCOUNT

Overview

A vivid picture of the progress of the construction of the road, despite the obstacles and challenges that it faced, can be found in the archival correspondence of the Department of the Treasury between 1811 and 1824, when responsibility for the road was transferred to the Corps of Engineers. This correspondence is preserved by the National Archives of the United States. The body of archival documents and other materials includes letters from bidders, contractors, bondsmen, and ordinary citizens. It also provides a continuing chronological survey of the correspondence between the road superintendents and the U.S. secretaries of the treasury during that period. In particular, the exchanges between David Shriver, the first road superintendent, who served from 1811 to 1820, and Albert Gallatin, who served as secretary of the treasury from 1801 to 1813, constitute an invaluable source of information as to the genesis of the nation's first interstate highway from the vantage point of two significant figures who were closely involved in its establishment and administration and were profoundly dedicated to its success. After Gallatin moved to a foreign policy role, Shriver continued his correspondence with Secretary Alexander Dallas, who served during the balance of Madison's term, and then with Secretary William H. Crawford under President Monroe. When Josiah Thompson was appointed superintendent of the western portion of the Cumberland-to-Wheeling road, he joined the conversation regarding his portion of the road project. A brief recap of this archival record gives the reader a better sense of the problems that faced the highest-level administrators of the project and of the manner in which they confronted these problems during that unique period when the responsibility for the work resided in the Treasury Department under the continuing supervision of the president.[1]

What kinds of problems did these officials face? The award of contracts to qualified bidders on the most favorable terms was a frequent concern. The qualifications of contractors, their selection, the scope of their work, concerns as to their performance, their progress, and their payments were frequent subjects for the steady exchange of letters over the years of early building. Thus, the archival files are replete with proposals from eager contractors; requests from contractors for updates on their status; glowing recommendations or attestations from citizens familiar with their work; bonds to secure performance; earnest, sometimes desperate, requests for payments for past work or for awards of new contracts; complaints or concerns from or regarding contractors; reports on project progress or the lack thereof; receipts for payments and disbursements; and concerns regarding idle periods for laborers and their employers. The sometimes mundane, sometimes elevated discussion of an infrastructure project's progress is the stuff of which this account is made. In general, contract administration and budget execution were, unsurprisingly, key concerns.[2]

The routing of the road was also an important topic for consideration. Superintendent Shriver furnished from time to time suggestions as to variations of the route that had originally been surveyed by the commissioners during the Jefferson administration. Shriver's suggestions were provided in order to save expense or improve the quality of the road or the route so as to comport more closely with the nature of the terrain. Suggestions were also received from interested citizens on this subject. Similarly, recommendations as to variations in road-building methods or techniques were a common subject of discussion, whether initiated by the superintendent himself or by experienced contractors.[3]

Money was a constant concern. Quite apart from the continuing debates in Congress about appropriations for the road, as summarized in part 1, over the several decades beginning with the commencement of the work in 1811 and the turnover to the states in 1838 superintendents pondered regularly about ensuring payment for contractors who had completed their work and about whether funds would be available to let new contracts.[4]

The ever-present need for road repair constituted yet another oft-repeated theme. David Shriver, for example, would dutifully remind the secretary on appropriate occasions regarding the perpetual problem of repair and upkeep. If the National Road project constituted a national investment, that investment had to be preserved. This problem seemed to represent for Shriver a major obstacle to the sustainability of the project that transcended the others. Similarly, the submission of reports on the progress of the road was continually on his mind. Each year, generally in December, Shriver would report on the year's progress in road building and that expected for the year to follow. These reports were carefully reviewed by the secretary and then transmitted to the president with comments by the secretary, frequently handwritten on the back of the letter in question.[5]

One is impressed by the depth of involvement of both the secretary of the treasury and the president in the minute details of the road's making, its funding, its routing, and its progress, both in terms of review of annual reports and in terms of review and approval of individual contracts. The making of the National Road was a hands-on project for officials at the very highest level in early-America Washington in both times of peace and times of war. It was part of the agenda of the nation's establishment and of its founding fathers, Jefferson, Madison, Monroe, and Gallatin. Careful thought was given to the details of construction, the cities or towns to be joined, and the pace of the entire initiative from Jefferson's day forward. Presidents and their cabinet officers were evidently well aware that this was a task for posterity. Perhaps at no time in our history was the building and construction of one highway, as distinguished from the enactment of relevant authorization or appropriation legislation, so much the daily business of the highest officers of the land. That successful national-infrastructure investment was a critical objective for the founding generation becomes clear from a study of this archival material.

Routing Concerns

Even before construction of the road began, discussion again took place regarding the routing of the road, a subject which, as we have seen, had been considered by Thomas Jefferson in 1806 and again in 1808. (See chapter 2 above.) The matter again arose in May 1809, when a Mr. Oswalt petitioned the newly seated James Madison in favor of a bridge over the Big Youghiogheny. Oswalt expressed the fear that the existing bridge would be the "means of som one or other losing life or property or perhaps both."[6] The following year, in a letter of February 8, 1810, John Connell of Washington, D.C., urged that the road west be routed through Charleston rather than Wheeling. Gallatin noted on the face of the letter that the survey ordered by Jefferson had never been performed and that therefore the decision on the route of the road from Brownsville to the Ohio had remained "unconfirmed." Gallatin apparently believed that it was necessary to appoint three new commissioners to conduct a survey or have the former commissioners do it. Ultimately, it was decided that the eastern portion of the road would terminate in Wheeling.[7]

1811—Beginning Construction and Charting Progress

Given the apparent doubt as to its ultimate route to the Ohio, by what name was the road to be called in its earliest days? As construction began in 1811, the artery was generally referred to as the "U.S. Road from Cumberland to the Ohio." It was so described in a letter from Mr. R. Nelson attesting to the honesty and industry of one John Adams for purposes of work on that road.[8] The road was also referred to as "the road leading from Cumberland in Maryland to Brownsville in Pennsylvania" in a bond of May 8, 1811, assuring the performance of Charles Ranle and William Gather under a contract for "making and completing the second Section" of that road "entered into with Albert Gallatin as Secretary of the Treasury of the United States." Ultimately, it came to be called the Western Road, the Cumberland Road, or the National Road. (See figure 1.)[9]

By April 29, 1811, work was already underway. David Shriver wrote to Secretary Gallatin regarding possible changes in location for a contract awarded to a Mr. Cochran. The road had apparently been laid just above the bottom of the mountainside. Shriver was proposing that the road be raised at least two feet and that it be relocated and was seeking Gallatin's approval for the change.[10] He also noted that the contracts for McKinley and Randel had not yet arrived, although both were at work. In May, Henry McKinley was complaining of the "disagreeable situation" in which he found himself as a result of Gallatin's failure to send a response to Shriver. McKinley had completed a portion of the road and was "partly out work" for thirty-seven hands and twenty horses. McKinley earnestly urged the secretary to "look in to" his situation.[11]

Road-building issues became a concern of the first summer of construction. On July 1, 1811, Shriver wrote Gallatin regarding road-building techniques, urging the width of the road be as great as possible. The contractors were complaining of aspects of the specifications that they had not understood or appreciated and were finding difficult to observe. Shriver therefore proposed an alternative that might solve the problem and still avoid injury to the road. He also inquired as to the status of the road and to whether a determination had been made regarding the rolling of the road. In the following fall, Shriver informed Gallatin of progress on the bridges. Shriver promised to be sure that the masons not receive money until they were entitled to it.[12]

The timing of contractor payments soon became an issue. In his letter of October 21, 1811, Shriver complained to Gallatin of his concern regarding the payment of contractors before a sufficient number of perches had been completed. (*The Oxford Universal Dictionary* 3rd ed., defines "perch" as "a rod of a definite length for measuring land, etc. hence a measure of length, esp. for land, etc., a standard measure, 5 1/2 yards but varying locally.") However, by October 29 Shriver was sufficiently satisfied with the progress made by the contractor, Henry McKinley, and advised Gallatin that he had drawn, on Draft no. 2, $850 in payment for "40 perches of the first section of the Western Road."[13]

By December 1811, Shriver was ready with another report on the issue of progress payments. The contractors were "filling out" the side roads and preparing to draw money. Because the ground was frozen, it was difficult to make further progress with the work. The main concern of the letter was whether Shriver might make advances to the contractors (given the situation of the laborers).

Shriver wondered whether this would be consistent with the progress payment provisions of the contract; he also worried about the reaction of the laborers if not paid during the winter break. Gallatin's clerk noted the issue on the back of the envelope; Gallatin's response is unclear.[14]

Shriver's duties included the preparation of an annual report on the progress of the project. In mid-January 1812, Shriver submitted such a report in response to the law's requirement that Congress receive periodic reports regarding the road. He therefore rendered to Gallatin what he regarded as a "concise view" of that progress and the "present state of the Western Road." He reported that "the leveling and shaping [of] the bed of the road [was] compleat (with a few exceptions) for about five miles." The "stone for the pavement" had been laid on a greater part of the road and for about four miles had been broken so as to be "nearly compleat." He thought it therefore probable that the first ten miles would be completed by the following August 1 (August 1, 1812). Shriver recognized that the expense of the masonry, lime, and other aspects of the "bridging" could not be "exactly estimated" but regarded the entire cost of the ten miles to be $75,000. He thought the expense of succeeding sections would be comparable. Shriver called for no changes to the law, but he did suggest that provision be made for repair of the road once it was "received" from the contractors and that a reliable basis to sustain the investment financially be established. He was concerned, given the use of the road and the terrain, about its likely state in the absence of such repair. He therefore "respectfully" suggested "the propriety of demanding such a toll as [would] be sufficient to keep [the road] in good and perfect order."[15]

On the back of the letter, Gallatin asked Shriver to give him the terms of each contract regarding the price per perch for each section and the length of each, as well as the price of masonry work per perch for which Shriver had contracted. He sought also the amount of Shriver's annual salary. This he believed would enable him to make his own report to Congress.[16]

On January 25, 1812, Gallatin had produced for the president a first draft of a report to Congress as required by the law calling for the laying out and making of the road. He included a summary of the cost of the three contracts with McKinley, Randle, and Cochran for the ten miles, $60,338.25, along with the cost per perch under each contract, ranging from $14.50 to $22.50, as well as copies of the contracts. He also provided information as to the masonry work as well as the $1,800 annual salary paid to Shriver, concluding that the cost of the ten miles would be from $75,000 to $80,000. Gallatin estimated that the first ten miles would be completed in August 1813. As $125,000 had been appropriated, Gallatin estimated that about $50,000 would be available for the next portion of the work, which would enable completion of about seven more miles. Shriver had suggested the desirability of completing eleven miles rather than seven, taking the road as far as Tomlinson's, approximately twenty-one miles west of Cumberland, where the "old" road (presumably a reference to the old Braddock Road) and the "new" road would meet. This would necessitate a "further appropriation" of $30,000. Gallatin also included, in a positive vein, a reference to Shriver's recommendation on repairs, but noted that this could be done under the authority of Maryland.[17]

To all this Gallatin added a broader postscript to inform President Madison regarding the significance of the project: "From the nature of the contracts and from the manner in which the work has been executed, it will, it is believed, satisfactorily appear, that the chain of mountains which divides the Atlantic from the Western States offers no real impediment to an easy communication; and that roads may generally be made as perfect, as convenient and on the same terms, across those mountains as in any other part of the Union." Gallatin may have been reflecting on his own report of 1808 in the Jefferson days that had proposed a broad program of essential national investment in internal improvement binding the new nation together. National unity was its underlying goal.[18]

1812—Shriver's Concerns about Contractors and Building Methods

Contractor concerns again occupied the administrators in the summer of 1812. In August of that year Shriver again wrote to Gallatin, commenting on two contracts proposed for execution regarding further work on the road. One was with John Adams and Charles Kinney and the other with James Cochran, who had held a previous contract for part of the first ten miles. Shriver was forwarding them for the approval of Gallatin and the president. Shriver enclosed as well statements of the other proposals so that Gallatin would be in a position to review the different bids. His comments on the various contracts and proposal provide an interesting window on the problems of building the road in this early period. Gallatin indicated his approval of the contracts but noted that he did not recollect whether the contracts of the prior year had been approved by the president or by himself. He was advised that they had been approved by the president.[19]

Shriver observed that he had been at first "fearful" that the different contractors would "combine." He admitted, however, that his fears had been "groundless." He now feared instead that the contractors had "bid the work lower than they can do [the work] for." This, he expected, would give him "grate trouble" because the contractors might therefore "slite" the work. As to the masons, Shriver had rejected their first proposal as too high. They had responded with a second and presumably lower proposal. Shriver noted his view that the mason, Bing, was "an old hand, and [was] as good, and as honest a workman as any other." Shriver recommended the proposals as "sufficiently low, considering the difficulty of getting materials." Shriver also informed Gallatin that only one proposal had been received for lime. Shriver believed that a bid could not be had for lower, given the difficulty of obtaining lime and the distance involved. No provision had been made for alteration of the route or location, Shriver observed, as he believed "we shall not alter for the worse" and no price break could be anticipated if the alteration was for the better.[20]

Shriver told Gallatin that, after he attended to the remaining contracts, he would spend a day or two "on the road" to get a view of the ground south of "our location" (presumably the end point of the work already done). This would aid him in preparing to review the work of Adams and McKinley when they commenced their performance. Shriver suggested that it might be well to let as much further work as the money on hand would permit. He also noted that Cochran had obtained (presumably through a bid) two additional sections. McKinley, Shriver observed, was "sorely smote." He had done "first rate work" except coarse breaking, which he was mending. As to progress, Shriver informed Gallatin that he would soon be obliged to draw on the secretary for Cochran's work "an amount which will have him on a footing with McKinley and Randle." He continued: "The whole sum I am authorized to draw 'on account of the expense in opening the western road' is drawn and applied." He therefore requested Gallatin to authorize him to draw a further sum of about three to five thousand dollars. Finally, he noted that the routing alteration of the fifteenth, sixteenth, and seventeenth miles had caused a loss of about eleven perches but had permitted the work to be let at a lower amount.[21]

Although on the road, Gallatin acted promptly on Shriver's letter. The secretary directed (by a note on the back of the letter) that the contracts be prepared and laid on his table on his return. He noted that he did not recollect whether the contracts of the prior year had been approved by the president or by himself. He further directed that a letter for Shriver be prepared approving the contracts and authorizing Shriver to draw for $5,000 more. The clerk dutifully noted below Gallatin's direction that the prior year's contracts had been approved by the president.[22]

In November 1812, Shriver continued his disquisitions on the work of the contractors, focusing particularly on matters such as the breaking of the stones, the width of the road (which he regarded as of paramount importance), the manner of payment where work was not complete, the matter of tolls, and experimentation with improved pavement cover. In a letter of November 7, the superintendent began by commenting on the work of McKinley, perhaps prompted by Gallatin. Shriver noted that he considered McKinley's work to be "nearly equal" to the contract except for stone breaking and the fact that in two places the width of the road was less than thirty feet. Shriver then amplified on his views regarding the importance of stone breaking. "The finer they are broken the smoother the road will be when traveled." He continued: "McKinley's [upper] stratum will not pass the 3 [inch] ring nor do I believe [that] they would pass a four [inch]." He compared the road in this respect to other arteries and concluded that "it [is] as strong or stronger, than it would be if finer, but the traveling on it will be uncomfortable in about the degree it may be coarse or finely broken." Shriver promised further efforts in this direction.[23]

Regarding the width of the road, Shriver reported that he had offered the contractors, if they would give a thirty-two-foot surface, the alternative of permitting them some leeway in other respects. Shriver mused as to the effect of these considerations on payment. To delay paying the contractors anything at all would cause great difficulty for them. He recommended that a further payment might be made while reserving a sum sufficient to cover any coarse breaking or other defects, recognizing that traveling on the road would consolidate the pavement, and thereafter the coarse stone could be broken. Shriver saw this partial payment approach as the best option. To reinforce his position on stone breaking, Shriver enclosed a draft letter on the subject to be sent to contractors, seeking comments from Secretary Gallatin on this subject.[24]

Shriver also undertook to report on the ground west of the twenty-one-mile point but expressed doubt that he could improve the location selected by the commissioners from that point. He also enclosed a draft bill (prepared by a senator in the Maryland state legislature) designed to authorize the collection of tolls, presumably by the state. Finally, Shriver suggested experimentation with some effort to cover the pavement with the type of earth and gravel found on the banks of the road.[25]

Thus, while progress had been made on the first twenty-one miles, a host of administrative, contracting, and specification problems urgently called for resolution. Shriver spared no effort in raising these points for the attention of the secretary. In his year-end report of December 21, 1812, however, Shriver focused on progress, perhaps moved by the need to report positively to Congress. He thus affirmed that "contracts for the first ten miles of the western road are completed with but few exceptions" and that "the contractors are paid," except for "a small sum" to ensure "the final completion next spring," evidently a reference to his strategy of the November letter. He also assured Gallatin that "the road is open and used daily by travelers." On the "second letting," the additional eleven miles, the contractors had made "considerable progress" and were at work "with a considerable number of hands." There was every probability that this work would be completed by November 1813. In sum, the $150,000 would be sufficient, Shriver commented, for the completion of the first twenty-one miles.[26]

As to the next ten miles, Shriver expected that the cost on the average would be the same as the proceeding span, subject to additional sums for bridges. Shriver hoped that the work would progress with more expedition so that ten miles more might be let in the ensuing spring (1813). Accordingly, Shriver requested payment for an additional four or five miles and for a bridge across the Little Youghiogheny; to lessen the expense, a sawmill would be used in the spring. Shriver also advised Gallatin that the Maryland legislature was expected to pass a law authorizing the president to receive tolls for the purpose of repairing the road and to protect against abuse. Tolls thus became an early and continuing theme and conundrum for the high-level administrators of this major national-investment project. Nevertheless, Gallatin apparently approved of the report as a whole, noting the need for two copies of Shriver's letter to accompany the report to the president.[27]

1813—Alterations in the Route

Routing concerns again occupied the administrative correspondence in the spring of 1813. Shriver favored Gallatin with a series of letters proposing alterations in the routing of the road over sections between mile 21 and the Big Youghiogheny just over the Pennsylvania border. In a letter of April 3, 1813, he explained that during the preceding winter and the following spring of 1813, he had been engaged in examining the ground of the route plotted by Jefferson's commissioners on the west side of Tomlinson's (now Grantsville, Maryland) to Uniontown. (This apparently covered roughly the remaining eleven or twelve miles in Maryland and the succeeding twenty-five or so miles to Uniontown.) (See figure 2.)[28]

Despite extensive exploration, Shriver was apprehensive about the condition of the ground for future road-building purposes. He told Gallatin: "The ground generally from Pack-horse ridge 28 miles from Cumberland to Union town is bad and some of it extremely so." At the same time he thought that little would be gained by fixing the location on "nothing but good ground in a country like this." Nevertheless he recommended that the government should "endeavor to avoid bad ground as much as possible" even if this meant an increase in the distance. Shriver also indicated to Gallatin his need for additional human resources to complete the project; he expressed the desirability of hiring an assistant who might help in the measurements and mentioned in this context a nephew, John Shriver, who he thought might help with the work.[29]

A little more than two weeks later, on April 19, Shriver appeared to be in a better frame of mind when he wrote to Gallatin enclosing a plat of his work as far as the end of fifty-two miles on the commissioners' route (in other words, about thirty-three miles in Maryland and nineteen in Pennsylvania). Among other accomplishments, Shriver reported that he had succeeded in crossing the "winding ridge" "on very good ground" and "without much loss of distance." He further indicated little difficulty in reaching the "Yoghiogeny," as it was then designated, but "great difficulty" on the west side of the river. For want of time he had then connected his plat with the commissioners' route in order to report expeditiously on the matter. Considerable distance could be saved only at the cost of using "ruff" ground. For the stretch of the road from Tomlinson's to the end of fifty-two miles on the commissioners' route, the "ground" was "good" with a few exceptions and, on the whole, "superior" to the Commissioners' location. He expected that the contractors would be satisfied. In short, Shriver was recommending his plot as a preferred alternative to the commissioners' route. As to timing, Shriver advised Gallatin that, after the president had determined which "route we should pursue," it would take as much as four weeks to grade the route before the work could be let.[30]

To Shriver's letter of April 19, Gallatin appended a note to President Madison, advising that the secretary was of the opinion that the alteration proposed by Shriver would "in every respect of ground, expense & course, be beneficial." Gallatin added his thought that, in confirming this, the president should reserve the right of making any further alterations that Shriver might recommend between the seventeenth and thirty-fifth miles. The clerk indicated that on May 20, the president had agreed to this course of action. Shriver was so advised on May 21.[31]

Accordingly, on May 31, Shriver again wrote to Gallatin, enclosing his grading notes from miles 20¾ to the Youghiogheny, constituting thirty-eight miles and 280 perches from Cumberland. (See figure 2—about thirty-three miles in Maryland and five in Pennsylvania, just past what is now Addison). Shriver thought that the contractors would encounter little difficulty in meeting one another's work. He then turned to the challenges of constructing a bridge over the little crossing of the Yough and suggested some procedures that he thought would facilitate that process. To push all this forward, Shriver dutifully enclosed a draft advertisement for the work and suggested that it be published in the usual way with a closing date of August 2. Thus was the work slated to proceed in the wake of Shriver's preceding winter and spring exploration of the terrain toward Union Town.[32]

1814—Continued Progress

By December 1814, Shriver was ready with another progress report. This one was addressed to Alexander Dallas, who had succeeded Gallatin as secretary of the treasury when the latter was assigned to the task of participating in the representation of the United States at the negotiations for concluding the War of 1812. To update the progress on the road, Shriver reminded Dallas that the first ten miles of the road were completed and that the second letting was now "generally used by the traveler." Only the incidence of heavy rain had precluded the full completion of that portion.[33]

As to the third letting (on the portion that had been the subject of Shriver's 1813 correspondence, summarized above), the task had been subdivided into nine sections involving, in total, approximately eighteen miles in length. Shriver undertook to advise Dallas of the progress that had been made on these sections. The results were mixed. Of the eighteen miles, eight were in a state of "great forwardness," and on ten "but little progress" had been made. Shriver then estimated the time that it would take the three contractors in question to complete the ten miles during the course of 1815. It would require substantial effort, but once completed, this work would take the road into Pennsylvania, stopping on the east bank of the Youghiogheny River.[34]

Shriver also reported that he had "nearly completed" a "location" from the end of the work contracted for (near the Yough) to Uniontown, an additional span of about twenty-one miles. (See figure 2.) Shriver preferred to defer this report until he had additional time to reexamine the route; he first wanted to fix on "the best ground and shortest distance" through what he termed "this mountainous country." He expected to have notes on this matter in the following spring. Shriver estimated that the twenty-one-mile span might constitute another year's contract work and would take the project further north to Uniontown.[35]

Shriver recognized, as he told Dallas, that the Big Youghiogheny River must be bridged, with the work commencing in the next season (presumably 1815). Shriver noted the experience with the bridge over the little crossing and estimated that the Big Yough bridge would cost $40,000; he recommended stone despite the cost. Without knowledge of existing appropriations, Shriver calculated a cost of $7,500 per mile to continue the Cumberland Road. Shriver closed his 1814 report, as he done in its predecessors, with a reminder that legislation might be needed to provide for the repair of the road and prevent abuses to the work by "mischievous persons."[36] A note penned on the back of the letter indicated that the report had been sent to President Madison on December 31, 1814.[37] Madison's second term had a little more than two years to run, but already considerable progress had been made in making the National Road that his friend and predecessor, Thomas Jefferson, had initiated.

1815—Shriver and Dallas Correspond on Continuing Problems and Progress

In 1815, Shriver explored a number of practical problem areas including a slippage of the road, bridging and bridge building, and lime supply, as well as the chronic need for road repair following almost immediately upon the initial construction of the road. In this vein, on March 25, 1815, Shriver reported to Dallas that a part of the road (about five to six perches) had "sunk 4 to 5 feet." This part of the road had been made on the side of a steep ridge. Shriver sought authority to make repairs on that part of the road and on other parts that had been subject to comparable accidents. He could give no figures as to cost, adding his view that "cost what it may, the road must be kept in order."[38] As usual, Shriver was concerned about the continuing availability of funds. Specifically, he asked Dallas about the extent to which available funds would be sufficient to permit the award of contracts at the "next letting." In raising this point, he noted that an answer would enable him to determine the next sections for his contractors.[39]

During the summer of 1815, as his July 29 letter informed Dallas, Shriver was engaged in the evaluation of proposals for the new sections. Such evaluations required him to share a candid appraisal of each contractor's qualifications. He expressed doubt as to whether the work of one of them could be practicably completed at the bid price. In the absence of experience with that contractor, and based on the proposal, Shriver expressed concern regarding the qualifications of the contractor. Thus, Shriver was placed in the role of a modern-day contracting officer, in a negotiation context, weighing the qualifications of a contractor based upon the record.[40] By August 3, Dallas was in a position to recap the various proposals. As to further work on the road, he directed that it be divided into several contracts. As to bridge proposals, Shriver was given broad authority.[41]

1816—The Last Year of the Madison Administration

By the end of 1816, the correspondence and other reports on the progress of the road indicate that it was close to exiting Pennsylvania. In the two-year period between the beginning of 1815 and the end of 1816, the road had advanced through Uniontown and Washington, Pennsylvania, and was nearing the western boundary of Pennsylvania. Proposals were being received in Alexandria, Pennsylvania (the last town in that commonwealth before the Pennsylvania-Virginia border). Only eleven miles lay between this point and the proposed eastern terminus at the Ohio River in Wheeling.[42] The proposals in question had to do with work on various sections of the road extending west from Washington, Pennsylvania. One contractor proposed to finish in twenty-four months the eighth section, involving one mile and 226 perches at the cost of $29 per perch. These proposals were passed on for approval or other disposition to Secretary Dallas, who would forward them to President Madison for signature. From what one can gather based on a review of the correspondence, it appears that Madison, as well as Monroe after him, generally approved the recommendations forwarded by Shriver through the secretary of the treasury.[43]

1817—The Changing of the Guard: A New Administration

The year 1816 also marked the last full year of Madison's eight-year tenure. In November of that year, James Monroe was elected president. Madison left the White House in March of 1817, having issued on his last day in office the Bonus Bill Veto that initiated another period of uncertainty for the funding of the road. (See chapter 3, above.) The year 1817 also brought a new team of players to continue the discussions regarding the building of the road in Maryland, Pennsylvania, and Virginia. James Monroe himself was a supporter of internal improvements and interested in the completion of the road, but he shared, at least initially, the constitutional qualms of his predecessor. He was destined to work diligently to resolve the constitutional quandary presented by Madison's veto.[44]

On the practical side of the issue, Monroe would also be presented with the resolution of the day-to-day questions of implementation of prior appropriations that had faced Madison. The change of administrations brought a new secretary to the Treasury Department, William H. Crawford of Georgia, who was later destined to vie for the White House to succeed Monroe when his two terms were completed in 1825. Furthermore, an additional road superintendent was appointed to share the administrative burden that Shriver had shouldered alone since 1811. Monroe named Josiah Thompson as superintendent of the western section of the Cumberland-to-Wheeling road; Shriver remained in charge of the Cumberland-to-Brownsville portion and maintained his headquarters in the former city.[45]

Even though the administration had changed, many of the issues had not. A major concern related to repair. On April 28, 1817, Shriver wrote to Crawford with a terse reminder: "Our road requires repair." Each day additional injury was being done to the road and required attention. Shriver indicated that he had been giving thought to the best method for effectuating such repairs. He suggested the employment on an annual basis for a man and a cart to be responsible for the repair of the road for a ten-year period. Shriver then listed the advantages of such an approach, including the possibility that the man might become a resident of the area in question and might work at a more modest rate than if only employed during the summer. Shriver strongly recommended a trial of the approach to ensure the maintenance of the road. (It is not clear how Superintendent Thompson responded.)[46]

The administrative team did, however, attend to the day-to-day business of building the road. Thus, on November 20, 1817, Superintendent Thompson, writing from Tridelphia, advised Secretary Crawford that he had drawn on the secretary's draft no. 66 in favor of one George Dawson for $9,000 for "Mason work" done on a section of the road east of the Monongehela in the western division of the road.[47]

That same year, Thompson sent his annual report of December 15. A major portion of the western part of the Cumberland-to-Wheeling portion of the road already contracted for would be completed in 1818. Unfinished work was also being completed between Washington, Pennsylvania, and Brownsville. Work was also progressing near Wheeling. Difficulties with individual contractors were described as well as a damages issue involving several inhabitants of the area. In that same month, on December 31, 1817, Shriver filed a report for the eastern division, indicating that forty-six miles "and the balance of the work" to Uniontown was in such a state of forwardness as to justify a belief that it would be completed in the summer of 1818. The bridge over the Big Yough was likewise nearing completion. With this positive news as an opener, Shriver once more "strongly pressed" the need for an "ample provision for repairs." Shriver noted that "the whole of the produce for a considerable distance beyond the west side of the mountains will be transported over the road." Shriver also predicted a vast increase in travel over the road as well as the passage of double-loaded wagons. He urged that provision must be made for "broad wheels" (that would do less damage to the road), to be encouraged by taxing those vehicles with narrow wheels. Shriver expressed concern that some of his contractors' men had been left idle, a problem that he thought needed to be addressed. Finally, the superintendent indicated the cost of the road between Uniontown and the Monongehela would not exceed $10,000 per mile, including road making and bridging.[48]

In January of 1818, Thompson continued the dialogue with Secretary Crawford, writing to determine the status of payments for a number of contractors who were falling behind in the pace of their work while assuring the secretary that the work would be completed in due course, despite the distress of the contractors. He speculated about the remedies the government might have for enforcing the terms of construction contracts where the contractor had no property and where he lacked money of his own to fund overruns. He worried as well as to the permanency of the road built along the sides of the hill. In these cases it was necessary to "wall all deep fillings to prevent the road from running off." Thompson was writing from Washington, Pennsylvania, where he had evidently made his headquarters, twenty-five miles from Wheeling, where the artery was headed in its last stretch.[49]

So the correspondence between the four key players—the two superintendents, the secretary of the treasury, and the president—in the administration of the National Road's initial construction between Cumberland and Wheeling progressed over the course of the Monroe administration through its two eventful terms. Continuity, dedication, and the bond of trust that evidently grew out of the successful completion of the project characterized that correspondence and the work that it represented. Thus, toward the end of that administration, in June 1824, we find President Monroe's clerk forwarding to the chief executive a letter from Shriver and trying to save steps. Said Chief Clerk Jones: "As it would answer no purpose to send the enclosed letter to Crawford, and as full confidence may be placed in Mr. Shriver, will it not be advisable to direct him to pursue that course which in his opinion will be most in the public Interest." To this the president replied: "Let the direction proposed be given to Mr. Shriver."[50]

One is struck by the degree to which one discrete project, a road running about 130 miles from Cumberland, Maryland, to Wheeling would draw the close attention of so many high-level figures in this period, presidents and treasury secretaries among them. Why did the National Road draw such attention? Was it because these figures—Madison, Monroe, Gallatin, Dallas, and Crawford—recognized that they were engaged in an enterprise essential to the nation's future, one that would exemplify the importance of national investment to the economic future of the United States, and thus its general welfare? Significantly, Shriver recognized the importance of sustaining that investment over time. In letter after letter he stressed to his august superiors the importance of sustaining the road by keeping it in good repair. Shriver continued to give voice to his plea during his time with the road. In the end, the inability to keep the road in repair, through the application of adequate budgetary resources, forced the federal government to send it back to the states as unsustainable at the federal level.[51]

Other factors may also have been in play in ensuring that the National Road project received high-level attention from Gallatin and Madison. For example, Gallatin's intense participation may have been driven by a number of perspectives. He was deeply involved in formulating policy relating to growth of infrastructure for the Jefferson administration. As indicated in chapter 2, at the request of Congress he had authored a report to that body recommending the construction of a network of federally assisted interstate roads. At the time that construction began on the National Road, however, it represented the only portion of Gallatin's proposal that was in the process of implementation. No doubt, he wanted it to succeed. Gallatin was also, at the time, a resident of the area through which the road passed. His estate, Friendship Hill, was located some twenty miles from Brownsville, through which the road was slated to pass. Finally, quite apart from his role in the government and the locus of his residence, Gallatin was personally committed to the cause of national growth through infrastructure development. Madison was also in general a proponent of infrastructure development, where necessary, through federal financial assistance. In his seventh annual message, he had clearly articulated the need for such investment as a matter of policy. The recognition of this need must have been reinforced by the experience of the War of 1812, in which the United States had confronted a difficult military challenge on its own soil. Indeed, the Madison administration had kept the National Road project going, despite the challenges of the war, a testament to its belief in the importance of that investment both for times of peace and times of war. Madison reflected on this in that same seventh annual message, citing the need for steps to increase the nation's defense capabilities, including transportation infrastructure. It is true that Madison harbored doubts regarding the constitutionality of internal improvement expenditures, doubts that were reflected in his veto of the Bonus Bill in 1817. However, he acted on that principle on his last day in the White House. During his presidency, pragmatic considerations prevailed. His belief in the need for national infrastructure development where necessary and his administration's commitment to the project that had been commenced during the Jefferson administration may have compelled him to take an active role in its administration.

For economic as well as defense-related reasons, both Madison and Gallatin supported an "investment" role for the federal government, where private resources could not be expected to fund infrastructure or other necessary projects. Madison shared these policy views in his seventh annual message ("the great importance of establishing throughout our country the roads and canals which can best be executed under the national authority"). He did not abandon them in the Bonus Bill veto. Again Jeremiah Young points to Madison's recognition of the expediency of publicly funded internal improvements. These considerations may have prompted his active involvement in the National Road project during his terms as president, quite apart from his general duty under the Constitution to "take care that the Laws be faithfully executed."[52]

CHAPTER 10

The Culture of the National Road in Its Prime

Traffic and Travel

The glory days of the National Road spanned the 1820s (in the East), 1830s, and 1840s. By 1852, with the advent of the railroad, stagecoaches began to be taken off the National Road. Because the railroad continued to draw traffic from it, the road steadily declined in importance. By the time that had happened, the National Road extended approximately six hundred miles from Cumberland, Maryland, to Vandalia, Illinois. It had cost the federal government roughly thirteen thousand dollars per mile to build.[1]

In its prime, the National Road was a major artery that played a highly significant role in the life of the new nation, binding it together through better and faster travel, transportation, and communication. Reed B. Day, in his book *The Cumberland Road*, describes the scope of travel on the road during its prime: "From the time that the National Road was opened to the public in 1818, until the coming of the railroad in 1852, the Road carried the bulk of freight, mail, and passenger travel from East to West." In 1840, in the heyday of the road, two hundred thousand travelers passed over it. During that period, the road carried thousands of "movers" to the West. Conestoga wagons hauled goods between points on the road. Farm products of the West were transported to eastern markets. The products of the East wended their way along the road to enhance life in the West.[2]

The road was the highway of choice for prominent politicians from the West. Andrew Jackson used the road on his way back and forth from his home near Nashville, Tennessee. James Knox Polk traveled the road to his inauguration as eleventh president of the United States. Henry Clay, at various times member of the House and Senate from Kentucky and, ever the advocate for internal improvements, was a celebrated and frequent traveler along the old pike, and a number of pike towns bear his name. In May 1818, Ebenezer Fitch, a bridge contractor or builder, reported to his family: "The Hon. Henry Clay was along here last week on his way home to Kentucky with his family. He has ever been an advocate for Public Roads. He left his coach at Washington [Pennsylvania] and went to Wheeling on horseback on the United States road to view it with the bridges [and] was well pleased."[3]

The road dramatically reduced travel time for the renowned and the average citizen alike. A Conestoga wagon from Cumberland could reach Wheeling in eight days. An ox-drawn wagon required three to four weeks. A traveler on horseback could make the journey in four days, while a stagecoach required only two.[4]

Tolls

With the transfer of the National Road to the states in the 1830s and succeeding decades, tollhouses and tollgates began to spring up all along the road at established intervals. In Ohio, tollhouses were opened as early as 1831 with the consent of the federal authorities and pursuant to state law. In Pennsylvania, with its ninety miles of National Road, a total of six tollhouses were established after 1835. (Two survive today.) Travelers were now generally obliged to pay tolls for the use of an artery that had previously been toll-free during the period of federal support. As mentioned, in that period the charging of tolls by the federal government had been regarded as inconsistent with proper canons of federalism. With the takeover by the states, the states through which the road passed now were at liberty to charge tolls as a means of maintaining the road. The expectation that they would do so had been a driving force in the 1835 debate to "rid" the United States of the obligation to maintain the road.

A tollhouse would typically display on an outside wall or window an announcement showing the rates of toll applicable in the state. The rates in turn reflected the action of the state legislature in establishing the tolls by law and provided a litany of the types of vehicles that one might see along the pike. Thus, affixed to the Petersburg (now Addison) tollhouse in Pennsylvania, the first such edifice in the commonwealth as one traveled west from Maryland, was a table of rates advising that a horse and rider must pay, at that tollhouse, four cents; a led or drawn horse, mule, or ass must pay three cents; and a chariot, coach, coachee, stage, phaeton, or chaise with two horses and four wheels must pay twelve cents. A score of sheep passed for six cents. (See figure 4.)

The rates favored wagons with broad wheels. These, it was thought, would tend to preserve the surface of the road. Narrow wheels would tend to grind it down. Thus, a cart or wagon whose wheels exceeded eight inches in breadth

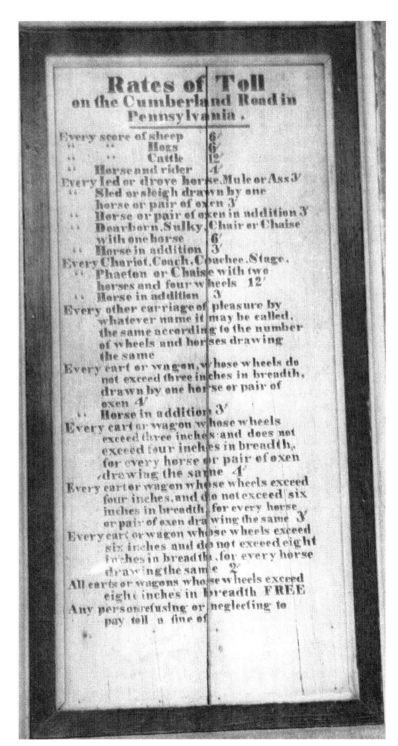

Rates of Toll
on the Cumberland Road in
Pennsylvania.

Every score of sheep   6'
  "   "   Hogs   6'
  "   "   Cattle   12'
  "   Horse and rider 4'
Every led or drove horse,Mule or Ass 3'
  "   Sled or sleigh drawn by one
         horse or pair of oxen 3'
  "   Horse or pair of oxen in addition 3'
  "   Dearborn,Sulky,Chair or Chaise
         with one horse   6'
  "   Horse in addition   3'
Every Chariot,Coach,Coachee,Stage,
  "   Phaeton or Chaise with two
         horses and four wheels 12'
  "   Horse in addition   3'
Every other carriage of pleasure by
         whatever name it may be called,
         the same according to the number
         of wheels and horses drawing
         the same
Every cart or wagon,whose wheels do
         not exceed three inches in breadth,
         drawn by one horse or pair of
         oxen 4'
  "   Horse in addition 3'
Every cart or wagon whose wheels
         exceed three inches and does not
         exceed four inches in breadth,
         for every horse or pair of oxen
         drawing the same 4'
Every cart or wagon whose wheels exceed
         four inches,and do not exceed six
         inches in breadth, for every horse
         or pair of oxen drawing the same 3'
Every cart or wagon whose wheels exceed
         six inches and do not exceed eight
         inches in breadth ,for every horse
         drawing the same 2'
All carts or wagons whose wheels exceed
         eight inches in breadth FREE
Any person refusing or neglecting to
         pay toll a fine of

Figure 4.   Sign Listing the Rate of Tolls on the Cumberland Road
in Pennsylvania (courtesy of the Museums of Oglebay Institute).

would travel the road "free" of toll. On the other hand, such a vehicle with wheel breadth between six and eight inches would pay two cents. Carts or wagons with narrower wheel breadth would pay higher rates. A person refusing or neglecting to pay the toll faced a fine of three dollars. To escape the toll, it is said, some travelers took to side roads where possible. The tollhouse and related gate remained a familiar feature of travel along the National Road from its period of extensive use in the 1840s through its period of decline after the advent of the railroad. Toll keepers evidently remained at their post until well into the late nineteenth century even though the road had substantially declined in significance and in some places had become primarily an avenue for local rather than interstate travel. Thus, Ierley depicts in his book a tollhouse near what is now Shadeland Avenue in Indianapolis that was not abandoned until about 1890.[5]

The increase and decrease in total tolls collected on the road following its transfer to the states in the mid-1830s provides some sense both of the road's progress and its later decline. In 1837, $39,843 was collected from tolls in Ohio. In 1839, toll revenues reached $62,496. By 1851, tolls had declined to $44,063 and never thereafter exceeded that figure. By 1876, tolls did not exceed $10,000 in that state. Despite the importance attached to them in the 1835 congressional debates on the road, tolls never provided sufficient revenues to maintain the road in a state of adequate repair. Until the transfer to the states, that responsibility largely fell to the federal government. The endless debates over ways and means to repair the road during the Monroe, Adams, and Jackson administrations testify to the difficulties that federal legislators faced in meeting that responsibility. After the transfer, the responsibility to keep the road in repair fell largely to the states. Did the eastern or western portion of the road raise more tolls? Archer Hulbert cites figures from 1840 to argue that more toll-bearing traffic traveled the road in Ohio than in Pennsylvania during that year. According to Hulbert, $51,365 was collected in Ohio; $18,489 was collected in Pennsylvania. It should be noted in this connection that the span of the road in Ohio was much greater than that in Pennsylvania.[6]

Billy Joe Peyton, in his account on the surveying and building of the road, provides us with the following observation: "Throughout its long and storied history the National Pike never did pay for itself, even after it became a toll road. One scholar estimates 'that the yearly expense of repairing the Ohio division of the road was $100,000.00 while the greatest amount of tolls collected in its most prosperous year [1839] was hardly half that amount $62,496.10.' Hence the governor of Ohio borrowed money for repairs as early as 1832, a plight shared by other states grappling to maintain their Road sections."[7]

Tolls, however, tell only part of the National Road story. The life along the road, whether federally or state funded, was the life of the wagoners, stagecoach drivers, and tavern keepers for whom it provided employment. It was also the experience of those who traveled the road, on a single occasion or more frequently. The mile markers, in some states made of cast iron and in others made of sandstone, enabled travelers to measure their progress east and west and the distance remaining before the next stop. Thomas Searight in his classic 1904 book *The Old Pike* gives a comprehensive account of these times and the individuals who made their livelihood along the old road. Searight's book gives a vivid impression of what he calls the "palmy" days of the road.

Stage and Wagon Drivers: Searight's Account

Challenges quite different from those that confronted the federal legislators in the Jackson years abounded. The difficulties of descending the steep hills, the snowstorms that stranded travelers at the taverns, the upsets, and accidents were all part of the daily life of the road. For some the road was a path to wealth and self-sufficiency. Wagoners would retire from service on the road, buy farms, and sell them later to the coal mines, making a sizeable profit on the transaction. As Searight puts it,

> We have in the story of these old wagoners, examples of the possibilities for achievement, under the inspiring genius of American institutions. Poor boys, starting out in life as wagoners, with wages barely sufficient for their subsistence, pushing on and up with ceaseless vigilance, attaining the dignity of farmers, in all ages the highest type of industrial life, and each bearing, though meekly, the proud title of freeholder. . . .
>
> The teams of the old wagoners, consisting[,] as a rule, of six horses were very rarely stabled, but rested over night on the wagon yards of the old taverns, no matter how inclement the weather. Blankets were used to protect them in the winter season. . . . Wagoners carried their beds, rolled up, in the forepart of the wagon, and spread them out in a semi-circle on the bar room floor in front of the big bar room fire upon going to rest. . . .[8]

Two categories or classes of wagoners plied the road, Searight tells us: the "regular" and the "sharpshooter." There were obvious tensions between the two. Searight explains why: "The regular was on the road constantly with his team and wagon, and had no other pursuit than hauling goods and merchandise on the road. The sharpshooters were for the most part farmers, who put their farm teams on the road in seasons when freights were high, and took them off when prices of hauling declined; and there was jealousy between the two classes. . . ."[9]

Stagecoach drivers vied against each other for speed. The arrival in town of the stagecoach, which could seat nine people, was a significant daily event. The stage would arrive at a tavern. A new team of horses would be hitched and the stage was off again to the next stop. News of a significant event, such as the results of a presidential election or the declaration of war, had to be delivered by stagecoach along the road, together with the mail. A stage could average sixty to seventy miles a day. The National Road was also a major national post road. In this respect, it achieved Washington's goal when he recommended that Congress pay "due attention" to the "post-roads." Moreover, the road ensured that mail would be received in a more expeditious manner. Mail from Washington might reach Wheeling in sixty-eight hours rather than the six to eight days that prevailed before the construction of the road.[10]

For many who made their livelihood on the road, including wagoners, stagecoach drivers, and tavern keepers, the golden age of the road was the high point of their lives and their vigor. An esprit de corps characterized the life of the road. Honesty, hard work, and responsibility were highly valued traits.

John Deets, the driver of a freight wagon from Baltimore to Wheeling in the 1820s and 1830s, describes the life and culture of the wagon driver in the 1820s and the occasional conflicts that arose:

> The pike boys had some hard times and they had some good times. They were generally very fond of sport, and mostly tried to put up where the landlord was a fiddler, so that they could take a hoe-down. Everyone carried his own bed, and after they had all the sport they wanted they put their beds down on the floor in a circle, with their feet to the fire, and slept like a mouse in a mill. They were generally very sociable and friendly with each other, but I must note one thing just here: Two of the boys met at David Barnett's, some three miles east of Hancock, and got into a dispute, which was not often the case. Elias Meek and Abner Benley were the two. Meek was for fight, Benley was for peace. But Meek pushed on Benley and Benley run, but Meek caught him. Then Benley knew he had to fight, and turned on Meek and gave him a wonderful thrashing, so that he was not able to drive his team for some time.[11]

Innkeepers and Tavern Keepers

Taverns and inns were located along the road. Generally, in the eastern segment of the road between Cumberland and Wheeling, they could be found at mile intervals. A renowned establishment was the Mount Washington Tavern in what is now Farmington, Pennsylvania, located along the National Road just above the site of Fort Necessity. Nathanial Ewing of Uniontown, a judge, bought the building in 1830 and later sold it to James Sampey, who ran it as a tavern. The tavern was principally designed to serve stagecoaches and travelers. Coaches of the Good Intent Line and a number of other stage lines would regularly stop there. Travelers could rest, drink, and dine at the tavern and move on after the horses were changed; or, they could rent a room for the night. Typically, men and women slept separately and dormitory style, with several persons sharing a bed. They slept fully clothed and could expect to be woken at five o'clock in the morning to resume the trip. The tavern consisted of a sturdy, handsome brick building of three stories, containing eleven rooms. Within the building one would find a kitchen, a parlor, a dining room, and several bedrooms on the second floor. Outbuildings included a stable, a shed, a smokehouse, and an outdoor privy. A Conestoga wagon (or two) might be parked in the shed awaiting the next leg of the journey.[12]

A typical meal at the tavern would have been served "family style" at a "long table." The traveler would not order from a menu but could select from a wide variety of offerings that might include, according to Robert C. Alberts in his informative book on the Mount Washington Tavern, "boiled smoked ham, boiled mutton, roast beef, fried speckled trout, fried chicken, fried potatoes, mashed pumpkin, mounds of country butter, hot bread, sauerkraut, preserves, pickles, pickled beets, pies, cake, cheese, and coffee." After dinner, the ladies might retire to the parlor, while the men would head to the taproom for a nightcap and conversation, until it came time to retire.[13]

The Mount Washington Tavern represents a typical stagecoach tavern catering to stagecoach passengers, who tended to be relatively affluent. An alternative category of hostelry was the wagon stand. It afforded food, drink, and lodging on a more economical basis and might cater to wagoners who could drink at the bar, dine, swap stories, and then bed down on the barroom floor, as Thomas Searight recounts in his work on the culture of the road.[14]

Some four miles west of the Mount Washington Tavern, one could find another tavern and inn called the Fayette Springs Hotel. It was constructed in 1822 and served as an inn and tavern for the life of the road. Its owner was Andrew Stewart, the member of the U.S. House of Representatives from Pennsylvania who frequently advocated for the interest of the road in that body. His contributions to the many debates in Congress on the road have been sketched above. Stewart was also a major real-estate investor in southwestern Pennsylvania. He opened the Fayette Springs Hotel on what is now the site of the Stone House Inn in 1822. It offered, according to the brochure available to today's guests, "a fine restaurant with top fiddlers entertaining on week-ends, a ten-pin alley, billiards, a porch swing and dancing into the wee hours." Stewart died at the age of eighty-one in 1872. His family sold the inn in the 1890s.[15]

Choice was not confined to two taverns. In the prime period of the road, the Pennsylvania traveler could find a tavern or inn virtually at mile intervals. Students of the road have since collected long lists of the many establishments that could be found in all the states of "the Pike." In Ohio, inns and taverns were found at ten-mile or closer intervals along Main Street in the various pike towns. In Old Washington, the traveler might stop at the stately, Italianate Colonial Inn. Just west of Zanesville, one could stop at the Headley Inn or the Smith House, which were within walking distance of each other. In Lafayette, the Red Brick Tavern served travelers, including prominent politicians such as Henry Clay, William Henry Harrison, and Martin Van Buren. In Springfield, Ohio, the weary road traveler could find respite at the Pennsylvania House, constructed in 1838–39, presumably to coincide with the advent of the National Road in that town. The inn, like the Mount Washington Tavern, was a "three-story, brick Federal style inn and tavern." The inn served as the terminal for the Ohio Stage Company. Along with stage passengers, it evidently also catered to drovers and wagoners. The parents of Dr. Isaac Funk, who helped author the Funk and Wagnalls dictionary, operated the inn in the 1840s. In Marshall, Illinois, the traveler might stay the night at the old Archer House, built in 1841. In Vandalia, like both Abraham Lincoln and Stephen A. Douglas, the traveler might visit the Charters Hotel.[16]

The Travelers

The accounts of travelers along the road in its prime give us the most vivid evidence of the National Road experience. In the absence of photographs, they provide us with detailed descriptions of that experience. Among them was the account by William Owen, traveling in 1824 by stagecoach with his father, Robert Owen. Robert Owen was a social reformer of the period who planned to establish a model community in New Harmony, Indiana. William Owen described a portion of the trip in western Pennsylvania, in December of that year, a time by which the National Road had been completed at least to Wheeling. He was entranced by the scenery that could be seen from the coach.

> Started per stage, as being the only conveyance, at ½ p. 5. We went 14 miles to breakfast and arrived about ½ p. 10 at Allegheny, having crossed the Savage Mount. The whole of the scenery was very romantic and beautiful, especially from the tops of the heights to which we ascended. The view was fine, alternate hill and dale, often enlivened by clear meandering streams and by large cleared fertile tracts of land or sometimes by neat little villages, one of which in particular reminded me of Swiss scenery, being composed of rustic log houses with rough wooded roofs, lying in a finely wooded valley in the Blue Mountains.

Owen also gives us an account of various encounters with other travelers: "We proceeded from Allegheny with 6 horses, to a beautiful valley in Pa., in which lies Smithfield, a nice little village whose situation struck me more than any I had yet seen. Here we met General Jackson, who had just arrived. He is a fine look-ing old man and widower. We overtook several parties of emigrants, all bound for the Ohio. They had usually a wagon with their utensils, and often a horse or two for some of the party to ride. They traveled 18 or 20 miles per day."[17]

In December 1829, John Gesaff wrote to his friend John P. Cockley of Baltimore regarding his journey in November of that year. He described this journey over the National Road to Laurel Hill in glowing terms, giving a pic-ture of a trip over the eastern portion of the road, a part of which Owen had described: "From the top of Laurel Hill you look down on a very fertile valley . . . in the midst of which is Uniontown, a beautiful place, which can boast of some very fine buildings, the farms are very handsomely situated and in excellent cultivation. This I think is the most splendid prospect I have ever seen." The letter continued: "Brownsville, a town twelve miles from [Uniontown], is a place I am told of considerable wealth. It is located on the Monongahela, a bold and beautiful river. Here I saw the first steam boat in the western waters."

The letter then describes the writer's somewhat restrained impressions of Wheeling: "From Brownsville, where I tarried two or three hours. I went on to Wheeling, nothing of interest attracting observation, save a neat monument by the way side, erected in honor of H. Clay. . . . In Wheeling are large commission stores and on the wharf there appears to be a great hum and stir of business. The Ohio River on which it is situated is properly styled the 'beautiful river' of the West." What the letter reveals is that, due to the construction of the National Road, one could make a fairly viable trip from the East over the mountains to Wheeling by the end of the first thirty years of the nineteenth century.[18]

The experience of Mary Eastman, age twenty-six, and her husband, Ornan, a graduate of Yale, an evangelist, and an agent for the American Tract Society, provides another perspective on the plight of road travelers in the early republic. Their long trip took them through a part of the road in Ohio:

> We left Columbus yesterday at noon. The road [apparently not the National] was very bad—a great deal of rain had fallen in 3 days, & the mud was very deep. There was a great deal of railroad [that is, wood rails placed across the road], & it was often broken through. We were tossed about most unmercifully, & an imaginative mind would have thought itself sometimes nearer the sky than the earth. There is nothing more calculated to keep one's eyes open, & learn to take care of one's self and stand on our own feet, than such a ride. There was only one man beside ourselves in the stage, and we had full scope for our limbs to play. No need of Calisthenics then; but great

danger if one's mouth is open, of such a jar as would break a tooth or bite the tongue. We were comforted in believing we had a strong stage & good drivers.

Finally, the couple reached the National Road, where their experience improved: "After we left Granville [near Newark, east of Columbus and north of the route of the National Road], the road was better & 12 miles farther, we came on the Great National Road, or 'the Pike,' as the people call it here [the new macadamized section from Wheeling west], which was very smooth & good, & we slept sweetly, undisturbed, until we reached Zanesville soon after 12."[19]

An account of a somewhat different nature is that of Eliza Steele, who enjoyed a long holiday tour during the summer of 1840 from New York to St. Louis and back to the East. Most of the return journey was by boat, a major part of it on the Ohio River from Cincinatti to Wheeling. However, at Wheeling, Mrs. Steele and her companions boarded a stage and traveled the National Road from that city east to Cumberland, Maryland, and then to Baltimore and her home in New York. Her vivid and well-crafted recollections of the journey along the National Road are contained in her book *A Summer Journey in the West*, published in 1841. Her journey over the National Road in July 1840 is an evocative account of a stagecoach journey across the eastern portion of the road during its prime.

On July 24, Eliza Steele and her companions set out by coach from Wheeling. She described her journey that day as "very delightful." The scenery evidently entranced her. "The country," she wrote, "is rolling, and alternatively pretty hill and dale scenery, and winding rivulets." The first part of the ride was through Virginia, but shortly the travelers reached the village of Alexandria (now W. Alexander) and entered Pennsylvania. She remembered driving over the National Road. "This is a firm McAdamized road," she wrote, "eighty feet broad, carried over mountains, vallies, and rivers, crossing the latter as well as every ravine and depression by well built stone bridges." Giving much credit to Henry Clay for the establishment of the road, she also noted the "bronze statue" of that statesman, "placed there by a widow lady . . . in gratitude for the benefit this road had produced to her property."[20]

Mrs. Steele described further stages of the experience at Washington, Pennsylvania: "At Washington, Pa., we dined; a pretty town, having three churches, hotels, and shops, with a college [Washington and Jefferson], a large building in the centre of pleasant grounds." She observed that the "dinner was good, but plain." The focus then returned to the scenery: "The hills, which we passed in the afternoon, were covered with rich pasture land, where sheep and cattle were making a fine feast. . . .While descending the side of one of these hills, we were told Brownsville, Pa. was in sight, and looking down, we beheld a town in the valley, with the pretty Monongehala glistening in the bright sun, as it wound

Figure 5. Engraving Showing a Man Wearing a Frontier Style "Hunting Shirt" Looking North along the Banks of the Ohio River. Wheeling and the National Road are in the Distance (courtesy of the Museums of Oglebay Institute).

its way around the hills. Rattling over a fine, strong covered bridge, we stopped to change horses before the principal hotel." In the same vein, Eliza Steele also described Brownsville as it then was: "This is a large manufacturing town, containing five thousand inhabitants. Steamboats are here built, and completely fitted up; and when the river is high, they run to Pittsburg; sixty miles distant. The hills are high around, abounding in bituminous coal and laid with strata of limestone and sandstone."[21]

That night (July 24) the party rode "up the hills and down the hills shut up [in] the stage coach." They were glad of their cloaks due to the cold weather, and at each stopping place they found fires. "They talked "merrily" but later "grew cold and weary and one after another sank into silence." At last they abandoned the vain attempt at sleep and tried to amuse each other with stories.[22]

At daybreak the next day, Eliza Steele lifted the curtain and thought she beheld a wide river. But this was an illusion. One of the travelers told her that "we were on the summit of a high mountain, and the deep valley filled with mist, with the opposite summits for a shore, made my river." She continued in a less solemn vein: "A bright sun soon dispersed the mist, and we were never tired of the variety of views we beheld upon every hand." She went on to describe the descent: "While descending one Allegheny we beheld another before us, like a high green wall reaching to the heaven, while a line across the summit showed the road we were to travel, so high and precipitous it seemed, that we wondered how we should ever reach the road."[23]

The travelers thus passed "both Laurel and Chestnut Ridges," and saw moose wood and box elder. Here Steele observed: "The road, although leading over mountain ridges and passes, is not a lonely one, as stages loaded with passengers were continually passing, and huge Pennsylvanian wagons with large Normandy horses, high collar, and jingling a bell to give notice of their approach." She further commented on the state of the road itself: "The fine broad smooth National road over which we were passing enabled the drivers to keep their horses upon a very quick trot." She confessed that, while she was "fond of rapid driving," it made her "rather nervous to dash at the rate of eight miles an hour, within two feet of a precipice down which we looked upon the tops of trees a thousand feet below." However, Steele conceded that there was "very little danger," because the driver could in a moment "cramp the wheel and check our speed."[24]

Eventually, Steele and her coach companions passed Smythfeld (later Somerfield and now below water) and Petersburg (now Addison), both in Pennsylvania, and Frostburg and Cumberland, in Maryland, the end of the National Road as such. In Cumberland, the party stopped to "change horses." Eliza Steele noted the town had "several large hotels, a college, court-house, and many shops." She described the status of the high mountain leading them into Cumberland as marking the Continental Divide (eastern) and noted that Cumberland marked the commencement point of the National Road. After Cumberland, Steele found a number of "pretty mountains" but none as high as those that they had crossed along the National Road.[25]

Emigrants and Immigrants

A somewhat different experience was encountered by those travelers who emigrated from the eastern part of the United States westward to the heartland, using the National Road as their route. Together with their families, they journeyed for the purpose of beginning a new life in another region rather than of visiting a different section of the country for business or public service. This continuing flow of emigrants drew the attention of travelers along the road who recorded their observations for their contemporaries and for posterity. For example, Daniel Drake, a medical doctor, who traveled extensively in the West and who produced a discourse on his observations in 1834, declared: "The emigration to the West is a perennial stream."[26]

Among the many emigrants who contributed to this stream along the National Road were Peter Hessong and his family. In 1838, Hessong journeyed from Fredricktown (now Frederick) in Maryland to Indianapolis in Marion County, Indiana. The family consisted of Peter and his wife, Catherine, and their five children—Benjamin F., four; Mary, eleven; Sarah, one; Eliza, nine; and John, six. Peter was thirty-six and Catherine thirty-one. After arriving in Indianapolis, they wrote to their parents, Jacob and Mary Kistner, about their journey of thirty days. Peter characterized it as "tiresome and discouraging," complaining about the inclement weather, the illness of their children, the bad roads, and other perils of the journey:

> It snowed unaccountable in the Allegh. Mountains, but before we reached Wheeling, Mary C. and Benjamin Franklin both were taken sick and we laid by one day one mile west of Norwich [Ohio] and applied to a Physician, and he Gave him a few powders and then thought he was out of danger, so we started again and before we got far he was taken worse than ever so we intened [sic] to lay by in Janesville [Zanesville] but could not get a room in the Tavern nor nowhere else. . . . [S]o on we came to a little town called Gratio [west of Zanesville] where we applied to a doctor, we [lodged] at Rodepoaches Tavern who said we were welcome to stay with him until our children were well since he said they had a very fine Doctor, so we applied to him and after three days we were able to travel again in good spirit.[27]

Peter complained emphatically about the state of the roads: "But such roads as we had from Dayton to Indianapolis I never saw in all my life. When we went through Dayton it rained as hard as it could pour down and continued raining for six days in succession." He advised his parents: "Now you may judge how the swamps were. It was just as much . . . as the horses could to get through, indeed Catherine did get mired once. I was walking and she drove into a mud hole. The horses stuck fast and then fell right down into the mire."[28]

Peter related in their letter that they had at first thought that Ohio and Indiana were "nothing but Bogs and Quagmires"; but as it turned out, the two states were "no such thing." He continued: "The Country is level to be sure, there are no mountains like those in Maryland." He had rented a farm five miles north of Indianapolis for a year for $120. He expected to shortly buy a farm. He had indeed been offered one for $1,400 but wanted to wait for a "good bargain." What had it cost the Hessongs to come to Indiana, including tolls? "I had to pay toll gates till we come to Columbus, Ohio, which we paid $11.16 and lodging." Provisions and horse cost him $49.77, making in all $60.93.[29]

Peter Hessong and his family and thousands like them sought opportunity through the purchase of farmland in Ohio and Indiana, escaping the limitations of the East. They suffered hardship along the journey and were beset by illness and poor roads, at least where the National Road had not been built. Yet, with all the rigors, dangers, and setbacks, the road enabled them to achieve their goal and arrive at their destination and seek out the opportunities it offered. For Hessong and his family, the road became a sort of "settlement corridor," enabling families to leave established communities in the East to find good farmland in the Midwest that would sustain them economically. At the same time, road historians suggest that the National Road largely followed settlements in the western states through which it passed rather than establishing them. A substantial degree of settlement had preceded the road in Ohio, Indiana, and Illinois. The long delay in construction, characterized by the constitutional, political, and sectional battles described above, ensured that there were substantial pockets of settlement alongside the route of the road by the time that it arrived. But the road also provided a pathway for settlers heading further west across the Mississippi.[30]

Tom Schlereth in his book *Reading the Road* assesses the role of the road in Indiana as a "conduit" of settlement in the early nineteenth century for certain groups of settlers such as the Quakers, who settled in eastern Indiana in significant numbers. The National Road, he says, marked the "westward trek of many nineteenth-century Friends," a significant number of whom settled in Richmond, Indiana, site of Earlham College, a prominent Quaker institution of higher education. According to Schlereth, a former director of the campus ministry of that college has drawn a map showing the sites of thirty-nine Friends meetinghouses established on or near the National Road during that era of settlement. Washington Street in Indianapolis was another thoroughfare for such migration.[31]

Immigrants from Abroad

The opportunity for work on the National Road and the easier access that it provided to the heartland brought forth a steady flow of immigrants who settled in communities along the road and contributed substantially to the growth of its faith-based institutions and to the breadth of its diversity. Thus, in Wheeling the numerous Irish immigrants working on the National Road and, later, the B & O Railroad swelled the membership of the Catholic churches in Virginia's northern panhandle and eventually justified the establishment of the Diocese of Wheeling-Charleston. A history of that diocese recounts:

> Among the immigrants that came to Wheeling were Irish laborers who had worked on the National Road project. The Irish joined a number of German immigrants who had been drawn to the city for its opportunities for skilled laborers. Requests for a priest soon followed and a church was completed by 1823. St. James Church was the first church built in the Diocese of Wheeling-Charleston and was used by the community until a second church was built in 1849. The community founded in Wheeling was made up of settlers who would prove to be representative of the Catholics western Virginia would attract over the course of the nineteenth and first part of the twentieth centuries: recently arrived immigrants who were employed on the great public and private works or in search of labor.[32]

In a similar vein, in Columbus, Ohio, the opening of the National Road and the Ohio and Erie Canal stimulated German immigration into that city, which became the capital of Ohio. One account of the growth of the German community in that city observes: "Though trips along the National Road could be arduous, it was much better than the rough traces and trails typical of the times. It created a reasonably reliable route between Ohio and eastern markets and facilitated the state's internal development as well." In the case of German immigration, the better traveling conditions that the road facilitated and the "failed revolution of 1848" in Germany contributed to the growth of the German population in Columbus and the establishment of a historic neighborhood now known as German Village.[33]

Visitors from Britain: Four Perspectives

Yet another perspective is provided not by an American stagecoach passenger or a family emigrating from the East to the heartland but by a procession of perceptive and articulate travelers from Great Britain. A number of these travelers, some of them renowned and all of them literate, recorded their impressions of travel along the National Road during the period of its prime. These firsthand accounts provide us with four somewhat varied perspectives of different segments of the road during that formative period and during various stages of its development in the 1830s, 1840s, and 1850s.

Frances Trollope was an English author and an observer of American manners. In 1830, she made a journey from Cincinnati, Ohio, where she had been residing, to Wheeling, Virginia (now West Virginia)—by steamboat. She then traveled the National Road from Wheeling to Cumberland and then to Hagerstown and Baltimore by stage. Trollope recounted that journey in her book *Domestic Manners of the Americans*, published in England some years later. The book as a whole caused a great stir, for it cast the Americans in a somewhat unfavorable light. Its author returned to England in near poverty. She was pilloried in the United States, but her book sold very well and catapulted its author into fame and a career as novelist and travel writer. Her son, Anthony Trollope, became a renowned and prolific novelist of the late nineteenth century. A number of his works have been dramatized on public television.[34]

Whatever the merits of her observations on American manners of the early republic, Frances Trollope's account of her National Road journey provides firsthand insight on the nature of travel over the road during the 1830s from the perspective of a foreign traveler with literary talent and power of observation who actually made the journey on the old pike during its period of extensive use. She began her account with some observations regarding her stay in Wheeling before commencing the stagecoach leg of the journey: "The weather was bleak and disagreeable during the two days we were obliged to remain at Wheeling. I had got heartily tired of my gifted friend; we had walked up every side of the rugged hill, and I set off on my journey towards the mountains with more pleasure than is generally felt in quitting a pillow before daylight, for a cold corner in a rumbling stage-coach."[35]

She described her first reaction to the vehicle in this "foreign land." She related: "This vehicle had no step, and we climbed into it by a ladder; when that was removed I remembered, with some dismay, that the females at least were much in the predicament of sailors, who, 'in danger have no door to creep out:' but when a misfortune is absolutely inevitable, we are apt to bear it remarkably well." Trollope noted that the coach "had three rows of seats, each calculated to hold three persons, and as we were only six, we had, in the phrase of Milton, to 'inhabit lax' this exalted abode, and, accordingly, we were for some miles tossed about like a few potatoes in a wheel-barrow." The initial discomfort was considerable: "Our knees, elbows, and heads required too much care for their protection to allow us leisure to look out of the windows; but at length the road became smoother, and we became more skillful in the art of balancing ourselves, so as to meet the concussion with less danger of dislocation."[36]

The scenery, viewed from the National Road, recompensed Trollope in some measure for the rigors of the coach journey: "We then found that we were travelling through a very beautiful country, essentially different in its features from what we had been accustomed to round Cincinnati: it is true we had left '*la belle rivière*' behind us, but the many limpid and rapid little streams that danced through the landscape to join it, more than atoned for its loss." Frances Trollope was generally aware of the circumstances of the road's construction, on which she commented: "This road was made at the expense of the government as far as Cumberland, a town situated among the Alleghany Mountains, and, from the nature of the ground, must have been a work of great cost."[37]

Like Uria Brown, Trollope commented favorably to her readers on the bridges that she crossed along the National Road: "I regretted not having counted the number of bridges between Wheeling and Little Washington, a distance of thirty-four miles; over one stream only there are twenty-five, all passed by the road. They frequently occurred within a hundred yards of each other, so serpentine in its course; they are built of stone, and sometimes very neatly finished." She also described a brief night's stay in Little Washington ("the hotel was clean and comfortable") and the journey to the western foot of Laurel Ridge (presumably the Washington–Uniontown leg) ("much less interesting").[38]

Trollope saved her rapture for the portion of the trip that crossed Laurel Ridge (presumably over Laurel Mountain and past what is now the Summit Hotel). Her reaction is comparable to that of Eliza Steele.

> The latter part of the day, however, amply repaid us. At four o'clock we began to ascend the Alleghany mountains: the first ridge on the Western side is called Laurel Hill, and takes its name from the profuse quantity of evergreens with which it is covered; not any among them, however, being the shrub to which we give the name of laurel. . . .
>
> The whole of this mountain region, through ninety miles of which the road passes, is a garden. The almost incredible variety of plants, and the lavish profusion of their growth, produce an effect perfectly enchanting. I really can hardly conceive a higher enjoyment than a botanical tour among the Allegheny mountains, to anyone who had science enough to profit by it.[39]

Then she returned, with less enthusiasm, to a description of the evening stay in the hostelry:

> The first night we passed among the mountains recalled us painfully from the enjoyment of nature to all the petty miseries of personal discomfort. Arrived at our inn, a forlorn parlour, filled with the blended fumes of tobacco and whiskey, received us; and chilled, as we began to feel ourselves with the mountain air, we preferred going to our cold bed-rooms rather than sup in such an atmosphere. We found linen on the beds which they assured us had

only been used *a few nights;* every kind of refreshment we asked for we were answered, "We do not happen to have that article."[40]

The following morning revived her spirits: "We now enjoyed a new kind of alpine witchery; the clouds were floating around, and below us, and the distant peaks were indistinctly visible as though a white gauze veil, which was gradually lifted up, till the sun arose, and again let in upon us the full glory of these interminable heights."[41] Trollope ultimately passed through Hagerstown and Frederick, Maryland, and arrived safely in Baltimore.

Another perspective is provided by the voyage of Joseph John Gurney, who traveled through Ohio along the National Road in 1837 on his way to Indiana. Gurney, a Quaker minister who resided in England and the author of several books on religion and morality, journeyed to the United States in part in order to visit many of the meetings of the Society of Friends (Quakers) in America, and in part to pursue his interest in prison reform. His commentary on the National Road in Ohio, while incidental to his religious mission, provides a valuable complement to Frances Trollope's description of her journey along the eastern section of the road some years earlier. His observations were contained in letters to a friend, Amelia Opie, which were published in 1841.[42]

Gurney described the National Road in eastern Ohio, at least, as "a macadamized turnpike, and a perfect contrast to the rough and almost dangerous ways" by which he had been traveling since entering the state (presumably Ohio). He was riding in "a light carriage . . . drawn by two good horses" belonging to his friend and traveling companion. The first part of his journey in Ohio took him to Norwich, which he called "a little *pseudo* Norwich." (Gurney was familiar with Norwich, England.) He regarded it as an "uninviting village of 700 inhabitants" but was gratified that it contained two meetinghouses. Gurney was more impressed with Zanesville, which he found to be a "neat and prosperous-looking town of about 7000 inhabitants" joined by a covered bridge to the town of Putnam across the Muskingum River. There he found "good frame houses being pleasantly intermingled with fine trees." Attendance at a large public meeting reassured him that the town's "inhabitants, varied as they are in point of denomination, are no strangers to the blessings of our common Christianity."[43]

From Zanesville, Gurney proceeded to Reynoldsburg. Along the way he found "two very tolerable houses of entertainment," noting that they were of greater frequency along that part of the National Road than on many of the "high roads" in England. He was impressed as well by the presence of limestone and the abundance of coal in the region. Journeying on to Columbus, he found the latter city "a baby metropolis bursting into life and already making some show of magnificence." He noted the large and handsome private dwellings, as well as the presence of a good institution for the education of the deaf and a state lunatic asylum. At Jefferson, Ohio, Gurney was obliged to "desert" the National Road, since "it was no further in a finished state." He found the road on the next leg of his journey "intensely bad and muddy."[44]

William Oliver, another visitor from Great Britain, came to the United States in 1841. His objective was more temporal than that of his countryman, Gurney. It was to discover whether emigration to the United States would be desirable for his fellow countrymen. Oliver was not particularly interested in American roads, but he spent a great deal of his time in Illinois and traveled east from that state across a portion of the National Road through Illinois, Indiana, and a part of Ohio during 1842. Oliver's report (published in 1843) gives some insights about travel over the western part of the road during that period, shortly after the debates of 1835 and the decision to transfer the road to the states through which it ran.

Oliver's account emphasized, more than that of Frances Trollope, the hardships of travel over the road, its hazards and uncertainties, the prevalence of illness for travelers and residents alike, and the challenge of finding adequate lodging. Oliver was traveling along the western segment of the road, while Trollope had traveled over it exclusively in the east. Oliver's description of the journey also dramatizes the degree to which the road was still undergoing initial construction in the early 1840s through the western states, at a time when congressional appropriations had terminated. (Between Springfield, Ohio, and its terminus in Vandalia, Illinois, it appears that the National Road was not fully completed with a macadamized surface and, as Oliver's description confirms, was in many stretches a largely dirt road. This status of the road is reflected in the maps contained in Jeremiah Simeon Young's 1902 study.[45]

Oliver's trip along the National Road began in Vandalia, Illinois, where he reported the prevalence of "bilious fever." He described the road for the most part as "nothing more than a track," although several miles had been completed east of Vandalia. Along the road, Oliver encountered snakes and wild turkeys. In contrast to the eastern portion of the road, with its multiplicity of taverns, lodging was difficult to find. On one occasion, Oliver and his traveling companion spent the night in the house of a farmer crowded with men, women, and children traveling the road, many overcome with fever. In Marshall, Illinois, although the place was "quite new," Oliver found that a "great number of lots had been sold and already partially built upon." There was, he noted, "one continued bustle of hewing, hammering and sawing going on." Oliver also took note of the progress on the road. "At several places in this neighborhood, large gangs of laborers were working at the National Road, cutting and embanking at some dark ravines and some stone piers for bridges were being erected, the materials for which were cut in large masses from a compact limestone, approaching in appearance to marble."[46]

Oliver found Terre Haute, Indiana, to be a "pretty place" with "some respectable stores and inns." However, some of the "inmates" of the hotel where he and his companion stopped were "lying dangerously ill in fever." Outside the town, Oliver found "numbers of workmen . . . busy on the National Road, raising it above the surface level of the bottom, and covering it with a thick layer of well-broken limestone." Along with the laborers, like Daniel Drake, Oliver noted the "stream of movers" who were "flowing west with unabated numbers." Among them, Oliver remarked on a number of Mormon families with "all their household goods" and farm animals bound to Missouri, where they were seeking a settlement "consisting entirely of that sect of religionists."[47]

Whenever practicable, Oliver noted, the National Road ran "in a straight line." This rendered "traveling exceedingly monotonous." He elaborated: "Hemmed in by a wall of forest the traveler can sometimes see a distance of many miles before him the cleared roadway diminished to a thread-like tenuity. Inns and villages, however, occur at no great distance from one another, so that the traveler on horseback or on foot has it in his power to halt and get rest and food when he requires them; and the accommodation is better than it is further west." Oliver portrayed the Indiana State House in Indianapolis as "built on the model of the Parthenon" and "of very imposing appearance." The city had some good hotels and a population of about two thousand. In Indianapolis, Oliver and his companion sold their horses and embarked by stage for Centreville, Indiana. Although the National Road was still a "track" in many places, the horses were "good" and the stage driver "fearless," very much "at the expense of the poor passengers' bones." In Centreville, Oliver noted the fine farms, the absence of poverty, and the beauty of the river.[48]

In Ohio, Oliver traveled by stage from Dayton to Springfield. He found the road macadamized in some places and "very bad" in others. Numbers of workmen were engaged on the road in that area. From Springfield, Oliver continued on to Columbus. On this part of the journey, the road was "excellent." From Columbus, Oliver took the stage to Sandusky, thus ending his journey on the National Road. He concluded that emigration to the United States was a good prospect for the poor, who would find better-paying jobs in the new country, but of less promise for others.[49]

Writing more than 150 years later, Thomas Schlereth, in his book *Reading the Road*, depicts the culture and typography of the National Road era in Indiana (1827–49) that Oliver must have observed. Schlereth invokes the role of Jonathan Knight, whose career is mentioned above, in connection with the establishment of Knightstown. Schlereth also identifies the blacksmiths, wagon shops, and drovers' stands that bordered the road. He describes the Huddleston House in Mount Auburn as a site where emigrants would camp on their way west. Travelers in Indiana might also stop at one of the numerous taverns and inns, such as the Vinton House in Cambridge City. For Schlereth, Centreville was the archetype of the National Road town, with its stagecoach stops and stately residences facing the road. In the twenty-first century it is now given over to a multitude of antique stores.[50]

J. Richard Beste traveled to the United States with his large family of eleven children in the early 1850s and spent considerable time in Indiana, particularly in Terre Haute. After returning to Europe, he completed a two-volume work on this journey to the "interior" of the United States. Like William Oliver, Beste was interested in the United States as "a scene for agriculture emigration." As a Catholic he, like Gurney, was also interested in the "religious state" of an emigrant's "future home."[51]

On the condition of the National Road, over which the family traveled by wagon, Beste sourly remarked: "After Mount Meridian, we found our road change sadly for the worse. It is true that it is marked in all the maps the 'National Road' . . . ; and it had been fenced in and laid down as such: but Congress, by subsequent decision, declared that the making and maintaining of roads was not a national affair, but should be at the charge of each State that wanted them."[52]

Beste was thus generally aware of the debates in Congress about the transfer of the road and indeed was writing twenty years after the 1835 debate described above. He described the mournful state of the portion of the road over which he traveled:

> The condition of this repudiated road, now therefore depended upon wants and traffic of each township through which it passed. The tract of country after passing Mount Meridian was but thinly inhabited: the road was little used, and still less attention was given to keeping it up. The water tables on each side were choked or washed away: water courses ran down the middle of it or furrowed it deep from side to side, or dug it into wide pits. Sometimes these had to be passed through almost on stepping stones: sometimes the rain-channels were bridged over by planks, so short that there was not [an] inch to spare at the sides of each wheel. Sometimes, where the gravelly top soil was quite worn away, and quicksandy bottom exposed beneath, a track just wide enough for the wheels, was made by corduroy road laid across the bog.[53]

The Dwellers alongside the Road: James Whitcomb Riley

If travelers from Britain like Trollope, Gurney, Oliver, and Beste had only a fleeting experience with the National Road, for others the National Road represented the daily experience of a childhood lived alongside it. Among these was James Whitcomb Riley, the Hoosier poet, who grew up in Greenfield, Indiana, along the National Road. In 1854, Riley's father, Reuben Riley, built a spacious two-story house fronting on the road, called Main Street. The house still stands at East Main Street in Greenfield. From the second-floor window of this home the young Riley could watch the ebb and flow of life along the road in the 1850s: the procession of livestock being taken to market, the lines of Conestoga wagons, the stagecoaches, and the individual riders. Riley later recorded some of his early impressions in a collection of poems entitled *A Child World.* The life he portrayed in that work was "characteristic of the rural, middle class, Midwestern family life" that he knew so well. In his later years, living in Indianapolis, Riley reflected on the role that the road had played in his childhood. He regretted that the rural life that he remembered was giving way to a more urban environment even in the half century that followed the era of the road in its prime.[54]

The Greenfield to which Reuben Riley moved in April 1844 was a small village of three hundred people. The legislation that provided for the establishment of the courthouse decreed that it be located along the National Road. Alongside that same artery Reuben Riley built a log cabin to house his family. James Whitcomb was born there in 1849. In 1855, in order to better house his family and reflect his stature as a lawyer in the community, Reuben Riley built a "simple old framed house" fronting the National Road. From his vantage point on the second floor, young Riley observed the road.[55]

As Riley's biographer, Elizabeth J. Van Allen, points out, for the poet, the "highway represented opportunity and adventure." The road also "held much romance for Riley and embodied the vision of the possibilities and hopes that the United States offered as a nation."[56]

One would like to believe, with Riley, that it still does.

CHAPTER 11

The Road as a Microcosm of Early-Republic America

The National Road was the iconic American internal improvement of its age. It was also the setting for a number of early social and political movements that characterized the era of which it was a part. These movements were not necessarily generated by the road or proponents of the road in Congress or elsewhere. Some took place as a consequence of, or incident to, the pattern of settlement that the road fostered. They also took place, it can be argued, because the natural barriers of the new nation were being breached. The National Road enabled people like Peter Hessong and his family to surmount the obstacles that had long been posed by the Allegheny Mountains and to head west to the heartland, seeking freedom, opportunity, land, and, perhaps, distance from traditional ways. With that freedom and the greater distance from the more established regions of the country, it became easier to challenge social restrictions and reshape traditional institutions. The road both represented and generated change from a variety of perspectives. Some of the changes that the road facilitated transformed the nature of travel upon it.

The road's primary significance was its status as "the most important" internal improvement in an era when internal improvement became a significant aspect of the national agenda as well as a key political and constitutional issue. At the same time, by providing some stations along the Underground Railroad, the road shielded from discovery those seeking freedom from the oppression of slavery. Slavery itself came to eclipse internal improvements as the paramount issue of the antebellum period. If the road facilitated the flight to freedom for some, it also hastened dispersal from ancient homelands for others. The influx of settlers, facilitated in part by the road or by other internal improvements that preceded it, inevitably worked to push Native Americans from lands on which they lived or upon which they had taken refuge as a result of earlier migrations.

Change was coming also for the women of the United States. Because of the spirit of freedom and opportunity that it spawned or because it constituted a suitable site to convene people for a statewide meeting, the road became the locus of gatherings or conventions that advanced the women's suffrage movement in Indiana. In this way, the National Road served as a microcosm of some the directions and movements that were bringing, sooner or later, momentous change to the nation.

Internal Improvements and National Growth

First and foremost, the National Road was an internal improvement. It is in that context that its impact as an instrument of change has been so clearly felt. Its building and operation reflected the general thrust for internal improvement in the form of roads, canals, and later, railroads in the United States. That thrust generally characterized the first half of the nineteenth century. The debates in Congress concerning the road dramatized for the young nation the importance of internal improvement for its growth and prosperity. Those debates identified as well the tensions and difficulties that confronted Congress and the people it served in establishing a coherent and fiscally sound policy regarding the role of the federal government in assisting and promoting such improvements in the form of roads and canals.

For the reasons stated above, the constitutional questions regarding the nature and scope of that role were a major aspect of the debates regarding the road. Equally sharp were the regional and sectional conflicts that played out the consideration of the appropriation measures for the road. In this framework, for over thirty years, from 1806 to 1838, as the major federally funded internal improvement, the National Road was a key item on the national agenda.[1] In this sense, the road represented a microcosm of the larger issue of internal improvements generally. During that period, all the presidents of the United States were profoundly engaged in the issues concerning the National Road and were major participants in the debates about it and about other national improvements in the form of roads and canals. The same may be said of many prominent political figures, including some unsuccessful aspirants for the White House such as John C. Calhoun, Henry Clay, and Daniel Webster.[2]

Political or policy decisions made respecting the National Road had significant consequences for internal-improvement law and policy in succeeding decades. James Monroe's constitutional compromise regarding the spending power and the outcome of the tollgate wars are examples. As the first federally financed highway, the National Road itself served as a major precedent for federal participation in internal improvements long after the stages had left the old pike.

The construction and operation of that old pike conclusively demonstrated that the infrastructure and transportation needs of the country were so significant to economic and social progress that they would ultimately have to be harmonized, and would often trump, constitutional, political, and policy considerations or values that seemed to run counter. America of the nineteenth century wanted federalism; it also wanted roads and canals.

To this day, and looking forward from this day across the span of the twenty-first century, it is broadly recognized that adequate infrastructure (and sustainable national investment in it) is essential to the growth and continued success of the American experience and to the maintenance of America's role in the global economy. For several generations in the early part of the nineteenth century, the National Road represented that reality and helped to establish that principle. In this sense, it was a microcosm of early-republic America.[3]

The Road as a Freedom Route: The Underground Railroad and the National Road

If internal improvement was essential to the economic and geographic growth of the United States, resolution of the issue of slavery was essential to its survival. During the period of the federal financing of the road (roughly 1806 to 1838) and until the Civil War, different reactions to slavery convulsed the United States. Among the responses were antislavery politics, the resistance to the extension of slavery in new states, the Abolitionist movement, and the operation of the Underground Railroad. Ultimately, the battle over the extension of slavery came to eclipse the scope and financing of internal improvements as the primary issue facing the nation and challenging its unity. Illustrative is the political journey of President John Quincy Adams as an internal-improvement advocate in the White House from 1825 to 1829 and Congressman John Quincy Adams as the eloquent postpresidential spokesperson for the repeal of the gag rule, which precluded the consideration of antislavery petitions in Congress. Illustrative as well is the political progression of Abraham Lincoln from advocate for internal improvement as a state and federal legislator in the 1840s to advocate for limitations on the extension of slavery as candidate for the Senate in 1858 and for the presidency in 1860.[4]

The National Road was a locus of one kind of antislavery activity. Underground railroad sites could be found at various points along the road, particularly in western Pennsylvania and eastern Ohio. In Washington, Pennsylvania, for example, Dr. Francis LeMoyne became a prominent leader in the state's Abolitionist movement and sheltered runaway slaves in his house along the National

Road. The Putnam area in Zanesville, Ohio, a very short distance from the National Road, was the site of the Putnam Presbyterian Church, built in 1835, where William Beecher, the brother of Harriet Beecher Stowe, was the first pastor and where Frederick Douglass spoke. Slaves were sheltered in the church basement on their way along the route of the Underground Railroad. Down the road in New Concord, Ohio, were a number of other such sites.[5]

The case of Francis LeMoyne is illustrative. His father, Dr. Julius LeMoyne, came to the United States in 1797 to escape the "turmoil" of the French Revolution and established himself in a stately house in Washington, Pennsylvania, fronting the National Road. Francis LeMoyne was a doctor as well as an ardent abolitionist. His house became part of the Underground Railroad. There slaves who were seeking to make their way to freedom in Canada could take refuge. (The Underground Railroad carried fugitive slaves to freedom in Canada, as fugitive slaves could not safely take permanent residence in the United States unless legally freed.) From time to time as many as twenty-five men and women fleeing the evil of slavery took shelter in the house. Dr. Francis LeMoyne is described as the "most famous figure" of Washington's Underground Railroad. He helped to found the Western Abolition Society and was a candidate of the Abolitionist Party for vice president of the United States. His house was regarded as a "haven for fugitives trying to escape bondage."[6]

The National Road in Pennsylvania was a part of the route of the Underground Railroad. The LeMoyne House served as a key station on this route. As noted in *Passages to Freedom*, a comprehensive and recent account of the history of the Underground Railroad, "Dr. [Francis] LeMoyne, who joined the Anti-Slavery Society in 1837, not only became an active promoter of abolitionist events but also offered his home in Washington, Pennsylvania as a place of shelter for runaway slaves. Free blacks, living in the surrounding county, had already established a network of escape routes leading from Virginia northward to Pittsburgh. Three of these pathways ran through Washington very close to Lemoyne's house." LeMoyne's activities were not confined to the Underground Railroad. He promoted the cause of education for women, established a college for African American students, and funded a public library.[7]

Notwithstanding the significant contributions of such important road-era figures as Dr. Francis Lemoyne, in assessing the role of the National Road and its relationship to the Underground Railroad one must bear in mind that the Underground Railroad was basically a south-to-north route, leading fugitive slaves to freedom in Canada, while the National Road was an east-to-west artery. Indeed, as indicated above, a major contribution of the National Road was to link the eastern seaboard to the West and to open up traffic, eastbound and westbound, across the Allegheny Mountains, which had operated as a barrier to that traffic prior to the opening of the National Road. The National Road was seen by its promoters and architects, Thomas Jefferson and Albert Gallatin, as a gateway to the West, joining the Potomac with the Ohio. Nevertheless, the significance of the National Road as a "stop" along the Underground Railroad should not be underestimated. Francis Lemoyne's house, now celebrated as a refuge in that railroad, was situated along an east-west segment of the road in Pennsylvania. A number of sites were situated along the road in Ohio and are still commemorated in that context. Visitors to a number of the bridges that carried National Road travelers are today reminded that fugitive slaves hid beneath those spans.[8]

If the National Road story embraces the story of fugitive slaves seeking freedom, it also embraces the story of Nelson Gant. Gant was born into slavery and gained his freedom in 1845. He settled in Zanesville, Ohio, in a house on the National Road. He owned a farm, and it is said that he would use his wagon to carry fugitive slaves from one station to another. Gant prospered, acquired properties, and became a self-made millionaire, a prominent citizen of the town, and a benefactor of his community. His house and his contributions are reflected in contemporary Zanesville, alongside what is now U.S. 40, the modern name for the National Road.[9]

The Road and the Plight of Native American People: The Migration of the Delaware Indians

As we have seen, Native Americans played a decisive role in the charting of the National Road. Nemacolin accompanied the Ohio Company expedition to Pennsylvania in 1752 and blazed the trail that was to become the route of the National Road from Cumberland to Redstone Old Fort. Nemacolin was a member of the Delaware Tribe. The interaction between the Delaware Indians and the National Road and between that tribe and the history of Indian displacement during the eighteenth and nineteenth centuries in the United States is recounted in a book by C. A. Weslager entitled *The Delaware Indians*. Weslager alludes to the role of Nemacolin in blazing the trail or pathway that preceded the National Road in Pennsylvania. Chapter 1, above, related Nemacolin's effort to the early history of the National Road and pointed out how his path constituted a sort of antecedent to the route of the National Road. Indeed, Nemacolin's path was "improved" by Colonel Washington during the events preceding the battle of Fort Necessity. The commissioners and surveyors who followed in the wake of the 1806 Cumberland Road legislation essentially followed Washington's trail of 1754. Weslager does not focus on Nemacolin's role but does recount evidence indicating Nemacolin's sense that has father had been "cheated" out of lands by settlers.[10]

If Nemacolin is part of the saga of the National Road, he is also part of the saga of the migration of his tribe, the Delaware Indians, to the western United States over a two-hundred-year period. Weslager chronicles this migration from what is now Delaware (and was then part of Pennsylvania) to the Susquehanna, to other parts of that commonwealth, including western Pennsylvania, to Ohio, to the Indiana Territory, and from there to Missouri, Kansas, and Oklahoma, where the Delaware tribes were essentially absorbed by or linked to the Cherokees. That migration illustrates one aspect of the Native American experience and the intersection of that experience with the road.[11]

The significant role that the Delaware Indians played in the battle at Fort Necessity in 1754 and in Braddock's march to Fort Duquesne in 1755 is discussed in chapter 1. Following those encounters, as Weslager recounts the history, the Delaware Indians in Pennsylvania and Ohio engaged in intermittent attacks on local English settlements in Pennsylvania, goaded on by the French during the French and Indian War. These attacks were followed by periods of short-lived peace. Evidently, the Delawares were moved by disappointments in their efforts to establish lasting rights to land as well as the rejection of their overtures by General Braddock. The colonists responded with attacks of their own, including an attack by three hundred troops near the Allegheny. By the end of the French and Indian War, many of the Delaware settlements in Pennsylvania had been dispersed. This process of dispersal was accelerated by Indian reverses in Pontiac's War. By 1768, most of the Delawares had departed Pennsylvania and settled, for a time, in Ohio, leaving room for settlements in such areas as Redstone (now Brownsville) along the Monongahela, which later figured in the establishment of the National Road.[12]

Following the battle of Fallen Timbers in which the Delaware, along with allied tribes, were once again defeated in battle, under the Greenville Treaty of 1795 the tribes dwelling in the Ohio Valley were required to again migrate to the West, this time to the Indiana Territory. The Delawares, then numbering about three thousand, established villages in the vicinity of the White River. In Indiana, they did not have land of their own but remained in the territory by leave of the host tribe (the Miami) and with the blessing of the United States. William Conner, a trader and interpreter, established a trading post near present Noblesville, Indiana, the site of present-day Conner Prairie, a museum and interpretive center near Indianapolis that portrays settlement in the early-republic period. He and his Indian wife, Mekinges, raised their family of half-white, half-Indian children and spoke the Delaware language. A modern-day exhibit in Conner Prairie reproduces such a trading post. The United States claimed title to the lands in Indiana, which became a state in 1816. Successive waves of migration to the Indiana Territory put pressure on the government to repossess these lands for settlement and to relocate the Indians to lands further west and across the Mississippi. Gen. William Henry Harrison played a strong role in this process. In addition, the government provided annuities to the departing Indians. The major relocation was provided for in a treaty of 1818. It was this relocation that evidently led to the departure from Indiana of William Conner's Delaware family. The main body of Delawares migrated from Indiana to Missouri and later to Kansas.[13]

Thus, the major portions of the migration to and from the Indiana Territory occurred prior to the completion of the National Road from Cumberland, Maryland, to Wheeling in 1821. (It is not clear how many settlers traveled the National Road west on segments of the road—which opened to traffic as early as 1812—to find residence in Indiana and thus served as an impetus for the departure of the Delawares to points west.) The construction of the road in Ohio and Indiana in the 1820s and 1830s apparently followed rather than antedated the Delaware migration from Indiana. Weslager does not ascribe to the road itself a large impact in compelling this migration. Nonetheless, the opening of the west by means of the National Road and other internal improvements must have had some considerable impact on that picture. Moreover, the whole process of opening up the West, a process to which the National Road made an important contribution, had a significant impact on the relocation of Indian tribes in general.[14]

In the late nineteenth century, the remaining remnant of the Delawares moved from Kansas to Oklahoma, where they mingled with the Cherokees. In providing this chronicle and taking us to modern times, Weslager traces the results of the proceedings regarding the Delaware Indians before the Indian Claims Commission in the twentieth century. This migration to the West was in part an element of the policy carried out by Thomas Jefferson, who initially believed that Indians should settle on farms along with white settlers and take up agriculture. In his second inaugural address, Jefferson recommended steps, including education, to achieve these goals. At the same time Jefferson believed that in the Far West, beyond the Mississippi, Indians could find space—and game—to practice their traditional ways of hunting in lieu of agriculture. This relocation and migration became an element of his Indian policy.[15]

Matters related to the future of Native Americans continued to arise during the administration of John Quincy Adams, who advocated and took steps to achieve the extension of the road through Ohio and Indiana. Gov. James B. Ray of Indiana reflected the perspective of his state when writing to Adams in 1825 regarding the situation of the Indians remaining in his state. Ray noted that a "large portion of the territory within the boundaries of the State of Indiana" was claimed by the Indians. He told the president that his jurisdiction should not "suffer that state of things to remain longer than that title can be extinguished upon fair and honorable terms." Finally, Ray offered Adams the following thought: "The tribes seem to entertain a wish to retire further from the scene of Civilization. Many of the most enlightened of them are beginning to discover that the Money which they receive for their . . . land produces amongst the . . . Indians a visible degeneracy from their fathers."[16]

Nemacolin represents two aspects of this picture. On the one hand, he was distressed by the loss of lands held by his father, and his descendants no doubt participated in the migrations described above. On the other hand, he also participated in events that led to the establishment of the National Road and thus contributed to the transportation progress that was part of its legacy.

The pathways that Native Americans were forced to follow to the Far West extended considerably beyond the National Road and its terminus in Vandalia, Illinois. The struggle that Native Americans faced continued long after the wagons and stages had left the National Road. The issues that are derived from that migration are an important part of the agenda of the United States today. A full discussion of those issues is beyond the scope of this account. Nevertheless, it seems appropriate to note that the National Road, whose route was first blazed by Nemacolin in 1752, along with many other roads, had a profound impact upon the destiny of Native American people in the United States. In the course of marking the unique heritage of the National Road, one may appropriately consider the efforts that have been made in our time to better that destiny and the need for yet further effort to achieve that end.[17]

The Women's Rights Movement

The women who traveled the National Road to find opportunity for their families in the heartland, to share in the work of their husbands, or to enjoy a summer tour of the West generally did not have the right to own property, manage their financial affairs, or vote for the presidents and legislators who were responsible for the future of the road on which they traveled. The National Road was the site of a number of events that were part of the initial efforts in Indiana and elsewhere to form organizations that would advocate for the civil and political rights of women. In October 1851, for example, the Congregational Friends called a convention to be held in Dublin, Indiana, an old pike town, the following year. Assembling in 1852, the convention was attended by both women and men and adopted resolutions for "political, social and financial rights for women." Moreover, its attendees established the Indiana Women's Rights Association, which ultimately became the Indiana Women's Suffrage Association.[18]

The life of Dr. Mary Thomas is illustrative of the early search for social change that accompanied the migration west along the National Road, the settlement of new communities on or near the road in the early nineteenth century, and the "new birth of freedom" derived from the Civil War. Raised as a Quaker in Maryland and for a time a resident of the District of Columbia, where her father took her to hear debates in Congress, Mary Thomas moved in her teens to Ohio and met and married Dr. Owen Thomas, also a Quaker. She graduated from Penn's Medical College for Women in Philadelphia in 1854 and eventually moved with her husband to Richmond, Indiana, where she resided and practiced for the rest of her life. During the Civil War, she provided medical care to wounded soldiers. After the war, she became a physician for the Home for Friendless Women in Richmond, was elected a member of the Wayne County Medical Society, and was the second female admitted to membership in the American Medical Association. She was active in the women's rights movement and became president of the Indiana Women's Suffrage Association.[19]

The National Road served as a site for the 1852 convention in Dublin, Indiana, presumably a convenient location because the road afforded a more easily traveled route. However, the road's role may be somewhat broader. It had served as a conduit for the earlier migration of Quakers to Indiana, perhaps influenced by the opportunity to settle in a new region of the country that would afford greater freedom to exercise their faith. In Indiana they founded a number of significant Quaker communities along the road. Thomas Schlereth, in his book *Reading the Road*, points to the number of small towns along the National Road that were founded by Quakers, including Richmond, Philadelphia, Greenfield, and Plainfield. Schlereth notes that College Avenue in Richmond, which borders Earlham College, was "believed to have the most Quakers per square foot of any street in the country." It is therefore not surprising, given the contribution of Quakers to the launching of the women's rights movement, that the 1852 convention convened along the National Road.[20]

In succeeding decades, as the National Road fell into desuetude and became the subject of nostalgia, fundamental change gripped the United States. A great civil war divided the land. That war was followed by a constitutional revolution from which emerged the Thirteenth, Fourteenth, and Fifteenth Amendments. They freed the slaves and afforded them civil rights. In the Nineteenth Amendment, and through interpretation of the Fourteenth Amendment, women gained suffrage and civil rights. Other laws were enacted to protect the rights of Native Americans. That progress in turn generated the need for further action to overcome the vestiges of slavery and discrimination. Responding to that need required a massive infusion of national investment delivered over many generations through educational, health, income maintenance, and other federally provided services and benefits. The urgent call for such investment was recognized by nineteenth-century presidents such as Abraham Lincoln, Ulysses S. Grant, and Rutherford B. Hayes, among others. It was given effect by twentieth-century presidents such as Franklin Roosevelt, Harry Truman, Dwight Eisenhower, John F. Kennedy, and Lyndon B. Johnson and further amplified and modified during the administrations of the chief executives who followed.[21] The constitutional underpinnings for this flow of assistance to give effect to the legal and constitutional changes made as a result of the Civil War were crafted in part through the constitutional history made by the National Road precedent, as described in chapters 3–7. The generations following the African American and Native American populations and the American women whose lives were affected by the National Road in the nineteenth century thus came to be beneficiaries of the National Road experience in the twentieth century. That process continues in the twenty-first century.

Part III

THE DECLINE AND REVIVAL OF THE ROAD, ITS ROLE AS A PRECURSOR OF THE INTERSTATE SYSTEM, AND ITS PLACE AS A NATIONAL SYMBOL

CHAPTER 12

The Decline and Revival of the Road

At least five epochs of technological change regarding surface transportation dominated the course of the National Road:

1. The era of road and canal building, of which the National Road was a part, that occupied the United States in the early nineteenth century and reached its peak in 1835
2. The rise of the railroad from 1850 to 1890, a period during which the "iron horse" replaced the road and canal as the primary mode of commercial and passenger transportation
3. The era of federally assisted highways that responded to the introduction of the automobile in the early twentieth century
4. The development of a network of modern limited-access interstate highways ushered in by the Highway Act of 1956 and the construction of the Eisenhower Interstate Highway System
5. The post-interstate period[1]

Each of these major epochs significantly affected the National Road or the transportation arteries that succeeded it in the twentieth century. That road was itself the product of the early nineteenth-century road-and-canal era in the United States and was perhaps its most significant and celebrated icon. It dramatically reduced the time required for the movement of passengers and cargo between the East and the Midwest.[2]

The Railroad Era

The railroad offered still faster and more dependable transportation services, thus further bringing together these two sections of the country. It began to eclipse the old pike in the early 1850s, and the latter slowly became no more than a rural and local byway. In the twentieth century, however, first the bicycle and then the automobile reversed the National Road's fortunes and contributed to its revival in the form of U.S. 40. It is in that form that it continues to attract travelers in the twenty-first century. Running parallel in some places to U.S. 40 and in some segments incorporating it are two superhighways that are part of the interstate system, I-68 and I-70. That system reflects the culmination of the long progression of federal assistance to interstate road building in the United States that began with the 1806 legislation that initiated the National Road.

The impact of the railroad on the National Road was felt gradually. "In their initial form," Craig Colten observes, "the American railroads were merely short lines serving waterfront cities with passenger service, and were no threat to the well-established land and water routes of the 1830s. By the early 1850s, however, the railroads had made the first of several trans-Appalachian crossings and began to compete with their predecessors: the turnpikes, toll roads and canals."[3]

In 1842, the railroad reached Cumberland, Maryland. In 1853, it came, in the form of the Baltimore and Ohio Railroad, to Wheeling. Soon, it was wending its way across the prairies of Ohio, Indiana, and Illinois.[4] For the National Road, the railroad proved a formidable and ultimately triumphant competitor. Produce and other freight could be transported more quickly, and passengers could travel without the weather-related hazards and other discomforts that confronted travelers on the National Road. People began to prefer to ride behind a locomotive rather than journey in a stagecoach or Conestoga wagon. By 1863, the "railroads had captured all the cross country passenger and freight traffic to the Mississippi River."[5]

The age of the railroad was greeted with little enthusiasm by advocates of the National Road. Those with close business or commercial ties to the road utterly detested the railroad and sought to dismiss its possibilities in any way they could. The owner of the Stockton Stage Line, for example, mounted his horse and raced a train. He won, but the railroad continued to take business from the stage lines. Congressman Henry Beeson of Uniontown took to the floor of the House to protest the unemployment and economic damage that the railroad could bring in its wake. His plea was to no avail.[6] Despite the laments and protests, the new technology prevailed over the old. After 1848, tolls from the road began to decline progressively. Stage lines stopped running, and wagons declined in number. The road fell into desuetude and disrepair.[7]

The National Road had been a product of federal financial assistance in the form of federal appropriations and leadership, and the railroad also became a beneficiary of federal dollars and federal policy. By the late 1850s, President James Buchanan, who, as a member of Congress, had pressed to transfer the road to the states in 1835, had modified his strict constructionist views about a national system of transportation sufficiently to enable him to advocate a federally assisted transcontinental railroad as a commercial and national defense measure. Federal land grants were provided to stimulate railroad growth. Despite the pressures of the Civil War, in his 1862 State of the Union address President Lincoln took time to propose that Congress support a transcontinental railroad.[8] Colten summarizes the impact of these developments. "During the second half of the nineteenth century, the railroad landscape became associated with progress, urbanity and prosperity. From the small town grain elevator to the grand railroad hotel, the complex of features that characterized rail travel became the signatures of a society on the move."[9]

By the turn of the century the impact of this technological change was profound. In 1902, Rufus Rockwell Nelson, traveling by horse and carriage between Frederick, Maryland, and Brownsville, Pennsylvania, lamented the state of the old National Road: "The coming of the railroad a generation and a half ago consigned the National Pike to the limbo of abandoned things. During a recent trip over it, few travelers were to be met with. Old taverns fast falling to ruins gape on either side, and the toll-keeper has little to do, while most of the pike boys are dead or bending under the weight of years." Nelson found Cumberland, Maryland, "almost deserted" and Brownsville "left stranded on the shore that is washed by the sea of Buried Hopes."[10]

Twentieth-century Revival: The Bicycle, the Automobile, and the National Old Trails Association and Related Organizations

Technology, however, continued to generate change. If the decline of the National Road had been ushered in by one new mode of transportation, its revival was signaled by the advent of two others. The arrival of the safety bicycle brought cyclists to the route of the National Road. They traversed its length, made hundred-mile rides, and frightened the horses. They also became an early force for improved roads. The League of American Wheelmen was one strong advocacy group that joined the call. With the advent of the automobile came renewed efforts in this direction.

A number of other organizations also took up the cause of good roads. Among them was the National Old Trails Association. It advocated for a national transcontinental highway that would follow the routes of some of the early roads that had been constructed in the nineteenth century, including the National Road and the Santa Fe Trail. This association called for the federal government to take the lead in the project by supplying funds and arranging for the construction of the road. During the period leading up to the adoption of Federal Aid Road Act of 1916, the organization, under the leadership of a number of its presidents including Judge J. M. Lowe, strongly advocated for legislation along these lines. Aligned with the National Old Trails Association was the American Automobile Association. Both groups wanted the federal government to build national, interstate highways and opposed the movement for federal aid to augment state highway funds for farm-to-market arteries and other projects selected by the state highway departments. In advocating its position, the Old Trails Association invoked the history of the National Road in calling for a more expansive federal role. The role of the association, which has been extensively chronicled by Richard Weingroff in a study for the U.S. Department of Transportation, is discussed more fully in chapter 14, which explores the place of the National Road as a national symbol.[11]

Congress responded to the call for better roads by appropriating funds to carry out an "inquiry" regarding the construction of roads in a way that would once more involve the federal government. Accordingly, the Office of Road Inquiry was formed in the U.S. Department of Agriculture to carry out this task. By 1916, over a century after the adoption of the 1806 law that initiated the National Road, Congress produced legislation providing a framework for a renewed federal role in road construction throughout the United States. The 1916 legislation constituted another chapter in the saga that had begun with the National Road and ushered in a series of federal legislative developments that significantly expanded the role of the federal government in infrastructure investment during the remainder of the twentieth century.[12]

The Federal Aid Road Act of 1916

The act that Congress passed and President Wilson signed in 1916, on the eve of World War I, established a new framework for federal-state cooperation that built upon, and in a sense improved upon, the earlier National Road legislation. The Federal Aid Road Act of 1916 provided for federal assistance in the context of state-owned and state-administered roads. Its focus was on post roads. It required, as a condition of receipt of federal funds, that states maintain the road for which federal funds were provided. It forbade tolls. Finally, it provided a formula for nationwide distribution of the funds among the states, so that legislators could not complain that they were being forced to support a solely regional project, as had been the case in the National Road era.[13]

The steps that led to the enactment of the 1916 Act provide some insights regarding the challenges confronting proponents of a federal role in the first two decades of the twentieth century, one hundred years after comparable challenges had faced the nation as it struggled to build the National Road. It was as if the nation had to relive the difficult process again. In 1835, the debates over the National Road had concluded with the transfer of that artery to the states. Roads were largely regarded as a state responsibility through the second half of the nineteenth century. In this context the roads deteriorated. Gen. Roy Stone, the government's engineer for road inquiry, sadly concluded that bad roads constituted a national "disease." In 1902, legislation was introduced in Congress to provide for federal aid, but it was not enacted. Constitutional and fiscal objections blocked it.[14]

An important factor in the movement toward better roads early in the twentieth century was the rural free delivery of the U.S. mail. In the late 1890s, the Post Office Department established experimental delivery routes in several towns in West Virginia. The absence of good roads presented a major obstacle to expansion of this service, despite the efforts of the postmaster general to encourage the installation of improved roads. Bills were introduced in successive sessions of Congress to provide federal funds to improve rural free-delivery routes. A major question, however, was whether this aid should be focused on maintaining and improving local roads or on building long-distance interstate highways. The American Automobile Association took the position that the main roads should come first. In 1913, Congress approved an experimental program regarding the improvement of post roads.[15]

Richard Weingroff of the U.S. Department of Transportation cites the factors that fostered a more extensive federal role regarding road investment, including support of farmers who wanted more efficient delivery of mail, the introduction of the automobile in the first decade of the twentieth century, and the founding of the American Association of State Highway Officials (AASHO).[16]

In 1916, the House and Senate took up a serious federal-aid bill. A proposal of the AASHO to provide $75 million over a five-year period to be apportioned to the states under a complex formula was incorporated into the Senate bill. Under that bill, states would establish highway agencies. These agencies would submit highway projects to the secretary of agriculture for approval. The Bankhead Bill passed the Senate. In the House, the bill supported by Congressman Dorsey Shackleford of Missouri proposed a $25 million federal-aid program. The bill that passed and became law on July 11, 1916, provided for a $75 million program of federal aid for highways over a five-year period, apportioned funds to the states on the basis of area, population, and post-road mileage, and was limited to post roads. The bill provided for a federal matching formula. The federal government would pay half the cost of a project. Unlike the pre-1835 situation of the National Road, under the 1916 act the states would bear the responsibility for maintenance, as a condition of federal project approval. The act in part represented the resolution of a debate between those like the National Old Trails Association, which advocated the construction by the federal government of national interstate and transcontinental roads, and those who favored federal aid to state highway agencies with the states responsible for construction and routing of the ensuing federally aided highways. The outcome of the dispute tilted in favor of the federal aid approach. President Wilson lauded the work of Congress represented by the act, stating the act would "add greatly to the convenience and economic welfare of all the people, and strengthen the national foundations."[17]

The bill had benefited from the contributions of Logan Waller Page, the then director of the Office of Public Roads. Under the bill, Page's office would approve state proposals. As Weingroff describes it, the 1916 act "served the social function of enhancing life in rural America by focusing on rural post roads rather than the long-distance roads favored by AAA and many others." In this framework, over a century after Congress enacted the original National Road legislation, Congress was again back in the business of meaningful support for internal improvements in the form of highways on a serious and nationwide basis. Moreover, the enactment of the 1916 act by a Democratic Congress and a Democratic president reflected the realignment of the Democratic Party as a proponent and supporter of public investment, as well as broad-scale federal regulation in such areas as antitrust legislation, Wilson had signaled this shift in his inaugural address in 1913 and in earlier pronouncements. The 1916 act, while perhaps modest in its own right, reflected a new recognition of the need for a federal role in financing road construction throughout the United States, a policy that had first engaged the nation in the National Road era of the early nineteenth century.[18]

The impact of the legislation was significant. It "provided," Karl Raitz observed, "monetary support toward construction of a hard-surfaced cross-country road network." Nevertheless, the 1916 act did not bring instant relief to America's motorists. In 1923, those traveling from Pittsburgh to Chicago were forced by road conditions to forgo the most direct route and travel the National Road from Washington, Pennsylvania, to Marshall, Illinois, and then head north to Chicago.[19]

Despite the change, the National Road did not become a forgotten chapter of American history. In 1916, as Congress was passing new road legislation, Robert Bruce took stock of the National Road by driving its eastern segment from Cumberland, Maryland, to Wheeling, West Virginia. He produced a book that recorded his travels. He noted that the road "has been from the first a unique American institution, and was for many years a vital factor in the life, politics and industry of the country." His book provides a brief snapshot of the road at the time that Congress was beginning to play a greater role in aid to road construction on a nationwide basis in the early twentieth century. Bruce described all the major historic sites such as taverns and bridges along the old pike in towns such as Frostburg, Grantsville, Addison, Somerfield, Uniontown,

Brownsville, Washington, and Wheeling. He paid appropriate homage to Fort Necessity, to Braddock's grave, and to Jumonville Glen. The two-lane road he found to be largely of macadam construction with some occasional stretches of brick. Here and there, unlike Rufus Nelson, he observed that the roadway was in "perfect condition." His photographs show that it was shared by both automobile and horse-drawn carriage traffic. He noted that the Cumberland-to-Wheeling drive had evolved into a "comfortable day's run." It seems clear that, despite the barriers that had confronted it, the National Road had survived to become a historic avenue of the automobile age.[20]

A 1918 report of the director of the United States Bureau of Public Roads, then Logan Waller Page, to the secretary of agriculture, in whose department the bureau was lodged, gives the reader some sense of the concerns of that bureau under the 1916 act. It included passages on the "war work" of the bureau in the form of such activities as supervision of highway construction at military facilities. With respect to the Federal Aid Road Act (the 1916 act), Page's report claimed progress in obtaining necessary state assents, the review of state highway department specifications, plans, contract and bond forms, the preparation of standard forms, and the financing of multiple highway projects. At the end of federal fiscal year 1918, federally assisted construction work was in progress in thirty states. Project agreements were entered into during the fiscal year involving approximately $6 million in federal aid, roughly the nominal amount of the federal funds spent on the National Road during its thirty-year status as a national project. What had changed, however, was the transformation of the relationship from a federally financed and federally constructed road project to the establishment of an ongoing partnership between the federal administering agency with stewardship over federal highway appropriations and the respective state agencies responsible for administering grants made to the states with those funds.[21]

Page's office faced serious challenges in the administration of the 1916 act, including the establishment of standards for the highways to be built in part with federal funds. Under the legislation, the secretary of agriculture had the authority to approve road types and standards, subject to the requirement that the project should be "substantial." Most of the miles submitted for federal aid were for gravel, sand-clay, or graded earth roads. For the most part, standards were set by the states through state agreement and the involvement of AASHO.[22]

The Federal Aid Highway Act of 1921

The 1916 act was succeeded by the Federal Aid Highway Act of 1921. It was a broader piece of highway legislation that seemed to further regenerate, although in a different mode, the federal role in infrastructure assistance that had been begun in 1806 with the first National Road legislation. In some respects, it reflected the 1806 legislation. It provided a framework for federal funds for highways, delivered some broad instructions as to road construction methods, and promoted interstate travel. In a number of other respects, however, the 1921 law demonstrated that the nation had learned much in the 115 years that had passed since Thomas Jefferson had signed the first National Road bill.[23]

Much of that learning had taken place in light of the experience with the administration of the Federal Aid Road Act of 1916 and problems encountered with the movement of personnel and equipment during World War I. One problem was the lack of emphasis on a "system of national highways under federal control," a concept that must have seemed to some a throwback to the era of the National Road. The eastern and north-central states pushed for such a system. Southern states, where counties played a larger role in road construction and administration, disagreed. In addition to these problems, states faced the challenge of a shortfall of funds under the 1916 act. To address these concerns, a bill was drafted with the assistance of AASHO providing that a state receiving federal aid must designate a "state highway system" embracing not more than 7 percent of all roads in the state. The federal funds would be targeted on this segment. Three-sevenths of the 7 percent would involve roads that were "interstate in character." The bulk of the federal funds could be directed to projects of this nature.[24]

These provisions were incorporated into the 1921 act. In effect, if not in terms, they pushed the federal government back into the role that it had played in the days of the National Road, albeit not in the same manner. Federal funds would again be directed at the construction of interstate highways. The National Road was such a highway. But, this time the federal government would not build the road; it would provide grants to state agencies that would have the responsibility to apply the funds to road-building activities that met the requirements of the program.[25]

Richard Weingroff, in *Clearly Vicious as a Matter of Policy: The Fight against Federal Aid*, summarizes the key provisions of the 1921 act as follows:

> Federal-aid highway funds would now be restricted to roads contained in a designated system of Federal-aid highways. The system would comprise up to 7 percent of all rural public roads in each State, but three sevenths of the system must consist of roads that were "interstate in character." . . . The roads that were "interstate in character" would have a right of way of "ample width and a wearing surface of an adequate width which shall not be less than eighteen feet, unless, in the opinion of the Secretary of Agriculture, it is rendered impracticable by physical conditions, excessive costs, probable traffic requirements, or legal obstacles."[26]

Weingroff further assesses the critical significance of the 1921 act in the following terms:

> The Federal Aid Highway Act of 1921 settled the long running dispute between advocates of long-distance roads and farm-to-market roads. The Federal Government would not build a system of national roads, as proposed by the AAA and other advocates. But it also would not devote its road funds to the county roads favored by farm advocates or let State and local officials use the funds on any road. That the legislation rejected the calls for Federal construction of national roads was a tribute to the efforts of MacDonald and others to make the Federal-aid highway program work, and their ability to find a compromise that both sides could consider a victory.[27]

In other respects, the 1921 act also marked new approaches that distinguished the system from that that had applied during the National Road experience:

1. The law provided for a formula to apportion money to all the states; the legislation would not suffer from the charge that it was a regional project for the benefit of one section of the country. Moreover, the legislation provided that the construction of the federally aided highways would be administered by state agencies rather than by federal officials as had been the case with the National Road.
2. The law specifically required that the states agree to *maintain* the roads with their own money, as a condition of receipt of assistance; the legislation would not suffer, because Congress would not be required to keep in repair those highways that it initially helped finance.
3. The law forbade tolls; the law would not suffer from a battle over the right of the federal government to charge tolls.
4. Priorities were set as between local and interstate highways.
5. The federally assisted highways were to be basically state administered, at least as long as the state lived up to its obligation to maintain the roads in question; projects would be selected by the state and approved by the secretary of agriculture (the responsible federal official). Thus, the legislation would not be subject to battles that challenged the authority of the federal government to assume an administrative role that seemed properly to be one that belonged to the states.
6. The legislation in effect made clear that the state maintained ownership of the roads within its borders, notwithstanding the provision of federal aid.[28]

In effect, while building on the precedent that the National Road afforded, the 1921 legislation provided a new framework that recognized principles of federalism, once fought over in the 1820s and 1830s with respect to the National Road, while providing a promising basis for federal-state cooperation in the area of transportation.

Federal Aid Legislation in the Coolidge and Hoover Administrations

While the 1921 act resolved a number of the major issues that imperiled the progress of federal-aid highway legislation, it did not put an end to controversy regarding the subject. Calvin Coolidge, who succeeded to the presidency upon the death of Warren Harding in 1923, gave his support to the continuation of a program of federal aid to highways but expressed misgivings about extending the concept to other arenas such as education and welfare. Weingroff observes: "The President's problem was with the Federal-aid concept, which was used for highways, but also for activities as diverse as vocational education, cooperative agriculture extension work, maternity and infant hygiene, and industrial rehabilitation." The cause of federal assistance for highway construction had not lacked for advocates in the era of the National Road. It did not lack for them in the mid-1920s. AASHO defended the concept as a "public necessity indisputably national in character." In support of this perspective, the organization reached for precedent to the time of the National Road. It cited James Madison's support for a federal role in road construction in his 1815 annual message as well as John C. Calhoun's eloquent defense of the concept in his capacity as Monroe's secretary of war. Though unimpressed with these arguments, Coolidge still signed into law federal-aid highway legislation to cover fiscal years 1926 through 1929.[29]

Herbert Hoover, who followed Coolidge to the White House in 1929, was obliged to grapple with the Great Depression, which began that year. Federal aid to highways played an important role in his initial efforts to respond to the crisis. The Emergency Construction Act of 1930 was the legislative vehicle for authorizing that role. Thus, federal aid for infrastructure became an instrument of pump priming in times of national economic distress. Later in his term, Hoover sought to take steps to balance his budgets by reducing highway-related spending. In order to achieve fiscal discipline, Congress in 1932 enacted a gasoline tax, not tied to the funding of new highway construction but aimed at increasing general tax revenue for budget-strengthening purposes. Later, that tax would take the form of a dedicated source of revenue for highway construction.[30]

Franklin Roosevelt

The election of 1932 brought Franklin D. Roosevelt to the White House to lead a nation still struggling with a massive economic depression. Roosevelt's New Deal generated a sea of change in the role of government in the economy. That role embraced the use of federal-aid funding for infrastructure as a mechanism of economic recovery. In 1934, under the National Industrial Recovery Act, highway funding was used as a means of stimulating employment on road construction projects, apparently to good effect. In 1937, conceiving that recovery was in progress, Roosevelt pulled back from such pump priming, but was soon forced by economic circumstances to return to public works spending as a means of economic stabilization.[31]

In the 1940s, with war approaching, FDR came to advocate for a program of national defense highways as part of the overall defense-mobilization effort. As we have seen, this tie between federal aid highway construction and national defense was not a new theme in American history. It had been sounded in the National Road era. Albert Gallatin, in his landmark 1808 report to Congress on surface transportation infrastructure, had recognized the relevance of federally assisted highway construction to national defense. Roosevelt's advocacy of the concept was consistent with Gallatin's vision. However, Roosevelt's position sparked a major battle with Congress over the contours of the Defense Highway Act of 1941 and the respective roles of Congress and the administration in approving highway projects, a battle described in detail in Richard Weingroff's account of the matter.[32]

As the war came to a close, Roosevelt again placed highways in the forefront of efforts to avoid a postwar depression, which were largely successful. He set in motion steps to explore the advantages of a system of national superhighways. An interagency committee was established to explore the possibility, and the Federal Aid Highway Act of 1944 was enacted with a distinct intention (among many others) to try to foster it. Building on the National Road experience and other precedents, the Federal Aid Highway Act of 1944 was enacted, carrying with it enthusiasm for the superhighway goal. However, the effort stalled, and the highways built did not constitute a true national interstate system of superhighways. By the time of Roosevelt's death, the series of landmark acts beginning with the 1916 act had clearly established a body of federally financed infrastructure, under the federal-aid framework, that was destined to last, expand, and grow. Despite the demise of the National Road in the nineteenth century, the establishment of a system of interstate highways had become, if not a legislative reality, a meaningful concept regarding which debate could proceed. More was yet to come.[33]

The National Grid System, U.S. 40, and the National Road

In 1925 a national grid system for numbering interstate highways was formulated. This system arose from the work of the Joint Board on Interstate Highways, established by the U.S. secretary of agriculture in response to the confusion generated by the multiplicity of locally and unsystematically named routes all over the United States. The roads in question constituted about 2.8 percent of the then total existing road mileage. The new grid system called for east-west highways with numbers ending in zero. North-south routes had odd numbers. The plan was submitted to AASHO, as the representative of the state highway departments and in recognition of state jurisdiction over the roads. The plan was adopted, with modifications suggested by AASHO in 1927. The numbering system is still controlled by AASHO.[34]

U.S. 40, which was incorporated into the new grid system, began in Atlantic City, made its way to Baltimore, and from there it proceeded to Hagerstown before arriving at Cumberland, Maryland. It then followed in a general sense the route of the National Road from Cumberland to Vandalia, from where it continued on to St. Louis and west of the Mississippi to San Francisco, California. In effect, U.S. 40 became a twentieth-century National Road for the automobile age. Today, when speaking of the National Road, people often identify it with or as U.S. 40.[35]

U.S. 40 was more than a product of the 1925 national route-numbering process that grew out of the work of the Bureau of Public Roads. In 1947, Phillip Jordan, driving it by auto and tractor trailer from Columbus, Ohio, wrote: "U.S. 40 never sleeps." Jordan linked it with the National Road. He said: "At no time in the National Road's long life of more than 140 years has it been busier." For Jordan, it was "a work road and a hauling route as well as a pleasant thoroughfare for swift running passenger cars." It was also "lined with new taverns, some doing business where Jacksonian taverns stood."[36]

An engaging survey of U.S. 40 in the era of the mid-1950s, provided by George R. Stewart in his book *U.S. 40: Cross Section of the United States of America*, also made the connection between the twentieth-century U.S. highway and the National Road. Stewart gave his readers, in both words and photographs, a transcontinental tour of U.S. 40, beginning in Atlantic City, New Jersey, and terminating in San Francisco, California. The part of that journey that encompasses the route from Cumberland, Maryland, to Vandalia, Illinois, appropriately emphasized the ties between the old National Road and U.S. 40. At the time of Stewart's journey, the Pennsylvania Department of Highways estimated that 50 percent of U.S. 40 in Pennsylvania was "relocated" from the

National Road. But, these relocations did not negate the old pike ties. Stewart concluded that "[o]n the whole U.S 40 still follows very closely the line of the National Road." Moreover, Stewart's words and pictures focused on the bridges, taverns, tollhouses, and public buildings that lined the old pike and that still survived almost 150 years after it was initiated in 1806.[37]

Stewart's observations are supplemented in Tom Schlereth's account, "A Road Guide to U.S. 40 in Indiana," found in his book *Reading the Road* (1997). Schlereth dates the U.S. 40 era as 1925 to 1960, which he regards as the golden age of the highway and as part of an "exuberant era of highway building." That era is memorialized in the road signs, hotels, and art deco motels that lined the road and became part of its typography, as well as the two-lane segments and the midcentury diners and White Castles.[38]

In the segment of U.S. 40 between Addison, Pennsylvania, and Washington, Pennsylvania, U.S. 40 and the National Road seem particularly intermingled in the fashion that Stewart observed. Vestiges of both are in evidence in Stewart's account. The National Road is represented by the surviving taverns and other edifices of its era, such as the tollhouses in Addison and outside Uniontown, the S-bridge in Claysville west of Washington, and the artifacts in the Interpretive Center at Farmington, as well as the Dunlop Bridge in Brownsville. At the same time, one can see a few mid-twentieth-century art deco motels of the U.S. 40 era in the Indiana segment.[39]

More than fifty years after Stewart's journey, Karl Raitz gave a vivid account of the evolution of the "U.S. 40 roadside" and the nature of its culture in the 1990s. He began it by acknowledging the contribution of the combustion engine: "The internal combustion engine is the first of a host of contingent technical and social ideas that, taken together, comprise a cascade of revolutionary inventions the product of which was no less than a radical transformation of American society." A part of that impact was felt on the National Road: "The engine's direct application to the truck and the automobile stimulated widespread alterations along the old National Road corridor and produced a new composite landscape: the US 40 roadside."[40]

Among the components of that "composite landscape," Raitz identified town and urban congestion, off-street parking facilities to combat the congestion and attract customers, roadside gas stations outside the town center to permit motorists to fill up without having to navigate an unfamiliar town center, auto camps, motor courts and, finally, motels and motel chains, the drive-in landscape, and the truck stop landscape. He concluded: "The conversion of the National Road into US 40 was the result of a complex combination of technical inventions and contingent social, economic and political processes."[41]

As did its predecessor, the National Road, U.S. 40 became a major east-west cross-country route. But its route was traversed by motor cars and trucks rather than stages and wagons. By 1926, 120 years after the initiation of the National Road, twenty million automobiles were registered in the United States. Seventeen hundred cars and trucks were daily traversing U.S 40 in eastern Ohio by the late 1920s.[42]

It is thus in the form of U.S. 40 that the National Road was revived in the twentieth century and survives to this day. As Phillip Jordan observed in 1947, the 2006 traveler along Route 40 could expect to pass many of the taverns that fed and entertained travelers along the National Road and still stand (or serve) today. Along Route 40 in many places one can see signs informing motorists that they are on the "historic National Road." The history of the National Road and a ride along Route 40 are closely intertwined.[43]

The Revenue Act of 1932 and the Gasoline Tax

In 1932, the nation was in the throes of a massive depression. President Herbert Hoover was faced with the need to confront this economic catastrophe. Among other concerns was the danger that the loss of federal revenues caused by massive unemployment and industrial dislocation would bring unprecedented deficits that would bankrupt the country. Hoover sought some means to increase federal revenues, while at the same time cutting government expenditures, in an effort to avoid what he regarded as fiscal ruin. Included in the package of revenue enhancements in the Revenue Act of 1932 was an excise tax on gasoline pegged at one cent per gallon. This tax, the administration believed, would help to fund a program of public works in the form of the highways, thus creating new jobs that would address the massive unemployment rates that threatened national stability and caused widespread economic and social misery. The bill was signed into law on June 6, 1932.[44]

Richard Weingroff has provided a brief history of the federal gasoline tax based upon a history of the tax by James Stouder Sweet entitled "The Federal Gasoline Tax at a Glance: A History." The National Industrial Recovery Act of 1933 extended the tax despite opposition from the highway interests. The Revenue Act of 1941 made the tax permanent and increased it to 1.5 cents. The Revenue Act of 1951 increased the tax to two cents as a revenue source during the Korean War. Initially, the tax was not dedicated to pay for road construction but was a general revenue measure.[45]

The gasoline tax represented a major innovation through which the federal government was ultimately able to tap a resource that would enable it to obtain funds from highway users in order to assist highway construction. It will be recalled that the inability or unwillingness of the federal government to impose a national user tax in the form of federally charged tolls had essentially brought to an end the first experiment in federal road building and road funding that that great artery represented. The gasoline tax was met with opposition, particularly by organizations that represented highway users, but it survived efforts to repeal it, and some two decades later it became the basis for the Highway Trust Fund that later enabled the nation to embark upon the interstate highway system.[46]

During the Great Depression road building and federal assistance to stimulate it became incorporated into the nation's efforts to restore the economy. Aid to the states became part of "a massive program of emergency public works." Under the National Industrial Recovery Act of 1933, $400 million was made available in the form of grants to states for highway construction, including urban streets that were extensions of the federal-aid system. Over 160,000 jobs were provided. With successive legislation, a billion dollars was "pumped" into highway construction in the period between 1933 and 1938 and 54,000 additional miles were added. Senator Carl Hayden of Arizona was a leader in this effort. The labor market aspects of the early-republic internal-improvement experience, the experience celebrated by John Quincy Adams, were being revived under twentieth-century federal-aid legislation to confront a nationwide economic crisis of that era.[47]

Thus, in addition to the geographic, social, and cultural incidents identified by those who traveled and celebrated U.S. 40 as the early twentieth-century version of the National Road, among them Stewart, Schlereth and Raitz, the first third of the twentieth century saw the beginnings of a road network that would eventually evolve into a modern interstate system of surface transportation infrastructure known as the Dwight D. Eisenhower Interstate Highway System, itself a model of sustainable national investment.

The National Road, the Creation of the Dwight D. Eisenhower Interstate Highway System, and the Post-Interstate Era

The Origins of the Dwight D. Eisenhower Interstate Highway System

During World War II, road construction became an important part of the military effort. After the war the great increase in automobile production helped to drive the continuing need for new and better roads. The production of automobiles increased from approximately seventy thousand in 1945 to almost 4 million in 1948. In 1947, 37 million vehicles were registered. This growth helped to drive the need for new and improved roads across the country. With growing urban congestion, Congress came to earmark funds for road construction in urban areas and for secondary roads.[1]

At the same time, the postwar period provided an impetus for advancing the then existing interstate highway system. An approximately forty-thousand-mile interstate network was projected. It included a route that tracked in part the line of the old National Road and its U.S. 40 counterpart. Nevertheless, inadequacy continued to plague the interstate system. The concept of limited access was not widely practiced. The Cold War and the struggle against Communism found the country ill-prepared in terms of road construction. The nation turned to toll roads as a solution that involved the expansion of the Pennsylvania Turnpike, built during the war, and the construction of turnpikes in Maine, New Hampshire, and New Jersey, without federal aid.[2]

At this stage, in 1954, President Dwight D. Eisenhower sought the assistance of the states in formulating what he called "a grand plan for a properly articulated system that solves the problem of speedy, safe transcontinental travel" among other major goals. The issues that the nation faced in giving effect to the president's plan included the question of tolls and toll roads, a conundrum that led to the termination of federal participation in the National Road in 1835 and in years following. A 1955 report reaffirmed the general principle that federally assisted roads should be toll free but contemplated the inclusion of some toll roads in the interstate system, where they already existed on the routes of that system. To implement President Eisenhower's call for a "grand plan," a federal interagency committee under Gen. Lucius Clay was appointed. It produced a blueprint calling for an over $100 billion program. In 1955, Eisenhower sent a highway bill to Congress calling for the funding of an interstate system through the issuance of bonds, the interest on which would be derived from proceeds of the federal taxes on fuel and lubricants. Legislation did not immediately emerge in the form that the president proposed.[3]

However, in June 1956, Congress finally passed and President Eisenhower signed the Federal Aid Highway Act of 1956, which provided for the massive and highly effective and popular interstate highway system, a network of modern controlled-access, multilane superhighways that would cross the United States, east and west and north and south. President Eisenhower was the moving force in the establishment of this major highway system. It involved cooperative federalism in that the federal government contributed the major share of the funds and a formula designed to achieve their equitable distribution. The federal government generally provided up to 90 percent of the cost, and the states undertook to construct and maintain the interstate highways. With respect to tolls, "[t]he decision reached in the 1956 Act was that toll roads, bridges, and tunnels could be included in the Interstate System if they met the System standards and if their inclusion promoted development of an interstate system." The 1956 act created the Federal Highway Administration (FHWA) to administer the interstate system. The Department of Transportation was established in 1966 to coordinate the various transportation agencies, including the FHWA. The interstate system had been originally authorized in 1944 to embrace 40,000 miles. The 1956 act increased it by 1,000 miles.

The Eisenhower Interstate System, despite problems of upkeep and funding, has made possible a highly efficient, modern system of highways to bind the country together in a way that evolved from the National Road experience. It is therefore fitting that the interstate system celebrated its fiftieth anniversary in 2006, the same year in which the National Road celebrated its two-hundredth anniversary. Both are key milestones in the direction of establishing adequate infrastructure in the United States.[4]

The origins of the interstate system have been appropriately marked by the U.S. Department of Transportation, in connection with the observance of the fiftieth anniversary of that system. Those origins go back to 1935 when President Roosevelt came to advocate for a system of transcontinental superhighways as part of the works program (described above) to stimulate the economy and job creation in a nation still suffering under the Great Depression. The Highway Act of 1938 commissioned a study of the subject. The idea also had the backing of state highway officials. Interestingly, the study of the background of the interstate system by Lee Mertz cites the National Road itself as a precedent for that system.[5] Among more recent antecedents of the interstate system is the Pennsylvania Turnpike, partially completed in 1940 and used extensively during World War II to facilitate the passage of military convoys through the Allegheny Mountains, reflecting the national defense aspects of the original National Road.[6]

The Role of Harry Truman and the Truman Administration

Richard Weingroff, in his work on Harry Truman entitled *The Man Who Loved Roads*, offers the following observation: "One of the little-known quirks of history is that Harry Truman could have been the father of the Interstate System." Truman's interaction, during his prepresidential years, with roads generally and with the National Road in particular is discussed below in chapter 14. What role did roads play during his presidency? Even before he entered into office, in April 1945 upon the death of Franklin Roosevelt, the enactment of the Federal Aid Highway Act of 1944 had provided for the designation of a 40,000-mile national system of interstate highways. However, inflationary pressures that followed the end of World War II precluded the Truman administration from supporting federally financed highway construction to the extent one might have predicted given his earlier involvement with the National Road as well as modern highway improvement issues.[7]

Therefore, in 1948, Truman could support only a "conservative" highway infrastructure program, and the Federal Aid Highway Act of that year authorized an appropriation at lower levels than that contained in the 1944 act. With respect to the designation of interstate highways, however, some progress was made. In 1947, the commissioner of public roads (Thomas MacDonald), together with administrator of the Federal Works Agency, announced the designation of over thirty-seven thousand miles of "future interstate highways." At the same time, funds were not specifically authorized for new interstate construction (building new interstate highways paralleling the existing system of "U.S. numbered highways"). Hence, substantial progress was not made on the construction, as distinguished from the designation, of the interstate system contemplated in the 1944 legislation. Rather, the priority was placed on meeting the mounting housing needs that had arisen in the wake of the war's end.[8]

In 1950, with a "highway boom" in the offing, Congress seemed prepared to authorize specific funding for the interstate system. However, the Korean War intervened. President Truman felt compelled to urge Congress to constrain nondefense spending. As Weingroff describes it, "The Federal-Aid Highway Act of 1950 authorized $500 million a year, with no special funding or enhanced matching ratio for the Interstate System." Ultimately, in 1952, in the Federal Aid Highway Act of that year, a token $25 million was appropriated for the interstate system for each year with a matching ratio of fifty-fifty. The president signed the legislation. It fell to the Eisenhower administration to greatly expand funding for the interstate program.[9]

Eisenhower's Leadership and the 1956 Legislation

A guiding force in the establishment of the system was President Eisenhower himself. Eisenhower is quoted as insisting that such a system is "as necessary to defense as it is to our national economy and personal safety." Once elected, he called for a "dramatic" plan to finance a system of highways that would not increase the national debt. He used his 1956 State of the Union address to press for passage of legislation that would provide a new network of interstate highways financed by the issuance of federal bonds. In that address, he said, "If we are ever to solve our mounting traffic problem, the whole interstate system must be authorized as one project to be completed approximately within the specified time. Only in this way can industry efficiently gear itself to the job ahead. . . . Furthermore, . . . the pressing nature of this problem must not lead us to solutions outside the bounds of sound fiscal management. As in the case of other pressing problems, there must be an adequate plan of financing."[10]

A major innovation involved in the Federal Aid Highway Act of 1965 was its financing mechanism. The act that the president signed in 1956 provided for a highway trust fund. Monies for the fund would largely be provided from the proceeds of a tax on motor fuels, as well as certain other federal excise taxes on highway-user products. From this fund, the federal government would furnish 90 percent of the costs of the system. The remaining 10 percent would come from the states. The system would thus be funded on a pay-as-you-go basis. As noted in the DOT historical study, this was "a landmark in Federal highway law since it established[,] for the first time, a linkage between federal excise taxes on highway users and Federal aid for highways." It was this "linkage" that had eluded the supporters of the National Road in the early nineteenth century. Another innovation was the application of the Davis Bacon Act to all contracts related to the system, thus ensuring that prevailing wages in the area would apply to that work. Finally, the program was to be treated as a single project under a unified authorization statute, the 1956 act.[11]

The legislative compromise that incorporated the use of a dedicated highway trust fund to be derived from the proceeds of the federal gasoline tax and other excise taxes was in part the product of efforts by Rep. Hale Boggs of Louisiana, who is credited with helping to craft and convert that concept to legislation. The legislation constituted "the largest highway construction program and, in fact, the largest single public works program ever undertaken by the United States."[12]

Richard Weingroff, in his comprehensive study *Clearly Vicious as a Matter of Policy*, provides a detailed description of the steps in the legislative process that led to the enactment of the act, including the various positions of the House, Senate, and administration on the nature of the program, particularly the approach to highway funding. Weingroff summarizes the administrative significance of the act as follows: "The legislation retained the structure of the Federal-aid highway program, but with construction of the Interstate System finally launched, the role of the BPR [Bureau of Public Roads] expanded. The importance of the Interstate System caused the BPR to expand its staff, not reduce it, while increased project oversight authority was delegated to its field office in each State, not decreased. The gas tax was increased to 3 cents, not eliminated as the States had desired." Indeed, at various stages of the legislative consideration leading up to enactment, President Eisenhower had fought to maintain adequate funding under the gas tax. For example, in his State of the Union address in January 1954, the president, speaking on the subject of national highways, strongly stated his views on the subject: "To protect the vital interest of every citizen in a safe and adequate highway system, the Federal Government is continuing its central role in the Federal Aid Highway Program. So that maximum progress can be made to overcome present inadequacies in the Interstate Highway System, we must continue the Federal gasoline tax at two cents per gallon. This will require cancellation of the ½ [cent] decrease which otherwise will become effective April 1st and will maintain revenues so that an expanded highway program can be undertaken." Eisenhower understood the connection between adequate federal revenues and sustainable national investment in infrastructure.[13]

It seems fair to suggest that the 1956 act, as finally adopted, through its reliance on a federal user tax and its insistence on pay-as-you-go had resolved some of the problems that had plagued the National Road, initiated 150 years earlier by Thomas Jefferson. The National Road had involved no user tax and was dependent upon federal appropriations (unless one regarded the 2 percent set aside from land sales as a user tax). It certainly depended upon no user tax for repairs. The "linkage" between federal excise taxes and federal aid was beyond the grasp of the supporters of the National Road. Nor had the National Road statutes involved the national distribution formula that accompanied the 1956 legislation. The authors of the 1956 legislation had succeeded in crafting a mechanism that had eluded the early-republic legislators, hard as they had struggled.[14] In providing new job opportunities incident to the construction of the interstate system, the 1956 interstate system legislators had carried forward a theme that John Quincy Adams had sounded more than one hundred years earlier when he had proclaimed that his favored program of internal improvement would provide jobs (and necessarily income) to thousands of workers, including the many who had come from abroad to work on such public projects as the National Road. In authorizing the "completion of an entire national system," rather than proceeding segment by segment as in the case of the National Road, the authors of the interstate system had also successfully broken with earlier traditions.[15]

The establishment of a nationwide system ensured that all states, not just one region, would participate. However, in its reach as an economic boost to the nation and in its purpose to provide for faster and safer ground transportation, it did reflect the efforts that began in Jefferson's day. Moreover, it embodied the recognition that adequate infrastructure was essential to the economic and social well-being of the American people.[16]

The Progress of the Interstate System after the Eisenhower Administration: Post-Highway Act of 1956; 1961–1989 (Kennedy to Reagan)

The administrations that followed the adoption and initiation of the 1956 act continued to implement the policy of maintaining and improving the federal-aid highway program and fulfilling the plans for the interstate highway system that Dwight Eisenhower had begun. The administrations of John F. Kennedy, Lyndon B. Johnson, Richard M. Nixon, Gerald Ford, Jimmy Carter, and Ronald Reagan all played significant roles in this saga, but their contributions covered the gamut of different perspectives and areas of focus, involving such emphases as safety, organization, consolidation, related transit concerns, energy conservation, and environmental considerations, as well as more traditional infrastructure issues. What emerged was a stronger, more extensive, more expensive, and more complex system of federally assisted highways. Despite the change that came with the passage of years, the underlying and fundamental issues would not have been unfamiliar to the founders and builders of the National Road.[17]

John F. Kennedy and the Role
of Infrastructure in the New Frontier

While he did not make interstate highways a centerpiece of his administration's program, as had President Eisenhower, President Kennedy readily included federal aid to highways in the body of concerns that he included in his aspirations for a "new society," or "new frontier." As Arthur Schlesinger Jr. puts it in his comprehensive account of the period, *A Thousand Days*, "The Nation at mid-century, urban, industrial, mobile, technologically kinetic, spiritually hyperbolic, confronted a swarm of hard and [insistent] problems." At the same time, the nation's labor force was largely employed and the national union was strong. A public education campaign was needed to spur action on a host of fronts. Kennedy undertook that campaign early in 1961. It included focus on health, education, and national resources. On February 28 of the year he sent Congress a message on highways. The message focused on the need for improvement and for continuing work to give effect to the promise of the 1956 act.[18]

Lyndon Johnson and the Establishment
of the U.S. Department of Transportation

Lyndon Johnson's contribution to the growth and progress of the system of interstate highways launched during the Eisenhower administration was largely organizational and safety oriented. At the same time, Johnson presided over significant progress in the laying out and construction of the interstate system. He saw transportation as one aspect of a broad program of national investment and renewal under the umbrella of the Great Society. Major and unprecedented investments in education, health care, the arts and humanities, and economic opportunity and antipoverty efforts were part of the Great Society. Landmark legislation emerged in the form of the Economic Opportunity Act of 1964, the Elementary and Secondary Education Act of 1965, the Higher Education Act of 1965, the Medicare and Medicaid legislation of 1965 and 1966, the National Foundation on the Arts and Humanities Act, and the Head Start Act—all products of this era of federal program growth.[19]

In 1966, Johnson turned his attention to transportation. He launched an effort to establish the new U.S. Department of Transportation that would bring, under one umbrella, federal activities administered by the federal government respecting highways, mass transit, aviation, and maritime matters. On March 2, 1966, Johnson sent to Congress his transportation message. It addressed the problems of the $120 billion industry, such as increasing congestion, accidents resulting in over fifty thousand fatalities annually, and aging plant and equipment. A bold and enlightened new agency could help to address these needs on a holistic basis. Johnson's plans called for the inclusion of the Federal Highway Administration in the new department along with a host of other transport agencies. This move put highway concerns in the heart of a cabinet agency, just as they were in the National Road era. Johnson was also able to sign in 1966 the National Traffic and Motor Vehicle Safety Act. While the safety and reorganization legislation expanded the federal enterprise, its effect was in balance largely positive. Robert Dallek observes: "The failures of the free enterprise system provoked an outcry for tough regulations which, according to safety experts, have played a crucial role in reducing highway deaths and injuries."[20]

The Nixon and Ford Administrations

Both the Nixon and Ford administrations made contributions to national legislative efforts to enhance investment in road infrastructure. In his signing statement on the occasion of the enactment of the Federal Aid Highway Act of 1973, President Nixon observed that it represented "a significant extension and reform of the Federal highway program." He cast himself as "a consistent supporter of that program over the years and as a strong proponent of improvements in that program embodied [in the act]." Among the improvements was a greater recognition of the need for mass-transit infrastructure, along with traditional highway needs. Nixon noted that one of the "most significant features" of the act "is that it allows the Highway Trust Fund to be used for mass transit capital improvements." He reiterated his support for this feature, explaining: "Under this act, for the first time, States and localities will have the flexibility they need to set their own transportation priorities. The law will enable them at last to relieve congestion and pollution problems by developing more balanced transportation systems where that is appropriate rather than locking them into further highway expenditures which sometimes make such problems even worse."[21]

On May 5, 1976, President Ford signed the Federal Aid Highway Act of 1976 but noted that the measure was an interim one, setting the stage for Congress to confront "critical" issues that Ford had posed. Ford's proposals included (1) restructuring the trust fund so as to confine it to the completion of the interstate system with other aid coming from the general fund, with a return of one cent of the gas tax to the states; (2) consolidation of categorical programs into three block grants; (3) placing emphasis in the interstate system on critical intercity routes; and (4) better control of federal spending for the program.[22]

Thus, by the bicentennial of the nation in 1976, bipartisan support for the federal-aid highway program was evident; emphasis was being placed on completion of the interstate system, alternative modes of federally assisted surface transportation infrastructure were advanced, and budgetary shortfalls were increasingly being identified. The Carter administration, while recognizing these issues, succeeded in identifying new issues that needed to be addressed in the context of advancing the nation's highway programs in a way that would present new challenges.

The Carter Administration, the Energy Challenge of the 1970s: Energy-Related Regulations under the Interstate Highway Program

President Jimmy Carter's principal contribution to the cause of federal aid for surface transportation related to energy and energy conservation. In his memoir *Keeping Faith,* Carter devotes a chapter to this critically important aspect of his presidency, one that continues to resonate thirty years after its completion. Carter saw the difficult effort to come to grips with the "energy crisis" of his time as the "moral equivalent of war." In an address to the nation on April 13, 1977, he said: "The energy crisis has not overwhelmed us, but it will if we do not act quickly." The core of this crisis concerned the overdependence of the United States on foreign oil. The dependence on foreign supplies of that substance had reached 50 percent by the time of his presidency. Much of the dependence was based on the use of gasoline in America's automobiles, many moving on federally aided or other categories of highways. Gasoline-driven autos had replaced the phaeton and Conestoga of the National Road. It had been a blessing for some, and a dedicated tax on gasoline had ultimately come to help finance highway growth. Carter described the problem as follows: "In the long run, available supplies of oil and natural gas would not be able to meet the demand for energy."[23]

In February 1977, dressed in a cardigan sweater and seated beside an open fire in the White House, Carter delivered his "fireside chat" on the subject. He said: "Our program will emphasize conservation . . . we will emphasize research on solar energy and other renewable energy sources." Despite multiple frustrations, Carter's program was largely enacted. Among other aspects of the program, the law authorized the government to impose speed limits on federally assisted highways, including the interstates. Noncompliant states would lose their federal funding. Application of these conditions triggered a lawsuit in which the federal conditions were upheld. The placement of conditions on the receipt of federal-aid highway funds was sustained. The case raises the sort of federalism issues that James Monroe had faced with respect to the National Road. How far can the federal government go in placing conditions on the use of federal-aid funds in order to carry out federal policies? The limitation, designed to carry out Carter's energy policies, was upheld as constitutional under the federal spending power; objections to the effect that the federal condition amounted to "coercion" and could not be affected under the spending power were rejected.[24]

Ronald Reagan and Federal Aid Highway Legislation

Two major highway measures characterized the Reagan administration. They provide a bridge to the so-called postinterstate period. The 1982 Surface Transportation Act, interestingly, increased the gas tax from four cents to nine cents per gallon in order to bolster the flow of dedicated revenues to the Highway Trust Fund, which had been established under the Federal Aid Highway Act of 1956. The act authorized one cent of this five-cent increase to be transferred to a mass-transit account that had been established under the Highway Trust Fund to help finance transit-related expenditures. The 1987 Surface Transportation and Uniform Relocation Assistance Act provided for highway programs through fiscal year 1991. It also extended the Highway Trust Fund through 1993. This set the stage for the enactment of the Inter-modal Surface Transportation Efficiency Act (ISTEA) in the administration of President George H. W. Bush, who succeeded President Reagan. On the other hand, Lou Cannon, who authored a major account of Reagan's presidency, notes that he did not take steps to "reduce U.S. dependency on foreign oil by imposing an oil import fee," and that "he did not accept the necessity of oil conservation." He also reversed the speed limits on federally assisted highways that had characterized the approach of the Carter administration.[25]

Thus, during the six administrations that followed after the landmark 1956 federal legislation that launched the Eisenhower Interstate System, that system had been largely constructed and laid out and was fully operative, a tribute to the perseverance and dedication of the nation in implementing Eisenhower's vision. But the nation had also faced multiple problems in related areas that needed to be confronted and that impacted upon the challenge of infrastructure investment, including the integration of transportation infrastructure programs within the jurisdiction of a single cabinet agency, the United States Department of Transportation, and the confrontation of energy availability, which was itself exacerbated by the growth of American mobility that came with improved highways and greater numbers of automobiles.[26]

The Continuing Influence of the National Road Experience and Federal Highway Legislation in the Last Two Decades, 1990–2009

In the early nineteenth century, at stake was the opening of an adequate road through the Allegheny Mountains that would carry commercial and passenger traffic to the west. This would bind the nation. Many obstacles were sur-mounted. The problems of financing the upkeep and repair of that road forced its return to the states so that they could keep it in repair through the collection of tolls. In the early twenty-first century, at stake is the maintenance and improvement of a system of federally assisted superhighways that will help the United States to maintain and improve its position in the global economy. Total transfer of financial responsibility for this road infrastructure to the states, as in 1835, is no long a viable option.[27]

ISTEA

Major federal highway legislation enacted during the period from 1990 to 2009 reflects the themes that characterize the history of the National Road that commenced in 1806 and the history of the interstate system that commenced in 1956, and it reflects the struggle to maintain and improve our system of surface transportation infrastructure in a way that comports with other priorities and aspirations of a mature but still growing nation. The Intermodal Surface Transportation Efficiency Act of 1991, Public Law No. 102-240, enacted during the administration of President George H. W. Bush, illustrates some of the themes and tensions that attend such national infrastructure investment in the post-interstate period.

The lofty declaration of policy in section 2 of the act reflects its key goals. Section 2 declares it to be the policy of the United States "to develop a National Intermodal Transportation System that is economically efficient and environmentally sound, provides the foundation for the nation to compete in the global economy, and will move people and goods in an energy efficient manner." The section announces that the Intermodal Transportation System "shall include a National Highway System which consists of the National System of Interstate and Defense Highways and those principal arterial roads which are essential for interstate and regional commerce and travel, national defense, intermodal transfer facilities, and international commerce and border crossings." Succeeding paragraphs refer to the achievement of national goals regarding "improved air quality, energy conservation, international competitiveness, and mobility" for elderly, disabled, and disadvantaged persons; "reduced traffic congestion, and *other* aspects of the quality of life in the United States; and adaptation of the system to "intelligent vehicles," "magnetic levitation systems," and other new technologies where possible. Section 2 further declares that the system, where appropriate, shall be financed by the Highway Trust Fund. Finally, section 2 states that the system "must be the centerpiece of a national investment commitment to create the new wealth of the Nation for the 21st century."[28]

In seeking to confront these issues, the House committee report on this legislation recognized the debt that Congress and the country owed to the lawmakers and administrators of 1806. "[I]n 1806, Congress authorized construction of the National Pike or Cumberland Road, which eventually lined the land west of the Allegheny Mountains and the eastern seaboard. At the same time, Congress established an important precedent by turning over the road to the respective states through which it ran." In signing the ISTEA into law on December 18, 1991, in Tarrant County, Texas, President George H. W. Bush used a cable spool at a construction site as a table. He emphasized the importance of the new act, declaring it to be "the most important transportation bill since President Eisenhower started the Interstate System 35 years ago." Thus, in its inception ISTEA was compared with the National Road and the Eisenhower Interstate System, both landmarks of the "national investment commitment" invoked in section 2 of the act.[29]

Even a cursory reading of the House report on ISTEA reveals that modern America's road legislators had overcome many of the fiscal, political, and constitutional challenges that confronted their counterparts in the National Road era. These modern legislators have also inherited a multitude of other doubting challenges, as reflected in the section 2 declaration of policy referred to above.[30]

Richard Weingroff has provided a comprehensive stage-by-stage account of the steps leading up to the enactment of ISTEA and of the conflicts and disputes involved in the Senate and House approaches to the bill and in the administration's aspirations for the bill. In summarizing the factors that led, after much division and gridlock, to passage, he observes: "[ISTEA] demonstrated the common ground that existed before 1991, such as agreement on the end of the Interstate era, increased flexibility for state and local officials, the need to preserve and increase the efficiency of the existing network, and the importance of intermodal links, and increased funding." In another study, *Clearly Vicious as a Matter of Policy*, Weingroff assesses the significance of ISTEA as follows: "ISTEA strengthened the statewide and metropolitan planning requirements to ensure [that] State and local officials considered priority issues that Congress wanted to emphasize, such as preservation of existing facilities, relieving congestion, access to ports and other intermodal facilities, efficient movement of freight, expansion of transit, and the overall social, economic, energy, and environmental effects of transportation decisions."[31]

Infrastructure Legislation in the Clinton and George W. Bush Administrations

These same surface transportation problems and others have been confronted during the administrations of Bill Clinton and George W. Bush. During the Clinton administration, Congress passed the Transportation Equity Act for the 21st Century, Pub. L. No. 105-178 (1998). It built on the foundation of ISTEA, but it also represented the breaking of new ground regarding the balancing of fiscal needs for infrastructure with other important investment priorities such as education and the environment. For the federal-aid highway program, it generally provided obligation ceilings ranging from $21.5 billion in fiscal year 1998 to $27.7 billion for FY 2003. The law also guaranteed each state a minimum percentage of the total apportionments for a fiscal year. For the interstate system, the Act set a maximum of 43,000 miles. The law enhanced the previously established system for addressing the needs of the interstate maintenance program and recognized environmental considerations by, among other things, providing for environmental restoration and pollution abatement projects. Congestion mitigation and air-quality improvement activities were carried forward for the new period of reauthorization under the act, along with a program favoring recreational trails. Thus, it appears that the scope and magnitude of a congressional highway authorization statute had vastly expanded in terms of subject, funding, nationwide distribution, and subject matter since the 1806 legislation that initiated the National Road, but many of the problems confronted were twenty-first-century versions of what confronted the early Congress that began the road.[32]

In signing the Transportation Efficiency Act for the 21st Century legislation into law, President Clinton, noting that it built on the ISTEA legislation of 1991, emphasized the interrelationship between federal transportation and other high-priority legislation, a relationship that also influenced the course of transportation appropriations during the period of the National Road. "This Act," President Clinton observed, "achieves our transportation goals while maintaining fiscal discipline. My Administration worked with the conferees to eliminate excessive funding that would have undermined key Administration priorities for the environment, child care and education. The resulting compromise . . . funds a record level of guaranteed transportation investment while preserving the budget surplus for Social Security first."[33]

His remarks on the substantive provisions of the bill illustrate the degree to which transportation legislation for the twenty-first century covers issues, such as those pertaining to safety and environmental priorities, that were less prominent in counterpart legislation in the nineteenth century. Thus, the president noted with approval that "the Act increases funding levels for key environmental programs to help communities meet standards for clean air and support environmental enhancements to our surface transportation system," but he expressed regret that the legislation failed to include language that would have helped to establish a uniform blood-alcohol-concentration level as the standard for drunk driving in the fifty states.[34]

The George W. Bush administration's budget for fiscal year 2006, two hundred years after the initiation of the National Road, emphasized the challenges that continue to require attention. "Highway and road congestion is an aggravating problem in all parts of the country. Congestion is also a growing problem at intermodal freight transfer facilities, like sea ports and rail yards." Further, the budget document proposed the following steps: "To ease gridlock, the Budget proposes highway and transit infrastructure spending of $283.9 billion over six years. This marks a 35 percent increase over the TEA 21 six-year spending total. This figure reflects the emerging consensus in Congress that was developed in a conference committee in 2004. . . . In addition to relying on new construction to reduce congestion, SAFETEA would fund research and development to increase the capacity of the existing highway system."[35]

The solution of the problems addressed in the post-interstate legislation discussed above will require a commitment of funds adequate to the transportation needs of a nation of 300 million (heading toward 400 million) people, a large element of state-federal cooperation and coordination within the kind of framework established by the 1956 and subsequent legislation, and the dedication of the leadership of the nation in the executive and legislative branches at the highest levels. That dedication characterized the building of the National Road in the early republic. It will surely be required in meeting the infrastructure needs of the nation in the twenty-first century.[36]

Despite the problems reflected in current legislation, the Eisenhower Interstate System represents a culmination of a 150-year-long effort to establish a successful and sustainable system of national investment in surface transportation infrastructure. For over fifty years the nation has benefited from a system of linked limited-access highways to move people and goods in an efficient manner. The problems of finding a reliable source of user-provided financial resources that afflicted the National Road have been solved in part through gas taxes and state-collected tolls where charged. However, in the twenty-first century there has arisen and been recognized a series of problems that challenge the sustainability of this system, such as those relating to funding, maintenance, safety, congestion, and environmental concerns. These are addressed below in chapter 16.[37]

As it faced these challenges, from the time of the National Road forward, Congress engaged in a continuous process of rebalancing the state and federal role in the process of federally assisted investment in infrastructure and in related areas. In the case of the first National Road authorization statute in 1806, the 1916 and 1921 highway acts, the Federal Aid Highway Act of 1956, providing for the construction of the interstate system, and subsequent post-interstate era laws such as ISTEA in 1991, TEA in 1998, and the Bush 2006 budget, such balancing and rebalancing took place. Throughout that process, one principle became increasingly clear: a reliable flow of federal investment funds was indispensable to infrastructure establishment and sustainability. The option tried in the 1830s—devolution of the road to the states with no clear stream of federal resources to support continuing infrastructure investment—was untenable. A reliable stream of federal aid funds, albeit in the context of a relationship that recognized the importance of state administration and jurisdiction, as Monroe insisted, was essential. President Eisenhower's 1954 emphasis on the maintenance of the gasoline tax put down an indelible marker on the subject in advocating for the interstate highway system that bears his name.[38]

CHAPTER 14

The National Road
as National Symbol

The Road as a Symbol of National Unity:
Reality or Myth?

Thomas Jefferson, the president in whose administration the Cumberland Road project commenced, saw it—and other internal improvement projects like it—as an instrument of national unity. In his sixth State of the Union message in December 1806 he told Congress, "By these operations [roads, canals, and other objects of public improvement] new channels of communication will be opened between the States, the lines of separation will disappear, their interests will be identified, and their union will be cemented by new and indissoluble ties."[1] Albert Gallatin, Jefferson's secretary of the treasury and a paramount force in the initiation and early construction of the National Road, observed that "good roads" would help to "strengthen and perpetuate [the] Union."[2]

James Madison, who signed into law appropriation measures for the road in amounts that were significant for his day, celebrated the unifying character of such projects. In his optimistic seventh State of the Union message after the close of the War of 1812, he took comfort from "the political effect of these facilities [roads and canals] for intercommunication in bringing and binding more closely together the various parts of our extended confederacy."[3]

Despite his intense struggle to find a satisfactory formula to justify, from a constitutional perspective, legislation designed to aid in the repair of the National Road, James Monroe saw that road, and other internal improvements, as strengthening "the bond of union." John Quincy Adams, in the same vein, unapologetically urged the country to embrace the "spirit of [internal] improvement." Among the internal improvements that he urged Congress to assist, the National Road was "the most important."[4]

Andrew Jackson, who signed measures extending the road on its westward route, despite his efforts to control internal-improvement spending and avoid overstrained constitutional construction, saw such improvements as unifying instruments for the nation.[5]

Less highly placed but no less important figures in this saga perceived it the same way. Rep. John Jackson of Virginia, supporting the adoption of legislation to appropriate additional funds for the National Road, presented a report of his committee promising Congress that barriers to east-west communication would be overcome if it continued to fund the work. "If Congress perseveres with becoming spirit in this great public work [the Cumberland Road], we shall soon see one of the best roads in the world over the chains of mountains which separate the Western from the Atlantic waters, and which, but a few years since, were supposed to present insurmountable obstacles to a safe and easy intercourse."[6]

Similarly, as Thomas Searight recounts, in 1832 Congressman T. M. T. McKennan argued that the National Road would "cement the bond of union" and "bring together the distant parts of this exalted Republic."[7] Cumberland Road superintendent David Shriver expressed the same sentiment in annually reporting to Secretary Gallatin on the progress of the work.[8]

The wagoners, stage drivers, tavern keepers, builders, and travelers involved in the life of the road during its prime recognized its significance to the nation. For example, Uria Brown saw it as having "more benefit than the Idea of man can possibly have any knowledge of." They believed to the core that they were engaged in a vitally important national undertaking that transcended the local scene. They pointed with pride to the wagonloads of eastern products headed west and the wagonloads of western farm produce headed to the markets of Washington and Baltimore. Incessant commerce was the binding force. For the sturdy and courageous band of pike boys, the improved transportation of the nation's products was a key aspect of national unity and pride.[9]

Archer Butler Hulbert, in his 1904 history of the project, observed: "[The National Road] was one of the great strands which bound the nation together in early days when there was much to excite animosity and provoke disunion." In 1953, George R. Stewart, in his book on U.S. 40, reminded his readers that the National Road "served to bind the whole nation closer."[10]

Was this vision of national unity achieved through a transportation artery real or mythical? After all, the legislative debates about the road, despite the soaring political rhetoric about unity, were punctuated by fierce battles over appropriations, over mounting costs, and over constitutional interpretation. Regional jealousies and sectional interests, not national harmony, were the stuff of which many of the debates were made. Southern legislators railed against the road as a costly regional project. Defenders of the road from the states through which it ran fought an increasingly difficult rearguard action during the over-thirty-year period of federal support (1806–1838). They repeatedly berated their opponents for subverting and betraying the purposes of the 1802 Ohio statehood legislation that set the stage for the road's initiation. Unity—of sorts—was achieved only through the legislation of the 1830s first authorizing state tolls and then transferring control to the states, which could then charge tolls, legislation that the road's supporters regarded as a bitter pill that they were forced to swallow in order to preserve the road in some form.[11]

The conflict also reverberated in the state houses. Long after the 1835 debates, the Indiana legislature pleaded with the state's congressional delegation to secure appropriations to continue the road. Citizens complained to their local representatives in Congress about the state of the road. Tranquility was not achieved until the use of the road decreased with the advent of the railroad. Unity was a worthy goal that foundered over the issue: who shall pay?[12]

Moreover the unity that the early-republic presidents and their successors sought was fracturing over the issue of slavery. As the road fell into modest use as a local artery after its transfer to the states and with the advent of the railroad in the 1850s, the country gradually slid into war and disunion over that deeply divisive issue. In his special session message of 1861, Abraham Lincoln epitomized the conflict as a "people's contest." By the same token, the National Road constituted a "people's" project. The people's appetite for it drove the nation's internal-improvement agenda for three decades.[13]

That the National Road generated conflict and "disunity" in the halls of Congress as it debated appropriations for the project should not be surprising. Even its own presidential supporters demonstrated their ambivalence about the road. Thomas Jefferson recognized the need for internal improvements but doubted the constitutionality of federal assistance to build them in the absence of a constitutional amendment. His friend and successor, James Madison, signed (and helped administer) a number of measures providing appropriations for the road but vetoed the Bonus Bill on constitutional grounds, while conceding the great value of the internal improvements that the bill was designed to promote and their contribution to national growth.[14]

James Monroe crafted a compromise solution to the problems posed by his predecessors under the General Welfare Clause that permitted him to sign legislation appropriating funds for the repair of the road. However, he balked at signing legislation that authorized the federal government to collect tolls along the road, a step that might have accelerated the pace and scope of federal involvement during the early republic and possibly avoided the 1835 legislation that ushered in the transfer to the states. Andrew Jackson recognized that federal participation in internal-improvement projects of national significance was institutionalized by prior practice but also pushed for retrenchment in the scope and pace of internal improvements. Only John Quincy Adams was definitively behind the internal-improvement movement and clear that a constitutional amendment was not necessary to finance it, but he was so politically weakened (in part because of his support for internal improvements and related projects) that he could not give full effect to his bold vision.[15]

This is not to say that these early-republic presidents were without strong convictions on the issues in question and lacking in dedication to the cause of internal improvement and the unity they said it would bring. Quite to the contrary, they were moved by exceedingly strong feelings in favor of internal improvement, but they were also deeply committed to the concept of a limited constitutional role for the federal government. They recognized the tension and conflict between those two roles, and it generated the ambivalence that appeared to characterize their acts. Madison saw the need for roads, but he also sought to preserve what he regarded as the integrity of the enumerated powers in the Constitution in limiting the legislative role of Congress—a value for which he had fought tenaciously since 1787. How to harmonize that tension between these two dimensions of the common good as these presidents saw it was the difficult challenge they faced.

Despite the conflict in Congress and the apparent ambivalence of early-republic presidents, the road did achieve some goals that in various ways and at various times contributed to American unity:

- It helped to open up a way to the West for travel and discovery. Americans, such as Eliza Steele, could learn from one another in a way that promoted unity.
- The road enabled European travelers, such as Joseph Gurney, Thomas Hulme, Frances Trollope, William Oliver, and J. Richard Beste to travel through the United States taking stock of its mores and its institutions and giving their own country a sense of this new world.
- The road provided an avenue through which emigrants, such as Peter Hessong and his family, could move to the heartland and establish new homes, while keeping ties with the old.
- The road served as an occasion for a compromise regarding the scope of the federal spending power that ultimately enabled Congress to craft legislation under which all Americans could jointly share the burden of helping the vulnerable and the elderly to meet their most pressing needs.[16]
- The road established a foundation for the federally aided highway system of the twenty-first century that helps to bind together today's nation of over 300 million individuals.

If the national unity that Jefferson and his successors so fervently invoked—through the powerful symbol of the National Road—sometimes eluded them, it was not because they failed to seek it or to appreciate the blessings that it would bring to their America. For them, despite the tension and the limited duration of the road as a federal enterprise, it stood as a symbol of unity achieved and unity yet to be achieved.

Westward Migration and Personal Freedom

Of equal significance, the road played a role in populating and settling the states west of the Ohio and beyond the Mississippi and thus bringing them into the ever-growing union. Searight, for example, recounts the numbers of wagoners and stage drivers who worked the road during their youth and then headed west to settle as farmers in Iowa and Kansas after its golden days had waned.[17] In that sense, the National Road became a symbol of unity to be achieved through westward migration as well as a symbol of the personal freedom and opportunity that could be achieved through that migration. As Joseph F. Wood notes: "Only with the American Revolution did Europeans both in Europe and America begin to experience a cosmographical shift in perception: America was transformed perceptually from a western outpost of Europe on the eastern margin of a great new world to an incipient national core from which might spread westward across a continental frontier an empire of liberty."[18]

Implicit or explicit in this vision was the notion that, by reaching for that frontier, Americans might achieve personal emancipation from the obstacles that precluded them from maximizing their opportunities in the established East. Wood observes: "Land to be had in the West would free Americans from laboring for others and living in urban squalor."[19] Traveling the National Road, tedious as the journey across it might be, would lead aspiring Americans to this land of opportunity. Multitudes followed the same or similar paths. To make good on the mystique of the West that tantalized these multitudes and their leaders alike, a viable artery of surface transportation through the daunting mountains, as Washington had envisioned, was essential. The National Road provided that pathway.[20]

Cementing the Growing Union

The six hundred miles of road served to join together six states—three in the East (Maryland, Pennsylvania, and Virginia) and three in what was then the West (Ohio, Indiana and Illinois). Moreover, in its inception, the road was seen as the primary route from the capital to St. Louis, the gateway to the Far West. The road amply served this function for the early republic. With the advent of the railroad that followed it and, for a time, supplanted it, the way west was charted, cleared, tamed, and macadamized.

The sixteen states in the Union at the time of the original authorizing legislation in 1806 expanded to forty-eight shortly after the turn of the century; the expansion in numbers continued with the admission of Arizona in 1912. To this unionizing process, the road contributed. The pathway over the mountains west of Cumberland in 1806, designed to join the eastern and western rivers (the Potomac and Ohio watersheds), has given way to the interstate system that traverses much of the same route west envisioned by Jefferson in that year. Interstate 70 now joins the original six states with St. Louis and continues on to Utah. From there motorists can follow southern or northern interstate routes to California. Jefferson's dream of a transcontinental road has been achieved not through the National Road alone but through the arteries for which it paved the way.[21]

The Romance of the Road in Poetry, Play, and Film

Beyond political rhetoric, the open road has from the beginning of the American experience tantalized Americans and stimulated poetic expression. James Whitcomb Riley was not the only poet to be inspired by the symbolism of the road. Walt Whitman, who wrote during and just after the era of road construction in the early nineteenth century, evoked the lure and the romance of the "open road" and its capacity to enable and individual to escape the burdens and obligations of daily life and find renewal:

> Afoot and light hearted I take to the open road,
> Healthy, free, the world before me
> The long brown path before me leading wherever I choose[22]

Not only did Whitman travel the "open road," but he also traveled the National Road and left us with a prose portrait of that experience. His account of the occasion, in a passage entitled, "Crossing the Alleghenies," published in March 1848, reinforces his poetic invocation and his sense of the symbolism that the road represented. Arriving in Cumberland, Maryland, he described that community as "the great rendezvous and landing place of the immense Pennsylvania wagons, and the drovers from hundreds of miles west." For Whitman the scene had "not a little the appearance of a caravan of the Steppes."[23]

At Cumberland, Whitman boarded a four-horse stagecoach of the National Road and Good Intent Stage Company, headed toward Wheeling. The "systematic" way in which the passengers were loaded intrigued him: "All the passengers' names were inscribed on a roll . . . and a clerk stands by and two or three negroes with a patent weighing machine. The clerk calls your name—your baggage is whipped on the machine, and if it weighs over fifty pounds you have to pay extra. You are then put on the stage, (literally put in, like a package, unless you move quickly,) your baggage packed on behind—and the next name called off—baggage weighed—and so on to the end of the chapter."[24]

Whitman's response to the discomforts of the trip over the mountains from Cumberland to Uniontown was not unlike that of Frances Trollope two decades earlier: "Up we toiled, and we down we clattered (for the first fifty miles it was nearly *all* up), over these mighty warts on the great beast of nature." For Whitman, the scene was compelling and totally American.[25]

Almost one hundred years later, during the New Deal days, the National Road became the subject of a play composed by workers in the Writers' Project of the Work Projects Administration (in the state of Ohio): *The National Road in Song and Story*. The dramatization was written to commemorate the one-hundredth anniversary of the completion of the road (in Ohio). The project was sponsored by the Ohio State Archaeological and Historical Society. Appropriately, the road itself had a part.[26]

In sum, whether in poetry or prose, drama or film, the symbolism of the road captured the imaginations of the creative Americans who traveled its length.

Nostalgia, History, and Tourism: The National Old Trails Association

One organization that clearly recognized the symbolic value of the National Road to reinforce the organization's advocacy on behalf of "good roads" was the National Old Trails Association. The association, which functioned early in the twentieth century, campaigned with great energy and purpose for a strong federal role in establishing a highway that would span the nation from east to west. Along with the Old Trails Association, the Daughters of the American Revolution (DAR) and the American Automobile Association also played key roles in that campaign. The vision of the National Old Trails Association was of an artery that would follow the routes of the old trails that had been constructed in the nineteenth century. Prominent among these trails was the National Road. The leaders of the Old Trails Association did not hesitate to invoke the history of the National Road in their efforts to spur national efforts on behalf of infrastructure development and investment to be carried out by the federal government.[27]

The National Old Trails Association was solidly in the camp of those who wanted a strong federal role in this process. It did not wish to settle for an enhanced "federal-aid" program that would provide funds to the states to improve state roads and ignore interstate arteries. The association clashed with those who favored the federal-aid model, such as Rep. Shackleford. Richard Weingroff of the U.S. Department of Transportation has provided a vivid picture of the National Old Trails Association and its contribution to the debates in the early twentieth century over road development and the federal role in that process.[28]

A portion of Weingroff's study is devoted to the contribution of Judge J. M. Lowe, who became the president of the association in 1912. In that capacity, Lowe became a vigorous and tireless advocate for the ocean-to-ocean old trails route. Significantly, he maintained that road building by the federal government should be looked upon not as a tax but as an "investment." Judge Lowe also strongly defended the constitutionality of federal appropriations for highway construction. In so doing, he sought support for that authority in the history of the National Road, particularly Jefferson's signing of the 1806 legislation that launched the road as well as the approval of National Road appropriations by later presidents.[29]

As of December 12, 1912, the National Old Trails Road Ocean-to-Ocean Highway followed the route of the National Road from Cumberland, Maryland, to Vandalia, Illinois, and then proceeded over other old trails to California. Judge Lowe sought to incorporate the history of the National Road into his plea for a federally constructed transcontinental road that included that route; at the same time he denied that the National Road represented a species of "federal aid." He said: "No such phrase occurs in the Act establishing the National or Cumberland Road. No such expression anywhere occurs in the history of that highway." In so contending, Lowe declined to deal with the distinction made in the Monroe Memorandum, which insisted on preserving state jurisdiction over the road, despite the infusion of federal funds. For Lowe, the solution to the legal issues surrounding the road enterprise was to have the federal government fund and construct the interstate highways. The states would then build lateral state roads intersecting the national road. Judge Lowe reiterated essentially these positions before Congress.[30]

Judge Lowe was no stranger to the route of the National Road. In 1913, for example, he went to Zanesville, Ohio, one of the old pike towns, to deliver a speech regarding the National Road and its history. He described it as forming a land bridge between the Potomac and the Ohio. He then recounted the enactment of the 1806 act and subsequent legislation funding the road from revenues derived from the sale of public lands. In short, Judge Lowe regarded the National Road and its history as a precedent for his position that the federal government should construct national highways serving interstate traffic. Despite that precedent, the effort to achieve legislation broke down in the disputes over whether direct federal construction or federal aid to states was the proper approach to achieving adequate road infrastructure in early twentieth-century United States. Antagonistic positions were taken in Congress and attacks were made by and against individual members of Congress who held differing positions. The year 1914 closed without substantive legislation. When legislation was finally enacted in 1916, it took the form of federal aid rather than establishment of a direct federal role independent of the state agencies.[31]

In 1926, Harry Truman of Missouri succeeded Judge Lowe as president of the National Old Trails Association. As described in Richard Weingroff's account, entitled *The Man Who Loved Roads*, Truman "periodically drove the National Old Trails Road from coast to coast and met with members of the association in each State to discuss improvements to their segments." Truman continued the tradition of his predecessor, Judge Lowe, in linking the history of the National Road to the work of the association. In his role as president of the association, Truman reinforced the historical importance of the National Road when he spoke at the unveiling of the Madonna of the Trail monument along the National Road in Wheeling, West Virginia, in July 1928. The statue of the Madonna of the Trail was built through the joint efforts of the Daughters of the American Revolution and the National Old Trails Association.[32]

In his biography of Truman, the noted historian and author David McCullough describes the latter's role in the association before his career took him to Washington, D.C., first as senator from Missouri and later as vice president and president of the United States. "Roads, highways, the new age of the automobile had become [Truman's] specialty," McCullough observed. "He was named president of the National Old Trails Association, a nonprofit group dedicated to building highways along the country's historic trails and to spreading the concept of history as a tourist attraction. (Writing from Kansas during one of many trips in behalf of the group, he told Bess, 'This is almost like campaigning for President, except that the people are making promises to me instead of the other way around.')"[33]

Truman did not discard his early affection for cars and good roads when he reached for political office. He campaigned for election to the U.S. Senate in 1934 by driving the back roads of Missouri and, once elected, he frequently drove between Independence and Washington on U.S. 40, traversing the National Road in the tradition of many statesmen from the West who had traveled that route in the nineteenth century.[34]

As George Stewart in his mid-1950s book on U.S. 40 aptly observed: "No other section of the [U.S. 40] route [the Cumberland-Wheeling portion] . . . has been so closely connected with the great events of our history, or has surpassed this one for its actual influence upon the course of history."[35]

Symbol of State and National Heritage for Today's Traveler: The National Road Heritage Corridor and the Six State Association

In the late twentieth and early twenty-first centuries, the National Road became a symbol in another sense—a symbol of national heritage to be preserved and celebrated, as well as an attraction for tourism in order to enhance the economic viability of an area that has suffered the loss of its mining and manufacturing base. This process has been aided and abetted by a creative mix of local, state, and federal interests. At the federal level, the National Scenic Byways Program, administered by the Department of Transportation, has played an important role. At the state level, various other programs have had a role. In Pennsylvania, for example, the state Heritage Corridor program has been central. In other states, state nonprofit organizations, such as statewide road alliances, have played a key role in preserving the heritage of the road and educating the public about it.[36]

STATE EFFORTS: HERITAGE CORRIDORS

The Commonwealth of Pennsylvania places great value on the part of its heritage represented by the National Road. It has developed an extensive system for preserving and promoting that heritage and its surviving artifacts. Under a program administered by the commonwealth's Department of Conservation and Natural Resources (DNCR), a number of heritage parks and corridors have been designated. These are multicounty areas that reflect its industrial or cultural history. For each park or corridor DCNR designates a nonprofit organization to be responsible for its preservation, protection, and promotion. This responsibility is carried out through interpretative and preservationist activities involving a wide range of strategies, including grants of financial assistance to restore particular sites; educational and informational projects; partnerships with local, state, or federal entities; outreach activities to schools and libraries; and other educational programs. The various activities are coordinated with a task force of governmental and private organizations representing such important state interests as transportation, parks, museums, art, recreation, tourism, and natural resources. The legislative leadership of the commonwealth through a network of identified state and federal legislators affects these coordination efforts.[37]

The National Road Heritage Corridor in Pennsylvania is one of the multicounty park-and-corridor organizations involved in this process. Its projects have included the restoration or replacement of the obelisk road markers along the length of the route of the National Road in Pennsylvania, as well as grants for the refurbishment or restoration of a number of sites dating back to the time of the road's construction and major use. It has made a major contribution to the establishment of an interpretive and educational center on the site of Fort Necessity in Farmington, Pennsylvania. Efforts to achieve coordination with other states through which the road passed is another aspect of the organization's functions. The partnership involved in these enterprises reflects in some sense the state and federal partnership that flourished during the inception and construction of the National Road. The preservation of the road as a symbol of our national heritage is thus proceeding more than two hundred years after Thomas Jefferson signed the original authorizing legislation in 1806. Coupled with this goal is that of regional revitalization in an area that has experienced job loss in the mining and steel industry. Job creation to assist low-income families is among the goals of the state's heritage park and corridor program.[38]

THE NATIONAL ROAD INTERPRETIVE CENTER AND THE ROAD'S ROLE AS A NATIONAL HERITAGE SYMBOL

On October 8, 2005, a new Fort Necessity National Battlefield / National Road Interpretative and Education Center was dedicated in a ceremony that appropriately marked the role of the road as a symbol of the history and heritage that it represented. The ceremony was held at the site of the new Interpretative and Education Center near the Fort Necessity Battlefield. The ten-year effort to establish the new center involved a strong partnership between the National Park Service, the Commonwealth of Pennsylvania, the National Road Heritage Corridor, and a number of private donors. The dedication ceremony included observations by representatives of the partners as well as by the Pennsylvania congressman John Murtha and the renowned historian and author David McCullough. Congressman Murtha represented Pennsylvania's Twelfth District from 1974 until his death in 2010 and was a staunch supporter of efforts to recognize the significance of the National Road in American history. At the dedication ceremony, he was honored for his efforts on behalf of the establishment of the center.

The center itself is housed in a new building that contains exhibits regarding the battle at Fort Necessity, the Braddock campaign of 1755, the French and Indian War, and the genesis, construction, and progress of the National Road, as well as the transformation of the nineteenth-century interstate artery into a national heritage corridor. The stages of the road's development are chronicled and represented by pertinent exhibits and objects, including Nemacolin's path and Washington's expeditions to southwestern Pennsylvania, as well as his interest in the opening of a road to the West. The exhibit also provides insightful information on the roles of Presidents Jefferson, Madison, Monroe, John Quincy Adams, and Andrew Jackson in the construction of the road and its continuation to Vandalia, Illinois. The exhibit traces the decline and revival of the road in the late nineteenth and early twentieth centuries. The progress from the bicycle era of the 1890s to the interstate highway system of the 1950s is graphically depicted. The exhibit also reveals the daily life of the travelers, wagon drivers, and stage drivers in tavern stops and other encounters along the road. The visitor, in a relatively short span of time, can come away from the center with a solid grasp of the road, its history, and its role as a distinct and important symbol of the American heritage.[39]

Between New Concord and Zanesville, Ohio, on U.S. 40, one finds the Zane Grey-National Road museum, which gives the visitor an insight into the different aspects of the National Road experience and ties that experience to the journey west of Wheeling and the Ohio River. The museum and its surroundings add to the enriching experience of traveling the National Road and contain many objects that communicate its history in a lively and accessible way. As Norris Schneider has observed, "Ohio can claim several 'firsts' in highway progress. Considering these records and the original enabling act which contained the provision for a highway connecting the Northwest Territory with the eastern states, it is appropriate that a National Road Museum to memorialize the historic importance of the famous highway should be located in Ohio."[40]

The National Road as a Symbol of America's Need for Sustainable National Investment in Infrastructure

The National Road can be seen as a symbol of the nation's continuing quest for an adequate system of surface transportation and, indeed, for adequate road infrastructure that would meet the economic and social needs of the United States and support increasing growth and well-being for its people. This would seem to be its primary symbolic significance. The National Road emerged because American leaders recognized the need for such a system at the very time that the nation's earliest governments were formed under the new Constitution framed in 1787.

Thomas Jefferson and Alexander Hamilton fought over the direction that the early republic would take, but they both agreed on the need for internal improvements to succor it. Federalists and Jeffersonian Republicans disagreed on the scope of the constitutional power to assist commerce, agriculture, and education, but they agreed on the need for roads and canals to stimulate economic growth. Jefferson took a narrow view of the role of the government's power to tax but still called upon Congress to enable him to help "chequer" the country with roads and canals. The National Road legislation of 1806 opened a chapter in American history that involved the federal government in the construction of an internal improvement that would help open up the West and bind it with the East. Over a thirty-year period the great debates about the road revealed the constitutional, fiscal, and programmatic conflicts involved in establishing adequate infrastructure for the new nation. Despite those conflicts, the National Road was seen as an essential, if sometimes frayed, pathway to American progress and vitality.[41]

The federal government undertook construction of the road, which eventually joined six states. At its prime, the National Road was the route that thousands of travelers and emigrants followed to the West. It opened the heartland, becoming an avenue of commerce and economic growth, and provided jobs for thousands of immigrants who came from the Old World to settle in the new. Eventually, it foundered because of sectional rivalry; the inability to achieve a reliable means, at least at the federal level, to fund its maintenance; the emergence of the railroad; and, perhaps, for many other reasons. But the essential truth survived: America needs an adequate surface transportation infrastructure to grow and prosper. That infrastructure network requires federal aid for its construction and maintenance. A sustainable and continuing source of that aid must be found consistent with sound principles of fiscal discipline and stability.[42]

In the twenty-first century, one may argue, the National Road continues as a symbol of the need, not only to maintain and improve the transportation system in place but to enhance and modernize it to meet the needs of the United States as a leader and prime participant in the global economy in the information age. Whatever perspective one applies to the significance of the National Road, it remains a genuine and meaningful slice of the American experience and, in that context, an enduring symbol of that experience. The need to follow the pathway to internal improvement and sustainable national investment that the National Road represents constitutes, as it did in 1806, a continuing national responsibility. Part 4 explores more fully this aspect of the important legacy of the National Road.[43]

Part IV

TWENTY-FIRST-CENTURY LEGACY

CHAPTER 15

The National Road and the Enduring Role of the Federal Spending Power

From one perspective, the story of the National Road may appear to be a somewhat dismal one. The road was constantly in a state of disrepair or "dilapidation." Its supporters were perennially put in the position of "begging" for appropriations to continue or repair it. Legislation regarding it was the subject of two major presidential vetoes. In the end, its best supporters were forced to vote to transfer it to the states through which it passed as the sole means of keeping it alive. As one commentator has noted regarding this experience: "[T]he country stood for three decades, hamstrung in the achievement of its greatest need. The clash of economic interest and constitutional doctrine resulted for the time being in a victory for the lawyers."[1]

Recapitulation

A short recapitulation will serve to illustrate. The National Road was first authorized in 1806. Construction did not begin until 1811. The War of 1812 limited but did not extinguish progress, and the road was largely completed to Wheeling by 1818, from which it continued, in fits and starts, through Ohio, Indiana, and part of Illinois. While appropriations were made through 1838, supporters of the road were never certain that federal funding would continue. The Bonus Bill was passed in 1817 to meet the financial needs of the road, but President Madison vetoed it. His call for a constitutional amendment to solve the problem and that of his successor, Monroe, met with opposition in Congress. Many in that body, as Senator James Barbour observed, felt that Congress possessed the authority to finance the investment that the road represented, without an amendment. To try to resolve the impasse, Congress passed the Gates Bill, providing for federally administered tollgates and toll collection that would furnish a source of local, user-provided funds for the road rather than federal funds, thus avoiding the constitutional issue. President Monroe vetoed that bill in 1822. He believed that federal control over tollgates and toll collection was itself unconstitutional. Efforts to revive the Gates legislation in 1829 and send it to John Quincy Adams, a president very friendly to internal improvements, failed. By 1835, if not earlier, it was clear that the sole available alternative to save the road was transfer control to the states, which could then collect tolls. The friends of the road, Senators Clay and Webster included, "reluctantly" joined in voting for the 1835 act that accomplished the transfer. The last federal appropriation for the road came in 1838. Not long thereafter, it was eclipsed by the railroads.

There is, however, a much more positive side to the story. In vetoing the Gates Bill, as we have seen, President Monroe furnished an explanatory memorandum that provided a way out of the constitutional difficulty. Congress could appropriate federal funds for roads, canals, and other improvements as long as it did not assume "jurisdiction" over them. Monroe found this authority in the Constitution's Spending (or General Welfare) Clause: Congress may tax (and spend) to provide for the "general welfare of the United States." While Monroe's compromise did not save the road as a national road, because the compromise ruled out a federal user tax through the medium of toll collection, it did provide a valuable legal and practical precedent for the future as well as a framework to keep the road moving and in some degree of repair for another two decades. This is summarized above in chapters 2–6.

The Monroe Memorandum, the "General Welfare" Concept, Participatory Democracy, and the Role of Government in a Growing Nation

The conclusions in the Monroe Memorandum are significant in a number of respects that transcend the immediate issue of establishing a constitutional basis in 1822 for congressional appropriations to repair the National Road, the issue to which Monroe's analysis was specifically directed. As applied in the interpretation of the authority of Congress to spend for the "general welfare," Monroe's conclusions helped to overcome the constitutional barriers to those appropriations, just as the National Road had overcome the geographical barriers posed by the Allegheny Mountains.

But those conclusions went much further. By providing a theory to sustain a broad reading of the authority of Congress to spend in order to "provide for . . . the general welfare of the United States," they ultimately came to invite Americans to explore the many ways in which citizens might help one another through the application of federal assistance to such matters as better education, better health care, and a reliable system of income security or support for the elderly, the poor, and the vulnerable in the United States. By rejecting the limitation of the "general welfare" concept only to the areas assigned to Congress under the enumerated powers in the Constitution (Art. I, sec. 8, cl. 2 and those that followed), Monroe's conclusions in effect substantially broadened the scope of what Congress could consider as objects of federal financial assistance and thus freed up federal revenues for these purposes, at least as a constitutional matter.

By the same token, Monroe's idea broadened the areas that could be the subject of participatory democracy in which an individual citizen might engage. The participating citizen could press his or her representatives to legislate about roads and canals and higher education in the nineteenth century. In the twentieth century, such a citizen could, for example, press for appropriations for elementary and secondary education, higher education, Social Security, and Medicare. In effect, Monroe's thesis to support appropriations for the National Road, as applied in other contexts over the decades, greatly expanded the scope of what federal lawmakers could consider under the rubric of the "common good" or "general welfare."[2]

This broadening process embraced a number of stages or phases, each of which involved a role for the people. First, the conclusions that Monroe reached were themselves arguably driven by the exercise of participatory democracy by early-republic citizens pressing for good roads and for access to the West, directly and through the actions of their representatives in approving successive appropriations for the National Road. The Virginia presidents and their successors who advocated for a federal role in internal improvements were driven to support them by popular will, as well as their own perceptions of the common good. Monroe wrote in order to provide a rational basis for explaining his own approval of appropriations for the road despite the absence of the constitutional amendment that Jefferson and Madison had recommended but that Congress was unwilling to propose.[3]

Second, in establishing a legal theory under which Congress could use the spending power (General Welfare Clause) as a basis for appropriations for the National Road and other internal improvements without such an amendment, the Monroe Memorandum offered a degree of flexibility (Madison would have said "ductility") that permitted greater scope for the exercise of participatory democracy in the early republic. The people's representatives could enact legislation, consistently with the Constitution, that aided areas of endeavor not spelled out in the enumerated powers in the constitution. In that era, internal improvements were a prime example. The alternative of seeking a constitutional amendment as a precondition to such legislation, while not without some advantages, would have largely constrained that process.[4]

Third, the legal theory that Monroe posed in 1822, along with earlier and later nonjudicial precedents (such as those provided by Hamilton and Story), established a framework that ultimately persuaded the Supreme Court in the 1936 *Butler* case to sustain Monroe's interpretation as the proper interpretation of the General Welfare (or Spending) Clause. The *Butler* precedent was in turn used by Justice Cardozo in his 1937 opinion in *Helvering v. Davis*, which sustained the Social Security retirement program under Title II of the Social Security Act of 1935. That opinion and others that followed confirmed the breadth of the permissible scope of the federal legislative role in many areas, At the same time, it necessarily provided a variety of fields in which voters could manifest participatory democracy, civic engagement, or "active liberty," whether at the polls or through other forms of support for causes or politicians advocating them. As Justice Rehnquist put the matter in *South Dakota v. Dole*, a twentieth-century application of Monroe's conclusion to a twentieth-century highway program, Congress was free to legislate in areas outside Article I's "enumerated legislative fields."[5]

Fourth, in the application of the Spending or General Welfare Clause to actual exercises of the spending power, the Court in *Helvering* and the cases that followed has adopted a relatively deferential stance providing Congress with a wide berth to determine what is or is not within the scope of the "general welfare." This in turn gives a broader range of subject matter to the people in the exercise of participatory democracy at the federal level. As Justice Cardozo put the matter in *Helvering*, "Nor is the concept of the general welfare static. Needs that were narrow or parochial a century ago may be interwoven in our day with the well-being of the nation. What is critical or urgent changes with the times."[6]

A full reflection on these stages of this history requires a consideration of three additional points. First, the uncoupling of the limits that some argued bound the "general welfare" concept was itself largely accomplished through Congress and the executive branch, not the courts. Monroe's legal interpretation was a response to a shared perception that Americans required a road across the Alleghenies that once built needed to be kept in repair. However, his opinion explaining that interpretation was the work of a president, not a judge. During the nineteenth century, as appropriations for the road proliferated, the judicial branch did not become institutionally involved. To be sure, Joseph Story, a great judge, played a key role in the matter, but he played it as a professor of law at Harvard Law School and as an author of a widely renowned set of commentaries on the Constitution, not as a justice of the Supreme Court, which he then was. The law-making steps in the process involved interaction between the presidents and the Congresses that were immediately concerned.[7]

Second, to suggest a nexus between participatory democracy and the legal precedents growing out of the National Road experience is not to concede a lack of basis for Monroe's conclusion, and for decisions of the Supreme Court that followed many decades later, in the language and original history of the Constitution. As has been suggested above, the literal language of the Constitution supported the reading that Monroe gave it. That textual support was emphasized by Hamilton in his *Report on Manufactures* and by Monroe himself. Madison, in his post–White House writings, conceded that the broad interpretation was consistent with the literal language of the General Welfare Clause. Moreover, there are historical indications that at least some framers recognized that the Constitution was susceptible to the interpretation during or close to the time of its adoption and ratification.[8]

Third, none of the interpretations of the General Welfare Clause *required* Congress to do anything. Whether or not to adopt spending legislation "to provide for the general welfare" was a matter left to the discretion of the people and their elected representatives.

How does the interpretation of the General Welfare Clause, first by the presidents, Congresses, and commentators who dealt with it in the nineteenth century, and then by the Supreme Court in the twentieth century, fit within the framework of a nation expanding in population, economic influence, and military power, and in its role on the world stage? One may reflect on this question by reference to one of those commentators, Justice Joseph Story, and his analysis of the matter in his 1833 commentaries on the Constitution. Story's view was essentially consistent with that of Monroe in his National Road–related memorandum of 1822. Congress could, under the Spending Clause, appropriate for purposes encompassed within the phrase "general welfare of the United States," although those purposes did not fall within the enumerated powers in Art. I, sec. 8. In summarizing his conclusions, Story focused on three factors: (1) "the language of the clause [the General Welfare Clause] conferring the power"; (2) "the nature of the power, which renders it in the highest degree expedient, if not indispensable for the due operations of the national government"; and (3) "the early, constant, and decided maintenance of it by the government and its functionaries, as well as by many of our ablest statesmen from the commencement of the Constitution." Story thus relied on text; precedent in the form of consistent practical application through legislative enactments, many of them related to the National Road; and expediency. His view was that a nation in the position of the United States, even when viewed from the vantage point of 1833, fundamentally needed to possess the constitutional power and flexibility to *invest* its resources for purposes that transcended the enumerated legislative fields in Art. I, sec. 8, cl. 2–17 of the Constitution. That degree of expediency could be served, without amending the language of the Constitution, as Monroe had concluded in his 1822 National Road memorandum, because the language of the charter and the nonjudicial interpretations that had been given to it, including those related to the road, justified that result.[9]

Alternative Constitutional Bases for Federal Infrastructure Investment: The Post-Road and Commerce Clauses

Rumination about the constitutionality of federal aid for highway and other infrastructure investment was not confined to the era of the National Road and the early republic. The issue also arose from time to time during the consideration of federal-aid proposals in the early twentieth century. For example, at the time of the passage by Congress of the Federal Aid Road Act of 1916, a congressional committee asserted that the legislation was clearly constitutional and that the matter was no longer a fit subject for legal debate. However, the committee based its constitutional conclusion on not one but on four separate provisions of the Constitution, including the General Welfare Clause, the Post-Roads Clause, and the Commerce Clause. Moreover, for a time the Post-Roads Clause was apparently used by Congress as the preferred constitutional authority for federal-aid highway appropriations, and the Supreme Court in *Wilson v. Shaw* opined that the Commerce Clause was a proper source. The congressional committee in question was the Joint Committee on Federal Aid in the Construction of Post Roads.[10]

In a 1915 report the committee sought to put to rest the constitutional issue with regard to the power of Congress to appropriate federal funds for roads. It said: "The constitutionality of the appropriations [for the National Road] was supported chiefly upon some or all of the following express Federal powers: To establish post roads, to regulate commerce, to declare war, to provide for the common defense, to promote the general welfare." Then the committee undertook to justify the constitutionality of such expenditures on the basis of the enacted federal legislation that had preceded in a variety of areas: "Even a cursory review of the ever-expanding activities of this Government, covering the purchase of Louisiana and Alaska, the improvement of harbors and interior rivers, appropriations for educational work, construction of reclamation projects, purchase of private lands for the formation of public forest reserves for protection of watersheds, demonstrates that a discussion of the constitutional question is purely academic." The committee concluded the discussion by noting its view that federal aid to "good roads" would "above all" "promote the general welfare."[11]

We have discussed the spending power, under the General Welfare Clause of the Constitution, at length. But what of the Post-Roads Clause? It was cited in the first annual message of President Washington and, as indicated, was apparently used as the basis for the 1916 act. However, in *South Dakota v. Dole* (1987), a leading Supreme Court case upholding the constitutionality of conditions established under the Federal Aid Highway Program statutes, the Court invoked the General Welfare Clause as the authority for the placement by Congress of a condition on a state's receipt of full funding under the act. The condition established a requirement that the state adopt a minimum prescribed drinking age if it wished to receive a full allotment of federal funds. In the light of this decision, the following paragraphs speculate on the considerations that may be relevant to the Court's choice of the spending power as the preferred constitutional basis for federal infrastructure investments and federal conditions relating to them.[12]

First, during the National Road era, the spending power in Article I, section 8, cl. 1, of the Constitution was put forward as the constitutional basis for federal assistance to infrastructure by those statesmen and commentators who concluded that such authority did exist. They included Monroe and Story with respect to roads, including the National Road. In particular, President Monroe's memorandum explored the issue at length and concluded that Article I, section 8, cl. 1, could support an appropriation of federal funds to be used for National Road construction and repair as long as the federal government did not assume jurisdiction over the road. Story cited Monroe on the point in maintaining the same position in his commentaries. John Quincy Adams and Andrew Jackson both relied upon the Monroe analysis in justifying the road appropriations that they signed. Moreover, both Madison and Monroe, with varying degrees of specificity, rejected the Post-Roads Clause and the Commerce Clause as viable alternatives on which to ground constitutional arguments for financial assistance to internal improvements.[13]

Second, in *United States v. Butler* (1936), the Supreme Court upheld the broad Hamiltonian reading of the General Welfare Clause as a basis for the enactment of the Agricultural Assistance Act (AAA):"It results that the power of Congress to authorize expenditure of public moneys for public purposes is not limited by the direct grants of legislative power found in the Constitution." A year later in *Helvering v. Davis*, the Court used the same authority to sustain the Social Security Act's Title II program of retirement security :"The conception of the spending power advocated by Hamilton and strongly reinforced by Story has prevailed over that of Madison." The same provision was used by the court in *Steward Machine Corp. v. Davis* to sustain Social Security's unemployment compensation program. Thus, in three New Deal–era cases, the General Welfare Clause was identified as sufficient authority for broad federal spending programs. (It is true that the AAA was struck down on other grounds, but that did not nullify the ruling on the breadth of the spending power.) Moreover, the government briefs in those cases had argued the applicability of the General Welfare Clause to those cases rather than other provisions. Hence, by the mid-1930s, the spending power had arisen as a reliable source for arguing and sustaining constitutional authority for a variety of programs in a variety of areas.[14]

Third, by the time the Court came to decide the *Dole* case, this body of precedent had been established. The Court therefore cited and used it in sustaining the provision of federal assistance under the Federal Aid Highway Act of 1956, concluding that "objectives not thought to be within Article I's 'enumerated legislative fields' may nevertheless be attained through the use of the spending power and the conditional grant of funds." The federal-aid highway program was now one such objective.[15]

Fourth, the government's brief in the *Dole* case clearly indicates that the Department of Justice was relying on the spending power in Article I, section 8, cl. 1, of the Constitution as the basic authority undergirding the federal-aid highway program and the interstate highway system. That brief stated: "The Constitution empowers Congress to 'lay and collect Taxes, Duties, Imposts and Excises to pay the Debts and provide for the common defense and general welfare of the United States . . .' This Court has repeatedly recognized the breadth of this grant of authority to spend federal funds, observing that it is for Congress to decide which expenditures will promote the general welfare." The government's brief in *United States v. Butler* was to the same effect. The Post-Roads Clause and the Commerce Clause were not similarly invoked.[16]

Thus, both the government and the courts had found the spending power to be a reliable generic authority for federal programs in a broad range of areas. This is not to say that the Post-Roads Clause lacked advocates. For example, in a monograph entitled *The Post-Road Power in the Federal Constitution and Its Availability for Creating a System of Federal Transportation Corporations*, published in 1907, Edgar Howard Farrar argued strenuously that the clause afforded authority for federal construction of highways and the use of federally chartered corporations to administer and construct such improvements. Relying on cases involving the federal chartering of transcontinental railroad corporations, Farrar argued that this authority could be extended to road construction. Farrar also cited *Monongahela Navigation Co. v. United States* in support of his thesis and rejected the Monroe Memorandum as the product an "extinct sect" of internal-improvement opponents. (Farrar did not mention Monroe's support for the use of the spending power to authorize federal appropriations for the repair of the National Road. Nor did he mention that Monroe was a regarded as favorable to internal improvements and had signed legislation providing for federal funds to build or repair such improvements.) Whatever the merits of the authorities cited by Farrar, modern decisions upholding federal-aid appropriations for highways and conditions imposed under federal-aid legislation have relied upon the spending power rather than the Post-Road power as their basic constitutional authority.[17]

One further anomaly in this analysis must be noted: the manner in which the construction of the National Road was administered under the Madison and Monroe administrations. While the 1822 Monroe Memorandum insisted that the federal government, in providing funds for the construction of the National Road, could not assume jurisdiction over the road, as that function belonged to the state through which the road passed, the key administrative activities were carried out by the National Road superintendent (a federal official), the secretary of the treasury, and the president. A review of chapter 9 above illustrates how this procedure was carried out during the construction of the eastern portion of the road during the period from 1811 through 1818. It is unlikely that these officials were abandoning the principles of federalism that were espoused, for example, in Madison's Bonus Bill veto of 1817 and Monroe's Gates Bill veto of 1822. What seems more likely is that the federal officials in question were following the framework set forth in the 1806 appropriation legislation and the legislative acts that followed respecting the funding of the National Road. These laws vested in the president the determination of the direction of the road, subject to the consent of the states through which it was to pass, as well as the laying out and construction of the road. Madison and Monroe were simply following the directions of Congress in providing financing for the road. Moreover, the work was largely completed in that manner prior to the announcement, in 1822, of the conclusions reached in Monroe's Memorandum regarding the spending power, an analysis that was not fully accepted in Supreme Court decision law until the 1936 and 1937 cases regarding the AAA and the Social Security Act. Finally, it was under the federal-aid highway legislation of 1916 that the federal-aid legislation and the constitutional theory regarding it came to be aligned through a federal-aid statute that clearly made provision for a major state administrative role and the grant of federal funds to the affected states by a designated federal transportation aid agency.[18]

The evolution of the federal spending power as the primary source of constitutional authority for the federal-aid highway program of the twentieth century was recognized by Edward V. Kussy, who served as general counsel of the Federal Highway Administration for a significant period during the expansion of that program. He gave a speech entitled, "Surface Transportation and Administrative Law: Growing Up Together in the 20th Century." It contains Mr. Kussy's perspective on the constitutional basis for infrastructure investment by the United States during that period. In that speech, Mr. Kussy discussed the many grant conditions made applicable in the federal highway program, such as those relating to "social, economic and environmental policy." These he posited on the basis of the federal "spending power." In so doing, he invoked *South Dakota v. Dole*, quoted above.[19]

In this framework, Mr. Kussy observed:

> Grant programs are carried out as part of the constitutional power of
> Congress to spend money for the general welfare. Hence, this is often

referred to as the "spending power" of the federal government. The
law regarding the spending power of Congress is remarkably simple:
essentially it is defined by two important Supreme Court cases, both
dealing with transportation programs. . . . The Supreme Court expressly addressed the power of the Congress to condition its grants
in *South Dakota v. Dole*, a case dealing with the constitutionality of
a grant condition requiring states to set the legal age for drinking al-
coholic beverages at no lower than 21. This provision of the Federal-
Aid Highway Act was justified as a highway safety measure. Failure
to have such a law could result in the reduction of a state's federal-aid
highway apportionment.[20]

Thus the spending power under Art. I, sec. 8, cl. 1, of the Constitution, rather
than the Commerce Clause under Art. I, sec. 8, cl. 3, or the Post-Roads power
under Art. I, sec. 8, cl. 7, of the Constitution, has come to be recognized by
scholars and federal highway officials as the primary source of federal constitutional authority for federal aid to highways. This is believed to be consistent
with the history of the National Road, as discussed above. The proponents of
the road, notably Monroe, based the authority of Congress to appropriate for,
but not exercise jurisdiction over, the road under that spending power in his in-
fluential, transgenerational, and comprehensive 1822 memorandum. The choice
of the Post-Roads power (the power to "establish" post roads) might have been
inconsistent with this notion of powerful but limited authority of the federal
government to invest in infrastructure by helping states through federal funding. On the contrary, it might have been used to suggest a role for the federal
government that took the form of direct construction of, and assumption of
jurisdiction over, infrastructure within a state, the role rejected by Monroe in
his forward-looking but federalism-rooted 1822 memorandum and ultimately
rejected by Congress in the landmark 1916 and 1921 acts, which reserved to the
states jurisdiction over and ownership of roads constructed in part with federal-
aid funds. (See chapters 4 and 12.)

In sum, by 1987, two hundred years after the Constitutional Convention,
the accepted constitutional authority for federal-aid spending for highways, the
applicable statutory framework for that spending, and the manner of administering federal-aid programs had come into reasonable, if not perfect, alignment.[21]

In his book, *A Government Out of Sight*, Brian Balogh shares his conclusions
regarding the American citizen's conception of government in the nineteenth century, an era in which the National Road played an important role. Balogh states:

First and foremost, Americans eschewed visible, centralized, national
administration by the General Government. That citizens resisted a
national bureaucratic state does not mean that they did not ask the
national government to do a lot for them. But Americans rebuked

> Hamilton: they responded far more favorably when the General
> Government was inconspicuous, or at least hidden in plain sight.
> Combining national resources and private initiative proved to be a
> consistent formula for political success in policies ranging from land
> distribution to internal improvements.[22]

As this observation suggests, government in the nineteenth and twentieth centuries came to reflect a mix of mutually reinforcing federal financial assistance and
state or local administration. That mix allowed the nation to benefit from the
federal resources available for growth propelling national investment. At the same
time, delivery of those resources took place in a framework that engaged state
participation and preserved the opportunity for state and local innovation and
creativity. The efforts of Jefferson, Madison, Monroe, J. Q. Adams, and Jackson,
to pursue, in varying degrees, federally financed internal improvement, while
emphasizing the need to preserve state jurisdictional prerogatives, provided early
legal and policy precedents for this kind of mix. So did the choices of the twentieth century in favor of an aid to states framework for federal investment programs
related to infrastructure, education, and other objects of such investment.

The Spending Power and
Sustainable National Investment

As it has come to be interpreted, the federal spending power embraces a host
of federal activities in areas that were probably not originally contemplated by
the framers but nonetheless fall within the scope of the phrase "general welfare
of the United States," including aid to education, health, welfare, social insurance, Medicare and Medicaid, environmental assistance, the arts and cultural
institutions, energy requirements, and many others. The General Welfare Clause
in effect defines the areas for which national investment may be pursued. The
constitutional issues that once gave rise to a great debate over the scope of the
General Welfare Clause have largely been resolved. What remains is the resolution of an equally perplexing issue: can sufficient fiscal "room" be maintained for
sustainable national investment within the range of purposes for which federal
funds are now appropriated, including the massive but necessary entitlement
programs that consume an increasing share of our budgetary resources? This
issue is explored in the epilogue in the context of a discussion of sustainable
national investment in a contemporary context.[23]

CHAPTER 16

A National Road Perspective on America's Twenty-First-Century Infrastructure Challenges

Twenty-First-Century Infrastructure Challenges

What is the nature of the new challenges in surface transportation that the United States will face in the twenty-first century? In building the National Road the United States made its earliest serious effort to address its infrastructure needs on a national, interstate, and holistic basis, with the federal government providing the preponderance of the funding and much of the direction. The lessons of that experience would seem to be relevant today, whether the challenge is one of confronting massive congestion, improving safety, enhancing intermodality, supporting the role of the United States in a global economy, or surmounting other obstacles yet to be identified. The challenge of solving these problems on a fiscally sound, pay-as-you-go basis through a dedicated tax or other fund is one that the promoters of the National Road addressed, albeit unsuccessfully. Transportation leaders in the twenty-first century may learn from the experience and improve upon it. "Good roads" are as essential to the national well-being in the early twenty-first century as they were in the early nineteenth.[1]

Perspectives of the Department of Transportation's Report, 2006 Status of the Nation's Highways, Bridges, and Transit

Having traced the history of the National Road and the evolution of the federal role in the development of the nation's highway system, particularly the

211

interstate system, it seems appropriate to ask: where does the national highway system stand today? The Department of Transportation's status report for 2006 provides a snapshot of U.S. surface transportation infrastructure two hundred years after the initial authorization in 1806 for the National Road. It portrays a vast federally assisted and state-administered system of highways that, in part, reflects the origins of that system in the early-republic struggle to build that road. A major challenge, quantified in the report, is to keep the system in repair. The report provides information regarding the scope, conditions, and investment needs of that system. A separate break-out for the interstate highway system is provided, reflecting the current condition of that system at the end of the fifty-year period that began with its initial authorization under the 1956 legislation.[2]

The report's executive summary describes the critical federal role in the federal-aid highway program: "The Federal-aid highway program is a Federally assisted, State-administered program. Federal, State, and local transportation partners work together to deliver the Nation's highway program." The present system, it should be noted, evolved from the battles over financing, constitutionality, and jurisdiction that came to a head during the Monroe administration. In terms of ownership, "76.5 percent of highway miles were locally owned, States owned 20.4 percent, and 3.1 percent were owned by the Federal government."[3] With respect to operational performance, the report notes the percent of VMT (Vehicle Miles Traveled) under congested conditions rose from 2002 to 2004 but at a lower rate for the period from 1995 to 2002. Regarding safety, the fatality rate per 100 million VMT declined from 5.50 in 1966 to 1.44 in 2004. Nevertheless, the total fatalities in 2004 were 42,636.[4]

How much was spent on highways in 2004? The report notes that all levels of government spent a total of $147.5 billion for highways in that year. Of that, $70.3 billion was used for capital investment, and $36.4 billion was used for system rehabilitation. The effort to keep the roads in repair, as David Shriver, the first National Road superintendent, so consistently urged, continues to this day. The 2006 status report presents several different investment scenarios but does not recommend a particular level. It envisions the annual cost of maintaining highways and bridges for the twenty-year period from 2005 through 2024 as $78.8 billion per year. The average annual maximum economic investment, on the other hand, for the twenty-year period is $131 billion. The cost to maintain this scenario "represents the level of investments by all levels of government required to (1) maintain the existing level of bridge deficiencies in constant dollar terms, and (2) keep the physical condition and operation performance of the highway systems at a level sufficient to prevent average highway user costs (including travel time costs, vehicle operating costs, and crash costs) from rising above the existing level."[5]

What is the status of the interstate system? The 2006 report describes that system as consisting of 46,835 miles, of which 31, 477 were rural, 2,088 were small urban, and 13,270 were urban. A total of 55,315 bridges were included in the system. Users of the system drove a total of 267 billion miles on rural interstates, 25.7 billion miles on small urban interstates, and 433.9 billion miles on urban interstates. The bulk of the travel involved passenger vehicles. Fatality rates per 100 million VMT were 1.21 for rural interstates and .55 for urban interstates. Ride quality ranged from acceptable to good. With respect to current spending and future investment for urban interstates, the report observed: "[S]ignificant increases in funding for rehabilitation and expansion above current levels would be required to prevent both average physical conditions and operational performance from becoming degraded."[6]

The Perspective of the National Surface Transportation Policy and Revenue Study Commission

These highway needs have also been comprehensively discussed during the past decade in the report of a national study on the future of our transportation infrastructure by the National Surface Transportation Policy and Revenue Study Commission. The twelve-member commission includes the secretary of transportation, who chairs the commission. Three members are appointed by the president; two by the Speaker of the House; two by the House minority leader; two by the Senate majority leader; and two by the Senate minority leader. The members of the commission were appointed, pursuant to federal law, in order to study the problems facing transportation and to recommend steps that the United States should take to meet its twenty-first-century transportation needs. In its final report, issued in 2008, the commission concluded that the surface transportation system of the United States was at a "crossroads" and that the nation's "well-being, vitality and global economic leadership" were consequently at stake. The commission issued an urgent call to action. It also described—starkly—the "consequences of inaction." To this end, the report attempted to lay out in detail the scope of the investment needs for a transportation system that would respond to these challenges and recommended ten programs or priorities that it believed would constitute a framework for federal participation and funding, a framework for an adequate federal role.[7]

The commission's report suggests that its recommendations and observations should be seen as an extension of the process that began with adoption of the Federal Aid Highway Act of 1956. Without in any way diminishing the importance of that legislation as a starting point, it is suggested here that another point of departure is the experience of the National Road beginning 150 years earlier, with the enactment of the federal statute of 1806 that launched the National Road. In this way, one can better appreciate the scope of the American experience in seeking to establish an adequate body of infrastructure to meet its transportation needs, and one can weigh the force of the commission's recommendation in the light of the entirety of that experience.[8]

The points or precepts that the commission believes would best serve the national interest in a quality transportation system serve as a starting point. They include the following:

- facilities are well-maintained
- mobility within and between metropolitan areas is reliable
- transportation systems are appropriately priced
- modes are rebalanced and travel options are plentiful
- freight movement is explicitly valued
- safety is assured
- transportation decisions and resource impacts are integrated
- rational regulatory policy prevails[9]

To give effect to these principles, the commission report calls for ten recommendations that help to delineate the focus of its work, including (1) a national asset management program to rebuild America; (2) a freight transportation initiative to enhance U.S. global competitiveness; (3) congestion relief involving improved metropolitan mobility; (4) a national safe-mobility program; (5) a national access program for smaller cities and rural areas; (6) a program to serve high-growth corridors by rail; (7) a transportation investment program to support a healthy environment; (8) a program to accelerate the development of environmentally friendly replacement fuels; (9) a program for providing public access to federal lands; and (10) a coherent transportation research program for the nation.[10]

The first of the ten programs proposed by the National Transportation Policy Commission, reflecting the history of the National Road, "would put and keep the Nation's infrastructure in a state of good repair" and call upon states receiving federal assistance for capital projects to "implement a program of asset maintenance and support over the useful life of the asset." Federal contribution would be established at the 80 percent level.[11]

In describing the freight transportation aspects of its recommendations, the commission insists that the "[f]ederal government must return to its historic role of ensuring that the transportation needs of interstate commerce are met." (The elimination of "choke points" is a component of these needs.) This "historic role" was an important component of the National Road experience. Finding a "smooth way" to transport goods from the East over the mountains to the Midwest, from Maryland to the Ohio Valley, was a paramount commerce-related objective of the National Road. The Allegheny Mountains between Cumberland, Maryland, on the Potomac and Wheeling, West Virginia (then Virginia), on the Ohio constituted a major "choke point" of its era that had to be surmounted if early-republic America was to seize the economic opportunities that the West held out. By the same token, the commission report notes that by 2020 freight volumes will be 70 percent greater that they were in 1998. Without improvements to the surface transportation network, the report warns, freight transportation will become less efficient, "hampering" American competition in the global marketplace.[12]

In the area of congestion relief, the commission recommends that "a distinct program be established to fund projects that reduce congestion in our largest metropolitan areas."[13] In pushing for a national safe-mobility program, the commission points to the almost 43,000 people killed and approximately 2,575,000 people injured in highway crashes in 2006.[14]

In support of its "connecting America" recommendation, the commission recognizes that a reasonable surface-transportation system must "take into account the emergence of new cities, suburban and exurban areas, including communities in the Heartland." A purpose of the National Road, it will be remembered, was to connect the capitals of Ohio, Indiana, and Illinois.[15] In sum, many of the twenty-first-century surface-transportation challenges that the nation faces reflect the types of challenges that the nation faced, and for a time surmounted, in the era of the National Road.[16]

Costing Out and Financing
the Commission Recommendations

How much would it cost to give full life to this modern vision? The national commission report provides a summary answer to this question regarding the surface transportation improvements that it recommends. This is summarized in its part 2, chapter 4, in its table 4-22, which shows, at the high end, an annual gap of $200 billion through the twelve-year period from 2008 to 2020, for all modes; a $215 billion annual gap for the fifteen-year period, from 2020 to 2035; and a $252 billion annual gap for the next twenty years, 2036 through 2055.[17]

The commission report makes a number of broad recommendations for paying for its recommendations.[18] "The Commission strongly believes," states its report, "that, before the Federal financial support for surface transportation is increased, the Nation's surface transportation programs must be fundamentally reformed." A central recommendation of the transportation commission was "that legislation be passed in Federal FY 2008 to keep the Highway Account of the [Highway Trust Fund] solvent and prevent highway investment from falling below levels guaranteed in SAFETEA-LU." In this vein, it should be noted that in 2008, during the Bush administration, Pub. L. No. 110-318, was enacted in order to transfer federal funds to the Highway Trust Fund, because that fund had been depleted by a drop in receipts from the gasoline tax growing out of a reduction in driving during the economic downturn.[19]

In addition, the commission makes suggestions for surface transportation finance through 2025 involving increased federal revenues. In particular, declares the commission report, "We strongly support the principle of user financing that has been the backbone of transportation finance for the last 80 years," presumably a reference to the highway legislation of 1921 and certainly 1956. The commission appropriately points to the fuel tax as the most important component of the user-financing system, constituting almost 90 percent of total Highway Trust Fund revenues.[20]

The commission returns to this theme by emphasizing the importance of the fuel tax and specifying the attributes that make it particularly attractive, attributes that the proponents of the National Road must have sought in the debates of the 1820s and 1830s. The commission report states: "Among the attributes that make fuel taxes particularly attractive sources of transportation revenues are their (1) low administrative and compliance costs, (2) ability to generate substantial amounts of revenue, (3) relative stability and predictability, and (4) ease of implementation."[21] For surface transportation finance beyond 2025, the commission poses a number of federal and state revenue options such as mileage-based user fees. In this connection, the commission recommends that the next surface-transportation authorization act require a major national study to develop the specific strategies for transitioning to an alternative to the fuel tax.[22]

In a sense we are brought full circle to the 1806 legislation that spawned the National Road and that sought a reliable basis to fund it—namely, federal appropriations. We are seeking reliable alternatives to the funding source that has maintained an admirable interstate highway system since 1956: the fuel tax. The search for a sustainable financial foundation for long-term infrastructure investment for the United States, recognized as essential to the economic future of the nation, continues. In addition, the quest for sustainability, as defined by the transportation commission, includes elements, such as safety, congestion management, environmental concerns, intermodality, comprehensive service, and other issues that were only faintly recognized when Congress began the investment process with the act of 1806 initiating the National Road. These issues must be addressed successfully and effectively by those making surface transportation policy if a fully sustainable system of national investment is to be retained in the area of infrastructure.

It should be emphasized that those who formulated the idea of the National Road in 1806, including Gallatin and Jefferson, saw it as a national *imperative*. This same sense of urgency should move those who must pass on the transportation infrastructure agenda and the other investment imperatives that confront the nation in 2011 in light of the information in the reports described above.

Intergenerational Contributions and Responsibilities

Those who conceived and built the National Road responded to their generation's challenge. Despite the disappointment and frustration that may have been reflected in the legislative debates, during its years of high use the National Road facilitated the migration of tens of thousands of Americans to the Midwest. During those years, the populations of Ohio, Indiana, and Illinois greatly expanded. Westward movement across the Mississippi followed as a matter of course. Among those who migrated were the newcomers, the thousands of workers—Irish, Welsh, and other immigrants among them—who toiled to build the road and expand its benefits. Jefferson's dream of a gateway to the Far West was in that sense fulfilled even if the road, as a federally funded highway, stopped at Vandalia and ceased to be the object of federal appropriations at the end of the 1830s. From a nation of three million along the eastern seaboard, we have grown to a nation with a population of over three hundred million spread across a continent. That population continues to grow. As an artery intended to serve the common good, the National Road played a significant role in this process. Despite the disappointments and pitfalls, its founders and builders contributed much to the progress of the nation.

This story of progress is still graphically symbolized in many places along today's heritage corridor where the National Road (in the form of bridges, road segments, or tollhouses) survives. Successor arteries, such as U.S. 40 and Interstate 68 or 70, all closely parallel each other. The work of the sturdy builders of the early nineteenth century is tangibly preserved for posterity alongside that of succeeding generations.

The National Road represents an important chapter in the unique experience that is America. That it is now a recognized heritage corridor, a scenic byway, and the subject of a new National Park Service educational and interpretive center is a reflection of its unique contribution to the constitutional, economic, communication, infrastructure, and population development of the United States. Those who travel the road today are the beneficiaries of that experience as they are of the scenic, historical, and recreational attractions that it affords. However, as they travel, they carry the burden of their own generation to continue the work of essential national investment that the early builders began more than two centuries ago. For the National Road sends an unmistakable cross-generational message that an adequate road infrastructure, as part of a comprehensive, sustainable national investment agenda, maintained on a fiscally and environmentally sound basis, is indispensable to the survival and progress of the United States.

Epilogue

THE NATIONAL ROAD, THE AMERICAN RECOVERY AND REINVESTMENT ACT, AND SUSTAINABLE NATIONAL INVESTMENT IN THE TWENTY-FIRST CENTURY

The ARRA in Historical Context

In February 2009, in response to the recommendations of the Obama administration, Congress enacted the American Recovery and Reinvestment Act (ARRA) of 2009. It represented a massive effort to respond to the economic recession that had gripped the nation through 2008 as well as to finance major investments that would strengthen the national economy in the future. The new law provided for a comprehensive program of appropriations, tax cuts, and other measures, and provided for large-scale investments in infrastructure, education, energy, climate change, health, science, and other areas; a multitude of federal agencies were called upon to help administer various facets of the program. It reflected the call that the president included in his inaugural address of January 20, 2009, when he stated: "The state of the economy calls for action, bold and swift, and we will act not only to create new jobs but to lay a new foundation for growth."[1]

Was the American Recovery and Reinvestment Act, Public Law No. 111- 5, which emerged from this legislative process, wholly unrelated to earlier steps in the history of the nation that provided for national investment in the American economy? Or, despite its unique size and bold purpose, was the ARRA reflective of a continuing theme in the American experience that emphasized the public investment role of government in supporting the revival or growth of the economy when warranted? Though vastly different in scope, size, and significance, the National Road experience that began in 1806 and the ARRA stimulus legislation launched in 2009 can be seen as components of a continuing quest on the part of the American people to craft a viable and sustainable role for the government in supporting growth-producing investments in the American economy. That quest has not been without its frustrations, interruptions, and strong criticism. The history of the National Road well illustrates them. However, it has also produced large-scale benefits for the American people and has provided important precedents for the nation as a whole.[2]

President Obama's predecessors would have been amazed at the fiscal magnitude of the ARRA—some $787 billion.[3] However, they were not strangers to exhortations for major programs of national investment in their own time to stimulate the nation's economic growth and prosperity. A number of these legislative investments were made in the era of the National Road. Indeed, as the nation's first federally financed interstate highway, the National Road, while minuscule in comparison to the aggregate investments funded in the ARRA, constituted, in its time, an important and widely debated early-republic national investment in the nation's economy.[4]

The principal National Road–era presidents each in his own way urged the country to adopt what was in effect a policy of *sustainable national investment* involving infrastructure, education, science, and other areas that would enhance the nation's level of economic prosperity and help to unify its diverse geographic regions.[5] From a legal perspective, Joseph Story, as commentator rather than jurist, remarked favorably on the "the nature of the [federal spending] power, which renders it in the highest degree expedient, if not indispensable, for the due operations of the national government." His interpretation helped to establish a broad reading of the spending power that would support a policy of national investment when and where needed. The ARRA represents a twenty-first-century expression of that vision.[6]

To be sure, one must recognize that allusions to the era of the National Road do not imply that nineteenth-century investment problems and solutions are the equivalent of what is needed for a twenty-first-century America in or out of the throes of an economic crisis. The scope and reach of the global economy has expanded exponentially since the experience of the Early Republic. It requires infinitely more complex, expensive, and technological solutions. While they run parallel to each other in some places, Interstate 70 is not the equivalent of U.S. 40; likewise, U.S. 40 is not a replica of the National Road. Nineteenth-century solutions will not respond to the needs of the current generation. Nevertheless, as we grapple with the economic problems of 2011 and beyond, perspectives reflective of the nation's "founding principles" and early precedents may inform our search for contemporary solutions. The "smooth way" across the Allegheny Mountains that George Washington sought was designed to stimulate the American economy of his day. It was also intended to avoid the diversion of economic activity from the new nation to other sections of the North American continent not then under the control of the United States. American economic investment of the nineteenth century had as one element the defense and advancement of the American economy.[7]

The public investment tradition represented by the National Road survived its transfer to the states in the 1830s and its subsequent demise. Presidents of both major political parties became advocates for such national investment in infrastructure and education. Despite the rigors of the Civil War, President Abraham Lincoln supported aid to railroad projects that he thought would be, over time, of economic benefit to future generations; aid to higher education in the form of the Morrill Act to stimulate agricultural production; and aid that would encourage the settlement of the West through the Homestead Act of 1862. Rutherford B. Hayes followed Lincoln's lead, albeit unsuccessfully, by calling for federal aid to elementary and secondary education in a way that would assist newly emancipated Americans to take their rightful place in the nation's economic and political life. As Congress considered his stimulus package, President Obama noted the occasion of the two-hundredth anniversary of Lincoln's birth by paying tribute to Lincoln's role in fostering economic growth through such investments.[8]

In the mid-twentieth Century, federal investment efforts resulted in the launching of the Eisenhower Interstate Highway System through the Federal Aid Highway Act of 1956, another landmark in the pathway to sustainable national investment, designed to support, among other purposes, the economic goals of the United States. The Eisenhower administration supported aid to education through the enactment of the National Defense Education Act of 1957, which emphasized science and mathematics education. Both initiatives can be seen as part of a long-standing tradition in the United States to undertake sustainable national investment, at least in part, to stimulate the nation's economy over the long term through improved nationwide surface transportation and through improved schools, colleges, and universities.[9]

The educational component of this investment thrust was vastly enhanced in 1965 as part of the Great Society launched during the administration of Lyndon B. Johnson. The Elementary and Secondary Education Act of 1965 constituted landmark education legislation, designed in part to boost educational achievement for children through federally financed compensatory education programs to respond to the educational needs of the impoverished and educationally deprived. The Higher Education Act of 1965 expanded access to colleges and universities through the adoption of broad programs of federally assisted student financial aid, including what was to become the Pell Grant program (grants to needy students) and a range of student loan programs.[10] During the decades that followed, these twentieth-century programs were frequently reauthorized in part in order to enable them to better serve the nation's interests in improving its competitive posture in an increasingly globalized economy.[11]

This tradition of sustainable national investment in such areas as infrastructure, education, and science was strongly extended in 2009 in the form of the American Recovery and Reinvestment Act signed by President Obama on February 17, 2009.

It was designed to respond to the economic challenges facing the United States and to strengthen its capacity for economic growth in future years, and on that occasion, the president noted the ties to the nation's past investment history. He observed: "Because we know we can't build our economic future on the transportation and information networks of the past, we are remaking the American landscape with the largest new investment in our Nation's infrastructure since Eisenhower built an Interstate Highway System in the 1950s."[12]

Before his election, Mr. Obama had himself recognized the role of earlier generations of American leaders in crafting this tradition of positive government involvement as a compelling and driving force of American economic growth when he wrote in his book *The Audacity of Hope* that

> Hamilton's and Lincoln's basic insight—that the resources and power of the national government can facilitate rather than supplant a vibrant free market—has continued to be one of the cornerstones of both Republican and Democratic policies at every stage of America's development. The Hoover Dam, the Tennessee Valley Authority, the interstate highway system, the Human Genome Project—*time and again, government investment has helped pave the way for an explosion of private economic activity.* And through the creation of a system of public schools and institutions of higher education, as well as programs like the GI Bill that made a college education available to millions, government has helped provide individuals the tools to adapt and innovate in a climate of constant technological change.[13]

Stages of the American Recovery and Reinvestment Act: From House Bill to Conference Report—Conflict and Compromise

THE HOUSE BILL

The various stages of the enactment process leading to Public Law 111-5, the ARRA, reflect these considerations. In general, the thrust of the House-passed bill (H.R. 1) was to rely on a combination of tax cuts and spending programs (totaling over $800 billion) to achieve the related goals of economic recovery and reinvestment in the economy. The House bill contained some $355 billion relating to investments in highways, education, and energy.[14] The president, seeking prompt action on the measure, told his newly established Economic Recovery Advisory Board: "Now is the time for Congress to act. It is time to pass an economic recovery and reinvestment plan to get our economy moving."[15]

THE SENATE DEBATE: THE MCCAIN AMENDMENT

A different response came in the Senate in a form of an amendment broadly supported by Senate Republicans. The substantive and other differences in the Senate of the 111th Congress over the scope of H.R. 1 were the focus of a debate on a substitute amendment proposed by Senator McCain (R. Ariz.) on February 5 and discussed on that day. In introducing the amendment, Senator McCain criticized the stimulus package contained in H.R. 1 as too big and too costly, as unlikely to sufficiently stimulate the economy, and as likely to increase the national debt. He proposed an alternative that would cost $421 billion in place of the over $800 billion package before the Senate. The alternative was strongly weighted in favor of tax-cut provisions ($275 billion of the $421 billion appropriated), provisions for increased unemployment insurance benefits, extended food stamp benefits, and a $15,000 tax credit for first-time home buyers. At the same time Senator McCain's alternative recognized the need for long-term investment in at least one category; it called for $45 billion of spending in transportation infrastructure, comparable to the House-bill level. However, Senator McCain's amendment would have eliminated most of the other spending for long-term investments, including those for health care, energy, education, and technology. Senator McCain's concern with the H.R. 1 alternative before the Senate was that it would worsen the long-term budgetary situation of the United States.[16] Other Senators responded to these points in a manner supportive of the version of H.R. 1 ultimately passed by Congress.[17]

THE SENATE DEBATE: THE COLLINS-REID AMENDMENT COMPROMISE AND THE CONFERENCE REPORT

After the rejection of the McCain Amendment on February 5, the Senate adopted a compromise amendment negotiated by a group of senators including Republican Senators Susan Collins and Olympia Snowe, and Senator Arlen Spector, then a Republican. The compromise reduced the bill from the House level by about $100 billion, mostly by eliminating some education expenditures (including expenditures for school construction). The differences between the House and Senate bills were resolved in a conference report that produced the final stimulus bill, restoring some of the education investments and making other changes. The conference report was approved on February 13, 2009, and sent to the president, who signed the bill, as mentioned, on February 17. Despite its significance and its purpose, the ARRA remains, as Jonathan Alter has observed, "one of the most important but least appreciated pieces of legislation of modern times."[18]

The ARRA and Transformational Investments and the Role of State and Federal Administration

In signing the ARRA into law President Obama identified a number of transformational investments funded by the law, including those in such areas as infrastructure, education, energy, ("[I]n the process we will transform the way we use energy") and health.[19] While these initiatives were targeted on job creation to counter the severe national recession as a central and overriding objective, they were also directed at investment that would require a longer-term framework to produce the institutional and economic growth-oriented change envisaged. A comparable goal, it would seem, characterized the American tradition of economic growth-oriented investment exemplified early in our history by the National Road experience.[20]

The ARRA was thus both a "reinvestment" and a "recovery" measure. The investments provided through the appropriations enacted under the ARRA were intended to stimulate a struggling economy through job creation and enhancement of confidence. As Judge Richard A. Posner has observed, "[F]ortunately, there is more that government can do to arrest a downward economic spiral besides pushing down interest rates. It can offset the decline in private consumption and investment in a recession or a depression by increasing public investment."[21]

Following the enactment of the ARRA, the White House provided a breakdown of the bill dividing up its $787 billion into the following categories (1) tax relief, $288 billion; (2) state and local fiscal relief, $144 billion; (3) infrastructure and science, $111 billion, (4) protecting the vulnerable, $81 billion; (5) health care, $59 billion; (6) education and training, $53 billon; (7) energy, $43 billion; and (8) other expenditures, $8 billion. (It will be noted that, of the $437 billion in discrete investment categories 3–8, $164 billion is devoted to infrastructure, education, and science, which were also principal investment categories funded or at least discussed in the National Road era.) Jonathan Alter captures this long-term investment thrust when he observes: "Contrary to public perception, the vast bulk of stimulus spending went to worthy programs, mostly long-neglected infrastructure projects such as local sewage systems and sensible investments in future productivity such as clean energy, scientific and medical research, and electronic hospital records."[22]

In light of these figures, it has been urged that the ARRA was inappropriately enlarging the size and authority of the federal government, a concern that also characterized some of the debates over the National Road. If, however, the ARRA involved a major infusion of federal dollars to stimulate a lagging economy, it also involved a major infusion of resources directed to state and local governments to help them to carry out state functions despite deep state-budget shortfalls. The bulk of these appropriations are administered by federal agencies through grants made to state and local agencies under formulas contained in previously enacted federal statutes. While some have argued that these provisions of the ARRA unduly expand the role of the federal government and trend toward "big government," the effect of the law is largely to expand the authority and flexibility of state and local agencies by providing them with the resources to carry out programs of assistance or benefit to their constituents in such areas as education, infrastructure, and health. For example, under Title I of the Elementary and Secondary Education Act and the Individuals with Disabilities Education Act, funds appropriated under the ARRA for the education of the disadvantaged ($13 billion) and for the disabled ($12 billion) are distributed to the states (under existing laws providing for these programs) and then subgranted to local public school districts in accordance with statutory formulas provided in that legislation.[23]

Additional education funds are provided to the states under the state and local relief category so that educational services are not curtailed as a result of the economic contraction. The state and local agencies are thus empowered with greater resources to meet the educational needs of the population within the given state. The investment is of benefit to the nation as a whole because the skills of its citizens are enhanced through the educational services that are provided at the state and local level. Similarly, ARRA funds for highways ($27 billion) and transit ($30 billion) are largely administered by state highway or transportation departments. The administrative decisions that make these education investments transformational are made by the school administrators, principals, and teachers at the community level within the framework of the applicable federal law. The national economy as a whole benefits from the enhancements to skill building through education and infrastructure improvement through highway and transit investments. Long-term deficiencies or shortfalls in these areas are addressed. However, state and local officials make the key decisions regarding the administration and expenditure of the funds.[24]

A smaller amount of ARRA resources are directed at cutting-edge efforts to transform the American economy in the areas of health, energy, and technology through grants made directly from the federal government to the local or private agencies carrying out the activities receiving support. For example, $20 billion is appropriated for health information technology (HIT) to be administered by the Department of Health and Human Services; $16 billion is to be used for activities related to renewable energy through programs administered by the Department of Energy; $10 billion is made available for health research to be administered by the National Institutes of Health; $7 billion is appropriated for broadband technology to be administered by the appropriate federal agencies; and $4 billion is made available for National Institute of Science grants. The State Incentive Grant program, a part of the State Fiscal Stabilization Fund contained in Title XIV of the ARRA, represents another effort at transformational national investment. It provides $4.35 billion for FY 2010 from which grants will be made to states that have "made significant progress in achieving equity in teacher distribution, establishing a longitudinal data system," and achieving other milestones relating to education reform. The Department of Education has used this unprecedented discretionary fund to encourage states to participate in a "race to the top" designed to incentivize education reform at the state and local level.[25]

Whether administered through formula grants to the states or direct grants made by the administering federal agency, the former are designed to lead to transformational investments that may address major obstacles that impede economic growth and progress. This mix of administering agencies at federal, state, and local levels ensures that a federal-state-local partnership is involved in driving the transformations and that a direct federal role is limited to those areas where direct federal grants to the ultimate recipient or researcher are absolutely necessary, keeping expansion of federal authority and bureaucracy to a minimum.[26] Thus, the preponderance of state-administered (but federally assisted) programs in the mix provided by the ARRA reflects, in a sense, the compromise advocated by Monroe in his 1822 memorandum. There Monroe recognized the constitutional validity of federal appropriations for infrastructure investment. However, he also insisted that these investments be carried out in a way that did not involve assumption of federal "jurisdiction" over state functions or property.[27]

In light of this discussion, what is investment spending for purposes of an examination of the concept of sustainable national investment? As discussed here, such investment ideally or typically has a number of characteristics. It is: (1) government investment carried out through federal appropriation; (2) generally carried out for long-term purposes; (3) authorized by the federal spending power under Article I, section 8, clause 1, of the U.S. Constitution; (4) designed to stimulate economic change, growth, or stabilization; (5) based upon a congressional finding, express or implied, that it has a reasonable likelihood of success; (6) typically designed to overcome perceived obstacles to economic growth; (7) designed to encourage or involve widespread participation of the people in that growth; (8) *generally directed at activities that only the government is willing or able to fund or carry out;* (9) supported by enacted legislation; and (10) ideally initiated and carried out with a solid foundation of bipartisan support (or at least a temporary suspension of partisanship).[28] At least for a time, the key national investments in our history have reflected a number of these characteristics, including the National Road. For the most part, the national investments examined here are products of discretionary federal spending. That category of spending, it should be noted, provides an opportunity for adjustment and increases or decreases in the level of investment based upon the applicable program and fiscal circumstances.[29]

Financing the ARRA, Sustainable National Investment, and Fiscal Discipline: The Grand Balance

The National Road and other federally assisted internal improvement investments of the early republic were generally funded from surplus funds. A major question that confronted architects of the ARRA was whether to fund the package through increased taxes or through borrowing, which would involve adding to an already deficit-ridden budget. The thrust of economic thought at the time did not favor paying for the stimulus measure through increased taxes, an option that would tend to nullify its effect in stimulating an economy in or coming out of recession. Instead, any resulting increase in the deficit would presumably be corrected when economic circumstances improved. The observations of Judge Posner seem relevant: "But for a confidence-building public-works program to be effective in arresting an economic collapse, the government must be able to finance its increased spending by means that do not reduce private spending commensurately. If it finances the program by taxation, it will be draining cash from the economy at the same time that it is injecting cash into it. But if it borrows to finance the program . . . , the costs may be deferred until the economy is well on the way to recovery and can afford to pay them without endangering economic stability."[30]

This observation, however, should not be taken to suggest that fiscal discipline is unrelated to the future success of sustainable national investment. The question left unanswered in the ARRA is whether critical investments in infrastructure, education, climate change, and other areas of major federal concern can be fiscally sustained in the long term. Whether or not they are "paid for" at the time of enactment, they must eventually be "paid for" in the future through program changes or additional revenue that will address the substantial budgetary challenges that the American people must face. These grow out of the cumulative deficits as reflected in the national debt and the implicit unfunded obligations related to the entitlement programs, in particular Social Security, Medicaid, and Medicare. Such budget reform is believed necessary to avoid crowding future national investments out of the budget or the creation of

economic problems that cancel out the gains made through such national investments as those made in the ARRA.[31]

The very magnitude of the ARRA demands an effort to balance the investments for which it provides with a measure of fiscal discipline once the
sought-after recovery is substantially achieved. The prospects for the budget
deficit for fiscal year 2010 (as of this writing estimated to be $1.556 trillion or
10.6 percent of GDP), the increasing national debt ($13 trillion for fiscal year
2010), and unfunded obligations growing out of the entitlement programs pose
a danger that future budgets will afford insufficient room for the maintenance
of substantial investments in infrastructure, education, and other areas necessary to support adequate economic growth. The concern that such budgetary
"crowd-out" might take place has long been recognized. The need with respect
to the economic contraction that faced the nation at the end of 2008 merely accelerated and dramatized that prospect. Moreover, the growing fiscal challenge,
coupled with the magnitude of the stimulus packages, in the financial area (e.g.,
TARP) and job creation area (the ARRA in the 111th Congress) must not be
permitted to cancel out whatever gains these legislative changes produce. To
render a long-term program of public investment for the economy sustainable,
meaningful fiscal discipline would seem essential to complement and sustain it.

To this end, shortly after enactment of the ARRA, the president convened
a Fiscal Responsibility Summit at the White House to address fiscal deficits and
the growing national debt. He called for continuing bipartisan efforts to address
this challenge, and attendees reflected on the role of rising health care costs and
an increasingly aging population in contributing to the fiscal problems. At the
conclusion of the Fiscal Responsibility Summit, the president sought to reconcile the ARRA enactment and the debt-deficit challenge:

> We chose to move forward on a recovery package because there was
> strong sense among the vast majority of economists that if we did not
> try to fill a $1 trillion-a-year hole in demand, because of the drastic
> pulling back of businesses and consumers, that the recession would get
> worse, unemployment would increase, and as a consequence, tax rev-
> enues would go down and the long-term deficit and debt projections
> would be even higher. . . . [T]he reason that there is no contradiction,
> from my perspective[,] in doing the recovery package first, but now
> focusing on the medium and long term, is because our hope is that this
> economy starts recovering. We will have taken a hit, in terms of our
> debt and our deficit. But as Bob Greenstein said, the recovery package
> will account for about one-tenth of 1 percent of our long-term debt.

He recognized the fiscal problems that the nation faced in this context: "*The real
problems are the structural deficits and structural debt that we've been accumulating
and all of us are complicit in.*"

Subsequently, at the closing session of the Jobs and Economic Growth Forum, in December 2009 President Obama returned to the fiscal deficit and debt issues in the context of growth stimulating national public investment and summarized the key economic-balancing issue confronting the nation at the threshold of 2010 and beyond:

> We have a structural deficit that is real and growing, apart from the financial crisis. We inherited it. We're spending about 23 percent of GDP, and we take in 18 percent of GDP, and that gap is growing because health care costs—Medicare and Medicaid in particular—are growing, and we've got to do something about that.
>
> You then layer on top of that the huge loss of tax revenue as a consequence of the financial crisis and the greater demands for unemployment insurance and so forth. That's another layer. Probably the smallest layer is actually what we did in terms of the Recovery Act . . . we've got a 9-point something trillion dollar deficit. Maybe a trillion dollars of it can be attributed to both the Recovery Act as well as the cleanup work that we had to do in terms of the banks. . . .
>
> Now if we can't grow our economy then it is going to be that much harder for us to reduce the deficit. *The single most important thing we could do right now for deficit reduction is to spark strong economic growth.* . . . The last thing we would want to do in the midst of a—what is a weak recovery is us to essentially take more money out of the system either by raising taxes or by drastically slashing spending.[32]

It should be noted that the health information-technology investment provisions in the ARRA are designed to address the long-term Medicare fiscal shortfall by reducing the costs of providing health care services through better information technology. In addition to helping reduce costs through information technology and digital record keeping, it has been suggested that this project may also identify practices that lower massive health care costs; and lowering such costs is a goal that is essential to establishing fiscal discipline in the health care area. Moreover, to the extent that the ARRA's transformational and other investments produce significant economic growth, they will presumably contribute to improved fiscal results. Thus, arguably, a part payment is made by the ARRA stimulus package itself in the direction of addressing the structural debt and deficit problems that the president referenced.[33]

A detailed description of the various alternatives for achieving fiscal sustainability for the nation's body of national investments to spur economic growth is beyond the scope of this epilogue to a long account of one early national investment: the National Road. Crafting such a program presents an excruciatingly difficult challenge. It embraces the massive task of bringing our entitlement programs, particularly Social Security and Medicare, into actuarial balance without impairing the effectiveness of these programs in serving the senior community. Indeed, this challenge is the core problem. Several decades of high-level studies and recommendations on the subject have yielded multiple options but no consensus on the content of fiscal sustainability or the legislation to implement it. The consequence of inaction is to threaten the continuity of the kind of investment programs contained in the ARRA or comparable investments programs enacted separately in the future, as well as to endanger the nation's economic position.[34]

Moreover, the issue of how to pay for critical public investment programs resonates across the history of the nation from the era of the National Road, as described above, to the end of the twentieth century. Failure to find an adequate source of dedicated funding helped force the transfer of the road to the states. President Bill Clinton, a strong advocate of national fiscal discipline, struggled throughout his presidency to achieve a viable balance between his support for vital investment programs and his efforts to find adequate revenue to pay for them; by the end of his presidency he had achieved equilibrium.

Quite apart from an examination of detailed policy changes to address such deficits in the future, what is needed now is a candid, continuing, and solution-oriented national conversation that will engage the American people in a discussion of the long-term fiscal challenges that are presented and the dire consequences that face us if those challenges are not effectively addressed. The alternative of decreasing or suspending national investment expenditures for infrastructure, education, energy, or other areas in order to address the fiscal challenges involves equally dire consequences that must be a part of that national conversation. Only when the American people are fully engaged in confronting these issues will a comprehensive solution be possible. This engagement may be facilitated if the conversation is organized within the framework of an appropriate and high-level government agency, commission, or other entity. The conversation should be coupled with the establishment of an appropriate "special process" designed to formulate and present to Congress, on a bipartisan basis, effective long-term solutions designed to achieve long-term budget stability. The steps must begin forthwith so that whatever solutions emerge from it can be phased in over a sufficiently long period to be viable.[35]

In carrying out that conversation, participants may want to take account of the observations of the Committee for a Responsible Budget in its discussion of the June 2009 Long Term Budget Outlook of the Congressional Budget Office, which pointed to what it regarded as unsustainable debt levels projected by 2040 largely as a result of excess health-cost growth and population aging. In concluding its discussion, the committee suggested: "Some actions can be taken to address aging . . . including enacting policies to increase the size of the labor force, encourage longer work lives, or increased national saving and investment. But ultimately, the long-term budget outlook will ne-cessitate serious tax and spending changes. Absent such changes, we face the real threat of a fiscal and economic crisis more severe than what we've already endured." As indicated at the Fiscal Responsibility Summit and in other con-texts, there seems to be an understanding of this challenge and the necessity for striking a grand balance involving growth-fostering national investment within a framework of meaningful and steadfast fiscal discipline.[36]

Is There a Sufficient Wellspring of Support for Sustainable National Investment?

In his book *The Pro-Growth Progressive: An Economic Strategy for Shared Pros-perity*, Gene Sperling, currently director of the National Economic Council, strongly argues the case for public investment strategies that stimulate economic growth in a way that benefits a wide spectrum of the society. He says: "A pre-sumption in favor of minimalist government will . . . prevent us from addressing two of the paramount challenges to America's competitiveness: how to ensure that we have an increasing number of highly skilled workers and how to stay at the cutting edge of the technological change that creates whole new industries and drives job growth in the dynamism economy." Other scholars in the field of economics have provided their own perspective on the contribution of national investment to widely shared economic growth. Moreover, there is an impressive body of literature describing the positive economic results of such investment in terms of such factors as growth, income, jobs, and other benefits. Evidently, Albert Gallatin's observations of 1808 regarding the value of infrastructure investment in the early republic have their counterpart in the early twenty-first century. General perceptions of that value might be reinforced and more widely appreciated if an appropriate governmental office were charged with the responsibility of monitoring and reporting on the outcomes of long-term trans-formational investments, including but not confined to those provided for in the ARRA, on a government-wide basis.[37]

Bipartisan support for the ARRA was extremely limited in the Senate and lacking in the House. Nonetheless, it was sufficient to permit enactment. More-over, the implementation of the act received broader, bipartisan support among the governors who were called upon to administer it and whose states were primary recipients of its provisions. Thus, at the National Governors' Conference held in February 2009, both Governor Rendell of Pennsylvania, a Democrat, and Gover-nor Douglas of Vermont, a Republican, spoke in support of the bill. A number of other Republican governors, including Governors Crist and Schwarzenegger, were on record as actively supporting implementation of the act, as President Obama noted when he spoke to the conference. Looking to the future, a greater degree of bipartisanship may be necessary in Congress to facilitate the enactment of needed future national-investment legislation.[38]

In an effort to attract broad support for its stimulus program, the administration has made substantial efforts to ensure that the implementation of the ARRA is carried out in an objective, economic, and transparent manner. Vice President Biden was asked by the president to oversee the administrative efforts to achieve the rollout of the funds and to ensure their use in a "swift," "efficient," and "effective" way. An inspector general was also appointed as chair of the Recovery Act Transparency and Accountability Board to oversee this process. A Web site, Recovery.gov, was also established to ensure accountability and transparency.[38]

Thus, just as in the case of the National Road, accountability to be pursued through oversight of the investment at the highest level of the federal government was made a priority. President Obama stressed the investment aspects of this agenda when he told the governors: "From my perspective, providing all of you additional resources to rebuild roads and bridges and levees and dams that will enhance the quality of life of your state but also make it more economically competitive, that's not wasteful."[39]

Continuing the Reinvestment Strategy in the Long Term: Infrastructure and Education; The Twin Pillars

Time does not permit full discussion of all the areas for investment provided for in the ARRA. The focus here is on both infrastructure and education as examples. It was on education as a topic of national investment along with infrastructure that the leaders of the United States focused during the early republic. The relevant discussions between Presidents Madison and Monroe, at the time of latter's assumption of executive responsibilities, regarding the importance of both investment areas are depicted in chapter 4. The emphasis on infrastructure in the ARRA is not an isolated gesture; it is strongly reinforced in related legislation, Public Law 111-8, the Omnibus Appropriations Act, 2009. In Division 1, Title I, of that act, appropriations are made for fiscal year 2009 for the Department of Transportation, including substantial improvements for airports, air carriers, highways, mass transit, railroads, and high-speed rail. For example, under the Federal Aid Highways account, $40.7 billion is made available for federal-aid highways and safety construction programs for FY 2009.

Smaller sums are made available to improve railroad and mass-transit services. Taken together, the ARRA and the 2009 appropriation act afforded substantial sums to improve transportation infrastructure.[40]

A more detailed account of the steps that are being taken to advance the ARRA's transportation infrastructure goals has been provided in the Department of Transportation's Recovery Web site. For example, as that site indicates, on June 3, 2009, Vice President Biden and Department of Transportation Secretary Ray LaHood met with governors to discuss key transport related investment programs. In particular, plans were considered for implementation of the administration's high-speed rail initiative, for which $8 billion was made available in the ARRA and $5 billion in the 2010 budget. Vice President Biden observed that the high-speed rail investment would "transform [the nation's rail system] fundamentally." Secretary LaHood said: "America is ready to embrace a new level of passenger rail service that offers a safe, convenient and sustainable way to travel from city to city." The interdisciplinary effects of the high-speed rail investment were noted in terms of the potential that high-speed rail has "to reduce U.S. dependence on oil, lower harmful carbon emissions, and foster new economic development."[41]

In the area of education, both in the ARRA and in the related provisions of the Omnibus Appropriations Act, again substantial sums are made available for education activities on the thesis that effective education spending will lead to demonstrable economic growth. Conversely, a failure to effectively narrow the so-called achievement gap and to respond effectively to perceived shortfalls in high school–level and postsecondary-level graduation rates will cost the United States dearly in terms of lost economic opportunity.[42] The ARRA (Public Law 111-5) includes resources to carry out some of this reform work. As in the case of infrastructure investment, these educational initiatives in the ARRA are reinforced in the Omnibus Appropriations Act (Public Law 111-8) under the Department of Education and other headings. But this is just a start.[43] The Education Department's ARRA-related document, "Using ARRA Funds to Drive School Reform and Improvement," indicates some of the principles that the department is using to attain these goals with those funds. The document expresses a key goal of the department in the use of ARRA funds: "In America, all students should graduate from high school prepared for college and a career and have the opportunity to complete at least one year of postsecondary education. This means that we must dramatically improve student achievement and close the achievement gap." Noting that "[m]any school districts may need to use a portion of their ARRA funds to save jobs, " the document advises: "[E]very district and school should be considering how to use [ARRA funds] to improve student outcomes over the next two years and advance reforms that will have even longer-term impact."[44]

Current research suggests that other efforts, such as broadening early child-hood educational opportunities, encouraging socioeconomic integration in willing school districts, strengthening high school programs for disadvantaged students, creating smaller schools with lowered student-teacher ratios, significant changes to NCLB, social and health supports, and more student financial aid for postsecondary education may all contribute to closing that gap or accelerating increased achievement levels. Research in the future may demonstrate whether or how well those other strategies, individually or in combination, may contribute to that result. The use of ARRA funds as suggested above may help to achieve further clarity regarding the best options. Beyond ARRA, a higher level of sustainable national investment in education will be necessary over coming decades to implement these changes, assuming a strong likelihood of success, in an efficient and effective manner.[45]

Beyond the ARRA

It is probably too early to assess the total impact of the ARRA in responding to the economic crisis that faced the nation in 2008 and 2009. However, despite strong cross-winds, some promising signs have been recognized. For example, noted journalist Fareed Zakaria stated in a May, 2010 column that "evidence mounts that the United States has emerged from the financial crisis of 2008 in better condition than anyone predicted 18 months ago" and attributed this result in part to "an America that acted speedily, comprehensively and with ample resources." The ARRA can be considered a component of that response. The role of the ARRA in stimulating job creation to counter the effects of the recession will constitute a major factor in the assessment of its impact. The results of its transformational investments should also be taken into account in that regard. It is unlikely that the bold infrastructure- and education-related goals reflected in the above-described ARRA initial guidance documents will be fully achieved during the lifespan of the ARRA. Establishing a thriving high-speed rail service is likely to be a multidecade task, as the DOT materials suggest by reference to the "down payment" nature of the investment. All fourth-grade children are, unfortunately, not likely to be reading at the basic level or above by the time that the last ARRA dollar has been spent. Further well-conceived national investments, in good economic times as well as in bad, will be required to overcome the obstacles presented by deficient infrastructure, academic achievement and school completion gaps, and comparable problems in the health, energy, and science areas represented in the ARRA. Future Congresses, convening after the 112th, will be called upon to provide the necessary authorization and appropriation legislation. The people of the United States will be called upon, again and again, to engage in shared sacrifice for the general welfare to the end that these vitally needed investment programs will be paid for on a current and fiscally responsible basis, so as not to preclude future investments or nullify the potentially positive impact of a sustainable national-investment strategy. To add to the challenge, once the economy has recovered, it is likely that these investments will largely have to be provided on a budget-neutral basis, absent dire emergencies. Moreover, proponents of such investment will have to overcome deep misgivings on the part of a substantial segment of the American public, misgivings that can be resolved, if at all, only through effective efforts to reach for common ground on the role of sustainable national investment in American economic life. Administration of investment projects and policy on a basis that emphasizes, where practicable, the role of local, state and interstate agencies should be encouraged. Essential to the process as well is a coalition of national unity that responds to the nation's need for both sustainable national investment and genuine fiscal discipline over the long term.[46]

To ignore this need is to deny the government a significant degree of flexibility in responding to crises, such as the recent major recession, or in maintaining and improving vital assets such as infrastructure and educational capacity. Restricting this flexibility potentially jeopardizes the common defense and general welfare of the United States, objectives that have been recognized in the Constitution since its adoption.[47] As the fiscal commission has recommended: "We should cut red tape and unproductive government spending that hinders job creation and growth. At the same time, we must invest in education, infrastructure, and high-value research and development to help our economy grow, keep us globally competitive, and make it easier for businesses to create jobs."

This would seem to be the message of the ARRA. This was also the message of the National Road and the public investments that followed it during the nineteenth and twentieth centuries.[48]

James Monroe, the last of the Revolutionary era presidents and a strong supporter of the National Road, continued to search for a creative balance between targeted national infrastructure investment and the preservation of federalism. He recognized that such a balance could be achieved only within a sound fiscal framework. For example, in his 1823 annual message, he proposed a mechanism that would have permitted the federal government to arrange with affected states for toll collections to finance repairs on the National Road. Monroe also sought common ground on issues pertaining to the federal role essential to that balance. Thus, after his presidency, in 1828, he wrote to John C. Calhoun urging that southern states take steps to "diffuse a common feeling and bind the Union by the strongest ties . . . more closely together." He saw roads and canals as essential to the creation of those bonds. This search for balance involving sustainable national investment in infrastructure, education and other key areas of national concern in the framework of a dynamic federal system remains today an important portion of the legacy of the National Road experience.[49]

Appendix: National Road Time Line

1752	Nemacolin said to blaze trail from Cumberland to Redstone Creek
1753	George Washington travels to Fort LeBoeuf to warn the French to stay out of the Ohio Valley
1754	Washington leads expedition of Colonial troops to southwestern Pennsylvania, encounters force under Jumonville, builds military road, and fights battle at Fort Necessity
1755	Washington participates in ill-fated Braddock campaign in French and Indian War
1776	July 4, Declaration of Independence
1781	Battle of Yorktown; British defeated
1783	Treaty of Paris ends the war and confirms independence
1784	Washington travels to Virginia seeking the best route for a good road over the Allegheny Mountains
1787	Delegates in Constitutional Convention in Philadelphia approve United States Constitution containing a power to tax "to provide for the General Welfare of the United States"; the Constitution is submitted to the states for ratification
1788	A sufficient number of states ratify the Constitution
1789	George Washington is sworn in as the first president of the United States and delivers an inaugural address and a State of the Union address that recommend post offices and post roads
1791	Alexander Hamilton submits a report maintaining that bounties for manufacturing can be provided by Congress under the power to tax (and spend) for the general welfare
1794	Whiskey Rebellion takes place in southwestern Pennsylvania
1796	Zane's Trace expedition

1797	Washington delivers last State of the Union message and continues to propose public investment projects
1800	Thomas Jefferson is elected third president of the United States
1802	Congress passes and President Jefferson signs legislation calling for the admission of Ohio to the Union; legislation provides for reserving funds for roads to and through the state
1806	March 29, Congress passes and President Jefferson signs federal legislation providing for the laying out of a road from Cumberland, Maryland, to the Ohio River (National Road)
1806	Commissioners under 1806 act submit report to Albert Gallatin, secretary of the treasury under Jefferson, suggesting a route for the road
1808	Commissioners submit second report suggesting a deviation through Uniontown; Jefferson approves
1808	When Pennsylvania insists that the road must also pass through Washington, Pennsylvania, Jefferson at first disagrees but is persuaded by Gallatin to acquiesce
1808	James Madison is elected fourth president
1809	Madison takes office
1810	Act of February 4, 1810, appropriates an additional $60,000 for the road from Cumberland to Brownsville
1811	Construction begins on National Road, starting at Cumberland; Superintendent David Shriver reports to Gallatin
1812	Act of May 6 appropriates an additional $30,000 for the road from Cumberland to Brownsville
1812	War of 1812 commences
1815	Act of February 15 appropriates an additional $100,000 for the road
1817	March 3, Madison vetoes Bonus Bill and then leaves the White House
1817	March 4, James Monroe is inaugurated
1822	Congress passes bill providing for federally administered tollgates on the Cumberland Road
1822	Monroe vetoes Gates Bill on constitutional grounds but sends memorandum to Congress concluding that Congress may appropriate federal funds for the Cumberland Road under its power to spend for the general welfare of the United States
1823	Act of February 28, 1823, appropriates $25,000 for repairs for the road from Cumberland to Wheeling, Virginia; act is approved by Monroe
1824	Monroe signs bill authorizing federal road surveys
1824	Election of 1824 is thrown into the House of Representatives, which selects John Quincy Adams

1825	Act of March 3, 1825, appropriates $150,000 for construction of road from right bank of the Ohio River to Zanesville, Ohio
1825	March 4, John Quincy Adams delivers pro-internal-improvement inaugural address
1825	December, Adams sends first annual message to Congress promoting an internal improvement policy including funding for the National Road
1826	Act of March 3, 1826, appropriates funds for continuation of the road.
1827	Act of March 2, 1827, appropriates $30,000 for the repair of the road from Cumberland to Wheeling
1828	Act of May 19, 1828, appropriates $175,000 for the completion of the road to Zanesville, Ohio
1828–29	Congress debates but does not pass another Gates Bill
1829	Act of March 2, 1829, appropriates $100,000 for the road "westwardly" from Zanesville; Act of March 2, 1829, appropriates funds for the continuation of the road in Indiana; Act of March 3, 1829, appropriates $100,000 for repair of the road east of Wheeling
1829	March 4, Andrew Jackson is inaugurated as the seventh president of the United States, delivers an inaugural address that gives less priority to internal improvements
1831	Jackson vetoes Maysville Road bill and issues an accompanying veto message explaining his constitutional and policy views
1831	Act of March 2, 1831, makes various appropriations for the continuation of the road in Ohio, Indiana, and Illinois
1831	Congress consents to state legislation in Ohio establishing tollgates
1833	Act of March 2, 1833, makes appropriations for the repairing of the road east of the Ohio, and continuing it in Ohio, Indiana, and Illinois
1834	Congress debates merits of appropriating funds for repair of the road in order to induce states to assume responsibility for it
1834	Act of June 24, 1834, in which Congress appropriates funds for continuation of the road in the three western states and an additional $300,000 to repair the road in Maryland, Pennsylvania, and Virginia in order to carry into effect laws of those states, providing for transfer to the states
1835	Congress debates merits of a further appropriation of $346,000 for the same purposes and approves such an appropriation, which is signed into law on March 3, 1835
1835	States east of the Ohio assume responsibility for the road
1836	Act of July 2, 1836, appropriates additional funds for the continuation of the road in Ohio, Indiana, and Illinois, including funds for bridging

1837   Andrew Jackson leaves office and Martin Van Buren becomes the eighth president of the United States

1838   Act of May 25, 1838, provides funds to continue the road in Ohio, Indiana and Illinois so that finished parts can be transferred to those states; last major federal appropriation for the road

1848   Act of August 11, 1848, transfers road in Indiana to that state

1856   Act of May 9, 1856, transfers road in Illinois to that state

1916   Federal Aid Highway Act of that year is enacted

1921   Federal Aid Highway Act of that year is enacted

1926   National Road becomes part of U.S. 40

1956   Congress passes and President Eisenhower signs the Interstate Highway Act of 1956 providing for a system of limited-access highways

1992   President George H. W. Bush signs the Intermodal Surface Transportation Efficiency Act of 1992

2005   On August 8 the Fort Necessity / National Road Interpretive and Educational Center is opened in Farmington, Pennsylvania, on the site of Fort Necessity

2006   Two-hundredth-year anniversary of the National Road

2011   Two-hundreth-year anniversary of the commencement of construction of the National Road.

Notes

Chapter 1. Washington's Role

1. George Washington, *Writings*, ed. John Rhodehamel (New York: Library of America of America, 1997), 17, 34 (report of January 16–17, 1754); for more detailed background on these journeys, see Douglas Southall Freeman, *Washington: an abridgement in One volume by Richard Harwell of the Seven-Volume George Washington by Douglas Southall Freeman* (New York: Macmillan Publishing Company, 1968), 36–89; George R. Stewart, *U.S. 40: Cross Section of the United States of America* (Boston: Houghton Mifflin Company, 1953), 86 (Nemacolin's role); C. A. Weslager, *The Delaware Indians: A History* (New Brunswick, NJ: Rutgers University Press, 2003), 222 (Nemacolin).

2. See Freeman, *Washington* (abridgment), 48–65 (detailed description of the expedition).

3. George Washington, *The Writings of George Washington*, ed. John C. Fitzpatrick (Washington, DC: GPO, 1931) (United States George Washington Bicentennial Commission), (Washington, *Writings*) 1:43–44; Stewart, *U.S. 40*, 87 (widening Nemacolin's trail; emphasis added).

4. Washington, *Writings*, 38 (letter to Gov. Dinwiddie from Great Crossing), 33 (exploration of river), 40 (letter to Gov. Dinwiddie, May 29, Great Meadows), 55 (journal entry of May 27); see Freeman, *Washington*, 53–54 (encounter with French force under Jumonville on May 28); see also Alan Axelrod, *Blooding at Great Meadows: Young George Washington and the Battle That Shaped the Man* (Philadelphia: Running Press, 2007), 458–84.

5. Washington, *Writings*, 71, 73 (letter of June 3, to Dinwiddie regarding the fort), 86 (on the march; journal, June 21), 89 (letter of August 11 to William Fairfax); see Freeman, *Washington*, 48–65 for the details of the battle at Fort Necessity; see George Washington, *George Washington's Journal for 1754*, ed. Donald H. Kent (Eastern National, 2004), 22 (journal entry of June 27, which is not in the Bicentennial Commission edition of Washington's writings).

6. See Norris F. Schneider, *The National Road: Main Street of America* (Columbus: Ohio Historical Society, 1975), 2.

7. Washington, *Writings*, ed. Rhodehamel, 54, 56 (letter to John Augustine Washington, July 2, 1755).

8. Stewart, *U.S. 40*, 88–89.

9. George Washington, *George Washington's Diaries: An Abridgement*, ed. Dorothy Twohig (Charlottesville: University of Virginia Press, 1999), 261–67 (entry of October 4, 1784, quoted language is at 265–66); for an account of the entire journey from September 1 through October 4, 1784, see ibid., 244–67.

10. For an account of the conversation between Washington and Gallatin, see Henry Adams, *The Life of Albert Gallatin* (1879; reprint, New York: Peter Smith, 1943), 56–59. The encounter evidently took place on September 1784 near Morgantown (then Virginia, now West Virginia). See ibid., 59. If the advice requested was regarding the best route from Cumberland to the Ohio, it is puzzling, as Washington was quite familiar with that route as a result of his experience in 1753, 1754, and 1755. Was Washington seeking an alternative route in the area of Morgantown? See also Washington, *Writings*, ed. Rhodehamel, 559, letter to Benjamin Harrison (Oct. 10, 1784) ("But smooth the road once, & make easy the way for them, & then see what an influx of articles will be poured in upon us . . ."); see also, Joel A. Achenbach, *The Grand Idea: George Washington's Potomac and the Road to the West* (New York: Simon & Schuster, 2004), 113–14 (encounter with Gallatin), 121–25 (October entry regarding Potomac route).

11. J. D. Richardson, ed., *Compilation of Messages and Papers of the Presidents, 1789–1902*, 10 vols. (Washington, D.C.: GPO, 1903), 1:65, 66; U.S. Const., Art. I, sec. 8, cl. 7; Richardson, *Compilation*, 1:584–85 (Madison's Bonus Bill veto); for further discussion see generally chapter 15 below.

12. Richardson, *Compilation*, 1:66 (seminaries of learning).

13. Alexander Hamilton, *Report on Manufactures: Communication to the House of Representatives, December 5,1791, from Alexander Hamilton, Secretary of the Treasury, on the subject of Manufactures*, as reprinted in H. Doc. No. 171, 63rd Cong.1st Sess. (1913) (Hamilton's interpretation of the General Welfare Clause).

14. Ibid.; see also Theodore Sky, *To Provide for the General Welfare: A History of the Federal Spending Power* (Newark: University of Delaware Press, 2003), 93–99.

15. Thomas Jefferson, *The Writings of Thomas Jefferson*, ed. Andrew A Lipscomb, Library Edition, 20 vols. (Washington, D.C.: Thomas Jefferson Memorial Association, 1903), 1:285–92 (account of conversation between Washington and Jefferson on February 28, 1792, in which Jefferson complained about Hamilton's interpretation of the Spending Clause in the latter's Report on Manufactures; Jefferson records no response on the part of Washington who apparently remained silent).

16. Ibid.

17. See Jerry A. Clause, *The Whiskey Rebellion: Southwestern Pennsylvania's Frontier People Test the American Constitution* (Harrisburg: Pennsylvania Historical and Museum Commission, 2002); Richardson, *Compilation*, 1:162-68 (Washington, sixth annual address, Nov. 19, 1794 (Whiskey Rebellion)).

18. U.S. Department of Transportation, Federal Highway Administration, *America's Highways, 1776–1976 A History of the Federal-Aid Program* (Washington: GPO, 1976), 16; see Richie Longfellow, *Back in Time, Zane's Trace*, U.S. Department of Transporta-

tion, Federal Highway Administration, Ohio Division Office (2008) (http://www.fhwa
.dot.gov/infrastructure/back0803.cfm).

19. See generally, Sky, *To Provide for the General Welfare*, 105–08.

Chapter 2. Jefferson, Gallatin and the Legislation of 1806

1. Act of March 29, 1806, ch. 19; a rod is 16.5 feet.

2. Act of April 30, 1802, ch. 40.

3. *American State Papers* (hereinafter, ASP), Doc. 195, 9th Cong., 1st Sess. (American State Papers are available through the Library of Congress website, www.loc.gov/American memory.)

4. *Annals of Congress*, Senate, 9th Cong., 1st Sess., 22–26 (December, 19, 1805), 43 (December 27, 1805); ibid., House of Representatives, 322 (December 30, 1805) (House receives Senate bill).

5. Ibid., House of Representatives, 835–38 March 21, 1806 (debate on Cumberland Road bill).

6. Ibid., 839–40 (March 24, 1806) (House passage); Joseph Wood, "The Idea of the National Road," in *The National Road*, ed. Karl Raitz (Baltimore, MD: Johns Hopkins University Press, 1996), 112–13, Achenbach, *The Grand Idea*, 231–33.

7. See H. Adams, *Life of Albert Gallatin*, 298–99; Albert Gallatin, *The Writings of Albert Gallatin*, ed. Henry Adams, 3 vols. (New York: Antiquarian Press, 1960), 1:76–79 (letter to William B. Giles, M.C.); see Reed B. Day, *The Cumberland Road: A History of the National Road* (Apollo, PA: Closson Press, 1996), 9; Joseph Wood, "The Idea of the National Road," 115, 116.

8. H. Adams, *Life of Albert Gallatin*.

9. Richardson, *Compilation*, 1:378–79, 405, 408–10; for background on this debate, see generally Sky, *To Provide for the General Welfare*, 93–105.

10. The difficulty with the Ohio admission legislation was that the funds generated, albeit from the proceeds of land sales, were still federal funds. To appropriate them for the needs of the road, Congress still needed a rational justification under the Constitution. In the absence of the spending power under Art. I, sec. 8, of the Constitution, there does not appear to be such a justification. Under the theory of Jefferson and Madison the spending power was unavailable for internal improvements. Henry Clay, in a March 13, 1818, speech before the House regarding internal improvements, attributes Jefferson's signing of the Cumberland Road legislation to that president's reliance on the compact under the Ohio statehood legislation as well as the consent of the three states (Maryland, Pennsylvania, and Virginia) to the project. Clay hastens to add his own view that such consent would not furnish the authority if the power to construct roads and canals (or, presumably, the power to aid such construction) did not exist independently of it. See Henry Clay, *The Papers of Henry Clay*, ed. James F. Hopkins, 11 vols. (Lexington: University of Kentucky Press, 1961), 2:460, 479–80. See Jeremiah Simeon Young, *A Political and Constitutional Study of the Cumberland Road*, (Chicago: University of Chicago Press, 1904), 37-40 (quoted language is at 40–41).

11. See p. 12 above.

12. Jefferson, *Writings*, 12:65–66 (letter of May 25, 1808, to Mr. Leiper) ("chequer" our country with roads and canals).

13. See Richardson, *Compilation*, 1:378–79, 405, 409–10 (calls for an amendment).

14. See Dumas Malone, *Jefferson the President, Second Term 1805–1809* (Boston: Little, Brown and Company, 1974), 553–60; see also p. 18 above (compact theory).

15. See Young, *Political and Constitutional Study*; Brian Balogh, *A Government Out of Sight: The Mystery of National Authority in Nineteenth-Century America* (Cambridge: Cambridge University Press, 2009), 114–25 (noting Jefferson's perspective on the financing of internal improvements including the National Road).

16. Merritt Ierley, *Traveling the National Road: Across the Centuries on America's First Highway* (Woodstock, NY: Overlook Press, 1990), 37–38 (role of Elie Williams), 38–39 (Elie Williams's journal).

17. *ASP*, Doc. 220 (9th Cong., 2d Sess., January 31, 1807).

18. Jefferson, *Writings*, 11:194 (letter of April 21, 1807 to Albert Gallatin).

19. ASP, Doc. 243 (10th Cong., 1st Sess. Feb. 19, 1808).

20. Ibid.; Young, *Political and Constitutional Study*, 22.

21. Jefferson, *Writings*, 12:31 (letter of April 22, 1808 to Albert Gallatin).

22. *South Dakota v. Dole*, 483 U.S. 203 (1987).

23. Gallatin, *Writings*, 1:395; Day, *Cumberland Road*, 13–14.

24. Albert Gallatin, *Report of the Secretary of the Treasury on Roads and Canals*, S. Doc. No. 250, 10th Cong., 1st Sess. (1808), (language is at 724, 725); see 1:5. Department of Transportation, *America's Highways, 1776–1976*, 17–18; H. Adams, *Life of Albert Gallatin*, 350–52.

25. Gallatin, *Report*, 724–25.

26. Ibid. See also Balogh, *A Government Out of Sight*, 125–28 (on Gallatin's Report and role).

27. Gallatin, *Report*, 724–25.

28. Ibid., 724–25 (emphasis supplied).

29. Ibid., 725; see also ibid., 738.

30. Ibid., 725.

31. Ibid., 740–41.

32. Ibid., 741.

33. See generally, Malone, *Jefferson the President*, chap. 26.

34. Jefferson, *Writings*, 12:117 (letter of August 6, 1808, to road commissioners).

35. *ASP*, Doc. 258 (10th Cong., 2d Sess., Dec. 18, 1808).

36. H.R. No. 67, 10th Cong., 2d Sess. (February 16, 1809).

37. Jefferson, *Writings*, 12:323, 325 (letter of October 11, 1809, Jefferson to Gallatin).

38. Wood, "Idea of the National Road," 109.

Chapter 3. Madison

1. See Act of February 14, 1810, Act of March 3, 1811.

2. *Annals of Congress*, House of Representatives, 11th Cong., 1st Sess., 465–66. It does not appear that the National Road was initially regarded as a toll road or a turnpike,

as the original authorizing legislation did not provide for tolls; it was only after the road was transferred to the states (or tolls were collected with the consent of the states) that the National Road became, in part, a toll road. See chapters 6 and 10 below.

3. *ASP*, Doc. No. 311 (12th Cong., 1st Sess., Feb, 1, 1812).

4. Ibid. (contract).

5. *ASP*, Doc. No. 317 (12th Cong., 1st Sess., April 14, 1812).

6. *ASP*, Doc. No. 339. (12th Cong., 2d Sess., March 1, 1813).

7. *ASP*, Doc. No. 356 (13th Cong., 2d Sess., January 18, 1814).

8. *ASP*, Doc. No. 357 (13th Cong., 2d Sess., January 24, 1814).

9. *ASP*, Doc. No. 379 (13th Cong., 3d Sess., January 2, 1815).

10. *ASP*, Doc. No. 381 (13th Cong., 3d Sess., January 24, 1815) (Smith report).

11. Richardson, *Compilation*, 1:562, 567–68 (Madison, seventh annual message); *ASP*, Doc. No. 458 (15th Cong., 1st Sess., April 20, 1818).

12. Richardson, *Compilation*, 1:562, 567 (seventh annual message, quoted language; emphasis added).

13. See James Madison, *Letters and Other Writings of James Madison , Fourth President of the United States*, 4 vols. (Philadelphia, PA: Lippincott and Co., 1865), 3:34, 35 (Madison's letter to Jefferson of February 15, 1817) ("compass by law only" denotes the absence of an accompanying constitutional amendment); see Sky, *To Provide for the General Welfare*, 138–41 for background; see also Robert V. Remini, *Henry Clay: Statesman for the Union* (New York: W. W. Norton and Co., 1991), 142–43 (Clay's views; Calhoun's role); John Lauritz Larson, "'Bind the Republic Together': The National Union and the Struggle for a System of Internal Improvements," *Journal of American History*, 74, no. 363 (1987): 377–85 (comprehensive discussion of the Bonus Bill veto and the factors that motivated Madison's action); see also Clay, *Papers of Henry Clay*, 2:308 (Clay's speech of February 4, 1817, in favor of the bill, citing the advantages of internal improvements).

14. See, e.g., *Federalist* no. 41 (Madison); Madison, seventh annual message, Richardson, *Compilation*, 1:562, 567–68.

15. Richardson, *Compilation*, 1:584–85 (veto message).

16. See Ralph Ketcham, *James Madison: A Biography* (Charlottesville: University of Virginia Press, 1995), 609.

17. See *Federalist* no. 15; see Sky, *To Provide for the General Welfare*, 19–25.

18. See Sky, *To Provide for the General Welfare*, 99–101.

19. Richardson *Compilation*, 1:585.

20. Ibid.

21. Young, *Political and Constitutional Study*, 53.

22. Richardson, *Compilation*, 1:562:567–68 (seventh annual message).

23. Ibid., 1:584–85 (veto message); Young, *Political and Constitutional Study*, 54; Balogh, *A Government Out of Sight*, 132–35 (noting the Bonus Bill veto and subsequent failed effort to obtain approval for a constitutional amendment, which Madison had proposed).

24. See Sky, *To Provide for the General Welfare*, 212–19 (Madison's 1830 letter to Andrew Stevenson).

25. Ketcham, *James Madison*, 610.

26. See Sky, *To Provide for the General Welfare*, 33–54 (provides a summary of the legislative history); cf. Young, *Political and Constitutional Study*, 37–40.

27. *Annals of Congress,* House of Representatives, 14th Cong., 2d Sess. 1059–62 (House override vote, March 3, 1817).

28. See Ketcham, *James Madison,* 610.

Chapter 4. Monroe's Compromise

1. Richardson, *Compilation,* 2:4, 8, 11, 18.

2. Madison, *Letters and Other Writings,* 3:50–51, 54–55.

3. Richardson, *Compilation,* 2:142–43 (Monroe veto message of May 4, 1822). For a comprehensive illustration of Clay's views, see Clay's speech on internal improvements of March 13, 1818, in Clay, *Papers of Henry Clay,* 2:467 (responding to views attributed to President Monroe that the Constitution did not confer power in Congress to establish a comprehensive system of internal improvements). The speech examines the precedents on the subject, including President Madison's veto of the Bonus Bill of 1817 (ibid., 480–82) and President Monroe's message at the opening of the then current session of the Congress (ibid., 483–89). It challenges the views taken by these presidents, in sometimes acerbic terms; evidently, Clay was relying on the post-roads clause in the Constitution, Art. I, sec. 8, cl. 7, as a basis for federal aid for internal improvements (Clay, *Papers of Henry Clay,* 474–79).

4. See Madison, *Letters and Other Writings,* 3:50–51 (November 29, 1817) (letter to Monroe regarding the utility of a constitutional amendment pertaining to education).

5. Richardson, *Compilation,* 2:144–83 (Monroe Memorandum).

6. Ibid.

7. Richardson, *Compilation,* 2:144, 173. The memorandum is discussed in detail in Sky, *To Provide for the General Welfare,* 148–59; see also Young, *Political and Constitutional Study,* 66–70.

8. Richardson, *Compilation,* 2:157–59, 161–62.

9. Henry Ammon, *James Monroe: The Quest for National Identity* (Charlottesville: University of Virginia Press, 1990), 392; see also Harlow Giles Unger, *The Last Founding Father: James Monroe and a Nation's Call to Greatness* (Philadelphia, Da Capo Press, 2009), 294 (national road as fulfilling Washington's and Monroe's dream).

10. See pp. 41, 200–3.

11. See *United States v. Butler,* 297 U.S. 1 (1936). Sky, *To Provide for the General Welfare,* 304–13.

12. See Wood, "Idea of the National Road," 116. See also Balogh, *A Government Out of Sight,* 136–39 (discussing Monroe's memorandum and its significance).

13. See *Annals of Congress,* House of Representatives, 17th Cong., 1st Sess., 1690–94 (debate on Gates Bill, April 26, 1822); ibid., 1734 (sent to Senate, April 29, 1822).

14. Ibid., Senate, 17th Cong., 1st Sess., 443–44 (Senate debate, May 3, 1822).

15. Ibid., House of Representatives, 17th Cong., 1st Sess., 1803–5 (veto message. May 4. 1822).

16. Richardson, *Compilation,* 2:144–83; U.S. Department of Transportation, *America's Highways, 1776–1976,* 198; see also Merrill D. Peterson, *The Great Triumvirate:*

Webster, Clay and Calhoun (New York: Oxford University Press, 1987), 81–82 (commentary on congressional debates on internal improvements, including the National Road and the General Survey Act, during the Monroe administration).

17. *Annals of Congress*, House of Representatives, 17th Cong., 1st Sess., 1872–75 (failed override vote, May 6, 1822).

18. Ibid., Senate, 17th Cong., 2nd Sess., 84–92 (Senate debate, January 7, 1823).

19. Richardson, *Compilation*, 2:185, 191 (Monroe, sixth annual message, December 3, 1822).

20. Act of February 28, 1823, chap. 17.

21. Act of March 3, 1825.

22. Young, *Political and Constitutional Study*, 76.

23. Thomas Searight, *The Old Pike: A History of the National Road with Incidents, Accidents, and Anecdotes Thereon* (Uniontown, originally self-published by the author 1894); Young, *Political and Constitutional Study*, 55–77 (Monroe veto and memorandum in the context of the road).

24. Ierley, *Traveling the National Road*, 59, 60–63 (Blane).

25. See chapter 5 and 6 below.

Chapter 5. John Quincy Adams

1. Sky, *To Provide for the General Welfare*, 167–97 (summary of role of J. Q. Adams in internal improvement controversy).

2. Richardson, *Compilation*, 2:294–99 (inaugural address); 2:299, 307–08 (first annual message); see generally Mary M. W. Hargreaves, *The Presidency of John Quincy Adams* (Lawrence: University Press of Kansas, 1987), 65–87 (account of Adams's domestic policies, including those relating to internal improvements); Daniel Walker Howe, *What Hath God Wrought: The Transformation of America, 1815–1848* (New York: Oxford University Press, 2007), 251–55.

3. John Quincy Adams, *Memoirs of John Quincy Adams*, ed. Charles Francis Adams, 12 vols. (Freeport, NY: Books for Libraries Press, 1969), 7:79–80 (constitutional amendment); 6:450–52 (Cumberland Road). James Barbour was a native of Virginia, served as its governor from 1812 to 1814, and served in the Senate from 1815 to 1825, when he accepted a position in the cabinet of President Adams as secretary of war. http://bioguide.congress.gov/scripts/biodisplay.pl?index=10000127.

4. Act of May 19, 1828 (National Road); Act of May 28, 1828 (C and O Canal); John Adams and John Quincy Adams, *Selected Writings*, ed. Adrienne Kech and William Peden (New York: Alfred A. Knopf, 1946), 375–78 (eulogy respecting Monroe).

5. Adams and Adams, *Selected Writings*, 389 (letter to Charles Upham); Lynn Hudson Parsons, *John Quincy Adams* (Madison, WI: Madison House, 1998), 200, see also Balogh, *A Government Out of Sight*, 139–50 (discussing the contribution of J. Q. Adams to the internal improvement debate).

6. Searight, *Old Pike*, 353–54; J. Q. Adams, *Memoirs of John Quincy Adams*, 9:356 (no entries in the diary by President Adams for the date of the Uniontown visit as indicated by Searight).

7. *Register of Debates*, House of Representatives, 20th Cong. 2d Sess., 240–44 (House debate, remarks of Rep. Buchanan, January 19, 1829).

8. *Register of Debates*, Senate, 19th Cong., 2d Sess. 349, 353–58, 364 (March 20, 1826); Act of March 3, 1826; Act of March 2, 1827, chapter XLIV; Act of May 18, 1828, chapter LVI.

9. *Register of Debates*, Senate, 20th Cong., 2d Sess., 119–25 (Jan. 23, 1828) (Smith-Noble debate); see Philip D. Jordan, *The National Road* (Indianapolis, IN: Bobbs-Merrill, 1948), chap. 10.

10. See chapter 4 above.

11. See *Register of Debates*, House of Representatives, 20th Cong., 2d Sess., 240–44 (January 19, 1829); ibid., Senate, 43–44 (January 20, 1829).

12. Ibid., House of Representatives, 360-61 (House debate, February 18, 1829).

13. Ibid., Senate, 74 (March 2, 1829).

14. Ibid., House of Representatives, 385–86 (March 2, 1829).

Chapter 6. Andrew Jackson

1. See Sky, *To Provide for the General Welfare*, 198–211.

2. Richardson, *Compilation*, 2:483–93 (Maysville veto message, May 27, 1830).

3. Ibid.

4. Ibid., 487.

5. Act of July 24, 1834; Donald B. Cole, *The Presidency of Andrew Jackson* (Lawrence: University Press of Kansas, 1993), 67; Wood, "Idea of a National Road," 118–19.

6. Sky, *To Provide for the General Welfare*, 209–10.

7. Searight, *Old Pike*, 52–56. See discussion at pp. 60–66 above.

8. Searight, *Old Pike*, 239.

9. See Richardson, *Compilation*, 2:483–85 (Jackson, Maysville Road appropriation veto message, May 27, 1830); See Jordan, *National Road*, 168 (Jackson views regarding the National Road).

10. *Register of Debates*, Senate, 23rd Cong. 2d Sess., 399–409 (Senate debate, Feb. 11, 1835).

11. Act of March 2, 1831, chap. 63; see U.S. Department of Transportation, *America's Highways, 1776–1976*, 198; Archer Butler Hulbert, *The Cumberland Road*, vol. 10 of *Historic Highways of America* (Cleveland: Arthur H. Clark, 1904), 10:73, 86, 92, 199.

12. *Register of Debates*, House of Representatives, 21st Cong. 1st Sess., 2726–2732 (House debate, May 3, 1832 (remarks of Rep. McKennan).

13. Ibid., 2730; see 43–46 above; Young, *Political and Constitutional Study*, 87 (discusses state law authorizing state tolls with the consent of Congress).

14. *Register of Debates*, 2737.

15. Ibid., 2737–42, 2748. http://bioguide.congress.gov/scripts/biodisplay.pl?index=S000899

16. *Register of Debates*, Senate, 22nd Cong. 2nd Sess. 486 (Senate debate, terminus, February 13, 1833).

17. Ibid., 23rd Cong. 1st Sess., 1141–43 (Senate debate, March 25, 1834).

18. Ibid., Senate debate, May 8, 1834, 1231–32, 1239–40; ibid., 1716–1717.

19. Ibid, House of Representatives, 4504–37 (House debate, June 16–17, 1834).

20. Ibid, 4504–12 (Polk amendment).

21. Ibid, 4520–21 (J. Q. Adams).

22. Act of June 24, 1834, chap. 68.

23. *Register of Debates*, Senate, 23rd Cong., 2nd Sess., 399–413 (Senate debate on transfer bill, February 11, 1835).

24. Ibid., 400–402.

25. Ibid., 402–5.

26. Ibid., 408–9 (Webster); see generally Claude M. Fuess, *Daniel Webster*, 2 vols. (Boston: Little, Brown and Co., 1930); see ibid., 1:325 (position on the Constitution: "Webster's conception of the Constitution led him to the conclusion that Congress had full power to carry out a policy of 'internal improvements'").

27. *Register of Debates,* 23rd Cong., Senate, 2nd Sess., 409–11 (Clay); see generally Remini, *Henry Clay;* see ibid., 212 (Clay's support for the National Road as a political plus).

28. *Register of Debates,* 23rd Cong., Senate, 2nd Sess., 410.

29. Ibid., 413.

30. Act of March 3, 1835.

31. Act of July 2, 1836; Act of March 3, 1837; Act of May 25, 1838; Jordan, *National Road*, 175; see U.S. Department of Transportation, *America's Highways, 1776–1976,* 198.

32. Craig Colton, "Adapting the Road to New Transport Technology," in *The National Road*, ed. Karl Raitz (Baltimore, MD: Johns Hopkins University Press, 1996), 198.

Chapter 7. The National Road

1. See Remini, *Henry Clay*, 225–36.

2. See pp. 54–55 above (1829 debate on the establishment of tolls for the National Road during the J. Q. Adams administration). On the American system and its relation to internal improvement legislation in the 1840s, see Sky, *To Provide for the General Welfare*, 233–34; see Jordan, *National Road,* 159–71; see ibid., 171–76 (efforts to gain appropriations for the western part of the road after the 1835 transfer legislation); on the debates during the Jackson administration, see ibid., 169: "Only die-hards failed to recognize that the period of Federal control of the National Road was about over. Southern opposition to further appropriations was unyielding; Jackson interpreted the Constitution strictly; Congressional aid was insufficient to maintain the pike in good condition and a toll system was impossible until the states took control. Westerners who had fought for years in defense of the highway, decided to retreat rather than surrender. If the road must be given up, then the relinquishment should take place gradually."

3. See generally chapters 4 and 5.

4. See chapters 1 and 2; Wood, "Idea of the National Road," 93, 115 (the road and internal improvements).

5. See chapters 2 and 3.

6. Wood, "Idea of the National Road," 104.

7. See chapters 4 and 5.

8. See chapter 6.

9. See *Springfield (OH) Republic* (editions concerning Van Buren administration and National Road) (disc containing selected articles from newspaper, courtesy of Springfield Heritage Center).

10. Ibid.; Richardson, *Compilation*, 4:5.

11. See Sky, *To Provide for the General Welfare*, 232–40.

12. See chapters 4, 5, and 6 above.

13. Paul Simon, *Lincoln's Preparation for Greatness: The Illinois Legislative Years* (Norman: University of Oklahoma Press, 1965), 76–105.

14. Ibid., 48–53; 83–91.

15. Ibid., 50–53; 171–88, quoted language is at 185.

16. See Abraham Lincoln, *Collected Works of Abraham Lincoln*, ed. Roy P. Basler, 9 vols. (New Brunswick, NJ: Rutgers University Press, 1953), 1:480, 485–86 (Speech of June 20, 1848 regarding internal improvements); Sky, *To Provide for the General Welfare*, 243–47.

17. See Sky, *To Provide for the General Welfare*, 247–49.

18. Ibid., 262–64.

19. See chapters 2–6 above.

20. See chapter 12 below.

21. *United States v. Butler*, 297 U.S. 1 (1936); *Helvering v. Davis*, 301 U.S. 619 (1937); See Jonathan Alter, *The Defining Moment: FDR's Hundred Days and the Triumph of Hope* (New York: Simon and Schuster, 2006), 312–13 ("One big worry was that the U.S. Supreme Court would rule any national program [of social insurance] unconstitutional. . . . These concerns were eased when Frances Perkins, chair of the Roosevelt appointed committee to study social security, bumped into Justice Harlan F. Stone at a party and Stone whispered: 'The taxing power of the Federal Government, my dear, the taxing power is sufficient for everything you want and need.'")

22. *Wilson v. Shaw*, 204 U.S. 24 (1907); at 33–34, quoting *California v. Pacific Railroad Company*, 127 U.S. 1, 39 (1887).

23. Cf. section 1125 of the Elementary and Secondary Education Act of 1965, as amended by the No Child Left Behind Act.

24. *South Dakota v. Dole*, 483 U.S. 203, 207 (1987).

25. See chapter 6 above.

26. *South Dakota v. Dole*, 483 U.S. 203, 212 (1987).

27. See chapter 3 above.

Chapter 8. Building the National Road

1. Billy Joe Peyton, "Surveying and Building the Road," in *The National Road*, ed. Karl Raitz (Baltimore, MD: Johns Hopkins University Press, 1996), 123–37.

2. Ibid., 144. The Bridgeport to Zanesville, Ohio segment was built in the macadam style, named after John L. McAdam, a Scottish engineer and road builder. That style involved flat layers of small, broken granite pebbles as a covering over the native soil. McAdam

insisted that water penetrating the road and filling the native soil beneath it would destroy a road. "Imperviousness to water" was, for McAdam, the critical element. See ibid., 140–41.

3. Simon, *Lincoln's Preparation for Greatness*, 57–60 (Lincoln's role in the move of the state capital of Illinois from Vandalia to Springfield).

4. Peyton, "Surveying and Building the Road," 146–47 (terminus at Vandalia); J. Q. Adams, *Memoirs of John Quincy Adams*, 9:113 (entry of March 20, 1834) (prospect of terminus at Jefferson City).

5. Gregory S. Rose, "Extending the Road West," in *The National Road*, ed. Karl Raitz (Baltimore, MD: Johns Hopkins University Press, 1996), 159,164–70; see Act of May 15, 1820, 16th Cong., 1st Sess., *U.S. Statutes at Large* 3 (1820): 604, and Act of March 3, 1825, chap. 98, 18th Cong., 2nd Sess., *U.S. Statutes at Large* 4 (1825): 128.

6. Rose, "Extending the Road West," 165–66.

7. Ibid., 167–68.

8. Young, *Political and Constitutional Study*, 28–30.

9. See figure 2 (1822 map of the National Road).

10. Peyton, "Surveying and Building the Road," 124.

11. Ibid., 132.

12. Ibid., 134.

13. Ibid., 135.

14. For information on Jonathan Knight, see http://bioguide.congress.gov/scripts/biodisplay.pl?index=K000285.

15. Ibid.; on Clay's role regarding the road, see chapters 6 and 7 above.

16. Communication from Daniel P. Cooke and Jonathan Jennings, U.S. House of Representatives to Honorable John Quincy Adams, March 3, 1825, Courtesy of Manuscript Section, Indiana State Library, original in Indiana State Library, L 79, Collection on Jonathan Jennings, box 1, folder 4.

17. Voucher, dated August 31, 1838, courtesy of Manuscript Section, Indiana State Library, original in Indiana State Library, S. 1807, Wm. Rockwood, folder 1; see also comparable vouchers in the same folder dated August 31, 1838, September 20, 1838, for various National Road–related services such as advertising and printing.

18. Petition from citizens of Somerset County, Pennsylvania, to Governor Curtin, January 11, 1862, courtesy Dickinson College Library, Special Collections, Carlisle, Pennsylvania. Changes in the routing or administration of the road did not go unnoticed by citizens in the communities which it served. In 1849, Marcus B. Chadwick, a resident of Eaton, Ohio, noted in his notebook or diary that the road in Ohio [in his vicinity] was then under the administration of local commissioners. Marcus B. Chadwick, notebook, p. 60, 1849 (book in possession of author; Chadwick is the great-grandfather of the author's wife). For an account of Marcus B. Chadwick, see Edward H. Chadwick, *Chadwick's History of Shelby County Indiana* (Indianapolis, B. F. Bowen and Company, 1909), 866–70.

19. Peyton, "Surveying and Building the Road," 139–43.

20. Ibid., 141–42.

21. Ibid., 141.

22. Ibid.

23. *ASP* Doc. No. 311, 12th Cong., 1st Sess., February 1, 1812 (American Memory) (Gallatin road contract); see also chap. 9, n. 1.

24. *ASP* Doc. No. 311 February 1, 1812.

25. Ibid.; Peyton, "Surveying and Building the Road," 134.

26. Notice to Road Contractors, *Springfield (OH) Republic,* May 28, 1841 (Courtesy, Clark County Heritage Center, Springfield, Ohio).

27. Peyton, "Surveying and Building the Road," 137.

28. Letter from James M. McAvoy to Hon. J. A. Wright, May 15, 1844, courtesy of Manuscript Section, Indiana State Library, original in Indiana State Library, L. 183, Joseph A. Wright box 1, folder 1.

29. Peyton, "Surveying and Building the Road," 142.

30. Adams and Adams, *Selected Writings,* 389 (letter to Rev. Charles Upham, February 2, 1837).

31. Ierley, *Traveling the National Road,* 53, 54 (observations of Adlard Welby, 1819).

32. Ibid., 54–55.

33. Letter from Ebenezer Fitch, May 1818, Washington, Pennsylvania courtesy of Bethany College, Wheeling, West Virginia) (addressee not given).

34. Ierley, *Traveling the National Road,* 49 (observations of Uriah Brown, 1816).

35. Ibid., 49–50 (same).

36. Ibid., 50 (same).

37. Thomas Hulme, "Thomas Hulme's Journal, 1818–1819," in *Early Western Travels,* ed. R. G. Thwaites, 10 vols. (Cleveland, OH: Arthur H. Clark Company, 1904), 10:77.

38. Ibid.

39. Rose, "Extending the Road West," 190–91.

40. Peyton, "Surveying and Building the Road," 136.

41. Ierley, *Traveling the National Road,* 49, 50.

42. Peyton, "Surveying and Building the Road," 136.

43. See Emery L. Kemp and Beverly B. Fluty, *The Wheeling Suspension Bridge: A Pictorial Heritage* (Charleston, WV: Pictorial Histories Publishing Co., 1999).

44. See *Pennsylvania v. the Wheeling and Belmont Bridge Company,* 54 U.S. 518 (1851) (Wheeling Bridge I); *Pennsylvania v. The Wheeling and Belmont Bridge Co.,* 59 U.S. 421 (1855) (Wheeling Bridge II); *Miller v. French,* 530 U.S. 327 (2000); Elizabeth B. Monroe, "Spanning the Commerce Clause: The Wheeling Bridge Case, 1850–1856," *Am. J. Legal Hist.* 32 (1988): 265.

45. See chap. 9.

Chapter 9. Archival Correspondence

1. See generally correspondence of the Treasury Department relating to the Cumberland Road, 1811–25 found in the Archives of the United States, Record Group 77, segment 79, as more fully described in this chapter; copies of letters cited are, for the most part, in the possession of the author; for more on Shriver and Gallatin, see chapters 2 and 8 above.

2. Ibid.

3. Ibid.

4. Ibid.

5. See letters on the repair issue from David Shriver to Albert Gallatin of the following dates described in the text: January 14, 1812, at p. 105 n. 15; letter of December 21, 1812, at pp. 108–9.

6. Petition in favor of bridge across the Youghiogheny River, May 25, 1809.

7. Letter of February 8, 1810, from John Connell of Washington, D.C.

8. Letter of 1811 from Mr. R. Nelson.

9. Bond of May 8, 1811.

10. Letter of April 29, 1811, David Shriver to Secretary Gallatin.

11. Letter of February 13, 1811, apparently to Shriver from Henry McKinley.

12. Letter of July 11, 1811, Shriver to Gallatin; see *Oxford Universal Dictionary*, 3rd ed. (London: Oxford University Press, 1955), s.v. "perch."

13. Letters of October 11 and October 21, 1811, Shriver to Gallatin.

14. Letter of December 2, 1811, Shriver to Gallatin; notation regarding issue, December 9, 1811 (by or on behalf of Albert Gallatin).

15. Letter of January 14, 1812, Shriver to Gallatin.

16. Notation of January 14, 1811, Secretary Gallatin.

17. Albert Gallatin, draft report of January 25, 1812.

18. Ibid.

19. Letter of August 3, 1812, Shriver to Gallatin.

20. Ibid.

21. Ibid.

22. Notation by Gallatin on back of letter of August 3, 1812.

23. Letter of November 7, 1812, Shriver to Gallatin.

24. Ibid.

25. Ibid.

26. Letter of December 21, 1812, Shriver to Gallatin.

27. Notation by Gallatin on back of Shriver's letter of December 21, 1812.

28. Letter of April 3, 1813, Shriver to Gallatin.

29. Ibid.

30. Letter of April 29, 1813, Shriver to Gallatin.

31. Notes by Gallatin and the president's clerk penned on the back of ibid.

32. Letter of May 31, 1813, Shriver to Gallatin.

33. Letter of December 19, 1814, Shriver to Secretary of the Treasury Alexander Dallas.

34. Ibid.

35. Ibid.

36. Ibid.

37. Note relating to ibid., indicating that it had been sent to the president on December 31.

38. Letter of March 25, 1815, Shriver to Dallas.

39. Ibid.

40. Letter of July 29, 1815, Shriver to Dallas.

41. Letter of August 3, 1815, apparently from Dallas to Shriver.

42. Advertisement for proposals in files of author.

43. Ibid.; see p. 110 for indications regarding Madison's general inclination to follow the course suggested by Shriver and Gallatin.

44. See chapters 3 and 4 above.

45. See letter of January 10, 1817, from Crawford to Elie Williams.

46. Letter of April 28, 1817, Shriver to Crawford.

47. Memorandum of Josias Thompson, November, 20, 1817, to William Crawford, secretary of the treasury.

48. Letter of December 15, 1817, Thompson to Crawford (annual report); letter of December 31, 1817, Shriver to Crawford.

49. Letter of January 20, 1818, Thompson to Crawford

50. Note of June 8, 1824, from Edward Jones, chief clerk to President Monroe, with notation from the president attached.

51. See chapter 3 regarding an account of Madison's policy dispositions in favor of federally assisted internal improvements. See chapter 6 regarding the transfer of the road.

52. Young, *Political and Constitutional Study,* 54 ("[Madison] was favorable to a national system of internal improvements").

Chapter 10. The Culture of the National Road

1. See chapters 3–6.

2. Day, *Cumberland Road,* 22.

3. See Searight, *Old Pike,* 239, 380; Day, *Cumberland Road,* 22 (quoted language); letter from Ebenezer Fitch, May 1818, Washington, PA (courtesy of Bethany College, Wheeling, WV).

4. See Colten, "Adapting the Road," 193, 197.

5. Ierley, *Traveling the National Road,* 102; toll rate announcement, Petersburg (Addison) tollhouse; see figure 2.

6. Hulbert, *Cumberland Road,* 114 (toll revenues for Ohio, 1831–77; the revenues totaled $1,139,795 for that period); ibid., 112 (comparative toll revenues for Ohio and Pennsylvania); for an indication of the shift of road responsibility to the states following the transfer in the 1830s discussed in chapter 6, see letter from Joseph B. Welsh to Eli Stifer, E. Bethlehem, PA, September 9, 1865 (expressing hope that Governor Curtin of Pennsylvania would not veto the Cumberland Road bill and discussing various concerns regarding the road) (letter courtesy of Dickinson College Library, Special Collections, Carlisle, PA).

7. Peyton, "Surveying and Building the Road," 123, 155.

8. Searight, *Old Pike,* 110–12.

9. Ibid., 110.

10. Ibid., 109; see chapter 1 above.

11. Ierley, *Traveling the National Road,* 86–88 (observations of John Deets, wagoner).

12. Robert C. Alberts, *Mount Washington Tavern: The Story of a Famous Inn, a Great Road, and People Who Used Them* (Eastern National Park and Monument Association, 1976) (information on menus is at p. 19), 11–12, 22; informational brochure supplied to guests at Stone House Inn, Farmington, PA; see Cassandra Vivian, *The National Road in Pennsylvania* (Charleston, SC: Arcadia, 2003), 48–49.

13. Alberts, *Mount Washington Tavern,* 13.

14. Ibid.

15. Regarding Stewart, see p. 61 above; regarding the tavern, see brochure supplied by the present Old Stone House in possession of author.

16. See Glenn Harper and Doug Smith, *A Traveler's Guide to the Historic National Road in Ohio: The Road that Helped Build America* (Columbus: Ohio Historical Society,

2005), 16 (Colonial Inn), 22 (Headley Inn and Smith House), 32 (Red Brick Tavern), 34–35 (Pennsylvania House).

17. Ierley, *Traveling the National Road*, 111, 114–15 (observations of William Owen, December 1, 1824.

18. Letter from John [Gesaff] to John P. Cockley, December 8, 1829, courtesy of Ohio Historical Society.

19. Ierley, *Traveling the National Road*, 115–16 (observations of Mary Reed Eastman, June 26,1833).

20. Eliza Steele, *Summer Journey in the West* (New York: John S. Taylor and Co., 1841), 266.

21. Ibid., 266–67.

22. Ibid., 268–69.

23. Ibid., 271 (July 25).

24. Ibid., 272.

25. Ibid., 272–74.

26. Daniel Drake, *Discourse on the History, Character and Prospects of the West* (Cincinnati, OH: Truman and Smith, 1834), 11.

27. Letter from Peter and Catherine Hessong to their father and mother, written from Marion County, Indiana, May 21, 1838 (courtesy of Manuscript Section, Indiana State Library, typed copy, S. 1186, Loury J. Silver) (typed copy) (original in Indiana Division, Indiana State Library).

28. Ibid.

29. Ibid.

30. See Rose, "Extending the Road West," 159, 170–76 (the road as a settlement corridor).

31. See Thomas Schlereth, *Reading the Road: U.S. 40 and the American Landscape* (Knoxville: University of Tennessee Press, 1997), 115–22 (Quaker settlements).

32. See Tricia T. Pyne, *Faith in the Mountains: A History of the Diocese of Wheeling–Charleston, 1850–2000* (Strasbourg, France: Editions du Signe, 2000), 6 (quoted language regarding diocese).

33. Jeffrey T. Darbee and Nancy A. Reccie, *Images of America: German Columbus* (Charleston, SC: Arcadia, 2005), 10 (quoted language regarding Columbus, Ohio).

34. Frances Trollope, *Domestic Manners of the Americans*, ed. Donald Smalley (New York: Vintage Books, 1960), 192–200 (the account is abbreviated in the quoted passages).

35. Ibid., 192.

36. Ibid., 192–93.

37. Ibid., 193.

38. Ibid., 193–94.

39. Ibid., 194.

40. Ibid., 196.

41. Ibid.

42. Joseph John Gurney, *A Journey in North America: Described in Familiar Letters to Amelia Opie* (1841; Reprint, New York: Da Capo Press, 1973), 27–35 (describes journey on National Road beginning on September 23, 1837).

43. Ibid., 27–28.

44. Ibid., 28–30, 33.

45. William Oliver, *Eight Months in Illinois: With Information to Emigrants* (1843; reprint, Ann Arbor, MI: University Microfilms, 1968), 99–112; Young, *Political and Constitutional Study*, frontispiece.

46. Oliver, *Eight Months in Illinois*, 103, 105.

47. Ibid., 106–7.

48. Ibid., 107–11.

49. Ibid., 112–13.

50. Schlereth, *Reading the Road*. See particularly part 2, "A Road Guide to U.S. 40 in Indiana: Past and Present," 61–74.

51. J. Richard Beste, *The Wabash; or, Adventures of an English Gentleman's Family in the Interior of America*, 2 vols. (1855; reprint, Freeport, NY: Books for Libraries Press, 1970), 311–12; for the journey of which this passage was a part, see 292–329.

52. Ibid., 311.

53. Ibid, 311–12.

54. Elizabeth J. Van Allen, *James Whitcomb Riley: A Life* (Bloomington: Indiana University Press, 1999), 16.

55. Ibid., 17–18; James Whitcomb Riley, *A Child World*, in *The Best of James Whitcomb Riley*, eds., Donald C. Manlove (Bloomington: Indiana University Press, 1982): xi–xv.

56. Van Allen, *James Whitcomb Riley*, 18.

Chapter 11. The Road as Microcosm

1. See generally chapters 2–6.

2. Ibid.

3. Compare Albert Gallatin's observations of 1808, quoted above at pp. 16–20, with the 1991 report on the Intermodal Surface Transportation Act of 1991, at pp. 177–79.

4. See chapter 5, above; Sky, *To Provide for the General Welfare*, 177–89, 193–97 (J. Q. Adams), 243–61 (Lincoln)

5. William J. Switala, *The Underground Railroad in Pennsylvania* (Mechanicsburg, PA: Stackpole Books, 2001), 73–75.

6. Switala, *Underground Railroad in Pennsylvania*, 81–82. Switala describes Dr. Julius LeMoyne's role in the Underground Railroad as well as the significance of his house as a refuge along the Underground Railroad. Switala also discusses the significance of the Cumberland-Uniontown route in *Underground Railroad in Pennsylvania*, 44–47.

7. David W. Blight, ed., *Passages to Freedom: The Underground Railroad in History and Memory* (Washington, D.C.: Smithsonian Books, published in association with the National Underground Railroad Freedom Center, 2004), 112 (quoted language); www.nationalroadpa.org (Web site of National Road Heritage Corridor).

8. See chapter 2 regarding Jefferson's role. On the Underground Railroad, see Switala, *Underground Railroad in Pennsylvania*, 81–82 (significance of LeMoyne's role).

9. See Harper and Smith, *Traveler's Guide*, 21 (Gant).

10. Weslager, *Delaware Indians*, 195, n. 15, see also ibid., 222.

11. Weslager, *Delaware Indians*, 261–439.

12. Ibid., 221–55; see also Charles N. Thompson, *Sons of the Wilderness: John and William Conner* (Noblesville, IN: Conner Prairie Press, 1988).

13. Weslager, *Delaware Indians*, 346–55.

14. Ibid., 331–33 (effect of settlement of Ohio).

15. Ibid., 331–32, 399–436.

16. Letter from Gov. John Ray to John Quincy Adams, president of the United States, [November] 25, 1825, courtesy Manuscript Section, Indiana State Library, original in Indiana Division, Indiana State Library.

17. See, e.g., Title VII-A of the Elementary and Secondary Education Act of 1965, as amended, by Title VII of P.L. 107-110 (relating to Indian education).

18. See information regarding "Indiana Woman's Suffrage Association Record Book, 1851–1886," available from Manuscripts and Visual Collections Department, William Henry Smith Memorial Library, Indiana Historical Society, Indianapolis, Indiana (see historical sketch, copy in possession of author); Web document, historical marker, Indiana's First Woman's Rights Convention, held October 14–15, 1851.

19. Biographical note on Dr. Mary F. Thomas (1816–88), www.mil.lib.in.U.S/history/biography/thomasmf..htm.

20. Schlereth, *Reading the Road*, .

21. See generally, Sky, To *Provide for the General Welfare*, chaps. 12 (Lincoln), 13 (Hayes), 14 (Roosevelt), 15 (Truman, Eisenhower, Kennedy, Johnson), 16 (other twentieth-century presidents).

Chapter 12. Decline and Revival

1. Colton, "Adapting the Road," 193–94.

2. See chapter 8 above.

3. Colton, "Adapting the Road," 203.

4. Schneider, *National Road*, 27–28.

5. Ibid.

6. Ibid., 27.

7. Ibid.; Hulbert, *Cumberland Road*, 114.

8. Richardson, *Compilation*, 5:436 (Buchanan, first annual message); 6:126, 128 (Lincoln, second annual message).

9. Colton, "Adapting the Road," 208–9.

10. Ierley, *Traveling the National Road*, 165 (quoting an excerpt from Rufus Rockwell Nelson, *By Horse and Carriage, Frederick to Brownsville*, 1902).

11. Richard F. Weingroff, *The National Old Trails Association*, Department of Transportation, Federal Highway Administration, Public Roads, www.fhwa.dot.gov/infrastructure/trails.htm; see also www.fhwa.dot.gov/infrastructure/not2.htm); see chapter 14 below.

12. Schneider, *National Road*, 28–31.

13. Federal Aid Highway Act of 1916, Act of July 11, 1916, chap. 245, *U.S. Statutes at Large* 39 (1916): 355.

14. Richard F. Weingroff, *Federal Aid Road Act of 1916: Building the Foundation*, U.S. Department of Transportation, Federal Highway Administration: Public Roads, vol. 60,

no. 1 (summer 1996), www.fhwa.dot.gov/publications/publicrecords/96summer/p9642. cfm.

15. U.S. Department of Transportation, *America's Highways, 1776–1976,* 80–86.

16. Weingroff, *Federal Aid Road Act of 1916. Wilson v. Shaw* is discussed at pp. 78–79 above.

17. U.S. Department of Transportation, *America's Highways, 1776–1976,* 86–87; Richard F. Weingroff, *Clearly Vicious as a Matter of Policy: The Fight against Federal Aid,* U.S. Department of Transportation, Federal Highway Administration, Public Roads www.fhwa.dot.gov/infrastructure/hwyhist01.cfm, at notes 17 and 18; see Weingroff, *Federal Aid Road Act of 1916.*

18. Weingroff, *Federal Aid Road Act of 1916.* See Sky, *To Provide for the General Welfare,* 296–99 (Wilson-led realignment of Democratic Party on spending power issues).

19. Karl Raitz, "The U.S. 40 Roadside," in *The National Road,* ed. Karl Raitz (Baltimore, MD: Johns Hopkins University Press, 1996), 289.

20. Robert Bruce, *The National Road: A Topographical, Historical and Pictorial Description of the the Old Highway from Baltimore and Washington across the Blue Ridge and Alleghenies to the Ohio River in Wheeling* (Washington, D.C.: National Highways Association, 1916), quoted language is at 7, 65.

21. Report of the director of public roads to Hon. D. F. Houston, secretary of Agriculture, October 14, 1918.

22. U.S. Department of Transportation, *America's Highways, 1776–1976,* 87–89.

23. Federal Highway Act of 1921, Act of November 9, 1921, 67th Cong., chap. 119, *U.S. Statutes at Large* 42 (1921): 212; Richard F. Weingroff's comprehensive study, *Clearly Vicious as a Matter of Policy,* contains an informative discussion of the debates and legislative activity leading up to the enactment of the 1921 act that focuses on the competing perspectives at issue; see the text at the Website between notes 39 and 104.

24. U.S. Department of Transportation, *America's Highways, 1776–1976,* 106–8.

25. Ibid.

26. Weingroff, *Clearly Vicious as a Matter of Policy,* text following his note 96 ("Federal Aid Highway Act of 1921").

27. Ibid., text following his note 103.

28. Federal Highway Act of 1921.

29. Weingroff, *Clearly Vicious as a Matter of Policy,* text following his note 109 (Coolidge reaction) and following his note 117 (AASHO).

30. Ibid., following his note 123 (Hoover administration).

31. Ibid., following his note 142 (FDR administration).

32. Ibid., following his note 188 (Roosevelt, under "Highways for National Defense"), and following his note 193 ("National Defense Highway Act of 1941). See chap. 2 above (Jefferson).

33. Weingroff, *Clearly Vicious as a Matter of Policy,* under "National Interregional Highway Committee") (FDR administration, interstate highways).

34. Richard F. Weingroff, *From Names to Numbers,* U.S. Department of Transportation, Federal Highway Administration, Public Roads, www.fhwa.dot.gov/infrastructure/numbes.cfm.

35. Schneider, *National Road,* 35–36.

36. Ierley, *Traveling the National Road,* 199–200 (observations of Philip Jordan, 1947).

37. Stewart, *U.S. 40*, 94.

38. Schlereth, *Reading the Road*, 87–100 (U.S. 40 era in "A Road Guide to U.S. 40 in Indiana").

39. Stewart, *U.S. 40*, 182–87.

40. Raitz, "U.S. 40 Roadside," 285.

41. Ibid., 316.

42. Ibid., 290.

43. See Karl Raitz, ed., *Guide to the National Road* (Baltimore: Johns Hopkins University Press, 1996); Stewart, *U.S. 40*, 130–31.

44. Revenue Act of 1932, Act of June 6, 1932, chap. 209, *U.S. Statutes at Large* 46 (1932): 169.

45. U.S. Department of Transportation, Federal Highway Administration, "Ask the Rambler: When Did the Federal Government Begin Collecting the Gas Tax?" www.fhwa .dot.gov/infrastructure/gastax.cfm.

46. Ibid.

47. U.S. Department of Transportation, *America's Highways, 1776–1976*, 124–25; see epilogue below.

Chapter 13. Creation of the Interstate Highway System

1. U.S. Department of Transportation, *America's Highways, 1776–1976*, 154–57.

2. Ibid., 158–67.

3. Ibid., 172, 469, 473.

4. Federal Aid Highway Act of 1956, Public Law 627, 84th Cong., 2d Sess., *U.S. Statutes at Large* 70 (1956): 374, 397.

5. See Lee Mertz, "Origins of the Interstate," United States Department of Transportation, Federal Highway Administration, Public Road, www.fhwa.dot.gov/infrastructure.

6. Richard F. Weingroff, "Three States Claim First Interstate Highway," United States Department of Transportation, Federal Highway Administration, Public Roads (www.tfhrc.gov/pubrds/summer96/96su.18/htm.

7. Richard F. Weingroff, *The Man Who Loved Roads*, United States Department of Transportation, Federal Highway Administration, Public Roads, www.fhwa.dot.gov/ infrastructure/trumanpr.htm); see also www.fhwa.dot.gov/infrastructure/truman.htm; Federal Aid Highway Act of 1944, Act of December 20, 1944, chap. 626, *U.S. Statutes at Large* 58 (1944): 838.

8. Weingroff, *Man Who Loved Roads* (under headings, "President with a Full-Plate," and "For the interstates: one step forward, one step back").

9. Ibid., Federal Aid Highway Act of 1950, Public Law 769, 81st Cong., 2d Sess. (1950), *U.S. Statutes at Large* 64 (1950): 785.

10. Dwight D. Eisenhower, 1956 State of the Union address; See *Public Papers, Dwight D. Eisenhower* [1956], 1–18; see also Geoffrey Perret, *Eisenhower* (Holbrooke, MA: Adams Media Corporation, 1999).

11. U.S. Department of Transportation, *America's Highways, 1776–1976*, 173–74.

12. See House Committee on Public Works and Transportation, *Intermodal Surface Transportation Efficiency Act of 1991*, 102d Cong., 1st sess., 1991, Rept. 171(1), 1-2; see T. R. Reid, "The Superhighway to Everywhere: No 50, Interstates Moved America into Another Lane," *Washington Post*, June 28, 2006 ("The late Rep. Hale Boggs [D.-La.] solved the impasse by proposing a dedicated highway trust fund, financed mainly by the federal tax on gasoline.")

13. Weingroff, *Clearly Vicious as a Matter of Policy*, (under heading "Future Battles on Devolution"), following his note 306; Eisenhower, 1954 State of the Union address, in *Public Papers, Dwight D. Eisenhower*, [Eisenhower, 1954], 6, 18.

14. U.S. Department of Transportation, *America's Highways, 1776–1976*, 474.

15. See chapter 5 above.

16. See chapter 2 above.

17. The six presidential administrations involved all made significant contributions to the growth of the nation's interstate highway system in keeping with the tradition set by the National Road.

18. Arthur Schlesinger, Jr., *A Thousand Days: John F. Kennedy in the White House* (Boston: Houghton Mifflin Company, 1965), 656.

19. See, generally, Lyndon Baines Johnson, *The Vantage Point: Perspectives of the Presidency, 1963–1969* (New York: Holt, Rinehart and Winston, 1971); Sky, *To Provide for the General Welfare*, 333–38 (summary of general welfare–related legislation in the Johnson administration).

20. See Robert Dallek, *Flawed Giant: Lyndon Johnson and His Times, 1961–1973* (New York: Oxford University Press, 1998), 314–17; quote is at 317; National Traffic and Motor Vehicle Safety Act of 1966, Pub. L. No. 563, 89th Cong., 2nd Sess. (2006), *U.S. Statutes at Large* 80 (1966): 718; Johnson, *Vantage Point*, 329 ("primary assignment [of DOT] was to develop the first coordinated national transportation program").

21. Richard Nixon, Statement on Signing a Highway and Mass Transit Bill, August 13, 1973, *Public Papers, Richard Nixon*, [Nixon, 1973], 690.

22. *Public Papers, Gerald Ford*, [Ford 1976-II], 1472 (signing of Federal Aid Highway Act of 1976, May 5, 1976).

23. Jimmy Carter, (New York: Bantam Books, 1982), 91–124 (quotes are at 91 and 92).

24. Ibid., 93–94 (quoted language from the chat is at 94); the federal case mentioned in the text is *Nevada v. Skinner*, 884 F. 2d 445 (9th Cir., 1989); chaps. 3 and 4 (Madison and Monroe).

25. Regarding the Reagan administration, see Surface Transportation Assistance Act of 1982, Pub. L. No. 424, 97th Cong., 2d Sess. (1982); Surface Transportation and Uniform Relocation Assistance Act of 1987, Pub. L. No. 17, 100th Cong., 1st Sess. (1987), *U.S. Statutes at Large* 101 (1987): 132; Lou Cannon, *President Reagan: The Role of a Lifetime* (New York: Public Affairs, 1991), 739–40.

26. See pp. 173–76 above.

27. See chapter 7 above.

28. See Intermodal Surface Transportation Efficiency Act of 1991, Public Law 240, 102d Cong., 1st Sess.; *U.S. Statutes at Large* 105 (1991): 1914; see H.R. Rept., 171 (1), 102d Cong., 1st Sess. (1991).

29. Ibid.

30. Ibid.

31. Richard F. Weingroff, *Creating a Landmark: The Intermodal Surface Transportation Efficiency Act of 1991*, Department of Transportation, Federal Highway Administration, Public Roads, www.fhwa.dot.gov/infrastructure/rw01.htm; Weingroff, *Clearly Vicious as a Matter of Policy,* (under "Future Battles on Devolution").

32. Transportation Equity Act for the 21st Century, Pub. L. 178, 105th Cong, 2d Sess. (1998), *U.S. Statutes at Large* 112 (1998):107, Title I.

33. *Public Papers of the Presidents: William J. Clinton, 1998 I*, 924–25 (Statement on Signing the Transportation Equity Act for the 21st Century, June 9, 1998); see accompanying remarks, ibid., 924–25.

34. Ibid.

35. Budget of the United States Government, Fiscal Year 2006, http://www.gpo access.gov/usbudget/fy06/pdf/budget/transportation.pdf (Department of Transportation, at 237, 241).

36. See chapter 16 below regarding the Commission Report.

37. Ibid.

38. See pp. 170–72.

Chapter 14. Road as a National Symbol

1. Richardson, *Compilation*, 1:409 (Jefferson, sixth annual message).

2. Gallatin, *Writings, Gallatin, Report*, 724. Gallatin, *Report*, 725. The report is discussed above in chapter 2.

3. Richardson, *Compilation.*, 1:567 (Madison, seventh annual message).

4. Ibid, 2:177 (Monroe, 1822 memorandum); ibid., 2:307, 316 (Adams, first annual message).

5. See chap. 6 above.

6. *ASP*, Doc. No. 406.

7. Searight, *Old Pike*, 107.

8. See e.g., *ASP*, Doc. No. 311; see also chap. 9 above.

9. Searight, *Old Pike*, 109–233; see pp. 121–22 above.

10. Hulbert, *Cumberland Road*, 185; Stewart, *U.S. 40*, 85.

11. See chapter 6.

12. See, eg., copy of letter to the editor of the *Springfield (OH) Ohio, Republic,* February 3, 1854, regarding portion of road west of Springfield, courtesy of Clark County Historical Society, Springfield, Ohio.

13. Richardson, *Compilation* 6:30 (Lincoln, special session message of July 4, 1861).

14. See chaps. 2 and 3 above.

15. See chaps. 4 and 5 above.

16. See chapter 4; see also Young, *Political and Constitutional Study*, 70 ("In his veto message, [President Monroe] indicated a basis on which he and Congress could work together; viz., the federal government had power to *appropriate* money for internal improvements of a *National character*").

17. See generally Searight, *Old Pike*.

18. Wood, "Idea of the National Road," 96.

19. Ibid., 97.

20. See chapter 1 (Washington); chapter 10 (Peter Hessong).

21. See chapter 13 above.

22. Walt Whitman, "Song of the Open Road," *Selected Poems* (Dover Publications, 1991).

23. Walt Whitman, "Excerpts from a Traveler's Notebook" in *The Uncollected Poetry and Prose of Walt Whitman*, ed. Emory Holloway, 2 vols. (New York: Peter Smith, 1932), 1:181–86.

24. Ibid.

25. Ibid.

26. *The National Road in Song and Story*. Federal Work Agency, Work Projects Administration, 1940.

27. Richard F. Weingroff, *The National Old Trails Association,* part 1, *The Quest for a National Road*, United States Department of Transportation, Federal Highway Administration, Public Roads, www.fhwa.dot.gov/infrastructure/trails.cfm under heading, "Location of National Old Trails Ocean-to-Ocean Highway, December, 1912."

28. Ibid.

29. Ibid., under the headings "Judge J. M. Lowe" and "On the Road."

30. Ibid., under the heading "Location of the National Old Trails Ocean-to-Ocean Highway, December, 1912."

31. Ibid.

32. Weingroff, *Man Who Loved Roads.*

33. David McCullough, *Truman* (New York: Simon and Schuster, 1992), 171; on the Madonna of the Trail, see *Wheeling, West Virginia, Visitors Guide*, p. 7; Stewart, *U.S. 40*, 86 (historical significance of National Road).

34. Weingroff, *Man Who Loved Roads*, under heading: "Senator Truman Takes to the Roads."

35. Stewart, *U.S. 40*, 3–4.

36. National Scenic Byways Program.

37. Commonwealth of Pennsylvania, Department of Conservation and Natural Resources, Web site. www.denr.state.pa.us.

38. National Road Heritage Corridor, www.nationalroad.pa.org; Pennsylvania Heritage Parks Program, program manual (January 2005), p. 3

39. Fort Necessity National Battlefield / National Road Interpretative and Education Center, www.nrhc.com; recollections from a number of visits to the center and attendance at dedication ceremony.

40. See Schneider, *National Road*, 37.

41. See chaps. 1–7.

42. See chaps. 8, 9, 10.

43. See chapter 12.

Chapter 15. Enduring Role of Spending Power

1. Leonard D. White, *The Jeffersonian: A Study in Administrative History, 1801–1829* (New York: Free Press, 1951), 483.

2. See chapter 4 above; Ammon, *James Monroe*, 392.

3. See Richardson, *Compilation*, 1:584–85 (Madison, veto message); chapter 3 above (vote on override).

4. A constitutional amendment would have afforded the people an opportunity to approve, through the ratification process of Article V, a specific constitutional statement of the role of Congress under the spending power but might have required multiple amendments as the need for federal financial assistance to support different federal missions was identified from time to time. This process would probably have precluded or delayed needed change and altered the character of the founding charter, converting it into an overly detailed framework for federal spending measures.

5. *United States v. Butler*, 297 U.S. 1, 66 (1936); *Helvering v. Davis*, 301 U.S. 619 (1937); *South Dakota v. Dole*, 483 U.S. 203, 207 (1987).

6. 301 U.S. 619, 641.

7. Joseph Story, *Commentaries on the Constitution of the United States, Abridgement, 1833* (reprint, with introduction by Ronald D. Rotunda and John E. Nowalk, (Durham, NC: Carolina Academic Press, 1991).

8. For Hamilton's role, see chapter1; see generally Sky, *To Provide for the General Welfare*, 48–52 (debates on and drafting of General Welfare Clause; roles of Roger Sherman and Gouverneur Morris); see Antonin Scalia, *A Matter of Interpretation: Federal Courts and the Law; An Essay by Antonin Scalia: with Commentary by Amy Gutmann, Editor, Gordon S. Wood, Laurence H. Tribe, Mary Ann Glendon, Ronald Dworkin* (Princeton, NJ: Princeton University Press, 1997), 3, 37–47 (Justice Scalia's essay; constitutional interpretation).

9. Joseph Story, *Commentaries on the Constitution of the United States*, ed. Melville Bigelow, 5th ed., 2 vols. (Boston: Little, Brown and Co., 1891), 1:716–17; see ibid., 661 et seq. for the comprehensive analysis, which cited and relied upon Hamilton and Monroe, as well as J. Q. Adams and others. Compare *New York v. United States*, 505 U.S. 144 (1992) (opinion of Justice O'Connor). O'Connor observed that the spending power was among the principal constitutional sources of the growth of federal activity: "[T]he powers conferred upon the Federal Government by the Constitution were phrased in language broad enough to allow for the expansion of the Federal Government's role. Among the provisions of the Constitution that have been particularly important in this regard, three concern us here" (Justice O'Connor then names the Commerce Clause, the Spending Clause, and the Supremacy Clause) (505 U.S. 144, 157).

10. *Wilson v. Shaw*, 204 U.S. 24 (1907). *Wilson v. Shaw* is discussed above at pp. 78–79.

11. Committee Report, cited in Weingroff, *Clearly Vicious, as a Matter of Policy*, following his note 14, under the heading: "Establishing a Principle." The committee in question was the Joint Committee on Federal Aid in the Construction of Post Roads. The committee report may be found in *Federal Aid to Good Roads*, House Document No. 1510, 63rd Cong., 3d Sess. (1921), 14.

12. George Washington, first annual message, in Richardson, *Compilation*, 1:66; Federal Aid Road Act of 1916 (1916); *South Dakota v. Dole*, 483 U.S. 203 (1987).

13. Regarding Monroe, see chapter 4 above; regarding Adams, see chapter 5, above; regarding Jackson, see chapter 6, above; for Story's role, see Story, *Commentaries*, ed. Bigelow; Sky, *To Provide for the General Welfare*, 219–32.

14. *United States v. Butler*, 297 U.S. 1, 66 (1936); *Helvering v. Davis*, 301 U.S. 619, 640 (1937); *Steward Machine Co. v. Davis*, 301 U.S. 548 (1937).

15. *South Dakota v. Dole*, 483 U.S. at 207.

16. Brief of the United States in ibid., 29.

17. Edgar Howard Farrar, *The Post-Road Power in the Federal Constitution and Its Availability for Creating a System of Federal Transportation Corporations* (n.d.: self-published, 1907). See ibid., 20, for quote; *Monongehela Navigation Co. v. United States*, 148 U.S. 312 (1893).

18. See chapter 9, above, regarding administration of the road during the period 1811–18 and chapter 2 for a discussion of the 1806 act and the consent of the states theory.

19. Speech of Edward V. A. Kussy, deputy chief counsel of the Federal Highway Administration (retired), "Surface Transportation and Administrative Law: Growing Up Together in the 20th Century," in *Transportation Research Record 1527* (1996) (Distinguished Lecture to the Transportation Research Board), http://trb.metapress.com/content/2670284264725655/.

20. Ibid. 15.

21. See chapter 4, above. See also, Gabrielle Appleby, "The Provenance of the Federal Spending Power" (December. 11, 2008; paper presented at the postgraduate session at the Law and History Conference, held at the University of Adelaide, Australia, December 11, 2008), http://ssrn.com/abstract=1323166.

22. Balogh, *A Government Out of Sight*, 380. See also pp. 154–60, 199–204 above. Balogh emphasizes "associative action" as key to surface transportation infrastructure development in the twentieth century. Ibid., 384–97. To be sure, while the federal role in its building may have been muted, travelers on the National Road were by and large cognizant of its identity as a federally funded and built highway between 1811 and the turnover of the road to the states. See pp. 124–37 above.

23. See Alice Rivlin and Isabel Sawhill, eds., *Restoring Fiscal Sanity, 2005: Meeting the Long Run Challenge* (Washington, D.C.: Brookings Institution Press, 2005), 1–15 (dimensions of the fiscal challenge). Nancy J. Altman, *The Battle for Social Security: From FDR's Vision to Bush's Gamble* (Hoboken, NJ: John W. Wiley and Sons, 2005), 259–60 (causes of social security shortfall); 297–309 (coherent and relatively pain-free suggestions for closing the long-range social security actuarial gap); see Rivlin and Sawhill, *Restoring Fiscal Sanity*, 73–97 (health; presenting even more difficult challenges). From an "active liberty" perspective, the "constitutional room" for civic engagement afforded by the National Road–era spending power interpretations and their progeny would be vastly circumscribed if the projected fiscal problems raised by the entitlement programs were not effectively resolved in a timely manner, circumscribed not by constitutional limitations but by budgetary ones. On infrastructure related concerns, see Rahm Emanuel and Bruce Reed, *The Plan: Big Ideas for America* (New York: Public Affairs, 2006), 176–77 (high-speed rail) ("Today, a rail car takes three days to travel from Los Angeles to Chicago, the nation's transportation hub. Because of outdated, inefficient infrastructure, that same car then takes another three days to travel from the west side of Chicago to the south side").

Chapter 16. Infrastructure Challenges

1. See chapter 5, above (Monroe).

2. U.S. Department of Transportation, Federal Highway Administration, Federal Transit Administration, *2006 Status of the Nation's Highways, Bridges, and Transit: Conditions and Performance* (Washington, D.C.: GPO, 2007).

3. Ibid., Executive Summary ES-1, ES-2.

4. Ibid., ES-6, ES-8.

5. Ibid., ES-13-ES-14

6. Ibid., chapter 11, pp. 11-2–11-17.

7. National Surface Transportation Policy and Revenue Study Commission, *Final Report* (2008); ibid., pp. 3–5, http://transportationfortomorrow.com/final-report/index.htm.

8. Ibid., part 1; see supra chapter 12, above for discussion of the1956 act.

9. Ibid., 7–8.

10. Ibid., 10–11.

11. Ibid., 16–17.

12. Ibid., 17–19.

13. Ibid., 19–22 (congestion; recommending program to reduce congestion in largest metropolitan areas; emphasis is on public transportation and road pricing).

14. Ibid., 22–24 (safety: vying to cut surface transportation fatalities in half by 2025).

15. Ibid., 24–25 (connecting: emphasizing on communities left out in initial system).

16. See ibid., 25–27 (intercity: see map of proposed intercity passenger rail network at p. 29).

17. Ibid., exhibit 4-22; ibid., at 38–40 (recommendations for paying the bill including list of options to keep system solvent; (part 2, chapter 4) (long-term capital investment needs of the system, pp. 4–27).

18. Ibid., part 2, chapter 4.

19. Ibid. at 38–39.

20. Ibid., 40.

21. Ibid., chap. 5.

22. Ibid., 53, see also ibid., pp. 33–36 (proposed National Surface Transportation Council to oversee, on a permanent basis, development of strategic plan).

Epilogue

1. See Office of the Federal Register, National Archives and Records Administration, Daily Compilation of Presidential Documents, Administration of Barack H. Obama (GPO Access), Inaugural Address, January 20, 2009, p. 2 (hereinafter "Daily Compilation"); American Recovery and Reinvestment Act of 2009 (ARRA), Public Law 5, 111th Cong., 1st Sess., *U.S. Statutes at Large* 123 (2009) 115.

2. See chapters 1–7 above.

3. See generally H.R. No. 111-16, 111th Cong., 1st Sess. (2009) (Conference Report to accompany H.R. 1).

4. See chapters 2–6 above.

5. See chapters 3 and 4 above (Madison, Monroe); see chapter 1, above (Washington); Richardson, *Compilation* 1:66, 199–201 (Washington, first annual message; eighth annual message); ibid., 405, 408–9 (Thomas Jefferson, sixth annual message); Sky, *To Provide for the General Welfare*, 79–82, 105–8 (Washington); 118–21 (Jefferson, sixth annual message); see also ibid., 1:563, 567–68 (Madison, seventh annual message); ibid., 2:294–97 (J. Q. Adams inaugural); Sky, *To Provide for the General Welfare*, 167–97 (Adams "spirit of improvement"). On Jackson, see chapter 6, above and Richardson, *Compilation*, 2:483 (Maysville Road veto). See also Balogh, *A Government Out of Sight*, 112–50.

6. Story, *Commentaries*, ed. Bigelow, 2:716–17 ("expedient language"); See also *Budget of the United States Government*, Fiscal Year 2011, president's Message, Washington, D.C.: GPO, pp. 1–2.

7. On differences between National Road, U.S. 40, and Interstate 70, see chapters 8, 12, and 13 ; on the "smooth way," see pp. 8–9 above (regarding Washington).

8. See Daily Compilation, remarks of President Barack Obama at the Abraham Lincoln Association Annual Banquet in Springfield, Illinois, February 12, 2009, pp. 2–3 ("[Lincoln] recognized that while each of us must do our part, work as hard as we can, and be as responsible as we can—in the end, there are certain things we cannot do on our own. There are certain things we can only do together. There are certain things only a union can do. . . .We are the United States. There isn't any dream beyond our reach, any obstacle that can stand in our way, *when we recognize that our individual liberty is served, not negated, by a recognition of the common good*") (emphasis added).

9. On the Federal Aid Highway Act of 1956, see above, chapter 13; National Defense Education Act of 1958, Public Law 864, 85th Cong., 2d sess., *U.S. Statutes at Large* 72 (1958): 1580.

10. On ESEA, see Public Law 10, 89th Cong., 1st Sess. (1965), *U.S. Statutes at Large* 79 (1965): 29; see also Higher Education Act of 1965, Public Law 329, 89th Cong., 1st Sess., *U.S. Statutes at Large* 79 (1965): 1219.

11. See, e.g., Improving America's Schools Act, Public Law 382, 103d Cong., 2d Sess. (1994), *U.S. Statutes at Large* 108 (1994): 3518; No Child Left Behind Act of 2001, Public Law 110, 107th Cong., 2d Sess., *U.S. Statutes at Large* 115 (2002): 1425; see particularly section 1111 of the Elementary and Secondary Education Act of 1965, as amended by the No Child Left Behind Act (accountability and adequate yearly progress).

12. See Daily Compilation, remarks on signing the American Recovery and Reinvestment Act of 2009 in Denver, Colorado, February 17, 2009, p. 2.

13. Barack Obama, *The Audacity of Hope: Thoughts on Reclaiming the American Dream* (New York: Crown Publishers, 2006), 152–53.

14. See generally H.R. 1, 111th Cong., 1st Sess. (2009).

15. Daily Compilation, Feb. 5, 2009 (Remarks on the Establishment of the President's Economic Advisory Board), p. 1.

16. *Cong. Rec.*, 111th Cong., 1st Sess. (daily ed., February 5, 2009), pp. 1618–20 (remarks of Senator McCain).

17. Ibid., 1620–21 (remarks of Senator Durbin); ibid., 1629 (remarks of Senator Baucus).

18. ARRA; Daily Compilation, remarks on signing the American Recovery and Reinvestment Act, February 17, 2009; Jonathan Alter, *The Promise President Obama, Year One* (New York: Simon & Schuster, 2010), 81.

19. Daily Compilation, p. 3. To the same effect: "[F]rom the National Institutes of Health to the National Science Foundation, this recovery act represents the biggest increase in basic research funding in the long history of America's noble endeavor to better understand our world."

20. Regarding the National Road and the spending power generally, see chapters 2–7 and 15.

21. Judge Richard A. Posner, "How I Became A Keynesian: Second Thoughts in a Recession," *New Republic*, September 23, 2009, 34, 37.

22. See the White House Web site (breakdown of expenditures) at www.whitehouse.gov ("signed, sealed, delivered: ARRA," release, dated February 17, 2009; see also Daily Compilation, "What I am signing is a balanced plan with a mix of tax cuts and investments."); Alter, *The Promise*, 84.

23. Some assailed the ARRA as too expensive and large. Others argued that it was not large enough and "could have accomplished more than it did." See "After the Stimulus," editorial, *New York Times*, February 13, 2009; Robert J. Samuelson, "Obama's Stunted Stimulus," *Washington Post*, February 23, 2009.

24. See American Recovery and Reinvestment Act of 2009 ("ARRA"), Public Law 5, 111th Cong., 1st Sess (2009); H.R. Rept., 111-16, 111th Cong., 1st Sess. (2009) (Conference Report on H.R. 1; hereinafter "Conference Report"), appropriations for Department of Education, Conference Report, at 456–60); see appropriations under the following accounts: Education of the Disadvantaged ($10 billion for Title I, $3 billion for school improvement), Special Education ($12 billion), Student Financial Assistance (maximum Pell Grant, $5,350),

25. See ARRA, appropriations for Department of Transportation, Conference Report, 469–71, see accounts for highway infrastructure investment ($27.5 billion); National Railroad Passenger Corporation ($8 billion for high speed rail); Federal Transit Administration, $6.9 billion).

26. See, e.g., ARRA under the following appropriations: Conference Report, 485–505 (health information technology, and related issues); ibid., 426–28 (energy efficiency and renewable energy, $16.8 billion), ibid., 421 (National Science Foundation, research, $25 billion); for information on the state incentive grant program, see ARRA, title XIV, Conference Report, 505–9; Nick Anderson, "Scoring System for School Aid," *Washington Post*, November 12, 2009 (account of competition for Race to the Top funds provided under program).

27. On the other hand, channeling investments through state and local agencies may, under certain circumstances, limit the ability of the federal government to emphasize specific priorities.

28. This framework is distilled from the account of the political, economic, and social history of the National Road, chapters 2–7. These characteristics generally apply to the ARRA as well.

29. See chapter 5, above.

30. Posner, "How I Became a Keynesian," 37.

31. The investment-for-growth theme is continued in a number of the provisions made for spending for fiscal year 2010, apart from the investment provisions of the ARRA. A framework of this enhanced level of investment is provided by the Concurrent Resolution on the Budget for Fiscal Year 2010, S. Con. Res. 13, 111th Cong., 1st Sess. (2009). The framework is more specifically laid out in the conference report on the resolution, H.R. Rept. No. 111-89, 111th Cong., 1st Sess (2009); see particularly the discussion therein at 87–89 (transportation: function 400); 90–93 (education, training, employment and social services, function 500); see also discussion regarding early childhood education); 93–94 (health, function 550; income security, function 600).

32. See Daily Compilation, "Remarks and a Discussion at the Closing Session of the Fiscal Responsibility Summit," February 23, 2009, 11–12; see also remarks of David Walker, former comptroller general of the United States ("As a former Comptroller General of the

United States, I can tell you that we're $11 trillion in the hole on the balance sheet. And the problem is not the balance sheet, it's off the balance sheet—$45 trillion in unfunded obligations"), in ibid., p. 8; Daily Compilation, "Remarks at the Closing Session of the Jobs and Economic Growth Forum and a Question-and-Answer Session," December 3, 2009, p. 7 (response to question by Robert Kuttner); see also David M. Walker, Comptroller General of the United States, "Saving Our Future Requires Tough Choices Today," presentation at Tallahassee Community College, Tallahassee, Florida, January 14, 2008 (charts and statistics regarding presentation) (Social Security, Medicare and Medicaid constitute a substantially increasing percent of GDP by 2080; balancing the budget in 2040 could require actions as large as cutting total federal spending by 60 percent or raising federal taxes to twice today's level; faster economic growth can help but will not solve the problem); deficit figures are from the *Budget of the United States*, Fiscal Year 2011, table 1, p. 146; the fiscal year 2011 deficit is projected at $1.267 trillion, ibid.

33. On the need to address budget deficits and long-term unfunded liabilities, see Robert E. Rubin and Jacob Weisberg, *In an Uncertain World: Tough Choices from Wall Street to Washington*, paperback ed. (New York: Random House, 2004), 118–31 (effect of long-term budget deficits); 124–25 (pairing of investment and debt reduction); 361–67 (fiscal effect of $9 trillion deterioration after 2001); Rivlin and Sawhill, *Restoring Fiscal Sanity, 2005*; Scott Bittle and Jean Johnson, *Where Does the Money Go? Your Guided Tour to the Federal Budget Crisis* (New York: HarperCollins, 2008), 97–117 (budgetary consequences of not dealing with the deficit problem), 199 (priority given deficit reduction in the view of the general public); Committee for a Responsible Budget, *Twelve Principles for Fiscal Responsibility* (Washington, D.C.: GPO, 2008); regarding the danger of "crowd out," see Peterson-Pew Commission on Budget Reform, "Red Ink Rising: A Call to Action to Stem the Mounting Federal Debt," December 2009, 11 ("Greater levels of debt and higher interest rates mean rising interest payments for the government. As interest payments become a larger share of the budget they squeeze out other important tax and spending priorities").

34. See the statement of Lawrence Summers, chairman of the National Economic Council at Brookings Institution session, March 13, 2009); see also www.whitehouse. gov/issues/fiscal responsibility (indicates president called on congressional leadership to pass statutory pay-as-you-go rules so that new nonemergency tax cut or entitlement expansion is offset in the budget); ARRA, Conference Report on ARRA, H.R. Report 16, 111th Cong., 1st Sess. (2009); H.R. 1, p. 1630 (regarding health information technology). See Bill Clinton, *My Life* (New York: Alfred A Knopf, 2004), 491–97, 525, 533–38, 657–64, 891–93, 954–57.

35. See generally Rivlin and Sawhill, *Restoring Fiscal Sanity, 2005*); on social security, see Peter R. Orszag and John B. Shoven, "Social Security," in ibid., 63; on health see, Henry J. Aaron and Jack Meyer, "Health," in Rivlin and Sawhill, *Restoring Fiscal Sanity*, 73; Henry J. Aaron and Isabel V. Sawhill, "Bend the Revenue Curve: Health Reform Alone Won't End Deficits," *Washington Post*, October 3, 2009; "Stemming the Tide: Unprecedented Levels of Debt May Require Radical Solutions," *Economist*, November 21, 2009, 26–28; for observations on the possible consequences of inaction, see Robert J. Samuelson, "Could America Go Broke?" *Washington Post*, November 1, 2009 ("The arguments over whether we need more 'stimulus' (and debt) obscure the larger reality

that past debt increasingly restricts governments' economic maneuvering room"). See The Peter G. Peterson Foundation, *The Solutions Initiative*, May 2011, www.pgpf.org (contains comprehensive plans of six invited organizations for putting the United States on a fiscally sustainable long-term path; this document should serve as a useful starting point for a national conversation about the options. The role of national investment in infrastructure, education and science is reflected in a number of the plans. See also S. 652, 112th Cong., 1st Sess. (2011) (Senator Kerry of Massachusetts; establishes an American Infrastructure Financing Authority to facilitate investment in economically viable infrastructure projects).

36. See Committee for a Responsible Federal Budget, "The Long Term Budget Outlook" (June 29, 2009), at 4 (available at www.cfrb.org); see Transcript of Remarks by Senate Budget Committee Chairman Kent Conrad (D-ND) at Hearing on Bipartisan Process Proposals for Long Term Fiscal Stability, November 20, 2009, at www.budget.Senate.gov (quote is at last page of remarks). For fiscal reform proposals in the 111th Congress, see also H.R. 947, 111th Cong., 1st Sess. (2009) (Rep. Jackson); See also Social Security Administration, *Status of the Social Security and Medicare Programs: A Summary of the 2008 Annual Reports, Social Security and Medicare Boards of Trustees* (Washington, D.C., 2008). In the fiscal year 2011 budget, the administration declared that it supported the creation of a Fiscal Commission "charged with identifying policies to improve the fiscal situation in the medium term and to achieve fiscal sustainability over the long run." With respect to the long run, the administration statement indicated that the commission examination of policies would include "changes to address the growth of entitlement spending and the gap between the projected revenues and expenditures of the Federal Government." *Budget of the United States Government*, Fiscal Year 2011, 146 (note to table S-1). See also Daily Compilation, Remarks on Signing an Executive Order Establishing the National Commission on Fiscal Responsibility and Reform and an Exchange with Reporters, February 18, 2010 and Daily Compilation, Executive Order 13531–National Commission on Fiscal Responsibility and Reform, February 18, 2010. See also Testimony of Maya MacGuineas Before the House Budget Committee, March 10, 2011, at 8 ("entitlement reform must be at the center of any turnaround plan") available at http://crfb.org/document/testimony-house-budget-committee-crushing-burden-debt. See also "The Moment of Truth," the 2010 Report of the National Commission on Fiscal Responsibility and Reform, December 2010 (White House, Washington, D.C.).

The Commission's 2010 report proposed a comprehensive set of steps, including defense and non-defense discretionary budget cuts, tax expenditure reductions, and entitlement reform, designed to reduce the national debt by approximately $4 trillion in ten years. President Obama in a speech delivered on April 13, 2011 proposed his own framework for a comparable national debt reduction over a period of twelve years. His proposal employed a mix of spending reductions (linked with "investments we need to grow"); defense savings and reduced health care costs; and revenue enhancements achieved by limiting tax expenditures. (The 2001 and 2003 tax cuts for wealthy taxpayers would not be extended in the President's plan.) In addition the President's plan proposes a "debt failsafe" mechanism that comes into play if debt reduction targets are not met; it operates through "more spending cuts and more spending reductions in the tax code." Daily Compilation, Remarks at George Washington University, April 13, 2011, Washington,

D.C. (quoted language at pp. 3, 7–8); see also Committee for a Responsible Budget, *Analyzing the President's New Budget*, April 21, 2011, ww.cfrb.org.

The House of Representatives on April 15, 2011 approved a budget resolution for fiscal year 2012 involving a comparable reduction in national debt over the succeeding ten years effected in part through substantial spending reductions and restructuring of entitlement programs. Medicare would by fiscal year 2022 be converted to a "premium-support model" and Medicaid would be converted into a block grant. Debt would be reduced by $4.2 trillion. See House Concurrent Resolution 34, 112th Cong., 1st Sess. (2011); H. R. Rept. No. 112-58, 112th Cong., 1st Sess. (2011), at 1–42.

A plan proposed by House Democrats put forward by Budget Committee ranking member, Chris Van Hollen, achieves comparable debt reduction albeit over a longer time frame. It does so by freezing non-defense spending for five years, reducing defense spending, incorporating health care spending cuts in the president's plan, and matching the president's revenue policies; investments for infrastructure, education, and other purposes would be preserved. *Van Hollen Issues House Democratic Budget*, www.vanhollen. house.gov/News/DocumentSingle.aspx?DocumentID=236244.

It is hoped that these proposals, and others in the offing, will lead to an effective and properly timed bipartisan agreement that balances the need to extend and strengthen the recovery from the recent recession as well as the need to address excessive national debt in a timely manner. Such an agreement, it is hoped, would provide an *adequate revenue base* sufficient to meet the core needs of the nation requiring federal assistance, as determined by the people, including needs recognized in discretionary and mandatory programs serving disadvantaged and vulnerable populations. If these proposals lead to such an agreement, a follow-up step, it is believed, should be the establishment of a long term, equitable failsafe mechanism designed to preclude recurrence of economically dangerous debt levels in the future. See Peterson-Pew Commission on Budget Reform, *Getting Back in the Black*, Washington, D.C., November 2010, at 3–4, 15–17, 21, www.budgetreform.org (automatic trigger mechanism to enforce enacted debt or deficit reduction targets); Pete V. Domenici and Alice Rivlin, *A Sword of Damocles for the Debt*, *Washington Post*, May 16, 2011, p. A17. These steps are essential to the successful pursuit of sustainable national investment that helps drive economic growth, full-employment and widely shared prosperity for the United States.

37. See Gene Sperling, *The Pro-Growth Progressive: An Economic Strategy for Shared Prosperity* (New York: Simon and Schuster, 2005), 30–31; see also Joseph E. Stiglitz, *Making Globalization Work* (New York: W. W. Norton and Company, 2007), 25–59 (advantages of development); Jeffrey D. Sachs, *The End of Poverty: Economic Possibilities for Our Time* (New York: Penguin Books, 2006), 251–55 (in the context of addressing global poverty); Robert G. Lynch, "Enriching Children, Enriching the Nation: Public Investment in High-Quality Prekindergarten" (Washington, D.C.: Economic Policy Institute, 2007), www.epi.org/publicationsentry/bookenriching.

38. Support for stimulus package from governors; National Governors Association meeting; cspan.org. (February 2009); See Jackie Calmes, "Obama Gains Support from G.O.P. Governors," *New York Times*, February 17, 2009.

See generally Daily Compilation, Remarks to the National Governors Association, February 23, 2009, p. 2; see also White House, Office of the Press Secretary, "Vice

President Biden to Oversee the Administration's Implementation of the Recovery Act's Provisions," February 23, 2009 (announces appointment of the vice president and the appointment of Earl Devaney as chair of the Recovery Act Transparency and Accountability Board); found at www.whitehouse.gov); see also www.recovery.gov, June 10, 2009 ("More than $1 Billion in Recovery Funds Now Available for Ohio to Save Teaching Jobs and Drive Education Reform"); ibid., June 11, 2009 (ED-Program Plan: Enhancing Education through Technology Recovery Plan (provides framework for Education Department).

39. Daily Compilation, Remarks to the National Governors Association, p. 3.

40. Omnibus Appropriations Act, 2009, Public Law 8, 111th Cong., 1st. Sess. (2009).

41. See U.S. Department of Transportation, Press Release (DOT 74-09), June 3, 2009: Vice President Biden, Secretary LaHood Meet with Governors on Future of U.S. High Speed Rail; U.S. Department of Transportation, American Recovery and Reinvestment Act of 2009, Agency-Wide Recovery Action Plan, May 15, 2009 (available at www.dot.gov [Tiger], at 3). The overarching objectives of the DOT ARRA investment programs were separately summarized in a framework departmental document describing the effort as follows: "The Recovery Act also created new programs that reflect the intent of both Congress and the Administration to create long-term economic benefits by investing in a transportation network that can keep us competitive in the 21st century. The Recovery Act also includes $8 billion to jumpstart high speed and intercity rail programs in the United States. This investment is not likely to provide the immediate recovery benefits that could be achieved through investments in existing highways and transit systems, but it represents a down payment for our efforts to transform travel in the United States and helps ensure that we reap benefits from our transportation systems for years to come." DOT, American Recovery and Reinvestment Act of 2009, Agency-Wide Recovery Act Plan, May 15, 2009, p. 3.

42. See U.S. Department of Education, National Center for Education Statistics, *The Nation's Report Card, Reading 2007 (Trial Urban District Assessment Results at Grades 4 and 8)*, table 2, p. 9 (indicates that for 2007, 34 percent of fourth-grade public schools students in NAEP reading assessment were reading below basic, down from 38 percent in 2002; 66 percent were at or above basic, and 32 percent were at or above proficient); Kevin Huffman, "How to Get Top Grades in Education," *Washington Post*, January 3, 2010 (cites estimates of $1.3 to $2.3 trillion annual cost resulting from the international education achievement gap); see David Brooks, "The Biggest Issue," *New York Times*, July 29, 2008; on attainment rates, see U.S. Department of Education, IES, National Center for Education Statistics, 2008, "Educational Attainment," (percentage of young adults who had completed high school was about 88 percent; percentage of young adults who had completed a bachelor's degree increased from 27 percent in 1988 to 31 percent in 2008); information available at www.nces.ed.gov/digest/d08). See also Sarita E. Brown, "Making the Next Generation Our Greatest Resource," in *Latinos and the Nation's Future*, ed. Henry G. Cisneros (Houston, TX: Arte Publico Press, 2009), 83.

43. See Public-Law 111-8, appropriations for U.S. Department of Education for fiscal year 2009.

44. U.S. Department of Education, "American Recovery and Reinvestment Act of 2009: Using ARRA Funds to Drive School Reform and Improvement, " April 24, 2009,

at 1, 2, 6. To achieve its goals, the U.S. Department of Education ARRA document suggests five categories for consideration: "Adopting rigorous college-and career-ready standards and high-quality assessments; establishing data systems and using data for improvement; increasing teacher effectiveness and equitable distribution of effective teachers; turning around the lowest-performing schools; and improving results for all students, including early learning, extended learning time, use of technology, preparation for college and school modernization" (ibid., 2). See also materials relating to the Race to the Top; see Richard Cooper and Ron Pikens, "Stimulus Data Indicate Gains for Education," *New York Times*, October 31, 2009 (325,000 jobs reported for education).

45. See Bill Gates, "How Teacher Development Could Revolutionize Our Schools," *Washington Post*, February 28, 2011 (on the need for sustainable spending and increased teacher performance). See also, Elizabeth H. DeBray, *Politics, Ideology, & Education: Federal Policy During the Clinton and Bush Administrations* (New York: Teachers College, Columbia University, 2006), 27–37, 111–25. Gerson M. Ratner, "Why The No Child Left Behind Act Needs To Be Restructured to Accomplish Its Goals and How to Do It," 9 U.D.C.L. Rev. 1, 48–49 (2007); Nancy Conneely, "After PICS: Making the Case for Socioeconomic Integration," *Texas Journal on Civil Liberties & Civil Rights* 14:95 (2008):105–25 (Ms. Conneely is a former student of this author); for an account of the genesis of the No Child Left Behind Act, see Edward M. Kennedy, *True Compass: A Memoir* (New York: Hachette Book Company, 2009), 88–94.

46. See Daily Compilation, (Brookings Presentation), December 8, 2009 (ARRA producing 1.6 million jobs per CBO); Jackie Calmes and Michael Cooper, "New Consensus Views Stimulus as Worthy Step: Talk of Second Infusion," *New York Times*, November 21, 2009 (cites various economists for job-related data); Fareez Zakaria, *America Is No Greece*, Washington Post, May 14, 2010, p. A19. Executive Office of the President, Council of Economic Advisors, *The Economic Impact of the American Recovery and Reinvestment Act of 2009*, Fifth Quarterly Report, November 18, 2010 (Washington, D.C.); Congressional Budget Office, CBO Report, Estimated Impact of the American Recovery and Reinvestment Act for Employment and Economic Output, July 2010 through September 2010 (November, 2010) (increased full-time equivalent jobs by 2.0 million to 5.2 million). See also, Testimony of Alan S. Blinder, Gordon S. Rentscher Memorial Professor of Economics, Princeton University, to the Senate Budget Committee, September 22, 2010; Testimony of Mark Zandi, Chief Economist, Moody's Analytics, to the Senate Budget Committee, September 22, 2010 (Blinder and Zandi testimony available at http://budget.senate.gov/democratic/index.cfm/committeehearings?ContentRecord_id=c720d7a9-4ac9-4643-abe2-5d256bd3c40b&ContentType_id=14f995b9-dfa5-407a-9d35-56cc7152a7ed&Group_id=d68d31c2-2e75-49fb-a03a-be915cb4550b); Testimony of Josh Bivens, Macroeconomist, Economic Policy Institute, before the House Budget Committee, July 24, 2010 (available at http://www.epi.org/newsroom/testimony/an_assessment_of_the_american_recovery_and_reinvestment_act). For a contrasting viewpoint on the success of the AARA, see Testimony of John B. Taylor, Mary and Robert Raymond Professor of Economics, Stanford University, before the Senate Budget Committee, July 1, 2010 (available at http://www.stanford.edu/~johntayl/).

47. See *Budget of the United States Government*, Fiscal Year 2011, President's Message, p. 1 ("With investments in health care, education, infrastructure, and clean energy,

the Recovery Act saved and created millions of jobs and began the hard work of trans-forming our economy to thrive in the modern global marketplace . . ."); see also The Peter G. Peterson Foundation, The Solutions Initiative, May 2011, www.pgpf.org.; S. 652, 112th Cong., 1st sess. (2011) (Senator Kerry).

48. 2010 report of the National Commission on Fiscal Responsibility and Reform, at 12; President Barack Obama, 2011 State of the Union Address, January 25, 2011 ("Our free enterprise system is what drives innovation . . . throughout our history government has provided cutting-edge scientists and inventors with the support they need."), available at www.whitehouse.gov/state-of-the-union-2011.

49. See Hamilton, *Report on Manufactures*, 40 ("The phrase [in Article I, sec. 8, cl. 1] is as comprehensive as that could have been used; because it was not fit that the consti-tutional authority of the Union to appropriate its revenues should have been restricted within narrower limits than the 'general welfare'; and because this necessarily embraces a vast variety of particulars which are susceptible neither of specification nor definition"); Monroe, Veto Message of May 4, 1822, in Richardson, *Compilation*, 2:142, 166–67 ("[I]t becomes necessary that, like the power to declare war, this power [the spending power] should be commensurate with the great scheme of the Government and with all of its purposes").

50. See James Monroe, *The Writings of James Monroe Including A Collection of His Public and Private Papers and Correspondence,* Stanislaus Murray Hamilton, Editor (New York: AMS PresS), VI:325, 338 (seventh annual message, December 2, 1823); VII:173, 176 (letter to John C. Calhoun, August 4, 1828).

Bibliography

Published Works

Aaron, Henry J., and Jack Meyer. "Health." In *Restoring Fiscal Sanity–2005: Meeting the Long-Run Challenge*, edited by Alive M. Rivlin and Isabel Sawhill. Washington, D.C.: Brookings Institution Press: 2005.

Achenbach, Joel A. *The Grand Idea: George Washington's Potomac and the Road to the West.* New York: Simon & Schuster, 2004.

Adams, Henry. *The Life of Albert Gallatin.* 1879. Reprint, New York: Peter Smith, 1943.

Adams, John Quincy. *Memoirs of John Quincy Adams.* Edited by Charles Francis Adams. 12 vols. Freeport, NY: Books for Libraries Press, 1969.

Adams, John, and John Quincy Adams. *The Selected Writings of John and John Quincy Adams.* Edited by Adrienne Koch and William Peden. New York: Alfred A. Knopf, 1946.

Alberts, Robert C. *Mount Washington Tavern: The Story of a Famous Inn, a Great Road, and the People Who Used Them.* Eastern National Park and Monument Association, 1976.

Alter, Jonathan. *The Defining Morment: FDR's Hundred Days and the Triumph of Hope.* New York: Simon and Schuster, 2006.

———. *The Promise: President Obama, Year One.* New York: Simon & Schuster, 2010.

Altman, Nancy J. *The Battle for Social Security: From FDR's Vision to Bush's Gamble.* Hoboken, NJ: John W. Wiley and Sons, 2005.

American Society of Civil Engineers (ASCE). *2003 Progress Report, an Update to the 2001 Report Card; Report Card for America's Infrastructure.* www.ASCE.org.

American State Papers (ASP). www.loc.gov/Americanmemory.

Ammon, Henry. *James Monroe: The Quest for National Identity.* Charlottesville: University of Virginia Press, 1990.

Appleby, Gabrielle G. "The Provenance of the Federal spending Power." December 11, 2008. Paper presented at the post-graduate session at the Law and History Conference, University of Adelaide, Australia, December 11, 2008. http://ssrn.com/abstract=1323166.

Axelrod, Alan. *Blooding at Great Meadows: Young George Washington and the Battle that Shaped the Man.* Philadelphia: Running Press, 2007.

Annals of Congress. www.loc.gov/Americanmemory.

Balogh, Brian. *A Government Out of Sight: The Mystery of National Authority in Nineteenth-Century America.* Cambridge: Cambridge University Press, 2009.

Bastian, Richard W. "From Richmond to Terre Haute, Indiana." In *Guide to the National Road,* edited by Karl Raitz. Baltimore, MD: Johns Hopkins University Press, 1996.

Beste, J. Richard. *The Wabash: or, Adventures of an English Gentleman's Family in the Interior of America.* 2 vols. 1855. Reprint, Freeport, NY: Books for Libraries Press, 1970.

Bittle, Scott, and Jean Johnson, *Where Does the Money Go? Your Guided Tour to the Federal Budget Crisis.* New York: HarperCollins, 2008.

Bivens, Josh. Macroeconomist, Economic Policy Institute. Testimony Before the House Budget Committee, July 14, 2010.

Blight, David W., ed. *Passages to Freedom: The Underground Railroad in History and Memory.* Washington, D.C.: Smithsonian Books, 2004.

Blinder, Alan S. Gordon S. Rentscher Memorial Professor of Economics, Priceton University. Testimony Before the Senate Budget Committee, September 22, 2010.

Breyer, Stephen. *Active Liberty: Interpreting Our Democratic Constitution.* New York Vintage Books, 2005.

Brown, Sarita E. "Making the Next Generation Our Greatest Resource." In *Latinos and the Nation's Future,* edited by Henry G. Cisneros. Houston, TX: Arte Publico Press, 2009.

Bruce, Robert. *The National Road. A Topographical, Historical and Pictorial Description of the Old Highway from Baltimore and Washington across the Blue Ridge and Alleghenieo to the Ohio River in Wheeling.* Washington, D.C.: National Highways Association, 1916.

Cannon, Lou. *President Reagan: The Role of a Lifetime.* New York: Public Affairs, 1991.

Carter, Jimmy. *Keeping Faith: Memoirs of a President.* New York: Bantam Books, 1982.

The Civil Rights Project. *Hard Work for Good Schools: Facts Not Fads in Title I Reform.* Edited by Gary Orfield and Elizabeth H. DeBray. Cambridge, MA: Harvard University Press, 1999.

Clause, Jerry A. *The Whiskey Rebellion: Southwestern Pennsylvania's Frontier People Test the American Constitution.* Harrisburg: Pennsylvania Historical and Museum Commission, 2002.

Clay, Henry. *The Papers of Henry Clay.* Edited by James F. Hopkins. Lexington: University Press of Kentucky, 1959–.

Clinton, Bill. *My Life* (New York: Alfred A. Knopf, 2004).

Cole, Donald B. *The Presidency of Andrew Jackson.* Lawrence: University Press of Kansas, 1993.

Colten, Craig E. "Adapting the Road to New Transport Technology," In *The National Road,* edited by Karl Raitz. Baltimore, MD: Johns Hopkins University Press, 1996.

Comeau, Clifford, M. *Conditions and Performance of the Interstate System—after 40 Years.* Washington, D.C.: U.S. Department of Transportation, Federal Highway Administration. Summer, 1996.

Committee for a Responsible Federal Budget. "The Long Term Budget Outlook," June 29, 2009. www.cfrb.org.

Congressional Budget Office, CBO Report. "Estimated Impact of the American Recovery and Reinvestment Act for Employment and Economic Output, October 2010 through December 2010," February 2011.

Conneely, Nancy. "After PICS: Making the Case for Socioeconomic Integration." *Texas Journal on Civil Liberties and Civil Rights* 14, no. 95 (2008).

The Concord Coalition, "A Fiscal Wake-up Call." www.concordcoalition.org.

Council of Economic Advisors. *The Economic Impact of the American Recovery and Reinvestment Act of 2009*, Fifth Quarterly Report. Washington, D.C.: GPO, 2010.

Cunningham, Noble E., Jr. *The Presidency of James Monroe*. Lawrence: University Press of Kansas, 1996.

Dallek, Robert. *Flawed Giant: Lyndon Johnson and His Times, 1961–1973*. New York: Oxford University Press, 1998.

Darbee, Jeffrey T., and Nancy A. Reccie. *Images of America: German Columbus*. Charleston, SC: Arcadia, 2005.

Day, Reed B. *The Cumberland Road: A History of the National Road* Apollo, PA: Closson Press, 1996.

Debray, Elizabeth. *Politics, Ideology, & Education: Federal Policy During the Clinton and Bush Administrations*. New York: Teachers College, Columbia University, 2006.

Dionne, E. J., Jr. *They Only Look Dead: Why Progressives Will Dominate the Next Political Era*. New York: Simon and Schuster, 1996.

Drake, Daniel. *Discourse on the History, Character and Prospects of the West*. Cincinnati, OH: Truman and Smith, 1834.

Eisenhower, Dwight D. *Public Papers of the Presidents of the United States: Dwight Eisenhower*, Washington, D.C.: GPO, 1960.

Emanuel, Rahm, and Bruce Reed. *The Plan: Big Ideas for America*. New York: Public Affairs, 2006.

Farrar, Edgar Howard. *The Post-Road Power in the Federal Constitution and Its Availability for Creating a System of Federal Transportation Corporations*. N.p.: self-published, 1907.

Freeman, Douglas Southall. *Washington. An Abridgement in One Volume by Richard Harwell of the Seven-Volume "George Washington" by Douglas Southall Freeman*. New York: Macmillan publishing company, 1968.

Fuess, Claude M. *Daniel Webster*. 2 vols. Boston: Little, Brown and Co., 1930.

Gallatin, Albert. *Report of the Secretary of the Treasury on Roads and Canals*, S. Doc. No. 250, 10th Cong., 1st Sess. (1808).

———. *The Writings of Albert Gallatin*. Edited by Henry Adams. 3 vols. New York: Antiquarian Press, 1960.

Gates, Bill. "How Teacher Development Could Revolutionize Our Schools," *Washington Post*, February 28, 2011.

Greenspan, Alan, The *Age of Turbulence: Adventures in a New World*. New York: Penguin, 2007.

Greenstone, J. David. *The Lincoln Persuasion: Remaking American Liberalism*. Princeton, NJ: Princeton University Press, 1993.

Gurney, Joseph John. *A Journey in North America: Described in Familiar Letters to Amelia Opie*. 1841. Reprint, New York: Da Capo Press, 1973.

Hagel, Chuck. *America: Our Next Chapter: Tough Questions, Straight Answers*. With Peter Kaminzky, New York, Harper Collins, 2008.

Hamilton, Alexander. *Report on Manufactures*. 1791. Reprinted in H. Doc. No. 72, 63rd Cong., 1st Sess. (1913).

Hargreaves, Mary M. W. *The Presidency of John Quincy Adams*. Lawrence: University Press of Kansas, 1987.

Harper, Glenn, and Doug Smith. *A Traveler's Guide to the Historic National Road in Ohio: The Road that Helped Build America.* Columbus: Ohio Historical Society, 2005.

Hemp, Emery L., and Beverly B. Flaty. *The Wheeling Suspension Bridge: A Pictorial Heritage.* Charleston, WV: Pictorial Histories Publishing Co., 1999.

Howe, Daniel Walker. *What Hath God Wrought: The Transformation of America, 1815–1848.* New York: Oxford University Press, 2007.

Hulbert, Archer Butler. *The Cumberland Road.* Vol. 10 of *Historic Highways of America.* Cleveland, OH: Arthur H. Clark Co., 1904.

Hulme, Thomas. "Thomas Hulme's Journal, 1818–1819." In vol. 10 *Of Early Western Travels, 1748–1846,* edited by R. G. Thwaites. Cleveland, OH: Arthur H. Clark Co., 1904.

Ierley, Merritt. *Traveling the National Road: Across the Centuries on America's First Highway.* Woodstock, NY: Overlook Press, 1990.

Jefferson, Thomas. *The Writings of Thomas Jefferson.* Edited by Andrew A. Lipscomb. Library Edition. 20 vols. Washington, D.C.: Thomas Jefferson Memorial Association, 1903.

Johnson, Lyndon Baines. *The Vantage Point: Perspectives of the Presidency, 1963-1969.* New York: Holt, Rinehart and Winston, 1971.

Jordan, Philip D. *The National Road.* The American Trails Series. Indianapolis: Bobbs-Merrill Company, 1948.

Kaplin, William, A. *American Constitutional Law: An Overview, Analysis and Integration.* Durham, NC: Carolina Academic Press, 2004.

Kennedy, Edward M. *True Compass: A Memoir.* New York: Hachette Book Co., 2009.

Ketcham, Ralph. *James Madison: A Biography.* Charlottesville: University of Virginia Press, 1990.

Koegler, Karen, and Kenneth Pavelchak. "From Cumberland to Wheeling, West Virginia." In A *Guide to the National Road,* ed. Karl Raitz. Baltimore. MD: Johns Hopkins University Press, 1996.

Kussy, Edward V. A. "Surface Transportation and Administrative Law: Growing Up Together in the 20th Century." In *Transportation Research. Record 1527* (1996), http://trb.metapress.com/content/26702842647256551.

Larson, John Lauritz. "'Bind the Republic Together': The National Union and the Struggle for a System of Internal Improvements." *Journal of American History,* 74, no. 363 (September 1987): 377–85.

Lincoln, Abraham. *Collected Works of Abraham Lincoln.* Edited by Roy P. Basler. 9 vols. New Brunswick, NJ: Rutgers University Press, 1953.

Longfellow, Richie. *Back in Time: Zone's Trace.* U.S. Department of Transportation, Federal Highway Administration, Ohio Division Office (2008), http://www.fhwa.dot.gov/infrastructure/backaarc3.cfm.

Lynch, Robert G. *Enriching Children, Enriching the Nation: Public Investment in High-Quality Prekindergarten.* Washington, D.C. Economic Policy Institute, 2007.

MacGuineas, Maya. Testimony Before the Committee for a Responsible Federal Budget at the New America Foundation. House Budget Committee, March 10, 2011. Washington, D.C.

Madison, James. *Letters and Other Writings of James Madison.* 4 vols. Philadelphia: J.B. Lippincott and Co., 1865.

Malone, Dumas. *Jefferson the President: Second Term, 1805–1809.* Boston: Little, Brown, 1975.

McCullough, David *Truman.* New York: Simon and Schuster, 1992.

Mertz, Lee. "Origins of the Interstate." U.S. Department of Transportation, Federal Highway Administration, www.fwha.dot/gov/infrastructure???

Minder, Mike. *The Wheeling Suspension Bridge Reader.* Wheeling, WV: Nail City Publishing, n.d.

Monroe, Elizabeth B. "Spanning the Commerce Clause: The Wheeling Bridge Case, 1850–1856." *American Journal of Legal History* 32 (1988).

Monroe, James. *The Writings of James Monroe, Including a Collection of His Public and Private Papers and Correspondence,* Stanislaus Murray Hamilton, Editor. 7 volumes. New York, AMS Press, 1903. (Reprint, 1969).

Murray, Meredith A. *To Live and Die amongst the Monongahela Hills: The Story of Albert Gallatin and Friendship Hill.* N.p.: Eastern National, 1999.

The National Commission on Fiscal Responsibility and Reform. "The Moment of Truth." Washington, D.C.: White House, 2010.

National Road Heritage Corridor. www.nationalroad.pa.org.

National Surface Transportation Policy and Revenue Study Commission. Final Report (2008). www.transportationfortran.

Obama, Barack. *The Audacity of Hope: Thoughts on Reclaiming the American Dream.* New York: Crown Publishers, 2006.

Office of the Federal Register, National Archives and Records Administration, Daily Compilation of Presidential Documents, Administration of Barack Obama. GPO Access.

Oliver, William. *Eight Months in Illinois.* Newcastle-upon-Tyne, England: William A. Mitchell, 1843.

Oliver, William. *Eight Months in Illinois: With Information to Emigrants.* 1841. Reprint, Ann Arbor, MI: University Microfilms, 1968.

Orszag, Peter R., and John B. Shoven. *Social Security.* In *Restoring Fiscal Sanity, 2005: Meeting the Long-Run Challenge,* edited by Alice M. Rivlin and Isabel Sawhill. Washington, D.C.: Brookings Institution Press, 2005.

Parsons, Lynn. Hudson. *John Quincy Adams.* Madison, WI: Madison House, 1998.

Patterson, James T. *America's Struggle against Poverty, 1900–1985* Cambridge, MA: Harvard University Press, 1986.

Perret, Geoffrey. *Eisenhower.* Holbrooke, MA: Adams Media Corporation, 1999.

Peter G. Peterson Foundation Solutions Initiative (2011), www.pgpf.org "Solutions Initiative."

Peterson, Merrill D. *The Great Triumphate: Webster, Clay, and Calhoun.* Cambridge, MA: Oxford University Press, 1987.

Peyton, Billy Joe. "Surveying and Building the Road." In *The National Road, edited by* Karl Raitz. Baltimore, MD: Johns Hopkins University Press, 1996.

Posner, Richard A. "How I Became a Keynesian: Second Thoughts in a Recession." *New Republic,* September 23, 2009.

Preston, Daniel, ed. *The Papers of James Monroe: A Documentary History of the Presidential Tours of James Monroe, 1817, 1819, 1819.* Westport, CT: Greenwood Press, 2003.

Public Papers of the Presidents of the United States, Richard Nixon, 1973. Washington, D.C.: GPO.

Public Papers of the Presidents of the United States, Gerald Ford, 1976. Washington, D.C.: GPO.

Public Papers of the Presidents of the United States, William J. Clinton, 1998-I. Washington, D.C.: GPO.

Pyne, Tricia T. *Faith in the Mountains: A History of the Diocese of Wheeling-Charleston, 1850–2000.* Strasbourg, France: Editions du Signe, 2000.

Raitz, Karl, ed. *A Guide to the National Road* Baltimore: Johns Hopkins University Press, 1996.

———. *The National Road.* Baltimore: Johns Hopkins University Press, 1996.

———. "The U.S. 40 Roadside." In *The National Road,* edited by Karl Raitz. Baltimore, MD: Johns Hopkins University Press, 1996.

Ratner, Gerson M. "Why the No Child Left Behind Act Needs to be Restructured to Accomplish Its Goals and How to Do It." *University of the District of Columbia Law Review* 9, no. 1 (2007).

Remini, Robert V. *Henry Clay: Statesman for the Union.* New York: W. W. Norton & Co., 1991.

Richardson, J. D., ed., *Compilation of the Messages and Papers of the Presidents, 1789–1902.* 10 vols. Washington, D.C.: GPO, 1903.

Riley, James Whitcomb. *The Best of James Whitcomb Riley.* Edited by Donald C. Manlove. Bloomington: Indiana University Press, 1982, xii–xiii.

Riley, Richard W. "The Improving America's Schools Act and Elementary and Secondary Education Reform." *Journal of Law and Education* 24 (1995):513.

———. "Redefining the Federal Role in Education: Toward a Framework for Higher Standards, Improved School, Broader Opportunities and New Responsibilities for All." *Journal of Law and Education* 23 (1994): 295.

Rivlin, Alice M., and Isabel Sawhill, eds. *Restoring Fiscal Sanity, 2005: Meeting the Long Run Challenge.* Washington, D.C.: Brookings Institution Press, 2005.

Rose, Gregory S. "Extending the Road West." In *The National Road,* edited by Karl Raitz. Baltimore, MD: Johns Hopkins University Press, 1996.

Rubin, Robert E., and Jacob Weisberg. *In an Uncertain World: Tough Choices from Wall Street to Washington.* Paperback ed. New York: Random House, 1994.

Sachs, Jeffrey D. *The End of Poverty: Economic Possibilities for Our Time.* New York: Penguin, 2006.

Schneider, Norris F. *The National Road: Main Street of America.* Columbus: Ohio Historical Society, 1975.

Sculle, Keith A., and John A. Jakle. "From Terre Haute to Vandalia, Illinois" in *Guide to the National Road,* edited by Karl Reitz. Baltimore, MD: Johns Hopkins University Press.

Scalia, Antonin. *A Matter of Interpretation: Federal Courts and the Law: An Essay by Antonin Scalia; with Commentary by Amy Gutmann, Editor, Gordon S. Wood, Laurence H. Tribe, Mary Ann Glendon, Ronald Dworkin.* Princeton, NJ: Princeton University Press, 1997.

Schlereth, Thomas. *Reading the Road: U.S. 40 and the American Landscape.* Knoxville: University of Tennessee Press, 1997.

Schlesinger, Arthur, Jr. *A Thousand Days: John F. Kennedy in the White House.* Boston: Houghton Mifflin, 1965.

Schneider, Norris F. *The National Road: Main Street of America.* Columbus, OH: Ohio Historical Society, 1975.

Schultz, George, and John Shoven, *Putting Our House in Order: A Guide to Social Security and Health Reform.* New York: W. W. Norton and Company, 2008.

Searight, Thomas. *The Old Pike: A History of the National Road with Incidents, Accidents, and Anecdotes Thereon.* Uniontown: self-published by the author, 1904.

Simon, Paul. *Lincoln's Preparation for Greatness: The Illinois Legislative Years.* Norman: University of Oklahoma Press, 1965.

Sky, Theodore. *To Provide for the General Welfare: A History of the Federal Spending Power.* Newark: University of Delaware Press, 2003.

Sperling, Gene, *The Pro-Growth Progressive: An Economic Strategy for Shared Prosperity.* New York: Simon and Schuster, 2005.

Steele, Eliza R. *A Summer Journey in the West.* New York: J. S. Taylor and Co., 1841.

Stewart, George R. *U.S. 40: Cross Section of the United States of America.* Boston: Houghton Mifflin Company, 1953.

Stiglitz, Joseph E. *Making Globalization Work.* New York, W. W. Norton and Company, 2007.

Story, Joseph. *Commentaries on the Constitution of the United States.* Edited by Melville Bigelow. 5th ed. 2 vols. Boston: Little, Brown and Co., 1891.

———. *Commentaries on the Constitution of the United States, Abridgement, 1833.* Reprint, with introduction by Ronald D. Retunde and John E. Newalk, Durham, NC: Carolina Academic Press, 1891.

Switala, William J. *The Underground Railroad in Pennsylvania* Mechanicsburg, PA: Stackpole Books, 2001.

Taylor, John B. Mary and Robert Raymond Professor of Economics, Stanford University. Testimony Before the Senate Budget Committee, July 1, 2010.

Thompson, Charles N. *Sons of the Wilderness: John and William Conner.* Noblesville, IN: Conner Prairie Press, 1988.

Trollope, Frances. *Domestic Manners of the Americans.* Edited by Donald Smalley. New York: Vintage Books, 1960.

Unger, Harlow Giles. *The Last Founding Father: James Monroe and A Nation's Call to Greatness.* Philadelphia, PA: Da Capo Press, 2009.

United States Department of Transportation, Federal Highways Administration. *2006 Status of the Nation's Highways, Bridges, and Transit: Condition and Performance.* Washington, D.C.: GPO, 2007.

United States Department of Transportation, Federal Highway Administration. *America's Highways, 1776–1976: A History of the Federal-Aid Program.* Washington, D.C.: GPO, 1976.

———. "Ask the Rambler: When Did the Federal Government Begin Collecting the Gas Tax?" www.fhwa.dot.gov/infrastructure/gastax.cfm.

United States House of Representatives. *Report No. 16.* 111th Cong., 1st Sess. (2009). (Conference Report on American Recovery and Reinvestment Act of 2009).

Vale, Thomas R., and Geraldine Vale. *U.S. 40 Today: Thirty Years of Landscape Change in America.* Madison: University of Wisconsin Press, 1983.

Van Allen, Elizabeth J. *James Whitcomb Riley: A Life*. Bloomington: Indiana University Press, 1999.

Van Hollen, Chris. Vanhollen.hoase.gov/news/Document.Single.aspx?DocumentID=236244

Vivian, Cassandra. *The National Road in Pennsylvania* Charleston, SC: Arcadia, 2003.

Walters, Raymond, Jr. *Albert Gallatin: Jeffersonian Financier and Diplomat*. New York: Macmillan Company, 1957.

Washington, George. *George Washington's Diaries: An Abridgement*. Edited by Dorothy Twohig. Charlottesville: University of Virginia Press, 1999.

———. George Washington's *Journal for 1754*. Edited by Donald H. Kent. Eastern National, 2004. Reprinted article [title?], Pennsylvania H

———. *Writings*. Edited by John Rhodehamel. New York: Library of America, 1997.

———. *The Writings of George Washington*. Edited by John C. Fizpatrick. Washington, D.C.: GPO, 1931.

Weingroff, Richard F. *Clearly Vicious as a Matter of Policy: The Fight Against Federal Aid.* U.S. Department of Transportation, Federal Highway Administration, Public Roads. www.fhwa.dot.gov/infrastructure/hwyhist01.cfm.

———. *Creating a Landmark: The Intermodal Surface Transportation Efficiency Act*. U.S. Department of Transportation, Federal Highway Administration Public Record.

———. *Federal Aid Road Act of 1916: Building the Foundation*. U.S. Department of Transportation, Federal Highway Administration, Public Roads Website, [web address].

———. *From Names to Numbers*. U.S. Department of Transportation, Federal Highway Administration, Public Roads. www.fhwa.dot.gov/infrastructures/numbers.htm.

———. *The Man Who Loved Roads*. U.S. Department of Transportation, Federal Highway Administration, Public Roads. www.fhwa.dot.gov/infrastructure/trumanpr.htm.

———. *The National Old Trails Association*. U.S. Department of Transportation, Federal Highway Administration, Public Roads. www.fhwa.dot.gov/infrastructure/trails.htm.

———. "Three States Claim First Interstate Highway." U.S. Department of Transportation, Federal Highway Administration, Public Roads, www.tfhrc.gov/pubrd/summer96su8018.htm.

Weld, Charles. *A Vacation Tour in the United States and Canada*. London: Longmans, Green, Longmans and Robert, 1855.

Welhelm, Hubert G. H., and Artimus Kieffer. "From Wheeling to Columbus, Ohio" in *A Guide to the National Road*, edited by Karl Raitz. Baltimore, MD: Johns Hopkins University Press, 1996.

Weslager, C. A. *The Delaware Indians: A History*. New Brunswick, NJ: Rutgers University Press, 2003.

White, Leonard D. *The Jeffersonians: A Study in Administrative History, 1800–1829*. New York: Free Press, 1951.

Whitman, Walt. "Excerpts from a Traveler's Notebook." In *The Uncollected Poetry and Prose of Walt Whitman*, edited by Emory Holloway. 2 vols. New York: Peter Smith, 1932.

Wood, Joseph. "The Idea of the National Road." In *The National Road*, edited by Karl Raitz. Baltimore, MD: Johns Hopkins University Press, 1996.

Young, Jeremiah Simeon. *A Political and Constitutional Study of the Cumberland Road.* Chicago: University of Chicago Press, 1904.

Zandi, Mark. Chief Economist, Moody's Analytics. Testimony Before the Senate Budget Committee, September 22, 2010.

Archival Bibliography

Letter from Ebenezer Fitch, May 1818, Washington, Pennsylvania. Courtesy of Bethany College, Wheeling, West Virginia, and Oglebay Institute, Wheeling, West Virginia.

Remarks of Rep. James Buchanan, April 9, 1822, before the House of Representatives in opposition to an appropriation for the Cumberland Road. Copy of handwritten manuscript. Courtesy of Dickinson College Library, Special Collections, Carlisle, PA.

Communication to Honorable John Quincy Adams from Daniel P. Cooke and Jonathan Jennings, U.S. House of Representatives, March 3, 1825. Courtesy of Manuscript Section, Indiana State Library, original in Indiana State Library, L 79, Collection of Jonathan Jennings, box 1, folder 4.

Letter to President John Quincy Adams from Governor John Ray, [November] 25, 1825. Courtesy of Manuscript Section, Indiana State Library, original in Indiana State Library.

Letter to John P. Cockley from John [Gesaff], December 8, 1829. Courtesy of Ohio Historical Society.

Letter to Jacob and Mary Kistner from Peter and Catherine Hessong, May 21, 1838. Courtesy of Manuscript Section, Indiana State Library, typed copy, S. 1186, Loury J. Silver.

Voucher, dated August 31, 1838. Courtesy of Manuscript Section Indiana State Library, original in Indiana State Library, S. 1807, Wm. Rockwood folder.

Notice to Road Contractors, *Springfield (OH) Republic,* May 28, 1841. Courtesy Clark County Heritage Center, Springfield, Ohio.

Letter to Hon. J. A. Wright from James M. McAvoy, May 15, 1844. Courtesy of Manuscript Section, Indiana State Library, original in Indiana State Library, L. 183, Joseph A Wright box 1, folder 1.

Letter to the editor of the *Springfield (OH) Republic,* February 3, 1854, relative to the portion of the National Road west of Springfield, Ohio. Courtesy of Clark County Historical Society, Springfield, Ohio.

Petition to Governor A. G. Curtin of Pennsylvania from citizens of Somerset County, Pennsylvania, dated [January] 11, 1862. Courtesy of Dickinson College Library, Special Collections, Carlisle, PA.

Letter from Joseph B. Welsh to Eli Stifer, September 9, 1865. Courtesy of Dickinson College Library, Special Collections, Carlisle, PA.

For archival sources for chapter 9, see notes to chapter 9.

Index

abolition, 141, 142
Act of March 29, 1806, 15, 16, 18, 20, 30, 36, 39, 45, 66, 71, 87, 89, 152, 154, 158, 177–79, 181, 188, 190, 193, 195, 199, 207, 212, 214, 216, 217, 219, 238
Act of May 15, 1820, 87
Act of February 28, 1823, 47, 238
Act of March 3, 1825, 87, 88, 239
Act of March 3, 1826, 50, 53, 239
Act of March 3, 1829, 239
Act of June 24, 1834, 64, 239
Act of March 3, 1835, 65
Act of May 25, 1838, 66, 240
Act of August 1, 1848, 66, 240
Act of May 9, 1856, 66, 240
Adams, John, 106, 107
Adams, John Quincy, ix, 17, 48–55, 57, 58, 60, 61, 63, 65, 72, 76, 77, 87, 91, 94, 100, 103, 106, 107, 120, 141, 145, 146, 165, 172, 183, 185, 194, 200, 205, 209 238, 239, 247nn2 and 3, 263n9
Agricultural Assistance Act (AAA), 205, 207
Alberts, Robert C.: on tavern fare, 123
Allegheny Mountains, ix, 8, 9, 89, 124, 125, 128, 133, 139, 142, 169, 177, 178, 200, 215, 220, 237

Allegheny River, 6, 144
Alter, Jonathan, 223
American Association of State Highway Officials (AASHO). 155, 157, 158, 160, 162
American Recovery and Reinvestment Act (ARRA), 219, 222–35
American Revolution, 11, 12, 35, 189, 191
American System, 51, 63, 69, 72, 74, 249n2
Appleby, Gabrielle: "The Provenance of the Federal Spending Power," 269n21
Army Corps of Engineers, 91, 97, 101
Articles of Confederation, 35, 42
Atlantic City, New Jersey, 162
Atlantic Ocean, 15, 16, 25, 184
automobiles, x, 77, 151–53, 155, 157, 162–64, 167, 175, 176, 191

Bailey, Rep. John, 50
Balogh, Brian: *A Government Out of Sight,* 208–9, 245n23, 246n12, 247n5, 249nn15 and 26, 269n22
Baltimore, Maryland, 16, 60, 88, 90, 95, 122, 125, 126, 132, 134, 162, 164, 184
Baltimore and Ohio Railroad, 90, 131, 152

Bankhead Bill, 155

Barbour, Sen. James, 44, 50, 199

Bedinger, Rep. George, 16

Beeson, Rep. Henry, 152

Benton, Sen. Thomas, 55, 62, 63, 65

Beste, J. Richard, 137, 186

Biden, Vice President Joseph, 231–33, 279nn38 and 41

Big Youghiogheny River, 5, 7, 9, 21, 31, 32, 86, 97, 103, 109–11, 114

Bivens, Josh: testimony to Senate Budget Committee, 272n46

Blane, William: on the condition of the National Road, 48

Blinder, Prof. Alan S.: testimony to Senate Budget Committee, 272n46

Bonus Bill: veto of, 10, 29, 33–39, 41, 42, 45, 113, 116, 185, 199, 207, 238, 246n3

Braddock, Gen. Edward, 8, 86, 97, 144, 157; campaign of, 7–8, 193, 237

Bradford, William, 13

Brewer, Justice David, 78, 79

Brown, Uria: on the National Road, 95–97, 133, 184

Brownsville, Pennsylvania, 5–7, 16, 21–23, 26–29, 32, 48, 86, 97, 103, 104, 113–15, 125, 126, 128, 144, 153, 157, 163, 238

Bruce, Robert, 156

Buchanan, President James, 52, 54, 55, 60, 64, 65, 69, 70, 74, 152

Bush, President George H. W., 176–78

Bush, President George W., 179, 180

Calhoun, Rep. John C., 33, 35, 140, 160, 235

Campbell, Dr. Hugh, 51

canals, 10, 11, 19, 24–26, 28, 32, 33, 36, 38, 40, 44–46, 49, 50, 57, 71, 76, 116, 140, 141, 152, 183, 195, 195, 200, 201, 235, 243n10

Cannon, Lou, 176

Cardozo, Justice Benjamin, 78, 202

Carter, President Jimmy, 172, 175–76; *Keeping Faith,* 175

Cass, Lewis, 74

Chadwick, Edward: *Chadwick's History of Shelby County Indiana,* 251n18

Chadwick, Marcus B., 251n18

Cheat River, 9

Chesapeake and Ohio Canal, 50, 72, 90

Chestnut Ridge/Laurel Ridge, 5, 6, 86, 128

Cincinnati, 52, 89, 132, 1333

Civil War, 66, 69, 76, 80, 98, 141, 147, 148, 153, 221

Clay, Henry, 33, 35, 37, 40, 49, 60, 63, 65, 69, 70, 73, 74, 80, 90, 117, 118, 124–26, 140, 200, 243n10

Clay, Gen. Lucius, 168

Clayton, Sen. John M., 62, 74

Clinton, President Bill, 179, 230

Cobb, Sen. Thomas W., 53

Cochran, James, 104–7

Cold War, 167

Collins, Sen. Susan, 223

Collins-Reed Amendment, 223

Colton, Craig, 66–67, 152, 153

Columbus, Ohio, 86–88, 125, 126, 130, 131, 134, 136, 162

Commerce Clause, 34, 42, 46, 77–80, 98, 204–6, 208, 263n9

Committee for a Responsible Budget, 230, 267–68n32, 269–70n36

Committee of the Whole, 30, 54

Conestoga wagons, 117, 138

Congress, ix, x, 5, 10–15, 17–55, 57–63, 65, 66, 70–74, 76–81, 85–91, 96, 98, 100, 102, 105, 108, 115, 120 122, 123, 135, 137, 139–41 148, 152–56, 159–61, 167, 168, 170, 173, 174, 178–81, 183–86, 190, 191, 193, 195, 199–208, 216, 219, 221–23, 226, 228, 230, 231, 234, 237–40, 243n10, 246n3, 249n2, 262n4, 268nn34 and 36, 269n41

Constitution, the, 10–14, 18–20, 34–37, 39, 41, 42, 45, 47, 48, 50, 52, 53,

58, 70–72, 76–78, 80, 98, 116, 155,
    186, 194, 201–6, 208, 226, 235, 237,
    243n10, 246n3, 248n26, 249n2,
    263n9
Constitutional Convention, 10, 35, 45,
    208, 237
Coolidge, President Calvin, 160
Crawford, Rep. Thomas H., 61
Crawford, William H., 101, 113–15
Cresap, Thomas, 5
Cumberland, Maryland, 5, 9, 15, 16, 21,
    50, 85, 115, 117, 126, 145, 153, 156,
    162, 188, 190, 215, 238
Cumberland Road, ix, 5, 10, 15, 18–20,
    22–24, 26, 28, 32, 39, 40, 47, 60, 51,
    53, 57, 59, 64, 71, 79, 80, 87–89, 91,
    92, 94, 104, 111, 117, 143, 178 183,
    184, 190, 238, 243n10, 254n6. *See
    also* National Road
customs duties, 44

Dallas, Alexander, 101, 110–12, 115
Dallas, Sen. George, 62
Dallek, Robert, 179
Daughters of the American Revolution,
    191
Davis Bacon Act, 170–71
Day, Reed B.: travel on the National
    Road, 117
Defense Highway Act (1941), 161
Democratic Party, 156
Democratic-Republican Party, 12, 16,
    28, 37
Detroit, 24
Dinwiddie, Gov. Robert, 5–7
Domenici, Pete V. 269–70n36
Douglas, Gov. Jim, 231
Douglas, Stephen A., 124

Eisenhower, Dwight D., 148, 167, 168,
    170–73, 176, 178, 180, 181, 221
Eisenhower Interstate Highway System,
    165, 167, 170–73, 176, 178, 180, 221
Emergency Construction Act (1930), 160
eminent domain, 19

Ewing, Nathanial, 123
Ewing, Sen. Thomas, 62–64
excise taxes, 49, 169–71

Ferrar, Edgar H.: *The Post-Road Power
    . . .* , 206
Federal Aid Highway Act: 1916, 77,
    181, 240, 191, 204; 1921, 77,
    154–60, 181, 204, 240; 1938, 169;
    1944, 161, 169; 1948, 169; 1950,
    170; 1952, 170; 1956, 79, 169, 170,
    174, 176, 181, 204, 206, 208, 213,
    221, 240; 1965, 170; 1973, 174;
    1976, 174
Federal Highway Administration (HWA),
    168, 174, 207
federal spending power, 208–9
Federal Works Agency, 169
Federalists/Federalist Party, 12, 16, 34,
    45, 54, 71, 72, 194
Fenton, Rep. Charles, 54
Fillmore, President Millard, 61, 74
Ford, President Gerald, 172, 174–75
Fort Cumberland, 5
Fort Duquesne, 6, 8, 144
Fort LeBoeuf, 5, 237
Fort Necessity, 6–8, 86, 97, 123, 143,
    144, 157, 193, 237, 240
France/French, 5–8, 17, 144, 237
Frelinghuysen, Sen. Peter, 63
French and Indian War, 193

Gallatin, Albert, 9, 16–18, 22–26, 28,
    30, 31, 33, 36, 71, 81, 90, 92, 93,
    97, 101, 103–10, 115, 116, 143, 161,
    183, 189, 217, 231, 238, 242n10;
    Friendship Hill, 115; *The Report of the
    Secretary of the Treasury on Roads and
    Canals,* 24–26
Gant, Nelson, 143
gasoline tax, 160, 164, 165, 171, 175,
    181, 216
Gates, Bill, 272n45
Gates Bill, 40, 41, 43–46, 199, 200, 207,
    238, 239

General Welfare Clause (Spending
   Clause), 10, 12, 14, 34, 35, 37, 38,
   41, 42, 47, 70, 78–80, 185, 200–205,
   209, 242nn13 and 15, 263nn8 and 9
Georgia, 24, 53, 113
Giles, William B., 17
Gist, Christopher, 5
Grant, President Ulysses S., 148
Great Britain, 6, 8, 9, 14, 17, 26, 29,
   131, 135
Great Depression, 160, 161, 164, 165,
   169
Great Lakes, 24
Great Meadows, Pennsylvania, 6, 7
Gurney, Joseph John, 134, 135, 147, 186

Hamilton, Alexander, 11–14, 18, 19, 24,
   35, 37, 43, 71, 72, 194, 202–5, 222,
   237, 271n48; Report on Manufactures,
   11, 14, 18, 24, 35, 37, 203, 242n15,
   271n48
Harding, President Warren G., 160
Harrison, William Henry, 53, 73, 124, 145
Hart's Tavern, 59
Hayden, Sen. Carl, 165
Hayes, President Rutherford B., 148, 221
Helvering v. Davis, 78, 79, 202, 205,
   250n21
Hendricks, Sen. William, 53, 55, 62–65
Heritage Corridors, 192–93
Hessong, Peter, 129, 130, 139, 186
Highway Trust Fund, 165, 170, 171,
   174, 176, 178, 216
Hocking River, 13
Hoover, President Herbert, 160, 164,
   222
House of Representatives (IL), 75, 76
House of Representatives (PA), 17
Hudson River, 24
Hulbert, Archer B., 89, 120, 184
Hulme, Thomas: on the National Road,
   96, 186

Illinois, ix, 48, 51–55, 58, 60–62, 64–66,
   75, 76, 86–89, 98, 117, 124, 130,
135, 146, 152, 156, 162, 187, 190,
   194, 199, 215, 217, 239, 240, 250n3
Illinois and Muskegon Canal, 76
Indian Claims Commission, 145
Indiana, ix, 51–55, 58, 60–62, 64–67,
   73, 86–91, 94, 120, 124, 139, 130,
   134, 136–38, 140, 144–47, 152, 163,
   185, 187, 191, 215, 217, 239, 240
Indianapolis, 86, 87, 120, 129, 130, 136,
   138, 144
Indians, 5, 7, 39, 143, 145, 146, 148;
   Cherokees, 145, 149; Delaware, 143–
   45; and the Greenville Treaty, 144
infrastructure, 211–28, 230–35
Intermodal Surface Transportation
   Efficiency Act (1991), 176–79
internal improvements, ix, 11, 13, 14,
   17–20, 24, 25, 29, 32–34, 36, 38–43,
   45, 47–54, 58, 52, 63, 69, 71–77, 81,
   90, 113, 116, 118, 139–41, 145, 156,
   184, 185, 186, 194, 200, 201, 205,
   206, 239, 243n13, 245 n13, 246nn3
   and 16, 247n2, 248n26, 249n16,
   261n16
Internal Improvements Act (IL), 75
Interstate Commerce Clause, 46, 78–80,
   98
interstate highways, ix, x, 78–80, 89,
   101, 115, 151, 152, 155, 156, 158,
   159, 161, 162, 165, 167–81, 188,
   190, 193, 194, 206, 211–14, 216,
   217, 220–22, 235, 240, 260n17. See
   also Eisenhower Interstate Highway
   System

Jackson, President Andrew, ix, 48, 49, 52,
   55, 57–63, 65, 66, 69, 70, 72, 73, 77,
   88, 95, 117, 120, 121, 125, 162, 184,
   185, 194, 205, 238, 240, 239n2
Jackson, Rep. John G., 30, 184
Jefferson, President Thomas, ix, 7, 12,
   15, 28, 32–36, 39–42, 47, 49, 53, 58,
   60, 62, 71, 76, 77, 85, 87–89, 102,
   103, 106, 109, 111, 115, 116, 126,
   135, 143, 145, 158, 171, 172, 183,

185, 186, 188, 190, 193, 104, 201, 212, 238, 242n15, 243n10, 265n5

Jefferson City, Missouri, 62, 87, 88

Jeffersonian Republicans, 195

Jennings, Jonathan, 91

Johnson, President Lyndon B., 148, 172–74, 221

Jones, Chief Clerk Edward, 115

Jordon, Phillip, 162

Jumonville, Sieur de, 6–8, 85, 237

Kanhawas River, 9

Kennedy, President John F., 148, 172–73

Kent, Donald, 76

Kentucky, 13, 16, 33, 46, 57, 65, 72, 76, 117, 118

Kerr, Joseph, 20, 89

Kerry, Sen. John: and American Infrastructure Financing Authority, 272n48

Ketcham, Ralph, 37

King, Sen. Rufus, 44, 72

Kinny, Charles, 106

Knight, Jonathan, 74, 90, 136

Knightstown, Indiana, 90, 136

Korean War, 164, 170

Kussy, Edward V.: "Surface, Transportation and Administrative Law," 207–8

League of American Wheelmen, 153

Leib, Rep. Michael, 16

LeMoyne, Francis, 142, 143

Lewis and Clark Expedition, 17, 28

Lincoln, President Abraham, 75–77, 87, 124, 141, 148, 153, 185, 221, 222

Lincoln-Douglas debates, 76

Little Youghiogheny River, 86, 96, 97, 100, 109

Louisiana Purchase, 17, 19, 28, 71

Lowe, Judge J. M., 154, 190–91

MacDonald, Thomas, 169

MacGuineas, Maya, 269n36

Madison, President James, ix, 10, 17–19, 27–43, 45, 48, 54, 58, 71, 76–79, 89, 97, 101, 103, 105, 110–13, 115, 116, 160, 183, 185, 186, 194, 199, 201, 203, 205–7, 209, 232, 238, 242n11, 243n10, 245n13, 246n3, 253nn43 and 51; *The Federalist Papers,* 35–37

mails, x, 13, 42, 60, 117, 122, 155

Maine, 24, 31, 60, 62, 66, 76, 103, 113, 120, 144, 167

Maryland, ix, 5, 8, 9, 15, 16, 18, 20–22, 30, 31, 44, 50, 55, 59–61, 63, 64, 66, 85, 86, 89, 92, 95, 97, 104, 106, 108–10, 113, 115, 117, 118, 126, 128–30, 134, 145, 147, 152, 153, 156, 162, 187, 188, 190, 215, 239, 239, 243

Maysville Road, Kentucky, 13, 57–59, 61, 72, 239

McAdam, John L., 92, 126, 250n2

McCain, Sen. John, 223

McCullough, David, 191, 193

McKennan, Rep. Thomas, 60–62, 74, 184

McKinley, Henry, 92, 92, 104, 105, 107, 108

Mercer proposal, 54, 55

Mexican War, 74

Midwest, x, 47, 73, 87, 130, 138, 151, 215, 217

Mississippi River, 22, 152

"The Moment of Truth." *See* National Commission on Fiscal Responsibility and Reform

Monongahela Navigation Co. v. United States, 206

Monongahela River, 5–7, 9, 16, 21, 22, 125, 144, 206

Monroe, President James, vii, 17, 39–54, 58, 59, 61, 70–72, 76–80, 86, 88, 91, 101, 103, 113, 115, 120, 142, 160, 176, 181, 183, 185, 190, 194, 199, 200–203, 205–9, 212, 226, 232, 235, 238, 246nn3 and 4, 263n9

Monroe Memorandum, 52, 61, 70,190, 200–1, 206
Moore, Thomas, 20, 89
Morrill Act, 221
Morrow, Rep. Jeremiah, 16, 31
Murtha, Rep. John, 193
Muskingum River, 13, 134

National Commission on Fiscal Responsibility and Reform: 2010 Report, 269n36, 272n48
national grid system, 162
National Industrial Recovery Act, 161, 164
National Old Trails Association, 154, 189–91
National Road, ix–x, 5–8, 10–15, 17, 19, 20, 22, 24–26, 28–34, 36–53, 55, 57–61, 64, 66, 67, 69–81, 85–98, 100, 102, 103, 109, 111, 115–18, 120, 122, 124–26, 128–61, 163–65, 167–72, 174–76, 178–81, 183–95, 199–208, 211–21, 224, 227, 229, 232, 235, 238–40, 244n2; achievements of, 186–88; American emigrants and immigrants, 129–30; bidders on, 93, 101, 102; bridges of, 97–100; builders, 94–97; building methods/construction, 92–94, 102, 106–9; bureaucracy of, 91–92; contractors, 31, 90, 92–94, 100–102, 104–8, 110–12, 114; decline of, 151–53; eastern portion, 85–86; financial concerns, 20–55, 60, 61, 72, 77, 80, 95, 100, 102, 104, 107, 114, 120, 141, 146, 156, 157, 159, 170, 177, 205, 207, 212, 215–17, 227, 229; foreign visitors' impressions, 131–37; immigrants from abroad, 131–37; as infrastructure symbol, 194–95; innkeepers/tavern keepers, 122–24; and the media, 188–89; as a national heritage symbol, 193–94; never built portion, 87–89; physical beginning of, 103–6; political considerations, 113–

16; progress of, 110–13; repairs to, 45, 54, 60–66, 92, 105, 106, 112–14, 120, 171, 235, 238; revival of, 153–54; routing concerns, 102, 103, 109–10; scenery along, 124–26, 128, 132; stage and wagon drivers on, 121–22; superintendents and surveyors, 89–91; tolls on, 118–21; traffic and travel on, 117–18; travelers on, 124–29; western portion, 86–87
National Surface Transportation Policy and Review Study Commission, 213–15
National Traffic and Motor Vehicle Safety Act, 179
Native Americans. See Indians
Nelson, Rufus Rockwell, 153, 157
Nemacolin, 5–7, 21, 143, 144, 146, 193, 237; trail of, 5
New Deal, 78, 79, 161, 189, 205
New Orleans, 24, 32
Nixon, President Richard M., 172, 174–75
Noble, Sen. James, 53
North Carolina, 76
Northwest Ordinance, 17
Northwest Territory, 16, 40, 194

Obama, President Barack, 219–22, 224, 229, 231, 232, 269n36, 272n47; The Audacity of Hope, 222
Office of Public Roads, 156
Ohio, ix, 5–9, 12, 13, 15–18, 20–22, 24, 29, 31, 32, 34, 40, 44, 46–55, 60–67, 72, 73, 85–91, 98, 101, 103, 112, 118, 120, 124–26, 129–32, 134–36, 141–45, 147, 152, 162, 164, 185, 187–90, 194, 199, 215, 217, 237–40, 242n10, 243n10, 250n2, 265n6
Ohio Co. of Virginia, 5
Ohio River, 13, 15, 44, 46–48, 54, 61, 63, 64, 66, 67, 85–88, 98, 101, 103, 120, 125, 143, 184, 187, 190, 194, 215, 238, 239, 242n10
Ohio Valley, 6, 144, 215, 237
Oliver, William, 135–37, 186

Page, Logan Waller, 156, 157
Panama Canal, 79
Pennsylvania, ix, 5, 6, 8, 9, 13, 16–18, 21–23, 26, 27, 44, 48, 62, 55, 59, 60–64, 66, 74, 85, 86, 89–91, 94, 95, 97, 100, 104, 109–14, 118, 120, 122–24, 126, 128, 141–44, 153, 156, 152, 163, 167, 169, 187, 188, 192, 193, 231, 237–40, 243n10, 254n6
Pennsylvania Turnpike, 167, 169
Perkins, Frances, 250n21
Peterson-Pew Commission on Budget Reform, 267–68n32; *Getting Back to the Black*, 269–70n36
Peyton, Billy Joe, 89, 90, 92, 93, 97, 120
Pittsburgh, 6, 48, 98, 142, 156
Philadelphia, 16, 48, 147, 237
Post Office Dept., 155
Polk, President James Knox, 60, 63, 69, 74, 78, 117
Posner, Judge Richard A., 224, 227, 256n21, 267n30
post roads, 10, 13, 14, 98, 122, 154–56, 204, 208, 237
Post Roads Clause, 10, 36, 42, 204–6, 246n3
Potomac River, 9, 10, 15, 18, 21, 24, 29, 86, 95, 143, 188, 190, 215
Preston, Sen. William C., 64, 65

Quakers, 130, 134, 147

railroads, ix, 76, 79, 140, 151, 152, 200, 232
Raitz, Karl, 156. 163, 165
Randle, 104, 105, 107
Randolph, Sen. John, 53
Ray, Gen. James B., 145, 146
Reagan, President Ronald, 172, 176
Red Stone Creek, 6, 7
Rehnquist, Chief Justice William, 80, 202
Rendell, Gov. Ed, 231
Republicans, 54, 75, 194, 222, 223, 231

Revenue Act: 1932, 164; 1941, 164; 1951, 164;
Richmond, Indiana, 87, 88, 130, 147
Richmond, Virginia, 16, 87, 147
Riley, James Whitcomb, 137–38, 188
Rivlin, Alice, 246n23, 269–70n36
Roosevelt, President Franklin D., 78, 148, 161, 168, 169

Santa Fe Trail, 153
Sawhill, Elizabeth, 264n23
Schlereth, Tom: *Reading the Road*, 163; on the road as conduit to settlement, 130, 136, 137, 147; on U.S. 40, 163
Schlesinger, Arthur Jr.: *A Thousand Days*, 173
Schwarzenegger, Gov. Arnold, 231
Scioto River, 13
Searight, Thomas, 51, 59, 66, 89, 121, 123, 184, 187
Second National Bank of the United States, 33, 34
Seven Years' War, 8
Shackleford, Rep. Dorsey, 155
Sharp, Horatio, 6
Sherman, Roger, 37
Shriver, David, 30, 31, 89–90, 97, 101, 102, 104–6, 184, 212, 238
Simon, Paul: *Lincoln's Preparation for Greatness*, 75
Sky, Theodore: *To Provide for the General Welfare*, 242n14, 243n19 (chap. 1), 243n9 (chap. 2), 245nn13, 17, 17, 24, and 26, 246nn7 and 11, 247n1, 248nn1 and 6, 249n2, 250nn11, 16, and 17, 256n4, 257n21, 258n18, 260n19, 263nn8 and 13, 265n5
Smith, Sen. Samuel, 31
Smith, Sen. William, 53, 54
Snowe, Sen. Olympia, 223
Social Security, 35, 36, 78, 79, 179, 201, 202, 205, 207, 227, 230, 264n22, 268nn33 and 35
South Dakota v. Dole, 80, 202, 204, 207, 208

Southard, Samuel, 63
Spain, 9, 14
Spector, Sen. Arlen, 223
Sperling, Gene: *The Pro-Growth Progressive*, 231
Springfield, Illinois, 75, 87
Springfield, Ohio, 73, 86, 88
Springfield (Ohio) *Republic*, 72–73, 93, 124, 135, 136
St. Clair, Arthur, 16
St. Lawrence River, 25
St. Louis, 22, 24, 54, 87–89, 126, 162, 187, 188
stagecoaches, 88, 117, 123, 138
Steele, Eliza: travels the road, 128–29, 186
Steward Machine Corp v. Davis, 205
Stewart, Rep. Andrew, 44, 55, 61, 74, 123
Stewart, George R., 171; *U.S. 40*, 162–63
Stone, Justice Harlan F., 250n21
Stone, Gen. Roy, 155
Story, Joseph, 43, 76, 202, 203, 220 263n9
Supreme Court, 23, 43, 77–80, 98, 202–5, 207, 208
Surface Transportation Act (1982), 176
Surface Transportation and Uniform Relocation Assistance Act (1987), 176
Sweet, James Stouder: "The Federal Gasoline Tax at a Glance," 164

Talbot, Sen. Isham, 46
tariffs, 63, 69, 72, 90
Taylor, Sen. John (John Taylor of Caroline), 46
Taylor, John B: testimony to Senate Budget Committee, 272n46
Taylor, President Zachary, 61, 62, 74
Tennessee, 63, 76, 117
Texas, 74, 178
Thompson, Josiah, 101, 113, 114
tollgates, ix, 40, 41, 44–46, 52, 54, 55, 61–64, 118, 199, 200, 238, 239

tollhouses, 44, 59–61, 63, 65, 69, 118, 163, 217
toll roads, 30, 120, 152, 167, 168, 244n2
tolls, 24, 40, 42–45, 48, 52, 54, 55, 59, 60, 61, 64, 65, 69, 70, 81, 94, 107–9, 118, 120, 130, 152, 154, 159, 165, 167, 168, 177, 180, 187, 200
Tracy, Sen. Uri, 15, 16
traders/trading posts: William Connor, 144, 145
Transportation Equity Act for the 21st Century, 179, 181
Treaty of Ghent, 17, 31, 32
Tresaguet, Pierre: building methods of, 92
Trollope, Frances: observations about the road, 132–34, 137, 186, 189
Truman, President Harry, 148, 169, 170, 191
turnpikes, 30, 40, 45, 48, 75, 76, 95, 96, 134, 152, 167, 169, 244n2

Uncle Sam's Road. *See* National Road
Underground Railroad, 139, 141–43
Uniontown, Pennsylvania, ix, 9, 22, 28, 31, 32, 59, 61, 86, 87, 97, 109, 111, 112, 114,123, 125, 133, 152, 156, 163, 189, 238, 247n6
United States v. Butler, 43, 78, 80, 205, 206, 250n21
U.S. Department of Transportation, 13, 46, 154, 155, 168, 170, 173–74, 190, 234; National Scenic Byways Program, 192
U.S. Department of the Treasury, 11, 12, 14, 16, 17, 20, 23, 31, 38, 43, 47, 51, 57, 59, 63, 73, 92, 97, 101, 102, 104, 110, 113–15, 183, 207, 238
U.S. House of Representatives, 16, 17, 27, 30, 31, 37, 44, 46, 49, 51, 54, 55, 59–63, 75–77, 88, 91, 117, 123, 152, 155, 171, 178, 213, 222, 223, 231, 238
U.S. Senate, 15–17, 24, 30, 31, 44–47, 51, 53–55, 59, 60, 62, 64, 75, 88,

117, 141, 155, 171, 178, 191, 213, 22, 231

U.S. 40, x, 143, 152, 162–65, 167, 184, 191, 194, 217, 220, 240

Van Allen, Elizabeth J., 138

Van Buren, President Martin, ix, 66, 73, 124, 240

Vandalia, Illinois, 62, 75, 87, 88, 100, 117, 124, 135, 146, 162, 190, 194, 217

Van Hollen, Rep. Chris, 269–70n36

Virginia, ix, 5–10, 13, 16, 18, 21, 30, 33, 39, 44, 46, 53–55, 59, 60, 62–64, 73, 77, 85, 86, 98, 112, 113, 126, 131, 132, 142, 166, 156, 184, 187, 191, 201, 215, 237, 238, 239, 243n10

War of 1812, 13, 29, 32, 71, 110, 116, 183, 199, 238

Washington, President George, 5–14, 16, 19, 21–23, 31, 40, 43, 71, 77, 86, 122, 147, 187, 193, 204, 220, 237, 238, 242nn9, 10, and 15

Washington, D.C., 16, 22, 24, 50, 86, 103

Washington, Pennsylvania, 13, 22, 23, 26, 27, 60, 95, 97, 112, 114, 126, 141, 142, 156, 163, 238

Webster, Daniel, 60, 62–65, 69, 140, 200

Weingroff, Richard, 154–56, 190; *Clearly Vicious as a Matter of Policy*, 158–61, 164, 171, 178, 258n23; *The Man Who Loved Roads*, 169, 170, 191

Welby, Adlard: observations about the road, 94–95

Weslager, C. A., 145; on Nemacolin, 143

West, the, x, 8, 9, 12, 14, 19, 21, 24–26, 32, 48, 51, 63, 74, 86, 117, 125, 129, 142–46, 177, 186, 187, 191, 193, 195, 201, 215, 217, 222

(Great) Western Road, 89, 104, 105, 107, 108. *See also* National Road

Wheeling, West Virginia, 6, 13, 16, 18, 21, 23, 26, 32, 43, 44, 47, 48, 53, 60–62, 66, 85, 86, 88, 89, 90, 92, 94–96, 98, 101, 103, 112–15, 118, 122, 124–26, 129, 131–33, 145, 152, 156, 157, 188, 191, 194, 198, 215, 238, 239

Whigs, 16, 51, 59, 61, 69, 72–75, 90

whiskey, 133; tax on, 13

Whiskey Rebellion, 12, 237

Whitman, Walt, 188, 189

Williams, Elie, 20, 21, 89

Wilson, President Woodrow, 148, 154, 156

Wilson v. Shaw, 78–80, 204

women's rights movement, 146–48

Wood, Joseph, 16, 17, 28, 43, 58, 71, 187

World War I, 154, 158

World War II, 167, 169

Young, Joseph Simeon: "A Political and Constitutional Study . . . ," 18–19, 22, 36, 47, 88, 135

Zandi, Mark: testimony to Senate Budget Committee, 272n46

Zane, Col. Ebenezer, 13, 14

Zane's Trace, 13, 14, 98, 194

Zanesville, Ohio, 47, 50, 51, 53, 54, 60, 86, 91, 124, 126, 129, 134, 142, 143, 190, 194, 239, 250n2

About the Author

Theodore Sky is distinguished lecturer at Columbus School of Law, The Catholic University of America. Prior to taking up full-time teaching, Mr. Sky served for more than thirty years with the U.S. Department of Education. His wife is a clinical social worker and his two daughters are, respectively, a public school teacher and a librarian in a public library.

CPSIA information can be obtained at www.ICGtesting.com
Printed in the USA
269310BV00001B/2/P

9 781611 490206